MW00649918

The Prince and the Emperors
The Life and Times of Rabbi Judah the Prince

Dov S. Zakheim

The Prince and the Emperors

The Life and Times of Rabbi Judah the Prince

To Rimonne,
with lots of love,
Zayda
Sept. '21

Maggid Books

The Prince and the Emperors
The Life and Times of Rabbi Judah the Prince

First Edition, 2021

Maggid Books
An imprint of Koren Publishers Jerusalem Ltd.

POB 8531, New Milford, CT 06776-8531, USA
& POB 4044, Jerusalem 9104001, Israel
www.maggidbooks.com

Cover Photo: The Cave of Rabbi Yehuda HaNasi, in the Beit She'arim National Park, Israel, where Rebbe is interred

The publication of this book was made possible through the generous support of *The Jewish Book Trust*.

ISBN 978-1-59264-540-4, *hardcover*

Printed and bound in the United States

To Deborah

מָצָא אִשָּׁה מָצָא טוֹב
משלי יח, כב

and

To Chaim, Reuven, Saadya, and Ben

הִנֵּה נַחֲלַת ה׳ בָּנִים
תהלים קכז, ג

Contents

Preface

Torah and Greatness

Over the course of the centuries, leading rabbis have served as the primary representatives of the Jewish community to the non-Jewish elites of the day. Less frequently, such men – and they were always men – combined the roles of scholar and legal decisor on the one hand, and secular leader on the other. The talmudic figure Rabbi Judah b. Simeon, better known as R. Judah the Prince, R. Yehuda HaNasi, *Rabbeinu HaKadosh* (our Holy Rabbi)[1] or simply Rebbe,[2] was such a man.

1. See Y. Avoda Zara 3:1; Ecclesiastes Rabba 9:110; and Shabbat 118b, where on being asked why he was called "our Holy Rabbi," Rebbe explained that it was due to his extraordinary modesty. See, however, E. E. Urbach, "The Rabbinical Laws of Idolatry in the Second and Third Centuries in Light of Archeological and Historical Facts," *Israel Exploration Journal* 9, no. 3 (1959), 153n13.
2. "Who is Rebbe? He is Rebbe, he is R. Judah the Prince. R. Abahu said, 'He is Rebbe, he is R. Yudan, he is Rabbeinu HaKadosh'" (Y. Sanhedrin 11:3). Throughout this book I translate the Hebrew honorific for Rabbi Judah as Rebbe, as opposed to Rabi or Rabbi. I believe that Rebbe is the closest approximation to the actual Hebrew or Aramaic. Though "Rebbe" is most closely associated with the English transliteration of the title granted to hasidic leaders, the actual Hebrew (actually Yiddish) pronunciation of that title is "Rebbeh" as in "Lubavitcher Rebbeh." In fact, there is no clear way to transliterate the Hebrew term, as it appears without

Everything that we know about Rebbe, his father R. Simeon b. Gamaliel, or indeed the lives and activities of his fellow *Tanna'im* – the class of rabbis who flourished from the first century BCE through the third century CE – as well as their interlocutors both Jewish and non-Jewish, derives from texts that appeared as much as several centuries after their activities supposedly took place. Moreover, these texts do not offer an organized, coherent, or even consistent picture of the *Tanna'im*. What they offer are anecdotes scattered throughout a literature whose earliest manifestation was the Mishna, edited primarily but perhaps not solely by Judah the Prince around 215 CE, while other texts, notably some of the midrashim, appeared as much as four hundred years later. Not surprisingly, at times these texts offer variations on the same story, or even contradictory accounts; a given anecdote may also be attributed to different rabbis.

Tales of the rabbis were not biographies in the modern, or even ancient, sense of the term – nor were they meant to be. They were not self-contained portraits akin to those of Roman authors such as Plutarch, Suetonius, or the authors of the *Historia Augusta*. They often involved miraculous doings, akin to tales that supplemented those of Scriptural figures. There are few if any references to these individuals in other contemporary sources, be they non-Jewish histories or archeological finds, at least as of this writing. These tales were meant for Jewish audiences only, and were likely intended for the even-more-limited circles of rabbis and their acolytes who were among the literati of their day.

In the absence of sources to validate these biographical sketches, and because of their very nature, these tales have evoked a variety of reactions on the part of contemporary Jews and modern scholars. *Ḥaredi* (ultra-Orthodox) Jews accept these stories at face value, as did their ancestors, especially prior to the Enlightenment. On the other hand, many academic scholars, as well as many Jews who adhere to the more liberal streams of Judaism, doubt their authenticity. Still other scholars, as well as many Modern Orthodox Jews, consider that these stories contain at least a germ of truth and as such are a source of valuable

vowels in rabbinic literature. Many Sephardic congregations pronounce the word as "Reebee," but spelling it that way would be no less confusing to the English reader, and perhaps even more so.

information about life in the talmudic era. Appendix 2 discusses these various opinions at somewhat greater length.

This book adopts the last of these views in presenting a biography of R. Judah. Its premise is that the hundreds of anecdotes about R. Judah that address everything from his childhood to his education, his family life and household, his role of leader of the Jewish community, his numerous halakhic rulings and opinions, and his passing, offer a relatively accurate account of his long and successful life. As a general rule, this book treats as accurate those talmudic dicta that attribute to R. Judah specific halakhic (legal) rulings. The Sages were exceedingly careful about ensuring that any given legal ruling was correctly attributed to its actual author. Similarly, talmudic accounts that do not treat R. Judah as the primary actor but rather mentions him in passing, likewise are presumed to be relatively accurate.[3] On the other hand, this study is far more tentative about tales that clearly are meant to glorify R. Judah. In such cases, where speculation is in order, these stories will include words such as "possibly," "may," or "might."

It is from this copious and diffuse material that I have sought to construct a biographical account of the man. While the talmudic anecdotes about the rabbis often are mere appendages to serious discussions of law and practice, this study attempts the reverse. It focuses on the individual, as well as on many of his colleagues, students, and interlocutors, while along the way incorporating elements of the debates and halakhic decisions that compose the core of the Talmud. In this way, readers hopefully will not only obtain a holistic picture of Rabbi Judah the Prince, but will also be afforded some insight into the human and historical context that shaped the Mishna, and by extension the Babylonian and Jerusalem Talmuds that were its primary interpretations.[4]

---

3. Jacob Neusner points out that with respect to talmudic discussions of both political and economic matters, "because the information they provide comes *en passant*, we accept it without question as valid historical evidence." Jacob Neusner, "Some Aspects of the Economic and Political Life of Babylonian Jewry, Ca. 160–220 CE," *Proceedings of the American Academy for Jewish Research* 31 (1963), 165–66.
4. Rebbe's great predecessor, R. Akiba, has also been the subject of full-length biographies, while the rabbi turned heretic, Elisha ben Avuya, was the subject of Milton Steinberg's novel *As a Driven Leaf* (Milburn, NJ: Behrman House, 2015).

In providing that context, I have also devoted considerable attention to the careers of the two emperors who, I argue, were the models for the many stories of Rebbe and "Antoninus" that appear throughout rabbinic literature. An outline of their careers provides a backdrop to several of the talmudic tales of Rebbe's interaction with these powerful men, who in many ways were a rabbinic vehicle for demonstrating that Rebbe was as important a personage in the secular world as he was among the Jews of both Judaea and the Diaspora.

Many modern scholars perceive discrepancies between the Babylonian and Jerusalem Talmuds' respective reports on Rebbe's life and activities. They argue that the Babylonian Talmud, while it recognized his political role as ethnarch (leader of his community), nevertheless emphasized his importance as a scholar and leader of an academy. In contrast, the Jerusalem Talmud, though it similarly reflects "an understanding of the dual nature of the patriarchate...recognizes the political function as primary."[5]

Actually, the Babylonian Talmud recognized Rebbe's uniqueness as both a communal leader and scholar. As it states, "From Moses until Rebbe we do not find sacred learning and [secular] greatness combined in the one [person]."[6] The *Amora'im,* those Babylonian and Judaean rabbis who flourished after the compiling of the Mishna and Rebbe's passing, were in awe of someone who could interact freely, and virtually on an equal basis, with leading Romans, including the emperor, and yet at the same time lead an academy and not only compile the Mishna, but issue rulings on a host of Jewish legal matters that became normative halakha.

For the past two centuries, a trend has taken shape among certain circles of traditional Jews to shy away from matters secular, unless absolutely compelled to do so in order to earn a living. However commendable their commitment to study might be, Rebbe's life demonstrates not only that one can excel in matters both religious and secular, but that

5. Devora Steinmetz, "Must the Patriarch Know 'Uqtzin'? The Nasi as Scholar in Babylonian Aggada," *ATJ Review* 23, no. 2 (1998), 187.
6. Sanhedrin 36a and see Rashi, ad loc., s.v. *bemakom*. The author of the talmudic statement is variously given as R. Hillel the son of R. Wallas or Rabba the son of Rava.

only one who does so can aspire to emulate the greatest statesman and scholar of them all, Moses our Teacher.

Rebbe's life, activities, and scholarship have been an implicit if not explicit model for many of the greatest rabbinic leaders throughout the ages. Samuel ibn Naghrillah, who flourished in Spain in the eleventh century, was a successful general and vizier. In addition, however, as Rabbi Shmuel HaLevi HaNagid, he wrote an important introduction to the Talmud (*Mevo HaTalmud*) that has been incorporated into virtually all editions of the Babylonian Talmud since the publication of the seminal Vilna *Shas* in the latter part of the nineteenth century.

A century after Rabbi Shmuel, Rabbi Moshe ben Maimon – Maimonides, the Rambam – was not only an important physician and leader of his community, and indeed of all non-European Jewry, but also perhaps the greatest codifier in Jewish history, as well as the author of commentaries, responsa, and philosophical works. He studied Greek as well as Jewish philosophy and even cited Greek philosophers in his halakhic responsa.[7] The cornice atop the Butler Library of my *alma mater* Columbia University includes his name among those of the greatest ancient and medieval thinkers.

Don Isaac Abrabanel was finance minister and advisor to the fifteenth-century and early sixteenth-century rulers of Portugal, Spain, and the Kingdom of Naples. Yet he was also the leader of Spanish and Portuguese Jewry, and the author of lengthy and detailed commentaries on virtually every book of Tanakh, the entire Holy Scriptures. Rabbi Obadiah Sforno, the great biblical commentator, was a graduate of the papal university La Sapienza, better known as the University of Rome.

Rabbi Jacob Ettlinger of Altona (now part of Hamburg) was Germany's foremost rabbinic leader in the first half of the nineteenth century. The author of *Binyan Tzion* and *Arukh LaNer,* he attended the University of Würzburg and as leader of his community also served as a civil judge. Rabbi Ettlinger's great student, Rabbi Samson Raphael Hirsch, was the most famous leader of German Jewry

7. See R. Moshe ben Maimon (henceforth cited as Maimonides), *She'elot UTeshuvot Pe'er HaDor,* ed. David Yosef, 2nd ed. (Jerusalem: Makhon Or Hamizrah, 1994/5754), no. 143.

in the nineteenth century. He studied at the University of Bonn and later served as a member of the Moravian parliament. Rabbi Hirsch's contemporary, Rabbi Esriel Hildesheimer, founder of the rabbinical seminary in Berlin and a leading halakhic decisor, earned his doctorate at the University of Halle. He worked closely with secular Jewish organizations, notably the Alliance Israelite.

Rabbi Isaac Halevi Herzog, chief rabbi of Ireland and the first chief rabbi of the State of Israel, earned his doctorate at the University of Leeds. His thesis addressed the question of the source of *tekhelet*, the blue wool that was meant to be part of the *tzitzit* (ritual fringes) attached to the corners of clothing. Rabbi Joseph Ber Soloveitchik and Rabbi Menachem Mendel Schneerson, the Lubavitcher Rebbe, studied at the University of Berlin; Rabbi Soloveitchik earned his doctorate in philosophy there. All of these men were respected, indeed, remarkable communal leaders; Rabbi Herzog became the first chief rabbi of the State of Israel after having worked with both religious and secular Jews to represent the interests of the *Yishuv* to the British Government during the mandatory era.

My own father, Rabbi Zvi Hirsh Zakheim, of blessed memory, was in this tradition. A university graduate, he served the Jewish community of pre-war Vilna as its legal counsel. In that role, especially after September 1939, he had to grapple with many sensitive issues, notably negotiating with Nazi officials to save Lithuanian Jewish soldiers from concentration camps after they had been drafted by the Polish military and then captured by the Germans. As an attorney in Shanghai, China, having escaped from the Communist authorities in Lithuania, he engaged the Japanese authorities to ensure the subsistence of refugee yeshiva students and their teachers. In addition to playing a vital role in Jewish communal affairs, however, he was also not only a rabbi – having been ordained in the famed Ramailes yeshiva of Vilna – but also a talmudic scholar. His collation of commentaries on Tractate Sanhedrin, entitled *Zvi HaSanhedrin*, can be found on the shelves on many major yeshivas both in the United States and in Israel.

These men followed in Rebbe's footsteps. He remains a model for contemporary Jews.

Modern scholarship and, ironically, many leaders of yeshivas who abhor such scholarship, both may posit that a Jew must choose among communal leadership, secular statesmanship, and Torah study. But a careful look at Rebbe's life and activities demonstrates that one can and should aspire to all three.

Acknowledgments

The relationship between rabbis and the secular rulers of the lands in which they lived has been for me a source of deep and lifelong interest. For some years I have lectured on this theme in my synagogue, the Kemp Mill Synagogue of Silver Spring, Maryland. Rebbe was a subject of a number of those lectures. I especially enjoyed researching for them, not only because Rebbe is a role model for Jews who wish to be immersed both in their religion and in the world around them, but also because it required me to go back to many original sources of another of my long-standing interests, Roman history. One of my fellow congregants, the renowned expert on Middle East politics David Makovsky, urged me to expand the lectures into a book. What follows in the result of his advice, though any errors, omissions, or mischaracterizations that the reader might encounter are solely my responsibility.

I owe much to those who took the time to read and comment upon my manuscript as it went through several revisions. David Makovsky, diplomat and scholar at the Washington Institute for Near East Policy; Professor Rob Eisen of George Washington University; my brother-in-law, Professor Bernard Firestone of Hofstra University; and Adam Garfinkle, editor of the *American Interest,* read the entire manuscript (Adam offered to read it a second time!). My sons Keith (Chaim) and Roger (Reuven), as well as Roger's close friend Rabbi Yosie Levine, rabbi of the Jewish Center in New York, read several chapters and offered extremely helpful comments and suggestions. I also wish to thank Matthew Miller, publisher of Koren and its imprint Maggid Books, for his encouragement; and Rabbi Reuven Ziegler, Ita Olesker, my editor Esther Cameron, and Nechama Unterman, of the Koren staff. I am grateful to them all, and especially to my wife, Deborah, who kept pushing me to complete this effort.

Chapter 1

Rabbis, Rulers, and Romans

> "And the Lord said to her: Two nations are in your womb" (Gen. 25:23). Said R. Judah in the name of Rav: Do not read "nations" (*goyim*), rather "proud ones" (*ge'im*). These refer to Antoninus and Rebbe, upon whose tables were not missing lettuce, cucumbers, and radish, neither during the summer nor during the winter.
>
> Avoda Zara 11a

INTRODUCTION

Ever since the days of the Second Temple, rabbis have acted not only as religious guides, educators, and halakhic decisors, but also as communal leaders. In the latter capacity, they have often represented the views and interests of their communities to the governments of the lands in which they lived. For the better part of two millennia, those governments were either monarchies ruled by emperors, kings, sultans, or emirs, or subdivisions within the imperial or royal realms, such as dukedoms, provinces, or satrapies, ruled by high-ranking officials. In addition, in Europe there were many lands under the direct control of the highest officials of the Catholic church – popes, archbishops, and bishops, who had the power to determine the fate of Jewish communities within their jurisdictions and to whom Jews at times looked for protection from attacks by townspeople, peasants, and crusaders. When acting as community representatives to non-Jewish rulers and governments, rabbis were in the capacity of what came to be termed in the Middle Ages as the *shtadlan*, which literally means "intercessor" or "representative."[1]

The Talmud (actually the Gemara, as opposed to the Mishna) is replete with stories about rabbis who interacted with the Roman and later Parthian rulers of the day. In some cases, they pleaded for the easing of restrictions on Jewish practices, whether by meeting individually with the ruling authorities, or by forming delegations such as those that traveled to Rome to make representations to the Senate and to the emperor. At other times they advocated resistance against the authorities; before and during the Bar Kokhba revolt, many of them, most notably R. Akiba, supported outright rebellion. Still other talmudic and midrashic accounts speak of friendly relations between the rabbis and rulers, such as Mar Samuel's close ties to the Parthian emperor Sappur II.

Later generations saw similar interactions, again varying from close friendship to outright hostility and, as with R. Akiba and his colleagues, imprisonment and execution. A tenth-century rabbi, Hasdai ibn Shaprut, doubled as the foreign minister of Cordoba, ably representing Caliph Abd al-Rahman III in negotiations with various Christian rulers, including Holy Roman Emperor Otto I (912–973). And in the following century, as already noted, Samuel the Prince (Shmuel HaNagid) served in his "day job" as both vizier and victorious army commander-in-chief under Badis, caliph of Grenada.

Other rabbis were courted by popes and cardinals who sought their support in the political and philosophical disputes of the day. Such was the case with the sixteenth-century Italian rabbis Elijah Halfan and Jacob Mantino, who took opposite sides in the debate over whether Henry VIII could annul his marriage to Catherine of Aragon. Rabbi Mantino supported the papal stance that an annulment was not possible; Rabbi Halfan supported

1. For an examination of the *shtadlan*'s role and activities in early modern Europe, see Selma Stern, *The Court Jew: A Contribution to the History of Absolutism in Europe*, 2nd ed., trans. Ralph Weiman (New Brunswick, NJ and Oxford: Transaction, 1985).

Henry's position. Needless to say, Mantino received papal preferment: Pope Clement VII initially appointed him to a lectureship in Bologna and later to a professorship at Rome's La Sapienza, the papal university.

On the other hand, many rabbis suffered at the hands of non-Jewish authorities precisely because of their leadership roles in the Jewish community. Such was the fate of the thirteenth-century Rabbi Meir of Rothenberg (known as Maharam Rotenberg), who, while attempting to flee Germany, was imprisoned by Emperor Rudolf at the instigation of the Archbishop of Mainz. He died in prison after refusing to be ransomed by the Jewish community, lest that act establish a precedent that would plague future generations.[2]

Rabbi Don Isaac Abrabanel, son of a Portuguese financier, acknowledged leader of the Spanish Jewish community, biblical commentator par excellence, and unofficial finance minister to the Spanish, Portuguese, and Neapolitan courts, was twice exiled – once by choice, once under compulsion. The rulers of united Spain, Ferdinand and Isabella, offered Abrabanel the opportunity to convert to Christianity in order to avoid exile under the 1492 Edict of Alhambra that expelled the Jews (and Moors). Abrabanel chose exile.

One of the earliest and most prominent rabbis to interact on a regular basis with those who ruled was R. Judah the Prince (135–217 CE). He was based in Judaea, the land of his patrimony, which once was ruled by the House of David, from which he claimed descent. As leader of the Jewish community, he was a ruler in his own right; and he was recognized as a prince both by his own people and by the Romans.

However, R. Judah's position differed from that of many of the aforementioned rabbis. He was not a government functionary. Nor was he merely a proto-*shtadlan,* that is, a forerunner of those Jews who from late medieval times until well into the eighteenth century and even in contemporary times, represented the community as "court Jews." These men – they were only men – were generally quite wealthy, but they could

2. "Meir of Rothenburg: Jewish Rabbi and Scholar," *Encyclopedia Britannica,* www.britannica.com/biography/Meir-of-Rothenburg; see also Solomon Schechter and Louis Ginzberg, "Meir of Rothenberg," *Jewish Encyclopedia,* http://www.jewishencyclopedia.com/articles/10581-meir-of-rothenburg-meir-b-baruch.

not impose their will on the Jewish community. On the other hand, they could be and often were dismissed by the ruler to whom they answered, sometimes at the cost of their lives.

R. Judah's authority no doubt derived in part from Roman recognition of his unique position as leader of the Jewish community. He was certainly a wealthy man. But his status was not a function of his wealth but of his royal heredity. In addition, unlike the later court Jews, he had the power to impose his will on the community in religious matters. Again, this was in part because the Romans recognized his authority; but it was also because he was also a scholar of the first order. Moreover, again unlike later court Jews, his authority extended beyond the boundaries of Palestine, ranging across the vastness of the Roman Empire. In that respect, he was a forerunner of the many leading rabbis who ruled on matters put to them from all parts of the Jewish world.

Despite his prestige and authority, R. Judah did not wield his power arbitrarily. Like any of the rabbis who were his colleagues and contemporaries, as well as those who preceded and succeeded him, his legal opinions did not go unchallenged. Many were not incorporated into that corpus of Jewish law which is known as halakha. Yet a considerable number did become law, and his views were never dismissed out of hand.

If there was anyone whose position was truly similar to R. Judah's, it was the *Resh Galuta,* the exilarch, who led the Babylonian Jewish community. As a patrilineal descendant of King David, he could claim more blue blood than R. Judah, whose Davidic ancestry was matrilineal.[3] He too commanded the respect of the ruling Persian authorities. He too had the authority and ability to impose his will on the community; and at least during R. Judah's tenure, he was also a talmudic scholar.

Rabbi Judah the Prince has not been the subject of many biographies. In part this is due to the traditionalist view that the personal biographies of religious heroes if they may be so termed is irrelevant to the pursuit of Jewish knowledge, which should be limited to their

3. Y. Kilayim 9:3; see also R. Moshe Margolies, *Pnei Moshe*, s.v. *Rebbe hava anvan sagin*. The nature of their comparative ancestry was not a trivial matter; as Rebbe acknowledged, if the exilarch had come to Judaea, protocol would have demanded that Rebbe defer to him. See below, pp. 154–55.

contributions to law and ethics as articulated in the Talmud and commentaries. Equally, it is due to the fact that, as noted above, modern scholars are skeptical of biographical details of rabbinic lives that are only found in the Talmud and related sources.

As one of the greatest leaders Jewry has ever known, R. Judah the Prince deserves better. He was a brilliant Torah scholar, yet educated in the Greek fashion. He was a first-rate jurist, a talented administrator, and an accomplished statesman. He sought, with some success, to reverse the hostility that had colored relations between Jews and Romans since before the destruction of the Temple. He was not only a Jewish nationalist, but also an advocate of Hebrew. He was an out-of-the box thinker, suggesting reforms that would surprise contemporary Jews and that certainly surprised his contemporaries. And his greatest and longest-lasting accomplishment, his compilation of the Mishna, which preserved the Oral Law from being lost in a collective national amnesia, was effected in the purest Hebrew.

REBBE'S PEDIGREE

The Jews were able to practice their religion freely both before and after the Great Rebellion of 68–70 CE.[4] However, what that religion was to look like after the destruction of the Temple was very much an open question. The Temple had been the center of Jewish ritual, though synagogues had been established throughout Judaea while it yet stood. The priestly class had been in charge of that ritual; but their authority was increasingly challenged by the rabbis, who appear to have commanded considerably more popularity than the corruption-riddled priesthood. In the aftermath of Titus' victory, it was the Sages who stepped in to fill the void left by the ruin of the Temple and the priesthood's loss of its raison d'etre.

The rabbis asserted that their authority derived directly from Moses himself.[5] They viewed the collection of ancient, unwritten laws and traditions that they and their followers practiced as having been transmitted by God to Moses on Mount Sinai in parallel with, and as

4. See Martin Goodman, "Trajan and the Origins of Roman Hostility to the Jews," *Past & Present* 182 (February 2004), 11–12.
5. Mishna Avot 1:1.

an explanation and expansion of, the written Torah. They stated that these laws and traditions had been passed on orally from generation to generation, hence the term "Oral Law." Although the rabbis had taught the Oral Law while the Temple still stood, it was only in the Temple's absence that the Oral Law became the basis for widespread Jewish religious practice; in effect the Sages structured what many now call "rabbinic Judaism." Nevertheless, despite its centrality in Jewish life, the Oral Law remained oral and somewhat inchoate; it was not for another half century that R. Akiba would begin to structure the laws, and not for over another half century that Rebbe would at last put them in writing.

Even as they promulgated the Oral Law, the rabbis also identified the first patriarch as one of their own, Rebbe's ancestor Hillel the Elder, who flourished while the Temple still stood. Although the patriarchate later became a dynastic office, it was talmudic tradition that leadership of the Jewish community had originally been bestowed upon a group – the sons of Beteira – rather than an individual. However, the sons of Beteira had abdicated to Hillel, when he was able to resolve legal issues that the people of Beteira could not.[6] Hillel, a Babylonian, was a student of Shemaya and Avtalion, the joint leaders of the Pharisees; some four centuries later the rabbis of the Talmud asserted that Hillel was descended from King David through his maternal side;[7] but it is not clear whether that claim achieved widespread acceptance during Hillel's lifetime or only later, perhaps not until the second century CE when Rabban Simeon b. Gamaliel II and his son, R. Judah the Prince, served as patriarchs.[8]

Hillel's son Rabban Simeon succeeded him as patriarch, but little is known about him. He may have held the position for only a brief period. Far more is known about Rabban Gamaliel the Elder, who became patriarch upon R. Simeon's passing.

Rabban Gamaliel the Elder issued numerous rulings that became normative halakha, among them the granting of permission for a woman to remarry on the basis of a single witness's testimony that her husband

---

6. Pesaḥim 66a.
7. Genesis Rabba 98:8; Y. Taanit 4:2.
8. For a discussion, see Yitzhak Buxbaum, *The Life and Teachings of Hillel* (Lanham, MD and Boulder, CO: Rowan and Littlefield, 1973), 304n10.

was dead.[9] The Talmud reports that while seated on the steps of the Temple Mount he transmitted decisions to Jews both in the Galilee and the south, as well as to communities in Babylonia and Media.[10] He appears to have had ties to the family of King Agrippa I.[11]

Upon Rabban Gamaliel's passing, Rabban Simeon b. Gamaliel I succeeded him as patriarch. Not much is known about him, other than his dicta as recorded in various places in the Talmud. Josephus records that he was a leading opponent of the Zealots who initiated the civil war that raged during the Roman siege of Jerusalem that began in 68 CE.[12] He died during the siege, though it is unclear whether he was killed by the Zealots or by the Romans during the final stages of the fall of Jerusalem.

In the aftermath of the rebellion, it was Rabban Yohanan b. Zakkai and not a scion of Hillel whom the Talmud recognized as the man who saved rabbinic Judaism when the Temple was burned. The Talmud records that Rabban Yohanan convinced the then-general and future emperor Vespasian to permit him to maintain a Torah academy in Yavneh. The Talmud is somewhat critical of Rabban Yohanan for not seeking reprieve for the Jews, but it admits that Rabban Yohanan may have felt that this was more than Vespasian was prepared to give and that such a request would have resulted in none of his requests being granted.[13] In any event, it was as a result of this request, or at least of Rabban Yohanan's leadership, that the center of rabbinic authority moved from Jerusalem to the north of the province and ultimately to the Galilee.

Rabban Yohanan also asked Vespasian to preserve the family of Rabban Gamaliel, who claimed royal lineage from the House of King David. This particular request of Rabban Yohanan was of critical importance to the Sages, since Rabban Simeon b. Gamaliel was no

9. Mishna Yevamot 16:7.
10. Sanhedrin 11b; Mishna Sanhedrin 2:6; Y. Sanhedrin 1:2.
11. Rabban Gamaliel is mentioned in Acts 5:34–40 and in 22:3 where Paul is called his student.
12. Josephus, *The Jewish War* 3:9:158, ed. Gaalya Cornfeld (Grand Rapids, MI: Zondervan, 1982), 267n159c.
13. Gittin 56b. Presumably that is also why Rabban Yohanan did not ask that the center of rabbinical authority remain in Jerusalem, which had been a key center of rebellion.

longer alive. Indeed, upon Rabban Simeon's death, Rabban Yohanan effectively served as patriarch for the remainder of his life. Nevertheless, despite Rabban Yohanan's request on behalf of Rabban Gamaliel's family, the very fact that it was he who served as patriarch created a degree of ambiguity as to whether the patriarchate was fully dynastic, or whether it required mastery of all facets of the law.[14]

The relative freedom that Rabban Yohanan had obtained for the Jews permitted the rise of a new postwar generation of sages, known as the *Tanna'im*, whose names populate the Mishna. Rabban Gamaliel II, son of Rabban Simeon, succeeded Rabban Yohanan, thereby restoring the patriarchate to the descendants of Hillel. R. Gamaliel appears to have needed formal Roman approval to take office; he traveled to Syria, the provincial headquarters for Judaea, where the governor is reported to have confirmed him officially as patriarch.[15]

One of Rabban Gamaliel's main objectives was to maintain Yavneh as the center of religious authority for the Jewish community. Perhaps it was in order to do so that, in the manner of ancient and medieval kings, he would be accompanied by a retinue of students and others in a series of extensive travels throughout northern Judaea, visiting towns like Tiberias and Acre (Akko) among others.[16] At the same time, he was a vociferous opponent of both Roman philosophers and Jewish Christians. The prayer against blasphemers (*LaMalshinim*) that is considered to be the nineteenth blessing of the daily *Amida* has been attributed to him.[17]

Rabban Gamaliel II appears to have been a wealthy man; he was also quite arrogant and was prone to belittling others, especially his impoverished colleague, R. Joshua. His behavior so outraged his

14. For a discussion, see Jeffrey L. Rubenstein, *The Culture of the Babylonian Talmud* (Baltimore, MD: The Johns Hopkins University Press, 2003), 90–92. See also Pesaḥim 66a; Y. Pesaḥim 6:1.

15. Sanhedrin 11b; Mishna Eduyot 7:7. None of Rabban Gamaliel's successors is reported to have sought such approval; perhaps it was because the position was dynastic. Alternately, having mentioned such approval once in the case of Rabban Gamaliel, the Talmud saw no need to mention it again.

16. Tosefta Terumot 2:13; Tosefta Pesaḥim 2:11; Tosefta Shabbat 13:2; Mishna Avoda Zara 3:4.

17. Megilla 17b; Berakhot 28b.

colleagues that they unseated him and temporarily replaced him with the considerably younger R. Eleazar b. Azariah. He never fully regained his position, even after mending fences with R. Joshua, and was forced to share his leadership of the academy with R. Eleazar.[18]

On the other hand, Rabban Gamaliel was able to recover – or perhaps never lost – his secular authority; according to the Talmud, he traveled to Rome with R. Eleazar and R. Akiba to obtain the rescission of an anti-Jewish decree. At one point, however, he appears to have run afoul of the Romans and was sentenced to death. He was able to escape, and eventually the sentence was rescinded.[19]

Rabban Gamaliel's son, Rabban Simeon II, was at first less fortunate in his dealings with the Romans. The freedom of religious practice and teaching that Rabban Yohanan had obtained for the Jews came to an abrupt end in the aftermath of the rebellion of 132–35. The victorious emperor Hadrian imposed a series of crushing decrees after he had defeated Bar Kokhba, laid waste to Jerusalem, renamed it Aelia Capitolina, and expelled the Jews from the city. Hadrian's additional punitive measures included a ban on Jewish religious practices, notably circumcision, Shabbat, and the laws of family purity.[20] He dismantled the Jews' communal institutions, particularly the Sanhedrin, the lesser courts, and the patriarchate. He also ordered the closure of synagogues and banned the study of Torah, the latter decree presumably due to his not incorrect perception that the rabbis had provided the spiritual underpinnings for the rebellion.[21] In many ways he recreated the environment under which the Jews had suffered when Antiochus Epiphanes ruled the land,[22] but this time the Jews were exhausted and in no position to revolt once again. As will be shown below, it took several decades for

18. Berakhot 27b–28a.
19. Taanit 29a.
20. Me'ila 17a.
21. Gedaliah Alon, *The Jews in Their Land in the Talmudic Age (70–640 CE)*, trans. and ed. Gershon Levi (Cambridge, MA and London: Harvard University Press, 1980), 634–37, makes a strong case for the historicity of these decrees as the talmudic literature reports them.
22. Ibid., 646.

Jews and Romans to develop a *modus vivendi*, which reached its apogee under Rabbi Judah the Prince.

MUTUAL ANTIPATHY AMONG JEWS, ROMANS, AND CHRISTIANS

When Judah succeeded his father R. Simeon b. Gamaliel II as patriarch of the Jewish community of Palestine sometime after 165 CE, just over thirty years had passed since the Roman Emperor Hadrian had finally crushed the three-year rebellion led by Simeon Bar Kokhba. The rebellion had followed on the heels of a major uprising in 117 by the Jews of the Diaspora, particularly those in Cyprus, Mesopotamia, and Egypt, against Hadrian's immediate predecessor, Trajan. And that revolt took place less than a half century after the great rebellion of 68–70 that had led to the destruction of the Temple in Jerusalem.

Initially after their defeat in what Josephus termed "the Jewish War," the Jews had plausibly expected to rebuild the Temple in the near future. After all, they had done so after the First Temple was destroyed. Jeremiah had prophesied[23] that after seventy years the Jews would return from their exile. Indeed, exactly seventy years had passed between the destruction of the First Temple by the Babylonian king Nebuchadnezzar in 586 BCE, and the completion of the Second Temple under Darius in 516.

Moreover, whereas Nebuchadnezzar had not only burnt the Temple but also exiled the leading Judaeans together with King Zedekiah, whom he blinded as well, the Romans had not relocated the Jews to another land. As a consequence, there was some logic to what seemed to be the Jews' expectation, vis-à-vis the Temple's destruction and the outcome of their war with Rome, that "this too shall pass."

The Jews also may have taken heart from the fact that neither Vespasian, who commanded Roman forces in Judaea until he was crowned emperor in 68 CE, nor his son and successor Titus, who presided over the rape of Jerusalem two years later, revoked the status of Judaism as a *religio licitia* (recognized religion); "Jews enjoyed the same religious

23. Jer. 29:10.

liberty after that date as they had done before."[24] As noted above, the rabbis of the Talmud credited this development to the intercession of Rabban Yohanan b. Zakkai. Similarly, Domitian, who succeeded Titus in 81 CE, made few if any changes to official policy toward the Jews (with the exception of expanding the *fiscus Judaicus* tax to include non-practicing Jews and converts) during the first decade of his rule. All of these factors seemingly gave the Jews good reason to be optimistic about the prospects for construction of a third Temple.

But no Third Temple came into being. Just as in biblical Egypt "a new king arose who had no recollection of Joseph,"[25] Domitian turned on the Jews in the later years of his rule. As a later Church historian wrote, "It was also decreed that among the Jews the race of David be sought out by harsh torture and bloody inquisitions, and killed. He [Domitian] did this because he hated, but believed the holy prophets, thinking that someone who would be able to take his kingdom might still come from the seed of David."[26] Yet as happened at other times in both ancient and modern Jewish history, for example with the assassination of Caligula and Stalin's death just as the "Doctors' Plot" was unfolding, "it was ... the murder of Domitian (in 96 CE) which saved the Jews themselves from actual attack."[27]

Domitian's successor, Nerva, showed no particular empathy for the Jews. Moreover, the rebellions against Nerva's successor, Trajan, and then against Hadrian, ended any dreams of rebuilding the Temple. Hadrian may have viewed Judaism as a politically motivating force for the rebellion in Judaea. In this regard Judaism foreshadowed the role other religions played in agitating for the overthrow of a foreign overlord, for example, the role of the Catholic church, and its leader Pope John Paul II, in undermining the Communist Party's rule in eastern Europe. When seen in political terms, Judaism and the revolt that in Roman eyes it had spawned represented more than a local uprising.

---

24. E. Mary Smallwood, "Domitian's Attitude toward the Jews and Judaism," *Classical Philology* 51 (January 1956), 5.
25. Ex. 1:18
26. Orosius, *Seven Books of History Against the Pagans*, trans. and intro. A. T. Fear (Liverpool: Liverpool University Press, 2010), 341.
27. Smallwood, "Domitian's Attitude," 11.

Hadrian was well aware of the fact that in the year 116 CE, the same year when Trajan had successfully defeated Parthia, its primary rival in Asia and the Middle East, and reached the Arabian Gulf, the Jews had joined the people of Mesopotamia in a major rebellion against the conquering Romans. As noted, the Jewish rebellion spread elsewhere throughout the Empire until it was brutally put down by Trajan's general, Lucius Quietus. Trajan appears to have anticipated a possible revolt in Judaea, whose Jewish population had not joined the uprising of 116–117 CE; he stationed a second permanent legion there shortly after the revolt had been crushed.[28] At least one legion, the Tenth, remained stationed near what is now Jerusalem's Jaffa Gate well into the years of the Severan dynasty's rule.[29]

Hadrian, whose primary objective was to restore the peace and stability that had marked the reign of Nerva, may thus have had good reason to view a hostile Judaea as a potential ally of the restive Parthians. After all, the largest Jewish community outside Judaea, and the only one outside the bounds of the Roman Empire, was that of Parthian Babylonia. The Jews were "among the most powerful and loyal supporters" of the Parthians.[30] Indeed, it appears that Jews had fought with the Parthians against Trajan.[31] They had also served with Persian forces against the Greeks, so Hadrian had no reason to suppose they would not do so against the Romans.[32]

The Jews for their part would have had good reason to support the Parthians and oppose the Romans. The Parthians allowed the Jews

---

28. Goodman, "Trajan and the Origins of Roman Hostility," 26.
29. Martin Goodman, *Rome and Jerusalem: The Clash of Ancient Civilizations* (New York: Vintage, 2007), 473.
30. Neusner, "Economic and Political Life," 175.
31. See Shaye J. D. Cohen, *From the Maccabees to the Mishnah*, 2nd ed. (Louisville, KY and London: Westminster John Knox Press), 5, and E. Mary Smallwood, *The Jews under Roman Rule: From Pompey to Diocletian: A Study in Political Relations*, 2nd ed. (Atlanta, GA: SBL, 2014), 417–20. Eusebius wrote of Trajan: "The emperor, suspecting that the Jews of Mesopotamia would also make an attack upon those there, ordered Lusius Quietus to clear the province of them, who also led an army against them and slew a great multitude of them. Upon this victory, he was appointed governor of Judea by the emperor." Eusebius, *Ecclesiastical History*, 109–10.
32. Dov S. Zakheim, *Nehemiah: Statesman and Sage* (New Milford, CT and Jerusalem: Maggid, 2016), 21.

more autonomy than the Romans did in their empire; the exilarch in Babylonia had far more power at that time than any Jewish leader. There were economic concerns as well: Roman taxation appears to have been more onerous than the taxes the Parthians imposed.[33]

Moreover, the two communities maintained close ties. The Babylonian community followed the halakhic lead of the Judaean yeshivas, accepted the rulings of Sanhedrin as binding, followed the Judaean lead in setting the leap year, and paid taxes to support the patriarchate and the yeshivas. In many respects the relationship between the large, well-organized and economically stable Babylonian community and the leadership in Judaea foreshadowed that which has developed a great many years later between the American Orthodox Jewish community and the Israeli religious leadership.

Under these circumstances, it would not be surprising if Hadrian suspected collusion between the two communities in support of the

---

33. See, for example, Jacob Neusner, "Judeo-Persian Communities iii. Parthian and Sasanian Periods, "*Encyclopædia Iranica*, XV/1, 96–103, http://www.iranicaonline.org/articles/judeo-persian-communities-iii-parthian-and-sasanian-periods/. See also Ali Farazmand, "Administrative Legacies of the Persian World-State Empire: Implications for Modern Public Administration, Part 2," *Public Administration Quarterly* 26 (Fall 2002–Winter 2003), 407–408; and Mostafa Khan Fateh, "Taxation in Persia: A Synopsis from the Early Times to the Conquest of the Mongols," *Bulletin of the School of Oriental Studies, University of London* 4 (1928), 728–29. Fateh notes the existence of customs houses that affected Jews whose trade with Rome flourished under the Parthians.

The status of Jews under the Parthians contrasted sharply with their status under Rome; the revolts of 70 and 135 CE were both motivated in part by onerous taxation. Moreover, in the aftermath of the first Jewish rebellion, Vespasian imposed on the Jews an annual poll tax of two denarii, which was especially burdensome for poor heads of large families. See Smallwood, *Jews under Roman Rule*, 371–76; Alon, *Jews in Their Land*, 689; Saul Lieberman, "Palestine in the Third and Fourth Centuries," *The Jewish Quarterly Review*, 36 (April 1946), 345–47; and Aharon Oppenheimer, *Rabbi Yehuda HaNasi* (Hebrew) (Jerusalem: Mercaz Zalman Shazar, 2007), 55. Oppenheimer's study has been translated into English as *Rabbi Judah ha-Nasi: Statesman, Reformer, and Redactor of the Mishnah* (Tubingen: Mohr Siebeck, 2017). All references in this volume are to the original Hebrew edition, which provides more extensive detail than the English version. Both versions devote far less attention than the present volume to the Romans, Rebbe's family life and students, and the breadth of his halakhic rulings, and draw primarily from the two Talmuds, as opposed to other rabbinical and later Jewish sources.

Parthians and at the expense of Rome. Indeed, it may not have gone unnoticed by Hadrian and his court that leading rabbis commuted between Judaea and Babylonia; most notably, R. Akiba, who became the spiritual leader of the Bar Kokhba rebellion, traveled frequently abroad, including to Parthian Babylonia.[34] It is quite possible that R. Akiba's journeys were intended to strengthen the ties between the Diaspora and the mother country. But since at least one major historian speculates that his travels were really in preparation for the Bar Kokhba rebellion, it is plausible that the Romans viewed them in this light, even if that were not actually the case.[35] An independent Judaea allied to the Parthians represented a threat to Roman domination of Syria, itself a hotbed of opposition to Hadrian's rule. Such a situation would have been intolerable to Hadrian; and he therefore took the radical step of not only putting down the Jewish rebellion, but also undermining the religion and executing its leaders, who appeared to have been the moving spirits behind it. Given these developments, the Jews began to resign themselves to the reality that they were to remain under Roman rule for the foreseeable future.

The accommodation between the two peoples after the Bar Kokhba rebellion was therefore hardly an easy one. Jews despised the Romans as idolaters and conquering occupiers. They considered the Romans to be either actual or spiritual descendants of Esau, the archetype of Jacob's biblical adversary. One ancient tradition posited that the first Roman king was an outsider, Elifaz the son of Esau. This view reflected the reality of the second and third centuries, when Roman dynasties rarely lasted more than two generations, and outsiders like Septimius Severus were crowned as leaders of the empire.[36] Another talmudic tradition interpreted the biblical passage "The voice is the voice of Jacob, but the hands are the hands of Esau"[37] in terms of the suffering that the Romans had inflicted upon them:

34. He also traveled to Rome, but his visits there would have caused far less suspicion than trips to Rome's avowed geopolitical rivals.
35. See Alon, *Jews in Their Land*, 236, citing Heinrich Graetz.
36. R. Samuel Eliezer Halevi Adels (Maharsha), *Ḥidushei Halakhot VeAgadot, Avoda Zara* 10a, s.v. *umi.*
37. Gen. 27:22.

> "The voice" is the Emperor Hadrian who murdered sixty times sixty myriads [1.2 million Jews] in Alexandria of Egypt, twice as many as had left Egypt [during the Exodus]. "The voice of Jacob" is the Emperor Vespasian who murdered four hundred myriads [four million] in the city of Betar – and some say four thousand myriads [forty million]. "And the hands are those of Esau" is the evil kingdom [Rome][38] that destroyed our House and burnt our Temple and exiled us from our land.[39]

The level of exaggeration, common in rabbinic texts – there were not four million Jews in all of Palestine, much less in Betar – reflected the Jews' deep-seated resentment and bitterness after the failure of two bloody rebellions.

Many of the sages who served as the community's spiritual leaders felt that the two peoples could never be reconciled. They drew their inspiration from the prophecy of Obadiah against the house of Esau: "For the violence done to thy brother Jacob, shame shall cover you, and you shall be cut off forever."[40] Their attitude toward the Romans was summed up by one of the empire's fiercest antagonists, R. Simeon b. Yohai: "It is a well-known principle (*halakha beyadua*) that Esau hates Jacob."[41]

For their part, Romans thought the Jews uncivilized and capable of outrageous behavior, such as that falsely attributed to them by Judah's contemporary, the consul, senator, and historian Dio Cassius. Dio's description of the Jews' behavior during their revolt against Trajan in 117 CE typified the attitude of many leading Romans:

> The Jews…were destroying both the Romans and the Greeks. They would eat the flesh of their victims, make belts for themselves of their entrails, anoint themselves with their blood and

38. *Yalkut Shimoni* (*Bereshit* 115, p. 69) inserts the word "Rome" into this passage, which clearly does refer to the Roman Empire.
39. Gittin 57b.
40. Ob. 1:10.
41. H. S. Horovitz, *Corpus Tannaiticum… Pars Tertia: Siphre D'Be Rab,* reprinted as Haym Shaul Horovitz, *Kovetz Maasei HaTanna'im… Ḥelek Shlishi: Sifrei DeVei Rav* (Jerusalem: Or Olam, 5768/2008), 65.

> wear their skins for clothing; many they sawed in two, from the head downwards; others they gave to wild beasts, and still others they forced to fight as gladiators. In all two hundred and twenty thousand persons perished. In Egypt, too, they perpetrated many similar outrages, and in Cyprus... also, two hundred and forty thousand perished, and for this reason no Jew may set foot on that island, but even if one of them is driven upon its shores by a storm he is put to death.[42]

THE SLOW MARCH TO RECONCILIATION

It took many years for the Judaean Jewish community to come to terms with their Roman overlords, unlike the far quicker reconciliation between Jews and Germans after the Holocaust. Within five years after World War II had come to an end, the newly independent State of Israel entered into reparations discussions with the reconstituted Federal Republic of Germany, better known as West Germany. In 1965, just two decades after the Holocaust, West Germany and Israel entered into formal diplomatic relations.

It took considerably longer than twenty years for Romans and Jews to reach a *modus vivendi,* and even then on very unequal terms. There were no reparations. There was no revived Jewish state. Jerusalem was not rebuilt as a Jewish city. Palestine, as Judaea was now called, remained under Roman occupation, with at least two legions stationed on its territory.

Nevertheless, just as Jews and Germans began to come to terms with each other less than a decade after the Holocaust, Jews and Romans did manage to find some means of mutual accommodation, though the start of the process probably took twice as long and progress was halting at best. The first attempt to lift Hadrian's bans occurred early in the reign of his successor, Antoninus Pius. The Talmud recounts:

> The Government had once issued a decree that [Jews] might not keep the Sabbath, circumcise their children, and that they should

42. Dio Cassius, *Roman History,* trans. Earnest Cary (Cambridge, MA and London: Harvard University Press, 1914), 25:31:2.

> have intercourse with menstruating women. Thereupon R. Reuben son of Istroboli cut his hair in the Roman fashion, and went and sat among them [the Senate]. He said to them: If a man has an enemy, what does he wish him, to be poor or rich? They said: That he be poor. He said to them: If so, let them do no work on the Sabbath so that they grow poor. They said: He speaks rightly, let this decree be annulled. It was indeed annulled. Then he continued: If one has an enemy, what does he wish him, to be weak or healthy? They answered: Weak. He said to them: Then let their children be circumcised at the age of eight days and they will be weak. They said: He speaks rightly, and it was annulled. Finally he said to them: If one has an enemy, what does he wish him, to multiply or to decrease? They said to him: That he decreases. If so, let them have no intercourse with menstruating women. They said: He speaks correctly, and it was annulled. Later they came to know that he was a Jew, and [the decrees] were re-instituted.[43]

R. Reuben bar Istroboli almost succeeded but ultimately failed because it was discovered that he was a Jew.[44] Antoninus had retained many of Hadrian's chief lieutenants, who clearly had no love for the rebellious Jews. Indeed, not all the Jews had finally conceded defeat. Some continued to fight on, both in Judaea and in Armenia, until Antoninus crushed them once and for all.[45]

Given the antagonism that characterized relations between Jews and Romans early in his reign, it is not surprising that Antoninus Pius did not restore the patriarchate or the Sanhedrin immediately upon succeeding Hadrian, his adoptive father. Perhaps he had also inherited Hadrian's antipathy toward the Jews, Hadrian, after putting down the Bar Kokhba rebellion, had demolished the Jewish leadership, beginning with the patriarchate, which had embodied the independence of the short-lived

---

43. Me'ila 17a.

44. Ibid.

45. *Historia Augusta,* trans. David Magie (Cambridge, MA and London: Harvard University Press, 1921); *Antoninus Pius,* 5:4; Alon, *Jews in Their Land,* 655. The *Catholic Encyclopedia,* http://www.newadvent.org/cathen/01586a.htm, asserts that there was also a revolt in Palestine, but the overwhelming majority of historians disagree.

Judaean state, and which also had distant familial ties to the exilarchs in Parthian Babylonia, Rome's great rival (both were of Davidic blood, the patriarchs through maternal ancestry, the exilarchs through their paternal forebears). Faced with any rebellion against his own authority, however minor, Antoninus would have been in no mood to reconstitute these symbols of Jewish nationalism and international connections.

It was only later in his reign, when Judaea was finally at peace and Jews had come to terms with Roman authority that Antoninus began to ratchet back Hadrian's decrees by granting the Jews their religious autonomy. His first step in this regard appears to have been his decision to lift Hadrian's ban on Jewish circumcision.[46] Equally important, he permitted the Sages once again to expound and implement the law, at first as individuals only, but later through their rulings in the reconstituted Sanhedrin.

It took somewhat longer for Antoninus to permit the restoration of the patriarchate. Thus, when the sages gathered in the Galilean town of Usha in the aftermath of the rebellion in order to intercalate the calendar and, on another occasion, to foster the study of Torah, Judah's father Simeon ben Gamaliel, who by rights should have succeeded his father as patriarch, was not among them. As has been noted, he had gone into hiding during the war, reportedly "in Asia,"[47] and remained there for some time thereafter, presumably until the Jewish community came to terms with Roman domination.[48] It was only then, still later in his reign, that Antoninus authorized the restoration of the patriarchate and, by permitting Simeon to assume the post, in effect "pardoned" him.

Like the rabbinic leaders who preceded him to Usha, Simeon had been a student of R. Akiba, the spiritual leader of the Bar Kokhba revolt, whom the Romans had put to death in such cruel fashion that it is commemorated on Tisha B'Av, the saddest day on the Jewish calendar, and additionally by Ashkenazic Jews on Yom Kippur, its holiest day. It was for that reason that Simeon had gone into hiding during the war; R. Akiba had at one point also attempted to evade the Romans, but he had

46. Alon, *Jews in Their Land*, 647.

47. Bava Kamma 83a.

48. Alon, *Jews in Their Land*, 664–66.

been caught. Ironically, the very fact that Simeon was so closely associated with R. Akiba might actually have worked to his advantage when dealing with Roman officials. By demonstrating his willingness to work with them, Simeon was signaling to his colleagues among the sages, as well as to the community at large, that even a disciple of an implacable opponent of Rome was prepared to bury the hatchet in the interest of peace and tranquility in his ravaged land. In doing so he set an example for his son Judah, who further strengthened the patriarchate's relationship with Judaea's Roman overlords, to the point where later rabbis considered that he dealt with them as a virtual equal.

JEWISH AND ROMAN ATTITUDES TO CHRISTIANS

The challenges and upheavals of the century preceding Simeon's assumption of the patriarchate had left an indelible mark on the Jewish community's religious practices. It was during this period that the rabbis explicitly ruled that matrilineal descent should be the basis for determining one's Jewishness.[49] Aware of increasing Roman hostility toward conversion to Judaism, the rabbis raised the bar for the non-Jews to convert. Finally, the rabbis had to take account of Christianity, a growing religious movement that claimed to have its roots in Judaism but became increasingly hostile to the older religion, though it was the Romans who tormented the followers of the new faith.

In 109–110 Trajan persecuted Christians in Palestine and elsewhere in what was later termed the "Third Persecution."[50] The Christians resented the Jews, often seeking to entrap them with passages from Scripture in order to convert them. Nevertheless, Jews sometimes got caught up in the Roman net if they were suspected of being followers of what was then still a sect. That was the case of R. Eliezer, who was arrested

49. For an overview of the academic literature on the subject of Jewish matrilineal descent, see Susan Sorek, "Mothers of Israel: Why the Rabbis Adopted a Matrilineal Principle," *Women in Judaism* 3 (2002), https://wjudaism.library.utoronto.ca/index.php/wjudaism/article/view/197/175.

50. John Foxe, *Book of Martyrs*, ed. Harold J. Chadwick (Alachua, FL: Bridge-Logos, 2001), 11–12. See also Pliny the Younger's letter to Trajan regarding his own treatment of Christians and Trajan's reply. *The Letters of the Younger Pliny*, trans. Betty Radice (London: Penguin, 1969), 293–95.

because he was suspected of being a Jewish Christian, but who had merely remarked favorably on a scriptural interpretation by the Jewish Christian Jacob of Kfar Sekhania, a remark that he later bitterly regretted.[51]

Hadrian shared Trajan's apprehensions regarding both Christians and Jews. He continued the "Third Persecution" by massacring ten thousand Christians during his reign.[52] As previously noted, the Romans had long recognized Judaism as a legitimate religion and had not banned its practice outside Judaea even during the worst of Hadrian's persecutions. Christianity, on the other hand, was a breakaway Jewish sect that was seeking to establish itself as an independent religion.

Antoninus Pius did not look favorably upon the nascent faith either. In his eyes it was a movement that rejected his own form of worship. In this regard his views meshed with those of the Jewish leadership and the rabbinate. During his reign numerous Christians were put to death and the religion was subject to persecution, in marked contrast to the treatment of Jews. Nevertheless, Antoninus upheld an earlier ruling by the Emperor Trajan that forbade extra-judicial attacks (that is, attacks by uncontrolled mobs) against Christians.[53] He also tolerated the meetings of bishops, called synods, which successively pushed for a complete break with any vestiges of Jewish practice.

After his passing, Antoninus was universally remembered by Roman historians as a model leader. In the words of one of them, "almost alone of all emperors he lived entirely unstained by the blood of either citizen or foe...and was justly compared to Numa Pompilius [the legendary second king of Rome], whose good fortune and piety and tranquility and religious rites he ever maintained."[54] His successor, Marcus Aurelius, was a very different figure. Though he is best remembered as a stoic philosopher, his reign was punctuated by

---

51. Avoda Zara 16b–17a.
52. Foxe, *Book of Martyrs,* 12.
53. The third- to fourth-century church historian Eusebius wrote that after an appeal by the governor Plinius Secundus, Trajan limited his attacks on Christians to those who openly practiced their faith. Eusebius, *Ecclesiastical History,* trans. C. F. Cruse (Peabody, MA: Hendrickson, 1989), 3:33. See also Trajan's reply to Pliny, in *Letters of the Younger Pliny,* 295.
54. *Historia Augusta: Antoninus Pius,* 13:4.

warfare, bloodshed, and intrigue. Like Antoninus Pius, Marcus Aurelius was a favorite of Hadrian, who arranged his marriage to the daughter of a prominent Roman, had Antoninus Pius adopt him as a son, and elevated him to the Senate and other prominent offices.[55] Unlike Antoninus, however, he does not appear to have outgrown Hadrian's dislike of Jews, nor for that matter, of Christians. Marcus went beyond nasty words when dealing with Christians, however. He launched a major attack on them in 161 CE, torturing many of their leaders and burning them at the stake.

The Jews were not troubled by his actions. After all, Bar Kokhba had persecuted the Christians as heretics; while for their part the Christians in Judaea remained neutral during his revolt because they considered *him* a heretic. It was not until the fourth century, when Theodosius designated Christianity as the official religion of the Roman Empire, that Jews identified Christianity with Esau, a not-illogical extension of their previous view of Rome as Jacob's antagonistic brother. Early church historians asserted that the Jews had encouraged the persecution of Christians under Marcus. These historians were by no means unbiased; but given the Jews' attitude toward Christians at the time, their accounts have some ring of plausibility.

Marcus' hostility toward Christians clearly was greater than his reportedly negative feelings toward the Jews. Whatever those feelings may have been, they were not enough to prompt him to disestablish either the patriarchate or the Sanhedrin. Simeon ben Gamaliel was able to maintain his position as patriarch, and indeed to strengthen it even while Marcus ruled. R. Simeon thus laid the groundwork for his son Judah, who rendered that office more powerful than at any time since the destruction of the Temple.

Rebbe's Relations with Jewish Christians

The rabbis of the Talmud generally detested Jewish Christians. The Talmud has numerous tales of *Tanna'im* confronting, and invariably outwitting, the people they termed *minim* (sectarians), who would try to embarrass

55. His father-in-law was Lucius Ceionius Commodus; see *Historia Augusta: Hadrian,* 24:1, and *Marcus Antoninus,* 4:5–5:8.

the rabbis with quotes from the Scriptures. Rebbe does not figure frequently in these tales, but one incident demonstrates that Rebbe's attitude toward them was considerably more nuanced. The Talmud records:

> A certain *min*[56] once cited to Rebbe the verse, "He who formed the mountains did not create the wind, and he who created the wind did not form the mountains, for it is written: For, lo, He that forms the mountains and creates the wind."[57]

The Jewish Christian's implication was that there was more than one deity. When Rebbe replied, "You fool, turn to the end of the verse: 'The Lord of hosts is His name,'"[58] the *min* responded by asking for three days in order to prove his point. The Talmud continues:

> Rebbe spent those three days in fasting; thereafter, as he was about to partake of food, he was told, "There is a *min* waiting at the door." Assuming that it was the same individual who had challenged him three days earlier and had now returned to refute him, Rebbe cited a passage in Psalms: "They put poison into my food."[59] But it was not the same man; it was another Jewish Christian. Said he [the *min*]: "My Master, I bring you good tidings; your opponent could find no answer and so threw himself down from the roof and died." He [Rebbe] said: "Would you dine with me?" He replied, "Yes." After they had eaten and drunk, Rebbe said to him, "Will you drink the cup of wine over which

56. The text of the most commonly used Talmud (the "Vilna *Shas*") reads "a certain Sadducee." This was clearly a redacted version to avoid Church censorship; Sadducees believed in the oneness of God every bit as much as the Pharisees. The Munich manuscript (MsM) of the Talmud (1342) reads *mina*. R. Adin Steinsaltz follows the MsM version: R. Adin Steinsaltz, ed., *Talmud Bavli:* Ḥullin vol. 1 (Jerusalem: Israel Institute for Talmudic Publications, 2010), 366, and his comment s.v. *mi sheyatzar*. Regarding the identity of *minim* and where Rebbe may have encountered the *min*, see Stuart S. Miller, "The *Minim* of Sepphoris Reconsidered," *Harvard Theological Review* 86:4 (1993), 377–402, especially 395.
57. Amos 4:13.
58. Is. 47:4.
59. Ps. 69:22

> the Benedictions of the Grace [after meals] have been said, or would you rather have forty gold coins?" He replied, "I would rather drink the cup of wine." Thereupon a heavenly voice came forth and said: "The cup of wine over which the Benedictions [of Grace have been said] is worth forty gold coins." R. Isaac said: "The family [of that *min*] is still to be found among the notables of Rome and is named 'the family of Bar Luianus.'"[60]

Rebbe could not tolerate the first Jewish Christian because he was a scoffer. The second *min* was different; he was respectful of Rebbe's status and of his beliefs, and Rebbe treated him differently. Rebbe may have considered the man to be misguided because he had adopted the Christian faith, but he showed him no disrespect as a consequence of his views. He was even willing to sup and drink with him. The man responded by preferring the wine of blessing, which was integral to the Grace after Meals (*Birkat HaMazon*), to forty pieces of gold. His decision led to his receiving the gold as a reward: for every amen that he answered in response to each of the four blessings that are uttered in *Birkat HaMazon*, he was awarded ten golden pieces.[61]

REBBE AND ANTONINUS

There are over fifty references in the Talmud, and over fifty more in midrashic literature, to the relationship between Rabbi Judah the Prince and a prominent Roman official named Antoninus, beginning with the story of their near-simultaneous birth. Who this official actually was remains a mystery, although his identity has been the subject of scholarly debate for well over a century.

Most scholars agree that "Antoninus" was indeed a Roman emperor, one of whose names was Antoninus. But there the agreement ends, because there were several emperors who bore that name who were Judah's contemporaries. Judah was born in 135 CE and died on the fifteenth of Kislev, 217 CE, at the age of eighty-two. His life overlapped

60. Ḥullin 87a. It is possible that Luianus returned to Judaism. See R. Yosef Hayyim, *Ben Yehoyada*, vol. 3 (Jerusalem: Salem, 5758/1998), s.v. *vekorin*.
61. Rashi, s.v. *arba'im*.

with the reigns of nine Roman emperors: Hadrian (76–138); Antoninus Pius (86–161); his two adopted sons, Marcus Aurelius (121–180) and Lucius Aurelius Verus, who ruled as co-emperor until his early demise (130–169); Marcus' son Commodus (161–192); Pertinax (126–193); Didius Julianus (133–193); Septimius Severus (145–211); and Caracalla (188–217).

Of the nine, it is clear that Judah could not have possibly had any interaction with Hadrian, who died when Judah was a small child. Some scholars have identified Antoninus Pius with the talmudic Antoninus. Again, however, it is unlikely that the Roman would have had much to do with Judah. The latter did not assume leadership of the Jewish community of Palestine until sometime after 165, some years after Antoninus Pius had passed away.

Other scholars have argued, even insisted, that Marcus Aurelius is the Antoninus of the Talmud.[62] None of them identify "Antoninus" with Marcus' brother by adoption, Lucius Verus. Although Lucius fought in the East, he never visited Palestine. After leading successful wars in Armenia and Mesopotamia and then fighting for a relatively short time near the Danube, he returned to Rome and died shortly thereafter, possibly from a stroke.

On its face, there is some merit to the assertion that Marcus Aurelius was "Antoninus." Marcus bore the name Antoninus: his full name was Marcus Aurelius Antoninus Augustus. His philosophic bent, together with his intellectual approach, appear to be reflected in many of the talmudic legends that surround Judah and the emperor. Indeed, some have argued that his writings paralleled Jewish values.[63] In addition, Judah's reign as Prince may have overlapped with Marcus' rule for as many as fifteen years, if his father Simeon died as early as 165 CE. Moreover, Marcus Aurelius passed through Palestine in 175 CE, when Judah would have been forty and perhaps fully entrenched as the leader of the Jewish community.[64] Finally, it was against the Christians,

62. Luitpold Wallach, "The Colloquy of Marcus Aurelius with the Patriarch Judah 1," *Jewish Quarterly Review* (January 1941), 259–86; E. Mary Smallwood, *Jews under Roman Rule*, 485–86.
63. Wallach, "The Colloquy of Marcus Aurelius," 282–83.
64. Smallwood, *Jews under Roman Rule*, 482.

rather than the Jews, that Rome under Marcus Aurelius exhibited the greatest venom.[65] Christian historians labeled his reign as the Fourth Persecution.[66]

On the other hand, it is arguable that because of their very nature, the legends might not accurately reflect the give-and-take that could have taken place between Judah and his interlocutor. The authors of the Talmud may simply have appropriated a form of discourse with which they were familiar and attributed it to Judah and the emperor. In particular, those who argue that Marcus was the Antoninus of the Talmud assert that the nature of the reported dialogue reflects a Stoic source without which "a great many Antoninus traditions would appear well-nigh incomprehensible."[67] Marcus was indeed a great Stoic philosopher; yet at least one dialogue with Judah directly contradicts a major tenet of Stoic philosophy. The Talmud reports that "Antoninus" convinced Judah to accept the position that the soul enters the body from the moment of conception, that is, from the time the sperm mates with the egg.[68] But Stoic philosophy denied that the soul exists prior to birth.[69]

Marcus Aurelius was considerably older than Judah, perhaps by as much as sixteen years. It is unlikely that the mature emperor and the newly minted patriarch could have had the sort of intimate relationship that the Talmud describes. In particular, as discussed below, the Talmud is replete with cases of advice that Judah gave to the emperor, notably regarding court intrigue as well as highly personal family matters.[70] It

65. Frank McLynn, *Marcus Aurelius: A Life* (Cambridge, MA: Da Capo, 2009), 290–93.
66. Foxe, *Book of Martyrs*, 13–16.
67. Wallach, "The Colloquy of Marcus Aurelius," 274.
68. Sanhedrin 91b; *Yad Rama,* cited in R. Zvi H. Zakheim, *Zvi HaSanhedrin*, vol. 3 (Brooklyn, NY: Gross, 5752/1992), 208; *Yad Rama* dismisses as "mere dreams" Rashi's interpretation that what was meant was the moment when an angel takes the fertilized egg to Heaven to determine its future. Rashi, Sanhedrin 91b, s.v. *pekida* based on a statement by R. Hanina bar Papa; Nidda 16b; Genesis Rabba 34:12. All citations from *Midrash Rabba* are from the Hebrew version (New York: L. Goldman, 5713/1953).
69. Samuel Kottek, "Embryology in Talmudic and Midrashic Literature," *Journal of the History of Biology* 14 (Autumn 1981), 309–10. Kottek inaccurately cites Sanhedrin 91a–b; the dialogue appears only in 91b.
70. Avoda Zara 10a–b and see below.

seems hardly plausible that Marcus Aurelius needed, or would have accepted, such counsel from someone so junior to him.

Moreover, Marcus may well have been antagonistic toward the Jews, making it even less likely that he would look to their leader for advice on the affairs of state. He had grown up in Hadrian's shadow and, was "transfixed, as all elite Romans were, by the third and most horrible of all Rome's Jewish wars...the most serious threat yet to the Roman position in Palestine."[71] Surely the revolt must have colored his image of the Jews. Indeed, it is possible that Jews may have served in the forces of rebel general Avidius Cassius, who declared himself emperor in the mistaken belief that Marcus had died.[72] Perhaps not surprisingly, therefore, when he first heard of the revolt, Marcus reportedly told his legions, "Cilicians, Syrians, Jews and Egyptians have never been superior to you and never will, even if they should muster as many tens of thousands more than you as they now muster fewer."[73]

The Jews may have supported Avidius simply as "a matter of prudence to favour the side locally in power in the impending civil war."[74] Alternately, it is possible that Marcus was entirely wrong about the Jews' sympathies and erroneously accused them of siding with Avidius, whose rebellion he crushed in 175.[75] In any event, they appear to have got under his skin when he was in Palestine. As reported by the fourth-century writer Ammianus Marcellinus, "Marcus, as he was passing through Palestine on his way to Egypt, being often disgusted by the malodorous and rebellious Jews, is reported to have said with sorrow: 'O Marcomanni, O Quadi, O Sarmatians, at last I have found a people more unruly than you.'"[76] As one contemporary historian has noted, "The Jews may well have seized the opportunity [of Marcus' presence in Palestine] to make requests and representations to Marcus in person, perhaps in a

71. McLynn, *Marcus Aurelius,* 33–34.
72. See Menahem Stern, ed., *Greek and Latin Authors on Jews and Judaism: From Tacitus to Simpliciius* (Jerusalem: The Israel Academy of Sciences and Humanities, 1980), 406.
73. Dio Cassius, *Roman History,* 71:25:1.
74. Smallwood, *Jews under Roman Rule,* 482.
75. Alon, *Jews in Their Land,* 654. See also Dio Cassius, *Roman History,* 71:25:1.
76. Quoted in Stern, ed., *Greek and Latin Authors on Jews and Judaism,* 606.

somewhat vehement manner and with irritating importunity."[77] The Jews may therefore simply have irritated him, producing a reaction not unlike President Harry Truman's annoyance at the constant badgering by American Jews that he support the creation of a Jewish state. Under these circumstances, would the emperor really have looked to a Jewish leader for advice and counsel?

Finally, though many scholars posit that Judah's father Simeon had passed from the scene by 175 CE, there is no conclusive evidence in that regard. Judah may not even have been Prince of the Jewish community when Marcus passed through Palestine. In that case it is unlikely that they would have met, much less engaged in lengthy and serious conversations.

Commodus, the son of Marcus Aurelius, was also named Antoninus. He ruled alongside his father for three years, from 177 to 180 CE, and then ruled alone. He was a wastrel who antagonized both the military and the populace, and he was assassinated in 192. Though he accompanied his father to the Middle East in 175 CE, he was only thirteen years old at the time. It is highly unlikely that he would have interacted with Judah, twenty-seven years his senior, in any serious way. Commodus never visited the Middle East again. In any event, virtually no scholar has identified him with the Talmud's Antoninus.

Both Pertinax and Didius Julianus hardly ruled long enough to interact with Judah. Pertinax, one of the plotters against Commodus, was named emperor by a somewhat reluctant army on January 1, 193, the day after the latter's assassination. The son of a slave and a one-time schoolteacher, he had risen through the army to the rank of legionary commander and served subsequently in senior civilian posts, including proconsul of Africa. The Praetorian Guard invited him to accept the throne – on the promise of a substantial payment to them. His reign lasted but eighty-seven days, however; when it became clear that he would only pay half of what he had promised, the Guard summarily murdered him.

Pertinax was succeeded by Didius, who bought the throne in an auction conducted by the Praetorian Guard. Unlike Pertinax, Didius

77. Smallwood, *Jews under Roman Rule,* 483.

hailed from a prominent Milanese family.[78] He too had been a military man and a senior civilian official, serving as a legionary commander, consul, and provincial governor, succeeding Pertinax as governor of Africa. His ascent to the throne immediately aroused hostility among both the populace and rival generals, and he reigned for an even shorter period than Pertinax – just sixty-six days, at which point the Senate deposed him; and on its orders a soldier executed him on June 1, 193.

The other two emperors whose lives overlapped with Judah's were Septimius Severus, who was able to bring stability to the empire and who founded the royal line of the Severi, and his son Caracalla, who co-ruled Rome with Severus from 198 to 211 CE and then ruled alone for an additional six years. Several contemporary scholars have identified either of these two men as the Antoninus of the Talmud.[79] Septimius Severus was the first Roman emperor to be born and raised outside Europe. He hailed from Tripolitania, a region in what is now, for the moment, Libya. That he was not Roman born and was of Punic or Phoenician origin may have contributed to a talmudic legend that placed his birth in Judaea.

Severus traveled widely throughout the Empire, both as a senator and then as emperor. Like Marcus Aurelius he visited Palestine – in 198 CE, in the course of leading military operations against the Parthians and other nations on the Empire's eastern border. Judah would have been at the height of his power when Septimius Severus was in Palestine. If there was any time when Judah would likely have interacted with an emperor, it would have been in 198–99 CE, when Judah was in his early sixties. With Severus in his early fifties, there would hardly have been a noticeable age difference between the two men at that stage of their lives. Severus was well disposed toward the Jews; like Marcus Aurelius, he persecuted the Christians in what church historians labeled "the Fifth Persecution," though he initially had been well disposed toward them because he reportedly had been "ministered to by a Christian" during "a severe fit of sickness."[80]

78. Milan was then called Mediolanum.

79. Binyamin Lau, *Ḥakhamim,* vol 3: *Yemei Galil* (Tel Aviv: Yediot Ahronot, 2008), 339–40. See also Oppenheimer, *Rabbi Yehuda HaNasi,* 47–48.

80. Foxe, *Book of Martyrs,* 16.

Septimius Severus was not called Antoninus. But Caracalla, his son and for thirteen years his co-ruler, did bear that name; his full name was Marcus Aurelius Severus Antoninus Augustus. The Church father and historian Eusebius always referred to Caracalla as Antoninus. Moreover, he would have had two separate opportunities to meet Judah: once when he accompanied his father to Palestine in late 198 to the spring of 199, just as he had become co-emperor, and again in 215 CE, when Judah, still very much the Jewish leader, was nearing the end of his life.

Several recent studies have identified the Talmud's Antoninus solely with Caracalla.[81] Yet when Caracalla first met Judah, he was still a ten-year-old boy and had just been proclaimed as co-emperor by his father. He was unlikely to have interacted with Judah as an equal in the presence of his father. When Caracalla was in Palestine a second time, however, he was emperor in his own right. While he certainly would have interacted with Judah, since the older man was still at the helm of a community that Caracalla favored, their discussions were unlikely to have been of a philosophical nature. Caracalla was no philosopher like Marcus Aurelius, nor did he share his father's positive disposition toward others. He was reviled as a bloodthirsty character and was assassinated before he reached the age of thirty.

Despite his generally despicable character, however, Caracalla was not at all badly disposed toward the Jews.[82] Indeed, there is one additional and explicit piece of evidence regarding Caracalla's, and, for that matter, Septimius Severus', positive attitude toward the Jews – Jerome's commentary on the Book of Daniel. The fourth-century Church historian, explaining the verse "Now when they stumble, they will be helped with a little help,"[83] noted that "some of the Hebrews understand these things as applying to the princes Severus and Antoninus, who esteemed the Jews very highly."[84] Jerome's reference had to have been

81. Oppenheimer, *Rabbi Yehuda HaNasi,* 47–48; Alon, *Jews in Their Land,* 682; Peter Schafer, *The History of the Jews in Antiquity: The Jews of Palestine from Alexander the Great to the Arab Conquest,* trans. David Chowcat (Luxembourg: Harwood, 1995), 168. See also Stern, ed., *Greek and Latin Authors on Jews and Judaism,* 626.

82. See below, p. 90.

83. Dan. 11:34.

84. Jerome, *Commentary on Daniel,* 11:34.

to the Talmud. And the only rabbi that the Talmud identified as having interacted on favorable terms with an emperor named "Antoninus" was Rabbi Judah the Prince.[85]

Who, then, was the Antoninus of the Talmud? We probably will never know for certain. Indeed, there was no reason why the rabbis who compiled the accounts of Judah and the Roman emperor at least a century, and in some cases several centuries, after Caracalla's passing, would necessarily have been sufficiently well informed about Roman history to have distinguished between him and his father. All they really knew was that there was a tradition that an emperor named Antoninus was well disposed to the Jews, and that this emperor was a contemporary of Rabbi Judah the Prince.

Very few rabbis during the era of the *Amora'im*, which extended from the third through the sixth centuries, interacted with their rulers, and even for those who did, their relationships were not nearly as close or personal.[86] The majority of rabbis during that period never seem to have interacted much with officials other than tax collectors and other minor administrators, and appear to have had little understanding of the outside world. Their ideas about emperors, kings, and the like had very little basis in reality. Yet it was their musings about Rebbe and Antoninus that the Talmud records.

A discussion in Tractate Shevuot illustrates the relative lack of knowledge about secular officialdom on the part of most of the rabbis. In attempting to outline and rank different forms of leprosy, the rabbis resorted to comparing those rankings to the rankings among kings and other high government officials. This is similar to modern protocol, which determines seniority in a variety of contexts that can range from where one is seated at a dinner to where one stands at an official ceremony. In

---

85. Some have argued that "Severus" is actually Alexander Severus; presumably, then, "Antoninus" would be Elagabalus, whose full name was Marcus Aurelius Antoninus Augustus. See, for example, Jay Braverman, *Jerome's Commentary on Daniel: A Study of Comparative Jewish and Christian Interpretations of the Hebrew Bible* (Washington, DC: Catholic Biblical Association of America, 1978), 120–21. The case for Alexander falls apart, however, because Judah passed away before Alexander assumed the Roman throne.

86. Goodman, *Rome and Jerusalem*, 483.

the course of these comparisons, Rava (280–352 CE) noted that the two major types of leprosy could be compared to his fourth-century contemporary King Shapur the Great of Persia and to the Roman Caesar, possibly Constantine. At which point Rava's student R. Papa asked, "Which of them is greater? He replied: You eat in the forest! Go forth and see whose authority is greater in the world; for it is written: It shall devour the whole earth, and shall tread it down, and break it in pieces."[87]

Rava was acquainted with both King Shapur and the queen mother, Ifra Hormiz. He did not get along well with the king, though Ifra Hormiz respected him greatly. As one who therefore occasionally moved in government circles, Rava was aware of the power of the Roman emperor. He mentioned King Shapur first, presumably because he was the king's subject; but he knew that the Romans were still more powerful, and he probably was aware of the emperor's new capital in Byzantium, renamed Constantinople.

On the other hand, Rava's student R. Papa, though a wealthy brewer, was not nearly as worldly wise. Rava mocked his ignorance. "You eat in the forest" meant that R. Papa had no idea about the larger world around him. Yet R. Papa was more typical of his amoraic colleagues than Rava. Apart from their pursuit of a livelihood, they focused entirely on studying the texts or implementing them as community judges and decisors. Yet it was these men, who did not know much about the Roman emperor because they "ate in the forest," who produced the largest number of tales about Rebbe and the emperor they called Antoninus; they were therefore, at a minimum, likely to be prone to exaggeration.

Was the Antoninus of rabbinic literature a single individual? Might not the rabbis of the Talmud and Midrash, our two sources of information about Rabbi Judah the Prince and Antoninus, have created a composite emperor combining the personalities of Severus and Caracalla, precisely because they had no real knowledge of Rome or its rulers? Unlike Antoninus Pius, Severus and Caracalla ruled the Empire when Judah served as the Prince of Palestine's Jewish community. Unlike Marcus Aurelius, Severus and Caracalla were unequivocally friendly toward the Jews, a fact asserted by the ancients and confirmed by modern

87. Shevuot 6b.

scholars. Finally, unlike Commodus, the later emperors both had occasion to pass through Palestine when they, like Judah, were mature adults.

There is no clear evidence that the rabbis of the Talmud deliberately blended the two emperors into one personality. Nevertheless, writing more than a century, and often several centuries, after the events they were describing, it is plausible that they treated as one person the two emperors who both had visited Palestine and shown some favor to the Jews. The case for either of them being the Antoninus of rabbinic literature is strong, but the case for Antoninus as a composite of them both is even stronger. As a contemporary scholar has observed, "The production of a singular talmudic voice is effected in part through the condensation of various historical 'others' into a single literary figure."[88]

This volume therefore postulates that Antoninus was indeed a blending of Severus and his son. It will draw upon talmudic references to explore the parallels between the Prince and the emperors in terms of their lifestyles, leadership, politics, attitudes, and beliefs. It will focus primarily upon Judah, with the emperors as an ongoing backdrop to his life, so as to provide a more complete context and better understanding of Rebbe's relationship with the Romans in general and with the emperors in particular.

In one major respect. Judah's rise to power and greatness differed markedly from that of Septimius Severus. Judah was the ultimate insider. He inherited his position from his father, Rabban Simeon ben Gamaliel. who had to fend off a major "palace coup" to solidify his ancestral office as Prince of the Judaean Jewish community. Severus, on the other hand, though descended from a prominent family, was an outsider: he was an African, not a European, and prior to his becoming emperor no African had ever led the Roman Empire. He had to plot, fight, and even kill in order to reach the top of the "greasy pole."

88. Ron Naiweld, "There Is Only One Other: The Fabrication of Antoninus in a Multilayered Talmudic Dialogue," *The Jewish Quarterly Review* 104 (Winter 2014), 82. While advocating the principle of a blended "other," Naiweld sees a very different form of blending, namely, dialogues reflecting a "dualist thinker" blended with those reflecting a Hellenistic philosopher, suggesting a Palestinian origin. See ibid., 84, 102, and 102n69.

Moreover, Judah's role was that of religious as well as political leader. Though as the Talmud relates, he often yielded to the views of rabbinical colleagues who disagreed with him on points of halakha and at times simply outvoted him, he both carefully and forcefully preserved the prerogatives of religious leadership that was his family's legacy. Severus, in contrast, paid lip service to the Roman religion. He exploited its ceremonial nature in order to validate his rule, and he resonated to its superstitions. But he was not a religious man.

Severus' son, Caracalla, resembled Judah in that he too inherited his throne from his father, though unlike Judah, he ruled alongside his father for several years before succeeding him. Although Caracalla, like Judah, displayed openness to other religions and peoples, the similarities end there. Caracalla was by nature a cruel individual and did not live out his days; he was assassinated just six years after his father's passing.

In addition to providing a modified form of what Plutarch might have termed "parallel lives," this volume hopefully will demonstrate not only Judah's great contribution to the development of rabbinic Judaism, but also, as already noted, his worldliness and openness to ideas, concepts, and practices whose sources were in the non-Jewish world, yet whose intrinsic value was no less significant. His attitudes stand in marked contrast to many among post-Emancipation Jewry who sought to shut themselves off from the world around them. It is because of his very different attitudes, in addition to his scholarship and leadership, that Judah provides a model for contemporary Jewry as he has been for Jews throughout the ages.

Chapter 2

The Road to the Top: Rebbe

> When Rebbe was born they [the Romans] banned circumcision and his father and mother circumcised him. The emperor [Hadrian] sent for him and they brought Rebbe and his mother before him. But his mother had switched him for Antoninus and nursed the child until he was brought before the emperor who found him uncircumcised and he sent them in peace. His legate said, "I saw that they circumcised this child but the Holy One, blessed be He, constantly works miracles for them. And so they repealed the decree."
>
> *Tosafot,* Avoda Zara 10b, s.v. *amar,*
> derived from *Midrash Beit HaMikdash* 8

SIMEON BEN GAMALIEL'S CHALLENGE

Simeon ben Gamaliel seemed to be personally well suited to begin the process of reconciliation with Rome. As a descendant of Hillel the Elder and therefore a scion of the royal House of David, he was the head of the ruling house, whose task it was to interface and negotiate with the Romans. His father, Rabban Gamaliel II, had determined that the family's diplomatic duties rendered it imperative that his son – and other members of his household – should be able to communicate with the Romans in a language they understood and in terms that reflected their cultural idiom. Simeon therefore had command of Greek language and literature and possibly philosophy, which the rabbis proscribed for all but his family.[1] He dressed like a Greek. He was, in effect, fully acculturated to the surrounding Roman and Hellenistic environment.[2] As his father's designated successor, Judah was reared in the same manner.

Simeon's resumption of the role of patriarch was not without opposition from some of his learned rabbinic peers. Moreover, unlike R. Akiba and many other religious leaders who accepted martyrdom rather than cease teaching Torah despite Hadrian's decrees to that effect, R. Simeon simply had disappeared from the scene.[3] His behavior naturally prompted considerable resentment on the part of his erstwhile colleagues. In particular, as will soon be noted, R. Meir and R. Nathan, to whom the rabbis had looked for religious leadership in R. Simeon's absence, were openly hostile to R. Simeon upon his return from exile.

Nevertheless, it is noteworthy that neither they nor Simeon's, nor subsequently Judah's rabbinical colleagues, voiced objections to the patriarchate's assimilation of Greco-Roman culture. While in general the rabbis bitterly opposed what they termed "external books" and "Greek wisdom," they accepted the patriarchate's secular need to interact with Roman officials. They cited the precedent of Nehemiah, who was permitted to drink gentile wine due to his position as cupbearer to Artaxerxes, and expanded the exemption from their own dicta to include anyone who was "close to the government" (*karov lamalkhut*). As the Talmud put it, the rabbis "permitted those of the house of R. Gamaliel

1. See Sota 49b; Bava Kamma 83a, which discuss both the ban on the study of Greek philosophy and the exemption accorded to the family of the patriarch. Since the rabbis forcefully proscribed the study of Greek philosophy, had R. Simeon not been known to have been familiar with Greek philosophy no exemption would have been necessary.
2. Y. Avoda Zara 2:2; Lau, *Ḥakhamim*, vol. 3, 252–53.
3. The Yom Kippur and Tisha B'Av liturgical poems about the "Ten Martyrs" who died in the Bar Kokhba revolt both list Rabban Simeon among the ten. That clearly was not the case, however, since he escaped the Roman terror. It was his grandfather, Rabban Simeon b. Gamaliel I, who died during the earlier Jewish revolt of 68–70 CE.

to engage in Greek wisdom because they were close to the government."[4] The principle of *karov lamalkhut* was adopted in normative Jewish law. Maimonides would put it well centuries later: "A Jew who is close to the government...and finds it debasing to differ from other courtiers, may dress and cut his hair as they do."[5]

In addition to their recognition of the practical need for Simeon to relate to their Roman overlords, the rabbis' mild response to his adoption of Roman practices and behaviors was also due to Simeon's personality, which also must have helped smooth his relations with the Romans. He led his community "with a blend of sagacity, moderation and resilience combined with a capacity for decisive action in moments of crisis." Even more important to his success with both rabbis and Romans was his "friendly disposition, the ability to work with others, a strong awareness of the need for consensus, and at the same time the will to assert his authority and to insist on the prerogatives of his office."[6] In other words, he was the consummate politician, and there can be little doubt that the young Judah learned the art of politics at the feet of his esteemed father once the latter returned from exile.

THE PLOT AGAINST JUDAH'S FATHER[7]

R. Simeon's political talents were put to the test almost immediately upon his return from exile to claim his place as patriarch. As previously noted, the patriarchate was dynastic, but it had not always been so. It had originally been bestowed upon the people of Beteira. They had abdicated to Hillel I, a Babylonian who was a student of Shemaya and Avtalion, the joint leaders of the Pharisees, when he was able to resolve legal issues they could not.

In attempting to assert his authority, Simeon confronted a serious threat from R. Meir and R. Nathan, who in his absence had been serving

4. Bava Kamma 83a. See also Tosefta Sota 15:8.
5. Maimonides, *Mishneh Torah, Yad HaḤazaka, Hilkhot Avoda Zara* 11:3.
6. Alon, *Jews in Their Land,* 667.
7. The plot against Rabban Simeon is discussed in Horayot 13b. See also David Goodlatt, "Al Sippur HaKesher Neged Rabban Shimon ben Gamliel HaSheni" (The Story of the Plot Against Rabban Simeon b. Gamaliel II [Hebrew]), *Zion* 49:4 (1984), 349–74.

as the community's leading jurists and teachers. R. Meir was a disciple of R. Akiba; equally if not more important, he was the leading scholar of his generation. R. Nathan's ancestry was actually more prominent than R. Simeon's. A Babylonian by birth, he was the son of the exilarch, and could therefore claim a more direct descent from the House of David than could Simeon.

The two rabbis had led the Sanhedrin during R. Simeon's exile, with R. Nathan serving as the court president (*Av Beit Din*) and R. Meir as the chief judicial expert (*Ḥakham*). When R. Simeon returned as patriarch, he initially was tolerant of the fact that his colleagues were shown the same degree of respect that he received; the arrival of any one of them in court prompted those in attendance to rise from their seated positions. Once he became more settled in his role, however, Simeon downgraded their status, insisting that only his entry into the court (or anywhere for that matter) would cause people to rise until he was seated. The others were to be accorded a lesser degree of respect.

R. Meir was particularly outraged by the change in his status; when he first experienced what he considered to be an affront to his station, he stormed out of the assembly hall. He then suggested to R. Nathan that they entrap R. Simeon by posing legal questions to him that they were sure he could not answer. His ensuing embarrassment would surely result in his relinquishing his office. To ensure R. Nathan's support, R. Meir cleverly proposed that his colleague become the patriarch, while he would assume R. Nathan's position as president of the court.

Not surprisingly, R. Nathan was amenable to R. Meir's proposal. Because R. Nathan was the son of the exilarch, his assuming the post of patriarch would have given his family control over two of the leading Jewish communities and influence over the rest of the Jews worldwide. Similar power plays would be repeated throughout history: to cite but one example, Napoleon Bonaparte appointed his older brother Joseph king of Naples and then king of Spain, and his younger brother Louis king of Holland.[8]

8. A somewhat less exalted example was the plan that Colin Powell and his close friend Richard Armitage hatched whereby Powell would be Secretary of State and Armitage Deputy Secretary of Defense, effectively controlling two-thirds of America's national security apparatus. The plan fell apart when Donald Rumsfeld chose Paul Wolfowitz

The plot failed because R. Simeon's devoted assistant, R. Jacob b. Krushai, overheard the plotters and alerted him in time to master the difficult tractate (Uktzin) from which the two rabbis planned to ask him questions they assumed he would be unable to answer. Both rabbis were then expelled from the assembly. R. Simeon went further, seeking to excommunicate R. Meir, as he was the ringleader. He was unable to do so, however, because the rest of the assembly, led by R. Yose bar Halafta of Sepphoris (known in the Talmud as *Tzipori*) would not agree to his proposal.[9]

R. Nathan decided to mend his relations with R. Simeon and duly apologized. R. Meir adamantly refused to do so. As a punishment, he was no longer referred to by name when being quoted on a point of law; instead he was termed "others" (*aḥerim*).[10] No other leading rabbi apart from his own teacher, the blasphemer Elisha ben Avuya, who was called "the other" (*Aḥer*) was ever treated in this fashion. R. Meir was understandably resentful and never was reconciled to the patriarchate. Unlike R. Judah b. Ila'i and other fellow-students of R. Akiba, R. Meir never became a mentor to R. Simeon's son, Judah. The most that Judah was ever able to say about their relationship was that he saw "his back." Once he became patriarch, Judah also encountered opposition that could be traced back to R. Meir's attempted putsch and its bitter aftermath.

The memory of the plot against his father may well explain Judah's later emphasis on the dignity of his office and his demands that it be accorded utmost respect. In particular, Rebbe neither forgave nor forgot the slight against his father or the damage that was intended against the family's dignity. For years he referred to R. Meir as "the others." When at one point during a lesson he was teaching his son Simeon, the latter asked him who "the others" might be, he replied, "There are men who sought to undermine your dignity and the honor of your father's house." When Simeon quoted Ecclesiastes, "Also their love, and their hatred, and

over Armitage, who then became Powell's deputy. See Dov S. Zakheim, *A Vulcan's Tale: How the Bush Administration Mismanaged the Reconstruction of Afghanistan* (Washington, DC: Brookings Institution Press, 2011), 29.

9. Horayot 13b.
10. Ibid.

their envy, is now long perished,"[11] indicating that bygones should be bygones, Rebbe replied with a quotation of his own: "The enemy has disappeared, the swords are forever."[12] Simeon demurred once more: "Your passage applies only when their actions are successful; these rabbis failed." Rebbe, despite seeing that his argument had been refuted, could not come to terms with the past: he repeated the lesson by stating "It was said in the name of R. Meir," but could not bring himself to say "R. Meir stated."[13] As we shall see, Judah's attitude to R. Meir may not only have stemmed from the latter's treatment of his father, but also from his being snubbed by the great teacher.

R. Meir and R. Nathan may not have been the only centers of opposition to Simeon and the family of the patriarch. It is possible that the descendants of Rabban Yohanan ben Zakkai, who had managed that daring escape from Jerusalem during the siege of Vespasian in 68 CE, may also have laid claim to the patriarchate. After all, it was Rabban Yohanan who was reported to have convinced Vespasian to permit the Jews to maintain rabbinic leadership at Yavneh and thereby preserve rabbinic Judaism. The rivalry with Simeon's house had begun under Simeon's father R. Gamaliel II, who reestablished his family's hold on the patriarchate after the Roman victory, and was only settled in favor of Simeon's family in the next generation, namely that of R. Judah the Prince.[14]

EARLY CHILDHOOD

Tradition has it that Judah was born in Usha, the town in the Galilee not far from Tiberias, to which the rabbis had repaired after the destruction of Jerusalem, and where Simeon reappeared from his self-imposed exile. His father was descended from the tribe of Benjamin,[15] his mother, from the royal house of David. Judah was his father's first-born. As has been noted, the patriarchate was dynastic; the founder of the dynasty

---

11. Eccl. 9:6.
12. Ps. 9:7.
13. Horayot 14a.
14. Burton L. Visotzky, *Aphrodite and the Rabbis: How the Jews Adapted Roman Culture to Create Judaism as We Know It* (New York: St. Martin's Press, 2015), 138.
15. Y. Kilayim 9:3; see also Margolies, *Pnei Moshe*, ad loc., s.v. *Rebbe hava anvan sagin*.

was Judah's ancestor, Hillel I.[16] Judah was the first patriarch since his father's earlier namesake, Hillel's grandson Simeon ben Gamaliel I, to be born into a functioning patriarchate that was neither threatened nor forced to relocate by hostile forces. An obscure midrash relates that the Roman Emperor Antoninus was born about the same time as Judah. Judah's mother, having been summoned to bring the baby before the emperor, found herself spending the first evening of her voyage at the inn of Antoninus' father. His wife, seeing the dire straits in which the Jewish mother had been placed, agreed to "lend" her own uncircumcised baby to the distraught woman and take charge of the Jewish infant. When Hadrian discovered that the baby was uncircumcised, he turned on the mayor of Usha, who had reported the circumcision, and sentenced him to death. When Judah's mother returned the baby Antoninus safely to the inn, the Roman mother told her Jewish counterpart, "Since the Holy One, blessed be He, worked a miracle through me, and through my son for your son, we will be related by marriage forever."[17]

The story of Judah's relationship with the future Roman emperor during his infancy is pure fancy. No Roman emperor was born in the same year, much less at the same time as Judah. Nor was the ban on circumcision lifted until well after Hadrian's passing. Judah never was related to any emperor. Still, the story is indicative of the awe with which later generations held Judah because of his ability to interact with the highest Roman officials, indeed the emperor himself, in a way no one ever did before or after. To explain that oddity, the rabbis needed to outline the origins of the relationship, so they invented a story that did so.

The Talmud asserts that Judah was born the day R. Akiba died.[18] There is considerable symbolism to the belief that the birth of a man who related well with the Romans took place on the day that they were torturing their most implacable opponent to death. Although in general, assertions that a great rabbi was born on the same day as another great rabbi passed away were meant to underscore rabbinical continuity,

16. Rubenstein, *Culture*, 91.

17. *Maasiyot*, 6, in Aharon Jellinek, ed., *Beit HaMidrash*, vol 6 (Vienna: Winter Brothers, 5638/1878), 130–31.

18. Kiddushin 72b.

the rabbis no doubt were aware of the contrasting views of Rome that the two men represented. Just as the rabbis of future generations saw the aristocratic Judah as virtually on a par with the emperor, the most powerful man in the Western world, so they also recognized that he represented a sea change from the ultra-nationalist attitudes that led the low-born Akiba to believe that Bar Kokhba was the messiah and to support his quixotic rebellion against Rome.

It was not that nationalism was absent from Judah's childhood environment. To the contrary, the house of the patriarch was the symbol of Jewish nationhood, even if it had to submit to Roman overlords. After all, Simeon had been associated with Akiba, and the Romans had put a price on his head. He may have come to terms with the Romans, but he did not shed his identity or his nationalist convictions. That Judah's first spoken language was Hebrew would indicate that Simeon's nationalism had never ebbed. Hebrew had been an important expression of Jewish identity since the days of Nehemiah. And like Judaism itself, it was not dependent on the existence of a Temple. There can be little doubt that Judah mastered Hebrew; the Mishna, his great work, is written in a most fluid form of that language.

PRIMARY EDUCATION

There were two major alternatives to Hebrew that were available to the patriarch and his family. One was Aramaic, the lingua franca of the region and the language of the common people. It was unlikely that Judah's family spoke Aramaic at home, however, except perhaps to servants. As an adult Judah disparaged the language, comparing it unfavorably to Greek, which he presumably was taught in the special school for the children of diplomats. As he put it, "Why [should people] in Israel speak Syrian Aramaic (*lashon Sursi*) – a gutter language – either [they should] speak the Holy Tongue [Hebrew] or Greek [the royal language]."[19] Interestingly, his disparaging attitude toward Aramaic was paralleled by the dictum of

19. Bava Kamma 82b–83a; see also Rashi, s.v. *lashon*, and R. Adin Steinsaltz, ed., *Talmud Bavli: Bava Kamma*, vol. 2 (Jerusalem: Israel Institute for Talmudic Publications, 1996), 358, s.v. *o lashon Yevanit.*

Rabbi Yose regarding eastern Aramaic in Babylonia: "Why [speak] Aramaic in Babylonia? Either the Holy Tongue or Persian [is preferable]."[20]

The upper classes, people like Judah, spoke Greek, much as the imperial Russian upper classes in their day spoke French rather than their native language. So too did Romans who held office in the Empire's eastern provinces, and indeed the emperors themselves.[21] Moreover, Jews living throughout the Roman Empire spoke Greek and had done so while the Second Temple was still standing.[22] Perhaps it was for these reasons that the Talmud relates, and there is no reason to doubt the veracity of its report, that Greek was taught to members of the patriarch's household. Greek may not have been the first language that newborns heard the patriarch and his family speak – that would have been Hebrew – but it surely was the family's second language, which the children must have begun to absorb at an early age.

Though it may have been the language of the upper classes, Judah saw it as preferable to Aramaic even for the lower classes. His view was that in Judaea Jews should speak either Hebrew or Greek, and he preferred Hebrew.[23] In this regard he emulated Nehemiah, who had insisted that only Hebrew be spoken in Jewish homes.[24]

Judah's attitude was therefore quite different from those of future Jewish leaders, some of whom not only venerated Aramaic but preferred Yiddish over both the local vernaculars and Hebrew.[25] To this day, some

20. Bava Kamma 83a; see also Tosafot, ad loc., s.v. *lashon Sursi.*
21. Management of the Roman Empire was essentially bilingual, with Greek being spoken both east of the Balkans and throughout North Africa.
22. Cohen, *From the Maccabees to the Mishnah,* 30–31; for an extensive examination of Jewish acculturation in the Greco-Roman diaspora, see Erich S. Gruen, *Diaspora: Jews Amidst Greeks and Romans* (Cambridge, MA and London: Harvard University Press, 2002).
23. Alon, *Jews in Their Land,* 714–15.
24. Neh. 13:24.
25. Indeed, in the mid-nineteenth century, a group of Hungarian Orthodox rabbis reacted to the emergence of the Reform movement by issuing a ban against preaching or listening to a sermon in any language other than that "spoken by observant Jews in that country," i.e., Yiddish. This ban was one of several that were promulgated in a pamphlet called *Judicial Decision,* which was published in 1865 by a group of Hungarian rabbis. Although the pamphlet clearly was addressed to European, Yiddish-speaking Jewry,

decisors argue that Yiddish is a holy language and should be the sole language of "Torah Jews," although it derives from medieval German – with an admixture of Russian, Hebrew, French, and even English – and not a word of it appears in Scripture, Talmud, or Midrash.[26] The Prince would not have agreed.

Ironically, over the centuries Aramaic took on a veneer of holiness, partly because it is the language in which the Talmud was written, partly because of a few Aramaic words in the Pentateuch[27] and the fact that Aramaic comprises the majority of the text of Daniel and more than a third of the Book of Ezra.[28] But Aramaic was simply the lingua franca of the Middle East for several centuries, especially among the masses. After the seventh century it would be replaced by Arabic.

Judah's view of the importance of Greek was influenced by that of his father Rabban Simeon. The latter not only knew Greek but venerated it to the point of issuing halakhic rulings that equated it with Hebrew. Because Rabban Simeon considered it superior to all other languages, he argued that even if one held that the Scriptures should not be written in a language other than Hebrew, an exception should be made for Greek.[29] In other words, a Torah written in Greek script had the same sanctity as one written in Hebrew script (termed *ktav Ashurit*). Indeed, a number of leading medieval scholars, notably R. Eliezer b. Yoel, known by his acronym Raavia (1140–ca. 1220), and R. Yom Tov ben Avraham Asevilli,

---

the phrasing was tailored to include permission for Sephardim to listen to sermons given in Ladino. For a discussion see Gil Student, "Rav Hildesheimer's Response to Ultra-Orthodoxy," *Ḥakirah* 24 (Spring 2018), especially 41–43.

26. See, for example, R. David Cohen, *HaSafa HaKedosha Yiddish* (Hebrew) (Brooklyn, NY: ArtScroll, 2013). For an analysis see Lewis Glinert and Yoseph Shilhav, "Holy Land, Holy Language: A Study of Ultraorthodox Jewish Ideology," *Language in Society* 20 (March 1991), 78–81.
27. Although there are only two explicitly Aramaic words in the Pentateuch – *yegar sahaduta* – there are many others that also appear to have Aramaic-like features. See Gary A. Rendsburg, "Aramaic-Like Features in the Pentateuch," *Hebrew Studies* 47 (2006), 163–76.
28. Just over four of the Book of Daniel's eleven chapters are in Hebrew; the remainder are written in Aramaic. Three of Ezra's ten chapters are in Aramaic, as are the majority of two others.
29. *Encyclopedia Talmudit*, vol. 37, 642–43.

known by his acronym Ritva (ca. 1260–ca. 1320), concluded that in R. Simeon's view, a Torah written not only in the Greek script but in the Greek *language* had the sanctity of one written in Hebrew.[30]

R. Yohanan bar Nappaha, a leading *Amora* who had studied under Judah as a young man,[31] explained R. Simeon's reasoning on the basis of the passage in Genesis, "God shall enlarge Japhet, and he shall dwell in the tents of Shem" (*Yaft Elohim leYefet veyishkon be'oholei Shem*).[32] The Torah identified Javan, the progenitor of Greece, as the son of Japhet.[33] Therefore, according to R. Yohanan, R. Simeon interpreted the passage as indicating that "the words of Japhet, namely Greece, shall be in the tents of Shem," the ancestor of the Jewish people.[34] Another explanation for R. Simeon's view was that Greek was the only language that could translate the Hebrew faithfully. Indeed, the Talmud asserted that the authenticity of Aramaic translations was due to its being a derivative of Greek (which it certainly is not!).[35] Although other rabbis disputed the validity of Greek as a translation of the Scriptures apart from the Pentateuch, R. Simeon's view prevailed: according to R. Yohanan, whose opinion was accepted as normative halakha, R. Simeon's opinion was to be followed in all but three halakhic disputes to which he was a party, and none of these concerned the status of Greek.[36]

Rav and Samuel, the leading *Amora'im* of their generation whose efforts led to the Mishna's acceptance as "the basis for Jewish law,"[37] went even further. They both asserted, as a corollary of R. Simeon's acceptance of Greek as a substitute for Hebrew, that one

30. See ibid., 643n374, citing R. Eliezer b. Yoel (Raavia), no. 549, and R. Yom Tov ben Avraham Asevilli (Ritva), Megilla 8b. For others holding this view, and for opposing views, see *Encyclopedia Talmudit,* loc. cit, 643, especially fns. 374–76.
31. Ḥullin 137b. R. Yohanan later said that he had difficulty comprehending his master's teachings, presumably because his scholarship was not yet fully developed.
32. Gen. 9:27.
33. Ibid., 10:2.
34. Megilla 9b.
35. Y. Megilla 1:9. Later commentators also claimed, quite erroneously, that Latin was a derivative of Greek. *Birat Migdal Oz,* quoted in *Encyclopedia Talmudit,* vol. 37, 646n405.
36. Ketubot 77a.
37. Rubenstein, *Culture,* 161.

could fulfill the mitzva of hearing the Megilla when it was read in Greek and when the listener did not understand what was being read.[38] Later authorities drew upon this latter ruling to hold that according to R. Simeon, Greek was an acceptable substitute for Hebrew in any matter which one was supposed to address in Hebrew – for example a vow – even if the individual involved did not understand either language.[39]

While the rabbis were prepared to tolerate those who spoke Greek even if they were not members of the patriarch's household, and ultimately accepted its validity as a substitute for Hebrew in certain circumstances,[40] they forbade to all but that household the study of what they termed "Greek wisdom." What exactly was meant by "Greek wisdom" has been the subject of varying opinions. Some have interpreted it to mean high Greek culture generally, e.g., Homer's *Iliad* and *Odyssey*, with which at least the upper Jewish classes were familiar.[41] Others translated the term more narrowly, arguing that it connotes "sophistry."[42]

The basis for the restriction was itself problematical. The Mishna that Rebbe himself edited attributed the ban to Titus' destruction of the Temple.[43] The Gemara, which normally expands upon the Mishna, instead gives a different basis for the ban, namely an incident that took place during the battle between the brothers Hyrcanus and Aristobulus for the Hasmonean crown.[44]

---

38. Megilla 18a.
39. R. Yoav Yehoshua Weingarten, *Ḥelkat Yo'av*, vol. 1, no. 1, cited in, *Encyclopedia Talmudit*, vol. 37, 64n398.
40. Later decisors disputed whether R. Simeon's ruling applied only to written Greek, to the Greek alphabet, or also to substitution of Greek for Hebrew where neither language was understood. See *Encyclopedia Talmudit*, vol. 37, 645–46, *passim.*
41. Steinsaltz, ed., *Talmud Bavli: Bava Kamma*, vol. 2, 357, s.v. *ḥokhma Yevanit.* The Greek classics were also part of the main curriculum "in the schooling of elite Roman youth." Barry Strauss, *Ten Caesars: Roman Emperors from Augustus to Constantine* (New York: Simon & Schuster, 2019), 178.
42. Rabbi Dr. I. Epstein, ed. *Sotah*, trans. Rev. Dr. A. Cohen (London: Soncino, 1994), 49b note b6.
43. Sota 49a.
44. Sota 49b, Bava Kamma 82b.

> When the sons of the Hasmoneans besieged each other, Hyrcanus was inside [Jerusalem] and Aristobulus outside [besieging him]. Every day [the people inside would] lower thirty denarii in a basket and [in exchange] would raise up the [lambs for the] daily sacrifice. There was among [Aristobulus' people] an elderly man familiar with Greek wisdom who said to them, "As long as they can maintain the [sacrificial] service they will never fall to you." The next day when the dinarii were lowered in the basket, they brought up a pig. When it reached the middle of the wall it stuck its nails in the wall and the land shook for a distance of one hundred and sixty thousand square parasangs. From that point on they said, "Cursed is the man who raises pigs and who teaches Greek wisdom."[45]

Leaving aside the exaggeration in this talmudic tale, many traditional commentators have noted that it is entirely inconsistent with the mishnaic version, since the conflict for the Hasmonean throne involved Pompey the Great, who predated Titus by over a century. Of course, the commentators sought to reconcile the two versions, e.g., by arguing that the pig represented Rome and that Roman intervention in the fratricidal conflict led to the destruction of the Temple.[46] In any event, by the time Judah was born, the ban on Greek knowledge, whatever it might have been, was firmly fixed in Jewish practice, while the exemption for the house of the patriarch was equally well established. That Judah himself could later transcribe the ban in the Mishna despite having been educated in the suspect "knowledge," indicated the degree to which he felt comfortable with the patriarchal exemption.

Although he may have restricted the study of Greek knowledge to his extended family, Rebbe did lay out a curriculum for parents to teach their children that was broader than that of Torah study. The rabbis outlined a parent's multiple responsibilities of a parent toward a male child. These included not only circumcision, redemption of a first

45. Bava Kamma 82b.
46. Maharsha, Sota 49b, *Aggadot,* s.v. *bepulmus*; and Maimonides, *Peirush HaMishnayot,* ad loc., s.v. *mishemet.*

born male from the Kohen after thirty days (the ritual known as *pidyon haben*), and teaching one's son Torah, but also teaching him a trade and finding him a suitable wife. R. Akiba added the need to teach one's son to swim. And Rebbe, in addition to all of the foregoing, added *yishuv medina* which can be translated as "secular studies that are necessary to function properly in society."[47]

THE USHA YEARS

Judah spent his childhood years at Usha. Already as a youngster he excelled at the study of the traditions and rabbinic rulings that came to be called the Oral Law, in addition to becoming proficient in Greek and its accompanying knowledge. He clearly had a retentive memory. He recalled that while still a young child, not having reached the age of thirteen, he had read aloud the Book of Esther in the presence of Rabbi Judah bar Ila'i, one of his earliest teachers, who acted as his foster-father. The Book of Esther runs to ten chapters and is not at all easy to read from a scroll. There are no vowels, and many of the words are of Persian origin. To this day it requires hours of practice before one can be confident of flawlessly reading the Megilla on Purim in the presence of the congregation, even if one has done so many times in the past. Interestingly, R. Judah b. Ila'i asserted that he had done the same in the presence of R. Tarfon when *he* was a child.[48]

Very bright children with overpowering intellects are often rambunctious, and talmudic accounts indicate that Judah fit that mold. He seems to have enjoyed finding loopholes in the law. Judah's mentor, R. Judah b. Ila'i, was also the father of his childhood chum Yose, who

47. *Mekhilta DeRabbi Yishmael, Parashat Bo*, 18:6. The translation is Marc Shapiro's; see Marc B. Shapiro, "Another 'Translation' by Artscroll, the Rogachover and the Radichkover," *The Seforim* Blog, http://seforim.blogspot.com/2018/06/another-translation-by artscroll.html.

    Shapiro speculates that when R. Yosef Rozin, "the Rogachover," cited this passage, he meant that Rebbe saw the teaching of appropriate secular studies as a parental obligation.

48. See the discussion in Megilla 20a. The rabbis rejected the views of both R. Judah bar Ila'i and Rebbe; normative halakha does not permit a child to read the Megilla for the congregation.

appears to have been inseparable from the younger Judah. Like him, Yose matured into one of the great *Tanna'im;* he figures prominently in the Mishna and related works. But the Jerusalem Talmud paints a very different picture of the two boys:

> Rebbe and R. Yose son of R. Judah were bringing a basket of figs to the back of the gardens, so as to avoid having to tithe them, when they were spotted by R. Judah b. Ila'i. He scolded them, "See what differentiates you from the early ones. R. Akiba would acquire three species specifically in order to tithe each species, and you bring the basket to the back of the gardens [to avoid the tithe]."[49]

That it was Judah, and not his young friend, who was the brains behind the incident of the figs, is illustrated by another talmudic tale. In this instance, the boys entered a garden and were about to eat figs that were overripe and so required no tithing. The gardener, citing their teacher's teacher R. Akiba, scolded the boys for trespassing on the property. Hearing of his father's teacher's ruling, Yose backed away, assuming that to eat the figs would be, in effect, to commit robbery. Judah reasoned otherwise and encouraged Yose to join him and eat the figs. He argued that the figs were no longer of use to the owner, and that the owner had, in effect, divested himself of them. He seemingly was not impressed by the reference to R. Akiba.

Both stories foreshadow Judah's independence of mind and his refusal to adopt conventional strictures if they could be avoided. They hint at a degree of contrarianism that flies in the face of the stifling conformity that many rabbis, from his day to ours, have insisted upon as essential to the integrity of Judaism. Judah's inclination pointed in a different direction: if the force of the law could be softened without undermining the law itself, he was inclined to do so.

JUDAH'S PRIMARY TEACHER: R. JUDAH BAR ILA'I

Judah had numerous teachers, including his father, and they did not all reflect a single point of view. Five of them were the last students of R. Akiba, the great nationalist and passionate opponent of the

49. Y. Maaserot 3:1.

Romans. These were R. Meir, R. Yose, R. Simeon bar Yohai, R. Elazar, and R. Judah bar Ila'i. Judah held R. Akiba, as well as R. Akiba's colleagues R. Tarfon, R. Eleazar b. Azariah, R. Yohanan b. Nuri, and R. Yose the Galilean, in the highest regard.[50] He described R. Akiba as "a well-stocked storehouse" of Torah, who organized Torah "in rings and rings," that is, every item individually.[51] He called R. Tarfon "a heap of stones or... a heap of nuts, when a person removes one from the pile they all go tumbling over each other."[52] What he meant was that when R. Tarfon would teach a scholar, he would cite the Torah and all the various branches of rabbinic literature to underscore his point. Judah had similar descriptions for the other three rabbis.[53]

Of R. Akiba's five students, Judah's first teacher, the man who appears to have filled the gap left by Judah's absent father, was, as noted, his friend Yose's father, R. Judah bar Ila'i. R. Judah was one of the greatest of his generation of *Tanna'im*. The Mishna records over six hundred

---

50. Judah's description of R. Akiba and four other great rabbis who preceded him appears in *Avot DeRabbi Natan* 18:1. It immediately follows, and is meant to parallel, a discussion of Rabban Yohanan b. Zakkai's five great students from 14:3–17:8, *passim*. Anthony Saldarini erroneously called them his students, while Judah Goldin described them as his "masters." See Anthony J. Saldarini, "The End of the Rabbinic Chain of Tradition," *Journal of Biblical Literature* 93 (March 1974), 105n25; *The Fathers According to Rabbi Nathan*, trans. Judah Goldin (New Haven and London: Yale University Press, 1955/1983), 195n1. Actually they were neither, as they passed from the scene in the fourth or fifth decade of the second century, around the time Judah was born. Indeed, it was talmudic tradition that Judah was born the day R. Akiba died (Kiddushin 72b). If these rabbis were his "masters" in any sense, it was that he received their traditions from his own teachers, notably R. Judah b. Ila'i, who was a student most notably of R. Akiba and R. Tarfon, as discussed below.
51. Thus Meir Etrog's understanding of Rashi's interpretation of this phrase. Meir Zev Etrog, *Me'orei Ohr: Avot DeRabbi Natan* 18:1 (Bnei Brak: Makhon Zichron Yerucham, 5761/2001), 206, s.v. *taba'ot*.
52. The translation is Goldin's, op. cit., 90.
53. He called R. Eleazar "a spice handler's basket," because he could respond to questions from each branch of the literature just as a spice handler had a product available to meet every individual buyer's request (ibid., 90–91). He called R. Yohanan b. Nuri "a basket of halakhot" and R. Yose "a fine gatherer without arrogance, " that is, "he was modest and was prepared to learn from anyone and treat what he learned as if it had been received on Mount Sinai" (Etrog, *Me'orei Ohr: Avot DeRabbi Natan* 18:3, s.v. *belo* and *meihar*).

of his halakhic rulings; and his name appears in every tractate of the Talmud bar the relatively minor Tractate Kinim. Indeed, he is cited in the Tosefta and the *Midrash Halakha* called *Sifra* more frequently than any other *Tanna,* of his or any generation. His authority was such that he prevailed in any halakhic dispute with R. Meir or R. Simeon, both of whom were great scholars in their own right.[54] Indeed, he served as halakhic decisor and authority for the patriarch's household.[55]

A native of Usha, where his young namesake was born and reared, R. Judah had studied under several of the great rabbis who flourished in Yavneh prior to the Bar Kokhba era, most notably R. Tarfon, who treated him as a son.[56] The teacher who made the greatest mark on his halakhic outlook, however, was R. Akiba. It was together with four of his fellow-students of that great rabbi that R. Judah somehow managed to begin the slow, but ultimately successful, process of reconstructing the Jewish community, its religious institutions, and the study of Torah in all of its aspects, in the wake of the Bar Kokhba rebellion.[57]

R. Judah also had the reputation of being a truly righteous man: one of the greatest of what the Talmud called *Ḥasidim.*[58] He was exceedingly spiritual: centuries before the mystics of Safed initiated the Friday night service, which quickly gained widespread acceptance among Jews regardless of specific tradition, R. Judah would dress in special linen robes with *tzitzit* so that he would appear to his students as "an angel of the Lord of Hosts."[59] Moreover, the Talmud relates that whenever it would relate an incident involving a *Ḥasid,* it was referring either to

54. Eiruvin 46b.
55. Menaḥot 104a and Rashi, s.v. *Rabbi Yehuda.*
56. Tosefta, Nega'im 8b.
57. The other four were R. Meir, R. Yose, R. Simeon, and R. Eleazar. For a brief but comprehensive biographical sketch of R. Judah bar Ila'i, see Mordekhai Margalioth, ed., *Encyclopedia of Talmudic and Geonic Literature: Being A Biographical Dictionary of the Tannaim, Amoraim and Geonim,* vol. 1 (Tel Aviv: Chachik, 1960), 395–403.
58. The term "*Ḥasidim*" has meant different groups at different times: the Talmud often referred to the early righteous (*Ḥasidim HaRishonim*). In medieval times, the term applied to extremely pious German Jews, exemplified by the twelfth-century scholar R. Judah the Hasid. Since the eighteenth century, it has been the appellation of the followers of R. Israel Baal Shem Tov and his rabbinic disciples and successors.
59. Shabbat 25b.

R. Judah, or to another R. Judah (Judah b. Bava) but to no one else.[60] R. Judah bar Ila'i was especially noted for his willingness to humble himself in order to mediate domestic quarrels. It is told that once a husband swore off his wife unless R. Judah or R. Simeon ate her cooking. R. Simeon refused, on the grounds it was a slight against Torah learning. R. Judah ate, placing a higher priority on family harmony.[61]

It was also of no small significance that R. Judah was a proponent of both having a trade and teaching a trade to one's son, going so far as to assert that if one did not teach a trade to one's son, he was teaching him to be a criminal instead.[62] R. Judah's views on work did not negate his recognition of, indeed emphasis on, the importance of Torah study. His point was that one could be both a scholar and a tradesman or craftsman.

As noted in the story of young Judah and the basket of figs, the elder Judah was certainly a stickler for the letter of the law. His often-stringent attitude toward the law did not spill over into what today would be called his *hashkafa,* or *Weltanschauung*. For unlike his colleagues R. Yose and R. Simeon bar Yohai, who were also students of R. Akiba, who was not only the greatest scholar of his time but also the ultra-nationalist whom the Romans tortured to death, R. Judah was an admirer of much of what Rome had to offer. The Talmud describes R. Judah bar Ila'i as "the chief speaker in every place," which was an official Roman appointment.[63] The Talmud's explanation of what the term meant sheds considerable light on the younger Judah's later attitude to the Romans as he matured into adulthood:

> R. Judah, R. Yose, and Rabbi Simeon [bar Yohai] were once sitting together and Judah the son of proselytes was sitting with them. Rabbi Judah opened [the discussion] by exclaiming, "How fine are the works of these people [i.e., the Romans]! They have

60. Bava Kamma 103b.
61. Nedarim 66b.
62. Kiddushin 29a.
63. See R. Moses Isserles, *She'elot UTeshuvot HaRema*, rev. ed., ed. R. Dr. Asher Ziv, no. 123 (Jerusalem: Mossad Harav Kook, 2018), 483–84. R. Isserles noted, however, that a royal appointee to a position of community leadership must also be acceptable to the community.

> established streets and markets, they have erected bridges, they have built baths." R. Yose [listened to these remarks but] remained silent. Rabbi Simeon bar Yohai replied and said, "All that they established they only did so for their own interests: they organized market places to house prostitutes; they have created baths to pamper themselves; they have built bridges to collect taxes." Judah the son of proselytes relayed their words to his immediate family, but they were overheard by the authorities. They decreed that Judah, who praised the government, should be promoted [hence he should be the first to speak in any rabbinical discourse]; Yose, who remained silent, should be exiled to Sepphoris; while Simeon, who denigrated the government, should be executed.[64]

R. Judah's positive attitude to the Romans must have affected the young Judah's outlook, softening his view on the occupiers of Judaea despite his father's absence. When R. Simeon finally returned and served as one of his son's teachers, his admiration for Greek culture and language could only have reinforced the attitude that R. Judah had conveyed to his younger namesake, and broadened his horizons well beyond the four walls of the yeshiva.

RIVALRY WITH ELEAZAR SON OF R. SIMEON BAR YOHAI

The future prince had his rivals, of course, even as a young student. Perhaps the most fearsome of these was Eleazar, son of R. Simeon bar Yohai. As a callow youth Eleazar, like his father, was a religious extremist, intolerant of those who were comfortable with a more moderate approach to Judaism. Indeed, he seems to have been even more radical than his father.

The Talmud relates that after the Romans put a price on R. Simeon's head, he escaped together with young Eleazar first to the *beit midrash* and then, when the hunt for them intensified, to a cave where they miraculously survived for a dozen years. At that point, the Talmud relates, the prophet Elijah informed them that the emperor, probably

---

64. Shabbat 33b. See Rashi, s.v. *rosh*, and also Maharsha, s.v. *kamma*, who argues that R. Judah was dissembling, and only spoke favorably of Roman accomplishments out of "fear of the government."

Hadrian, had died and they were no longer wanted men. When they emerged from the cave and came across a man working his fields rather than studying Torah, they were so enraged that, employing what can only be called superpowers, they burned every place that they set their eyes upon.

The Talmud goes on to note that Heaven was not at all amused by such manifestations of religious extremism. Not everyone was meant to sit in a yeshiva all their days, and there was nothing shameful about working the fields. A Heavenly voice (*bat kol*) called down to chastise the two men: "Have you emerged to destroy my world? Return to your cave!" R. Simeon and Eleazar, duly reprimanded, returned to the cave for twelve additional months – the maximum time for remaining in Gehenna – and then emerged again.

R. Simeon had learned his lesson; but the younger, hotheaded Eleazar had not. He continued to singe people with his glare, and his father had to heal all whom the young man had wounded. Finally, R. Simeon tried to pacify Eleazar by telling him that their own knowledge of the law was "sufficient for the world," and that he need not insist that all study the way the two of them had done. Shortly thereafter, they came across an old man who was running with two bundles of myrtles just before Shabbat. When they asked him why he needed two bundles, he answered one was for "remember" and the other for "keep," the two variants of the commandment to sanctify Shabbat. R. Simeon said to his son, "See how precious the commandments are to Israel," that is, even to ordinary Jews. It was only at that point, states the Talmud, that Eleazar was finally pacified.

Eleazar may have come to terms with the reality that not all Jews were meant to be scholars, but he had a combative personality that revealed itself in other ways. In particular, he did not hesitate to cut Judah down when they disagreed over a point of law while studying together in the yeshiva of R. Tarfon. Eleazar was at least half-a-dozen years older than Judah and had only recently emerged from the cave in which he and his father had sojourned for a dozen years. In Eleazar's eyes, his knowledge of Torah, together with that of his father, was "sufficient for the world." How could anyone else's views match up to his own?

The Talmud relates that initially Eleazar actually was supportive of Judah's interventions during R. Tarfon's lectures. If Judah asked a question and followed it with an explanation of his own, Eleazar would argue in favor of Judah's explanation. One day, however, the rabbis decided to elevate Judah to the rabbinical bench (students normally sat on the floor while their instructors would sit on a bench). When Eleazar saw that only Judah was elevated, he became very cross and stayed that way, even though he joined him on the bench shortly thereafter. In contrast to his previous reactions to Judah's questions and answers, now Eleazar would poke fun at him, asserting that he was wasting everyone's time since R. Tarfon had already provided the class with the most suitable response.

Judah resented his older colleague; whenever R. Eleazar "entered the scholars' college, the face of R. Judah darkened."[65] But his father, who instructed his son in the ways of diplomacy in addition to those of the Talmud, counseled him to swallow his pride: "He [Eleazer] is a lion the son of a lion; you are a lion the son of a fox." In other words, he was telling his son that R. Simeon bar Yohai outshone him when it came to Torah study, and that Judah should accept that reality. Rebbe's vaunted humility as an adult no doubt drew upon his father's shrewd management of colleagues with difficult personalities, even if it meant a degree of self-abnegation. But it also may have led him to recoil from religious extremism, which in any event would not have meshed well either with his open-minded outlook on matters Greek and Roman or with his later relationship with Septimius Severus and his son Caracalla.

Rebbe eventually reconciled with R. Eleazar, recognizing his scholarship and, in particular, his unrivaled expertise in matters of family purity.[66] Indeed, Rebbe performed a singular act of kindness after his erstwhile rival had passed from the scene. It appears that R. Eleazar had a wayward son, Yose, who spent most of his time in the company of prostitutes who adored him. Rebbe then did something that would shock many contemporary

65. Solomon Buber, *Peskita: VeHi Aggadat Eretz Yisrael Meyuḥeset LeRav Kahana* (Lyck, Germany [now Elk, Poland]: Mekitzei Nirdamim, 1868), 10:94b. See also *Pesikta deRab Kahana: R. Kahana's Compilation of Discourses for Sabbaths and Festal Days*, trans. William G. (Gershon Zev) Braude and Israel J. Kapstein (Philadelphia: Jewish Publication Society, 1975), 221.

66. Bava Metzia 84b.

Jews: he conferred rabbinical ordination on the young man. He then sent him to study with his maternal uncle, R. Simeon b. Issi b. Lakonia. Every day Yose wanted to return to his town, and presumably to his former way of life; but R. Simeon would remind him that he was now a rabbi and had to live up to a higher standard. At some point the newly minted R. Yose announced that he had overcome his passions, and he went to study in Rebbe's yeshiva. When Rebbe heard the man's voice (presumably he was sitting in the back of the class), he said that it sounded like that of R. Eleazar.

> He is his son, they [his students] told him. Thereupon [Rebbe] applied to him the verse: The fruit of the righteous is a tree of life and he that wins souls is wise. [That is,] The fruit of the righteous is a tree of life, this refers to R. Yose, the son of R. Eleazar, the son of R. Simeon; And he that wins souls is wise, to R. Simeon b. Issi b. Lakonia.[67]

Rebbe surely understood the magnitude of the risk he was taking; yet he was prepared to do so in order to light the spark that is in the heart of every Jew, no matter how alienated he or she might be from his or her heritage.

JUDAH'S OTHER MENTORS

Apart from R. Judah bar Ila'i, we do not know the chronological order in which his other teachers, apart from his father, became the younger Judah's instructors. He seems to have wandered from one yeshiva to another, seeking to absorb whatever he could from the community's leading scholars. Later he would recall some of these experiences and would base his legal rulings on that period of his life. For example, he related that while studying in the yeshiva of his rival Eleazar's father, R. Simeon b. Yohai, he and his fellow students would carry up towels and oil from the courtyard to an enclosure where there was a fountain where they bathed on Shabbat.[68] He spent some time in the yeshiva of

---

67. Bava Metzia 85a.
68. Shabbat 147b. The parallel text in Menaḥot 72a reads: Rebbe said, "When we were studying Torah at R. Simeon's in Tekoa we used to carry up to him on Shabbat oil and a towel from the courtyard to the roof, and from the roof to an enclosure, and from one enclosure to another enclosure, until we came to the fountain where we bathed."

R. Tarfon, his mentor's R. Judah's mentor. It was in this yeshiva that he first became a rival of Eleazar b. R. Simeon b. Yohai.

Judah so venerated the teachings of R. Yose, whose yeshiva he had also attended, that he even valued them above those of Beit Shammai and Beit Hillel. Years later he ruled that the minimum number of sheep triggering the requirement to provide the first fleece (*reishit hagez)* to the priests was neither two sheep (as Beit Shammai argued) nor five sheep (Beit Hillel's position) but rather the compromise number of four sheep, as R. Yose postulated.[69]

Judah's peripatetic yeshiva years were on occasion difficult and even unpleasant. In particular, he seems to have had a rough time at the yeshiva of R. Eleazar b. Shammua. The yeshiva was so packed with students that Judah barely had a place to sit. He later reported: "When we were studying Torah at R. Eleazar b. Shammua's six of us used to sit in one cubit."[70] Since a cubit is something less than two feet, the students must have been practically sitting on top of one another, a situation quite alien to a young man used to the comforts of the patriarch's spacious home.

Worse still, it appears that the students resented him. As he later recalled: "When I went to learn Torah at R. Eleazar b. Shammua's, the students ganged up on me like the cocks of Beit Bukia [who would attack any rooster that they did not recognize].[71] They did not let me learn but one item in our Mishna, namely, that if one copulates with a hermaphrodite, one is punished by stoning similar to the punishment for homosexual relations."[72]

Did the other students resent him because he was viewed as the pampered son of the patriarch? Why restrict him to that one law about especially peculiar relations? Did they deliberately jostle him – what he may have meant by the attacks of fighting cocks[73] from Beit Bukia – when he tried to absorb R. Eleazar's teachings, so that it was only where he sat

69. Ḥullin 137a; Y. Gittin, 6:7.

70. Eiruvin 53a.

71. Rashi, loc. cit., s.v. *shel.*

72. Yevamot 84a.

73. The contemporary scholar R. Adin Steinsaltz compares the cocks of Beit Bukia to fighting cocks. R. Adin Steinsaltz, ed., *Talmud Bavli: Yevamot,* vol. 2 (Jerusalem: Israel Institute for Talmudic Publications, 1989), s.v. *tarnegolim,* 368.

that five other students shared a space of one cubit with him? In other words, did they want to drive the privileged boy out of the yeshiva? It certainly would appear that way.

Interestingly, R. Eleazar did not intervene when Judah was being hounded by his fellow students. It certainly was not because he resented the patriarchy's close ties to Rome. On the contrary, a marvelous sixth- or seventh-century midrashic tale asserts that his attitude to Romans was far more positive than that of his countrymen. The story is revealing as well for its retrospective view of Roman behavior, and deserves to be quoted at length:

> R. Eleazar b. Shammua was walking on the rocks by the sea when he saw a ship ... sink in the twinkling of an eye with all on board. He spied a man riding the waves on a plank on the sea. At just that time the Jews were going up to Jerusalem for the Festival [Sukkot]. He said to them: "I descend from Esau, your brother; give me a little clothing to cover my nakedness because the sea stripped me bare and nothing was saved with me." They replied, "So may all your people be bare." He looked up and saw R. Eleazar walking among them and exclaimed: "I note that you are an old and honored man of your people, and you know the respect that is due to your fellow creatures. So help me and give me a garment to cover my nakedness because I was stripped bare by the sea." R. Eleazar b. Shammua was wearing seven robes; he took one off and gave it to him. He also brought him to his house, gave him food and drink plus two hundred dinars, drove him fourteen miles, and treated him with great honor until he brought him home. Some time later the evil emperor died; this man was elected king in his stead. He decreed that all men from the province [of Palestine] be killed and all women taken as captives. They [the people] said to R. Eleazar b. Shammua, "Go and intercede for us." He answered, "You know that this government does nothing without being paid." They said to him, "Here are four thousand dinars; take them and plead on our behalf." He took the money, and stood by the gate of the royal palace. He told the guards, "Go tell the king that a Jew is standing at the gate, and

> wishes to greet the king." The king ordered him to be brought in. On seeing him, the king leaped from his throne and prostrated himself before him. He asked him, "What is my master's business here, and why has my master troubled himself to come here?" He replied, "That you should have mercy on this province and annul the decree." The king asked him ... "Is it not written in your Torah ... 'Thou shalt not abhor an Edomite, for he is thy brother' (Deut. 23:4)? And am I not a descendant of Esau, your brother, but they did not treat me with kindness! And whoever transgresses the Torah incurs the penalty of death." R. Eleazar b. Shammua replied ... "Forgive them and have mercy on them ... I have with me four thousand dinars; take them and have mercy upon the people." The king said, "These four thousand dinars are presented to you in exchange for the two hundred which you gave me, and the whole province will be spared ... in return for the food and drink which you provided me.... Go in peace with your people whom I forgive for your sake."[74]

It is noteworthy that R. Eleazar was unable to receive *semikha* (ordination) from his teacher R. Akiba; the Romans tortured and executed him before R. Eleazar could complete his studies. One might have expected R. Eleazar to retain a lifelong hatred of the Romans, much as did his colleague R. Simeon b. Yohai. But that proved to be not the case at all. While this midrashic tale, set down long after R. Eleazar's passing, is clearly apocryphal,[75] its message of mercy toward all humans, even those of an alien culture, is unequivocal.

No doubt his teacher's merciful attitude to the Romans taught Judah the importance of showing kindness to all humans. It was a lesson he would impart to his own sons. Unfortunately, it is one that has

---

74. Ecclesiastes Rabba 11:1.

75. There is no evidence that a Roman emperor ever was washed up naked on the Judaean seashore; prostrated himself before a rabbi; or was so conversant with the Torah that he could cite a biblical verse in the course of a conversation. However, there may have been an incident involving a Roman official in Palestine and R. Eleazar that formed the basis for the tale.

all too often been honored in the breach by traditional Jews, even by those currently living in Western societies.

Given R. Eleazar's attitude to the Romans, it was not resentment of the patriarchy's relations with Rome that prompted him to remain silent in the face of his student's behavior. A man who cared for others as deeply as he did surely would have been sensitive to the hazing that Judah underwent. Why, then, did he look the other way? Perhaps he was unaware of the goings-on among his acolytes. We will never know. What has been reported, however, is that R. Eleazar had his own favorites. Rebbe himself related that when he approached R. Eleazar to summarize what he had learned at the academy, he found the master praising Joseph the Babylonian in the course of a colloquy regarding a ruling on a sacrificial ritual that had been issued by Rebbe's own mentor, R. Judah bar Ila'i.[76] It must have pained Judah that R. Eleazar clearly showed more fondness to an outsider from Babylonia than to himself. In any event, the yeshiva's atmosphere was clearly poisonous, at least as far as Judah was concerned, and it no doubt encouraged him to move elsewhere as soon as he could find another house of study.

Judah also attended lectures delivered by R. Meir, his father's old nemesis. He later attributed his own analytical capabilities to R. Meir's influence. R. Meir may also have reinforced the pro-Roman attitudes that Judah's father, his foster-father, and R. Eleazar b. Shammua all had imparted to him. According to talmudic legend, R. Meir – who was also called R. Nehorai[77] – was descended from the Emperor Nero, who converted to Judaism. Judaism had become increasingly popular among Romans during the first century, with thousands of Romans either converting outright or conducting themselves as "fellow travelers" of Judaism. Like many seemingly fanciful midrashim, therefore, this one may have exaggerated an actual event, in this instance the conversion of a senior Roman official to Judaism. If this were indeed the case, R. Meir could well have had a more positive view of Rome than his teacher, R. Akiba, and many of his colleagues. Indeed, R. Meir was known to be

76. Menaḥot 18a.

77. Both names mean "illuminates"; *Nehorai* is simply the Aramaic translation.

conversant in Greek and Latin literature;[78] perhaps this factor also contributed to the legend of his ancestry.

As with his experience in R. Eleazar's yeshiva, there was a deeply troubling aspect to Judah's studies under R. Meir. He never sat before his teacher, only behind him, and did not see his face. For Judah this was a source of lasting regret. Had he sat before R. Meir, he contended, "I would have been even sharper, as it is written, 'And your eyes shall behold your teacher.'"[79] He missed catching the nuances that his teacher's facial expressions conveyed, and that would have deepened his understanding of R. Meir's analyses.[80]

It says much about Judah's thirst for knowledge that he was prepared to study under the man who plotted against his father. R. Meir does not come off as well. As a veteran instructor, he was certainly aware of the importance of face to face contact with a student, as he no doubt was of the passage in Isaiah that Judah would later cite. Was R. Meir's treatment of Judah his way of getting back at the son of the patriarch whom he sought to depose?

R. Meir led a tragic life, and by the time Judah entered his yeshiva, he may have become an embittered man. His beloved teacher, Elisha b. Avuya, became the most infamous heretic in rabbinic literature. Two of Meir's sons died prematurely. And Beruria, Meir's brilliant and dear wife, who suffered with him when they lost their sons, could not cope with the stress of their loss. She committed suicide in circumstances that were never fully explained, but that appear to have been the result of an embarrassing incident which involved R. Meir himself.[81] The memory of having also failed to retain his position

78. For example, R. Meir related "300 fox fables," often identified with Aesop. See Sanhedrin 38b.
79. Eiruvin 13b; the Scriptural reference is from Is. 30:20.
80. See Maharsha, *Aggadot*, loc. cit., s.v. *hava.*
81. The Talmud does not explain what prompted Beruria's suicide. Rashi reports a story, whose source he does not provide, and which is nowhere to be found in the Talmud, that R. Meir tested his wife by encouraging a young student to seduce her. When she failed the test, she took her own life. See Avoda Zara 18b, which does not actually mention the incident. Rashi, s.v. *ve'ika,* discusses it in detail. It is not clear what might have been his source. For a discussion of what has been termed "the

as Judaea's most prominent legislator when R. Simeon ben Gamaliel reappeared on the scene may have been too much for R. Meir when he learned that the patriarch's son was attending his lectures. He simply may have been unable to control his resentment, which would explain his surprising indifference to the placing of one of his more brilliant students in a spot that no doubt was normally reserved for those less capable of absorbing his teachings. Under these circumstances, it is doubtful that Judah remained in R. Meir's yeshiva for very long. As had happened in R. Eleazar's yeshiva, Judah once again found himself unwelcome through no fault of his own.

Finally, Judah studied under R. Jacob b. Karsha'i, a close friend of his father's who had not only served as his assistant but prevented the coup against him from succeeding. Not surprisingly, there are no reports of any friction either with other students or with the master. Judah was able fully to absorb R. Jacob's teachings, and these were plentiful.

R. Jacob's lectures constituted a foundation for the Mishna that Judah edited, and they also served as a transmission belt for those rabbinic discussions that Judah chose not to include in the Mishna, called *baraitot*. R. Jacob's primary focus was on the importance of Torah education. He deemed it of such overarching importance that in his view one who interrupts his review of Torah study to admire his natural surroundings "endangers his soul."

R. Jacob had been a senior student of R. Meir, studying under the master well before Judah attended the latter's yeshiva. That Judah absorbed R. Meir's teachings was due not to the man himself, but rather to R. Jacob, who transmitted them to him. In that regard it is of no small significance that unattributed *mishnayot* (the Hebrew term is *stam mishna*) always reflected R. Meir's halakhic position. Whatever Judah may have felt about R. Meir, he did not let those feelings get in the way of providing what he perceived as the correct interpretation of the Oral Law.

Beruria affair," see M. Herschel Levine, "Three Talmudic Tales of Seduction," *Judaism* 36 (Fall 1987), 468–70. Levine writes (468n11) that Rashi "drew upon Talmudic sources," but offers none. There appear to be none extant.

As both the variety of Judah's experiences as a student and the story of the conversation among R. Simeon b. Yohai, R. Yose, and R. Judah b. Ila'i make clear, Judah's mentors did not share a single perspective on either halakha or the great political issues of the day. His behavior as patriarch appears to indicate that, as is often (but hardly always) the case, he was deeply influenced by his first teacher-cum-foster-parent R. Judah and by his father, R. Simeon. In addition, it is possible that his exposure to so many different points of view also shaped his personality as an independent thinker and halakhist. Indeed, if his teacher R. Judah b. Ila'i could follow a different path from his own teacher, R. Akiba, and openly admire the greatness of Rome, why should not Judah be true to his own principles?

Judah no doubt had one other teacher, of whom rabbinic literature rarely speaks: his mother. Apart from the story of her exchanging Judah for the infant Antoninus, we know virtually nothing about the wife of R. Simeon ben Gamaliel. She had to manage her household on her own for many years while her husband was in exile. Did she have an income? An inheritance? The Talmud and midrashim are silent. In what ways did she influence the young Judah? Again, only silence.

It is a shame that we know so little about a woman who must have brought up Judah and his siblings (though we have no idea who they were) under very difficult circumstances. Her economic situation must have been precarious. Unfortunately, rabbinic literature is very niggardly when it comes to the mothers of the rabbis. They rarely are mentioned, and even when they are, they are not identified by their own names. A notable exception is the foster mother of Abaye, a third-century *Amora*, whom he simply calls *Em* ("mother") when acknowledging her as the source of several of his rulings.[82] Few others get even that minimal degree of recognition.

82. For a discussion of Abaye's genealogy, see Aaron Demsky, "Abbaye's Family Origins – A Study in Rabbinic Genealogy," http://iijg.org/wp-content/uploads/2014/02/WUJS_Aaron_Demsky.pdf.

ADULTHOOD

Rabbinic literature is relatively silent regarding Judah's early manhood years and his development into a leader of his community. It does mention that, in common with many Jewish leaders harking back to King Saul, he was taller than his contemporaries.[83] There is no mention of his marriage or of the birth of his sons Simeon and Gamaliel or of his daughter, however. The only time his wife appears in any rabbinic writing is in the text of Rebbe's testament, in which he commands his sons to look after their mother. In fact, he was probably referring to their stepmother.[84] There is no indication that he was polygamous, yet the Talmud relates that he wanted to marry the widow of his former yeshiva rival, R. Eleazar.[85] Rebbe was an old man, probably in his mid-seventies, when he proposed to her sometime around the year 212 CE, the year of R. Eleazar's passing. Rebbe's first wife must therefore have died at some earlier date, and his command to his sons could only have been about their stepmother. That lady was not, however, R. Eleazar's widow.

R. Eleazar's wife, clearly no youngster either, was still exceedingly strong-willed. At one point during their marriage, she had walked out on R. Eleazar, taking their daughter with her. Now she gave Rebbe the back of her hand. The lady was not interested in Judah. He may have been a prince and a patriarch, but she felt that she would be marrying down! As noted, her late husband considered himself superior because he had studied far longer under his father, R. Simeon bar Yohai, beginning as a youngster, whereas Rebbe did not come to study under R. Simeon until he was older and had already received *semikha*. Moreover, R. Eleazar's wife was herself the daughter of a prominent rabbi, R. Issi b. Lakonia, whose son R. Simeon had cooperated with Rebbe in rescuing the young Yose from his wanton ways.

83. Nidda 24b lists numerous rabbinical figures who were exceedingly tall. Scripture describes King Saul as "from his shoulders and upwards he was taller than any of the people" (I Sam. 9:2).

84. See Ketubot 103b and Y. Ketubot, 12:3.

85. Bava Metzia 84b. See also *Pesikta* 10:94b for a variant of this tale.

That Rebbe had been her son's spiritual savior cut no ice with the former Mrs. R. Eleazar. She evidently had absorbed her husband's sense of intellectual superiority, which trumped Rebbe's genealogical status. In a word, she was a snob. As she put it, "A utensil that was used for holy purposes should now be used for profane ones?" Unwilling to accept rejection, Judah replied, "Perhaps he is greater than I am in Torah knowledge, but is he any better than me when it comes to doing good deeds?" She shot back, "As for Torah, I really don't know if he is your better, but when it comes to deeds, that I do know, for he accepted tribulations upon himself [such as hiding with his father in a cave for twelve years]."[86] The scion of the House of David, who was so proud of his ancestry that his student Rav accused him of whitewashing David's sin with Bathsheba, could not have been very pleased by the putdown.[87]

Rebbe appears to have been determined to have a companion in his old age. He did remarry, though the Talmud is silent as to the lady's identity or age. The Talmud does record, however, that in his parting words to his sons, Rebbe adjured them to look after their step mother.[88]

Judah and His Young Children

Rabbinic literature is generally indifferent to history and more specifically to the dating of events that took place outside the context of Scripture, though on occasion it can be very precise about such matters.[89] Thus we have no indication of when exactly Judah's four children – Gamaliel, Simeon, and his two daughters – were born. Was one or more of them born before Judah succeeded his father? That answer would depend on which tradition prevailed with respect to naming a child after a living person. This practice is permissible today in the Sephardic tradition but is avoided in Ashkenazic tradition. We simply do not know the tradition prevalent in Judah's family. Gamaliel may have been born while his grandfather was alive and may have

86. *Pesikta* 10:94b.

87. For a discussion of Rebbe's excuse for David and Rav's comment, see Shabbat 56a; see also Ephraim E. Urbach, *The Sages: Their Concepts and Beliefs*, trans. Israel Abrahams (Cambridge, MA and London: Harvard University Press, 1979), 495.

88. See Ketubot 103a. For a discussion see below, p. 295.

89. See, for example, the talmudic discussion of the precise dating of Nehemiah's petition to King Artaxerxes, Rosh Hashana 3a–b.

known him as a child. It would appear, however, that Simeon and his sister either were not born or were very young before Judah's father passed from the scene. In any event, there is no talmudic record of the elder R. Simeon having any interaction with his grandchildren.

We also know very little about the early lives of Judah's children or about his performance as a parent. It is possible that Judah was a doting father, since his father had been forced to be absent during much of his own childhood and his primary male role model was his quasi-foster father, R. Judah b. Ila'i. Again, however, rabbinic literature provides few insights in this regard; and as will be seen, in later years he could be a demanding, even harsh mentor.

Rabbinic literature does record Judah's teachings to his son Simeon, and some of them could well date to the years before he assumed the patriarchate, when both Judah's boys were still engaged in elementary-level studies. For example, the Talmud relates on several occasions that Judah taught Simeon that if someone robbed another of a cow to plow with, an ass to drive after, or any other significant item, and it was inherited by his children, they would be liable to restore it to save the good name of their father, so that people would not say their father had robbed it from someone.[90] It was the kind of ethical lesson that Judah might well have taught both his sons before they reached manhood.

There are considerably fewer examples of Judah imparting lessons to his other son, Gamaliel, until the day of his passing, when he confirmed his son as patriarch and gave him general instructions on how to conduct himself in his new role. It is possible to infer some of Judah's influence on his son from some of R. Gamaliel's own dicta. For example, both the Talmud and the Midrash relate a story that reflects both Rebbe's own sensitivity and his efforts to impart that sensitivity to his daughter and presumably to his other children. His daughter (whose name, like that of his wife, is never revealed) was about to kill a small animal that was in her way, something that small children are wont to do; Judah admonished her by saying: "Let it live, child; for it is written 'His tender mercies are over all.'"[91] Years later, when he was serving as

90. See, for example, Bava Kamma 111b and 113a. See also Rashi, op. cit., 111b, s.v. *ḥayavim*.
91. Bava Metzia 85a; Genesis Rabba, 33:3; the quote is from Ps. 144:9.

patriarch, Rabban Gamaliel II, basing himself on a passage in Deuteronomy, asserted that "one who shows mercy on creations will receive Heaven's mercy while one who shows no mercy on creations will not receive Heaven's mercies." It was a statement worthy of his father: if caring for animals was a virtue, how much more so caring for other humans.[92]

Moving to Beit She'arim

At some point during R. Simeon's patriarchate the Sanhedrin, the center of Jewish authority, moved from Usha to Shefaram. This was hardly the Sanhedrin's first move. During the turbulent years of the later Hasmonean period, it had relocated elsewhere in Jerusalem. As has been noted, the Talmud relates that subsequent to the fall of Jerusalem in 70, Rabban Yohanan b. Zakkai moved it to Yavneh, a town near the Mediterranean south of Jaffa. He succeeded in establishing the court as the central repository for rabbinic rulings, including appeals of rulings issued in other towns.[93] While Rabban Gamaliel II was patriarch the court moved to Usha in the Galilee, and back to Yavneh and then back again to Usha prior to R. Simeon's return from exile. It was later in Rabban Simeon's patriarchate that the Sanhedrin moved yet again, this time to Shefaram, the present-day primarily Arab and Druze city of Shefa-Amr, located at the entrance to the Galilee and about twelve miles from Haifa.[94] At the time the Sanhedrin moved there, it was a middle-sized Jewish town and apparently well organized.[95] Its ancient synagogue, destroyed and restored multiple times, dates back to the days of the Sanhedrin and is still in use. An Arab woman who lives across the street from the synagogue holds the keys to its gate.

92. Shabbat 151b. The quotation is from Deut. 13:18.
93. See for example Y. Kilayim 1:4 and Tosefta Kilayim 1:3, which record that the rabbis of Yavneh, following rulings of Beit Hillel, overruled students of Beit Shammai in two separate cases that involved the grafting of certain kinds of fruit. The two texts are almost identical, except that the Tosefta reverses the cases as they appear in Yerushalmi and the terms for the fruit vary slightly. For a discussion, see Saul Lieberman, *Tosefta Kipshuta: Order Zera'im*, vol. 2 (Hebrew) (New York: Jewish Theological Seminary Press, 2001), 598.
94. Rosh HaShana 31a, b; see also Rashi, ibid., s.v. *umiYavneh*, 31b.
95. Lau, *Ḥakhamim*, vol. 3, 370.

Sign at entrance of the ancient synagogue in Shefaram reads: "Ancient Jewish Synagogue from the Era of the Sanhedrin – Shefaram." On the right, the synagogue's exterior. (Photo: Dov Zakheim)

The Talmud is silent as to why R. Simeon saw fit to move the Sanhedrin from Usha, his hometown. Perhaps he moved to Shefaram to get away from R. Meir and his clique, who had held sway in Usha prior to his return and whose hostility to him remained undiminished. In any event, the Sanhedrin did not remain there very long. With R. Simeon's passing, it soon moved again, this time to Beit She'arim, which was located in the southern Galilee, about twenty miles east of present-day Haifa. The move appears to have been prompted by a plague of locusts which, the Talmud reports, occurred as R. Simeon died. The Talmud adds that there were additional unspecified troubles that took place at that time as well.[96] Rebbe's first act as patriarch may therefore have been to move the Sanhedrin, in accordance with the rabbinic maxim, "He who changes his place of residence changes his fortune (*meshaneh makom meshaneh mazal*)."

96. Sota 49b.

Since his father died at some point between 165 and 175, Rebbe could not have been more than forty years old when he succeeded him. He may even have been as young as thirty. Although, as will be seen, not all his rabbinical colleagues fully accepted his religious authority, there appear to have been few if any challenges to his inheriting the patriarchate. The rabbis believed that it had been granted to his family as a result of Rabban Yohanan b. Zakkai's intervention with Vespasian. Perhaps that is why there was little opposition to the move from Shefaram to Beit She'arim.

Rebbe was to remain in Beit She'arim for the better part of his life, and he was most closely identified with the place. As the Talmud put it when listing leading rabbis and the academies they had led: "Our Rabbis taught: *Justice, justice you should follow* means that you should follow the Sages to their *yeshivot* and courts. Follow R. Eliezer to Lod, Rabban Yohanan ben Zakkai to Berur Hayil, R. Joshua to Peki'in, Rabban Gamaliel to Yavneh...Rebbe to Beit She'arim."[97]

97. Sanhedrin 32b.

Chapter 3

The Road to the Top: Septimius Severus

Antoninus was the best of [the descendants of] Esau.

R. Yosef Hayyim
in the name of R. Hayyim Yosef David Azulai (Hida)

GROWING UP IN LEPCIS

Talmudic tales notwithstanding, Septimius Severus was not born on the same day as Judah the Prince.[1] Nor did his birth take place anywhere near Judaea, much less a day's walking distance from where Judah was born. His father was no innkeeper but a scion of a prominent, perhaps the pre-eminent, family of his city.

We do not know the exact day of Judah's birth, or even the year he was born. If he was born the day R. Akiba died, that could have been any time from 132 CE, at the beginning of the Bar Kohkba revolt, to as late as 137 CE, nearly two years after it ended. On the other hand, we do know the exact day Severus was born: April 11, 145 CE.[2]

1. The story appears in *Maasiyot,* 6, in Jellinek, ed., *Beit HaMidrash,* 130–31.
2. This is the view of Anthony Birley and most scholars. See Anthony R. Birley, *Septimius Severus: The African Emperor,* rev. ed. (London and New York: Routledge, 2010), 1.

Despite the exaggeration inherent in the talmudic tale, its story of the infant prince and the future emperor does hint at one true aspect of Severus' early years. Like Judah, he was something of an outsider, not being a native Roman, or even Italian. He was born in Roman North Africa, in the colony of Leptis or Lepcis,[3] the modern-day Lebda. During the first days of the empire the city was in the eastern part of the province of Africa Proconsularis; but it later became part of the separate province of Tripolitania, meaning the land of three cities (of which Lepcis was one), a name the region continues to bear to this day as part of war-torn Libya.

Lepcis and the other two cities of Tripolitania, Oea (modern-day Tripoli) and Sabratha, were founded by the Carthaginians. The name Carthage is actually a bastardized version of *qart-hadasht,* meaning "new city" in Phoenician and Canaanite, and akin to *kirya ḥadasha* in Hebrew. Unlike other parts of Roman North Africa, these three cities retained their Levantine heritage and language for two centuries after Rome defeated and destroyed Carthage in the Third Punic War of 149–146 BCE. Despite the fact that Carthage no longer existed, and indeed had been rebuilt as a Roman city, Rome's hatred of its ancient rival had never fully abated.

Severus' family had fully assimilated Roman culture. His paternal grandfather Lucius Septimius Severus, after whom he was named, was a barrister, a poet, and a Roman knight who was brought to Rome as a very young child and became "completely Italianized," speaking Latin without a trace of the Punic accent that marked the citizens of Tripolitania. After the assassination in 96 CE of the Emperor Domitian, who had commanded the allegiance of many of his friends, Lucius Septimius returned to Lepcis where he obtained a position as a municipal magistrate. When Trajan elevated the city to the rank of *colonia,* the highest status of a Roman city, and granted Roman citizenship to its inhabitants,

---

Mason Hammond, "Septimius Severus, Roman Bureaucrat," *Harvard Studies in Classical Philology* 51 (1940), 139, has Septimius' date of birth as 11 April 146, but this may be a typographical error.

3. Or Lepcis Magna; see Birley, *Septimius Severus,* loc. cit. This volume refers to the town as Lepcis.

Lucius Septimius was named prefect of the city. He then was promoted to the post of *duovir,* one of two judges who tried crimes against the state. By the end of his career, Lucius Severus had become one of the leading men, if not its most prominent official, in one of Roman North Africa's most prominent cities.

Lucius Severus left a legacy of public service that was continued by his relatives. His son, Severus' father, P. Septimius Geta, held no major political rank but was quite well off; he inherited land both in Lepcis and in several parts of Italy, including a farm in the ancient Etruscan town of Veii, just under ten miles from Rome, that Severus would himself later inherit. Severus' mother was Fulvia Pia, whose father, Fulvius Pius, was the scion of an old and respected family. All in all, therefore, the young Severus was born into privilege and prominence.

Septimius Severus was one of three children; he had an older brother named Geta after their father and a sister, Octavilla. Following in the footsteps of his father and grandfather, he was educated in both Latin and Greek literature, just as Judah's education in Greek culture was similar to that of his own father and grandfather. Severus also was fluent in Punic, the language of his ancestors, reflecting the family's attachment to their hereditary culture, just as Judah's family steadfastly adhered to the religion and culture of their own ancestors, however close their relationship to the Romans and their culture may have been. Punic was probably the language spoken in Severus' home, just as Hebrew was spoken in the household of the patriarch. In any event, though Severus was fully acculturated as a Roman, and was at least the third generation of his family to possess fluency in Latin, he evidently spoke Latin with a Punic accent, pronouncing "s" as "sh" (the Book of Judges recounts that the tribe of Ephraim pronounced "sh" as "s," which cost many of them their lives).[4] He may well have introduced himself to others as Sheptimius Sheverus.[5]

---

4. Judges 12:6.
5. Adrian Goldsworthy, *How Rome Fell* (New Haven and London: Yale University Press, 2009), 66. T. D. Barnes argues that Severus was not of Punic origin, but was rather descended from an Italian family that had migrated to Africa. His view is not shared by most scholars. T. D. Barnes, "The Family and Career of Septimius Severus," *Historia: Zeitschrift fur Alte Geschischte,* vol. 16 (March 1967), 94–107 *passim.*

Because Punic and Hebrew may have been closely linked linguistically,[6] Severus not only communicated with Jews in Greek, the language of the North African community, but also may well have been able to comprehend a few words of their native language, a fact that would have important ramifications for his future activities in Judaea.

Already as a child Severus demonstrated a domineering personality. He reportedly refused to play games with other children except to play judge. In that role he required that "rods and axes be borne before him, and, surrounded by the throng of children, he would take his seat and thus give judgments."[7] He was evidently a gifted public speaker; he culminated his education with his first "oration" at the age of either seventeen or eighteen, either just before or just after he left Lepcis.[8]

JEWS AND THE YOUNG SEVERUS

It is unclear whether Septimius Severus ever came across Jews when he was a boy growing up in Lepcis. He may well have, as there certainly was a community living there. Some Jews had migrated to North Africa together with the Phoenicians who had founded Carthage, and were therefore long-time residents. Many settled in the region around Carthage, in modern-day Tunisia; but certainly after its destruction, some would have gravitated to surviving Punic towns like Lepcis. Other Jews were more recent arrivals, having been exiled to North Africa after the rebellion of 66–70 and later after the Bar Kokhba rebellion.

Talmudic discussion of North African Jewry, apart from that of Alexandria in Egypt, is both oblique and scarce. At one point it refers to R. Hanan (or R. Abba – the Talmud is unsure) of Carthage, who related a case of a woman who had been captured as a slave. Her minor child testified that he had always been with her, indicating thereby that

---

6. There is considerable scholarly debate regarding the degree to which Punic and Hebrew, both North West Semitic languages, are related. See Geoffrey Khan, general editor, *Encyclopedia of Hebrew Language and Linguistics*, vol. 3 (Leiden and Boston: Brill, 2013), 71–76. See https://jewishstudies.rutgers.edu/docman/rendsburg/587-ehll-phoenician-punic/file. See also Strauss, *Ten Caesars*, 238.
7. *Historia Augusta: Severus*, 1:4.
8. Birley, *Septimius Severus*, 34, states that he was seventeen. *Historia Augusta* (*Severus* 1:5) asserts that he was eighteen.

she had never been violated, on the basis of which R. Joshua ben Levi – and some say Rebbe (!)– allowed her to marry a Kohen.[9] Since the issue involved a woman and child who were captured and enslaved, the incident may well have taken place in Roman North Africa, sometime in the second century or even later, which would explain why a rabbi from "Carthage" was aware of it and why Rebbe or R. Joshua ben Levi dealt with it.

The talmudic case underscores the point that the Romans brought Jews to North Africa, but also that there was a long-standing community there that produced rabbis of sufficient stature to be quoted in the Talmud. The older community clearly retained its Jewish identity, though recent scholarship has demonstrated that, as with so many Jewish communities past and present, local influences did affect the community's culture. Its leading figures, who no doubt were at least partially acculturated,[10] might possibly have come into contact with the Severi, who would have been, to some extent at least, their Roman counterparts. Unlike the patriarchs, however, the Severi made no claim to having royal blood. Severus may therefore indeed have met some Jews, and may even have learned some words in their language. Moreover, if Jews had shown any kindness toward him, it would also have affected his future attitude to them.[11]

SEVERUS LEAVES LEPCIS

Born into a privileged household, provided with a formal education, yet having fully imbibed his family's Punic heritage, Severus left Lepcis for Rome, "the Mecca of budding lawyers," in 162 CE.[12] In coming to the capital, Severus was following in the footsteps of his older brother Geta, who had embarked on a career in government service that normally led

9. Bava Kamma 114b; a slight variant appears in Ketubot 27b.
10. Gruen, *Diaspora*, 108n20; Smallwood, *Jews under Roman Rule*, 141; Cohen, *From the Maccabees*, 30–31.
11. Such has been the case many times ever since, most recently with respect to the warm relationship that Vladimir Putin has long maintained with the Chabad movement, reportedly due to the kindness shown to him by a Chabad family who were his neighbors during his childhood days in Leningrad.
12. Hammond, "Septimius Severus," 151.

to an appointment to the Senate. The young Severus was small in stature, but had a powerful body. He featured a turned-up nose, curly hair, and was clean-shaven, though he later grew a short beard. He was very energetic, and while not a talkative person, had an "active and original mind."[13]

Severus arrived in the capital city just at the time that Antoninus Pius was dying; he was succeeded by Marcus Aurelius. Thanks to the influence of Severus' relative, the Senator Gaius Septimius, Marcus Aurelius granted Severus the purple stripe that marked senatorial rank.[14] He was unable to enter the Senate, however, even as a quaestor, the lowest-ranking magistrate usually responsible for finances, until he entered his twenty-fifth year (the same minimum age as for entry into the U.S. House of Representatives). In other words, he had to wait some six years before he could attain the first rung of the ladder to political prominence.

Severus was interested in the law but apparently was not terribly successful as an advocate.[15] Like many who studied the law in his days or ours, he looked elsewhere for opportunities to climb the ladder of success. During those intervening years, he probably initially held some lower-ranking government positions, no doubt obtained through the influence of his family. Like all young, ambitious people who seek to make a name for themselves in government circles, Severus exploited his position to befriend both other rising stars as well as more established individuals, such as Marcus Aurelius' tutor, Marcus Cornelius Fronto, who could serve as his mentors.

Despite his Punic background and provincial upbringing, Severus was very much the Roman. It was for that reason that he saw the Senate, which was nowhere near as powerful as it had been during the Republic and even in the early years of the Empire, as the starting point for a successful career. Severus could have pursued a career as an equestrian serving directly under the emperor. It was the chosen profession of many provincials. Such service actually "offered more interest, opportunity, and promise of power than the senatorial career, which had become more

13. Birley, *Septimius Severus*, 42.
14. Ibid., 39.
15. Hammond, "Septimius Severus," 151.

and more restricted in scope."[16] There is some evidence that Severus actually did initially embark on the equestrian path to prominence, but he soon gave it up. The Senate offered both status and a host of contacts, political as well as social, that he reckoned – rightly, as it turned out – would further his career in a way that equestrian service would not.

Roman historians report that Severus also was exceedingly superstitious and was a strong believer in omens and astrology. In particular, he took note of several omens such as his having attended his first imperial dinner in the wrong costume and been given one of the emperor's togas to wear instead that seemed to indicate that he would someday inherit the imperial mantle. That Severus continually took note of omens points to the burning ambition that motivated him. In his mind at least, they pointed to a glorious future.[17] How glorious, even Severus himself could not have anticipated.

SENATOR AND QUAESTOR

As the oldest son of the recently restored patriarch, Judah's future was never in doubt. Once the coup against R. Simeon had failed, Judah was the unchallenged heir to his father's position. He was the crown prince, whose succession depended solely upon his father's passing. In contrast, Severus' route to the throne of Rome was neither simple, nor direct, nor foreordained. As a distinguished expert on Roman history has written, Severus "had greater difficulty than anyone before him in seizing the throne.... It was, indeed, a remarkable feat that Severus succeeded in reaching the throne at all."[18]

During the period while the young Severus was biding his time until he could enter the Senate, Rome was hit by the plague, which had been brought to the city by troops who had been fighting the Parthians in the east. With thousands dying, the wealthier classes retired to their country homes, a practice that continued for centuries even to the early

16. Ibid., 152.
17. Birley, *Septimius Severus,* 41; see also *Historia Augusta: Severus,* 2:7–9; 3:4–6; Herodian, *History of the Empire,* 2:3–6.
18. Michael Grant, *The Severans: The Changed Roman Empire* (London and New York: Routledge, 1995), 7.

years of the American republic, when yellow fever would strike cities like Philadelphia and New York. Although Severus was able to retire to the country farm in the central Italian region of Etruria, it was located too close to Rome for his health, and he returned to Lepcis in 167.

Once in Africa, it appears that Severus dropped all pretense of civility, his political ambitions notwithstanding. According to one of his Roman biographers, Severus' "early manhood was filled with follies and not free from crime."[19] He was prosecuted for adultery and represented himself before the court. He was found not guilty; it is not implausible that the magistrate hesitated to punish the scion of a prominent local family with connections in the capital.[20]

Sometime after that, he was back in Rome, where he was formally elected as a quaestor. With many others who had previously been elected having perished in the plague, Severus did not even have to wait until he was twenty-five in order to assume his new office. On December 5, 169, at the age of twenty-four and eight months, Septimius Severus took office as quaestor and member of the Senate. He was now one of six hundred men who still had a role, albeit a diminished one, in managing the affairs of an empire of sixty million people.

Although Severus was a fully assimilated Roman, he may not have been fully accepted by his colleagues, at least in private. "The Roman elite were certainly snobbish about Senators from the provinces. People joked about them not being able to find their way to the Senate house."[21] Severus' accent certainly did not help him in this regard.[22] Severus clearly was highly sensitive to his being something of an outsider, even when he had become emperor; perhaps he was aware that Hadrian had

19. *Historia Augusta: Severus*, 2:1.

20. According to the *Historia Augusta* (*Severus* 2:2–3), he was acquitted by Didius Julianus, "the man who was his immediate predecessor in the proconsulship, his colleague in the consulship, and likewise his predecessor on the throne." Julianus, who became proconsul in 175, was no longer a callow youth but rather a man of thirty, a senator, and an administrative official serving in Africa.

21. Mary Beard, *SPQR: A History of Ancient Rome* (New York and London: Liveright, 2015), 522.

22. Discrimination on the basis of accent certainly persists in many countries, for example in Britain, where regional accents are very pronounced and parvenus strive to adopt the plummy accents of the upper class; but also in the United States, where

been "mocked for his 'provincial' Spanish accent."[23] When Severus' sister came to visit him when he was already on the throne, he gave her presents and made her son a senator, but quickly sent them both home because he was embarrassed by her terrible Punic accent when she spoke Latin.[24] No doubt he felt that it drew attention to his own provincial background.

It is not clear exactly where Severus initially served as quaestor. In any event, in 171 Severus was ordered to serve a second term as quaestor supporting P. Cornelius Anullinus, proconsul of the southern Spanish province of Baetica, now Catalonia, which was still under the control of the Senate. Anullinus was at least ten years older than Severus;[25] but some two decades later, when Severus would become emperor, Anullinus would become his faithful subordinate.

Just before his scheduled departure in April 171, Severus learned of his father's passing and returned home to deal with family matters. While he was in Africa, the Moors attacked southern Spain, and Marcus Aurelius took temporary control of the province. With Baetica now under Marcus' direct authority, the Senate was given Sardinia as a sort of consolation prize, and it was therefore to Sardinia that Severus was dispatched from Africa.

MOVING UP THE ADMINISTRATIVE LADDER

Sardinia was not exactly a major stepping stone to future greatness; it was a Roman backwater. Moreover, less than half the quaestors were able to move up to the next level, that of praetor.[26] Severus was able to escape the island rather quickly, however, thanks to the fact that in 173

far too many northerners assume that anyone speaking with a southern drawl cannot be terribly bright. The drawl has been a source of amusement, if not ridicule, in countless films.

23. Adrian Goldsworthy, *Pax Romana: War, Peace and Conquest in the Roman World* (New Haven, CT and London: Yale University Press, 2016), 295.
24. Beard, *SPQR*, 522. Aelius Spartianus records that her inability to speak Latin properly "made the emperor blush for her hotly." *Historia Augusta: Severus*, 15:7.
25. Birley, *Septimius Severus*, 40.
26. Josephine Quinn, "Caesar Bloody Caesar," *The New York Review of Books* 65 (March 22, 2018), 25.

his relative, C. Septimius Severus, was named proconsul of Africa and proceeded to name his younger relative as one of his deputies (*legatus pro praetore*). The job was essentially that of administrative assistant,[27] not exactly an exalted position, but Severus took his new status far too seriously. In a display of arrogance, when he returned to his hometown and was embraced by a plebeian acquaintance, he had the man flogged.[28] As will be seen, once he was established as patriarch, Judah also had the ability to administer floggings to those who might flout his authority.[29]

While serving in Africa, Severus, now thirty, married Paccia Marciana, from the provincial upper class, though of Punic or Libyan, rather than Italian origin.[30] They remained married for ten years until her death. It is unclear whether they had children. The marriage must have been a strong one; once emperor, Severus erected statues in her honor, even though he was by then in a second marriage.[31]

Around the same time, his connections in Rome enabled him to become tribune of the plebs – a once-powerful position that included the right to initiate and veto legislation. By the time Severus was appointed, however, those responsibilities had lapsed, and his primary focus was on ensuring that magistrates did not "endanger the rights of Roman citizens."[32] Severus evidently performed well; in 176 he moved up the administrative ladder again, advancing to praetor, a higher level magistracy, by winning a contested election.[33] He was dispatched to Spain, his first post in the service of the emperor, and his career began to arc sharply upward. Within four years, that is, by 180, he was granted his first military command, in charge of the Fourth Legion in Syria[34] – his first taste of the Near East, where the two primary languages were Greek and Aramaic, the latter related to his own Punic mother tongue. Like

27. Hammond, "Septimius Severus," 155.
28. Birley, *Septimius Severus*, 51; *Historia Augusta* (*Severus*, 2:6) reports that the man was "beaten with clubs."
29. Berakhot 16b and Rashi, s.v. *ve'af al gav*.
30. Birley, *Septimius Severus*, 52.
31. *Historia Augusta: Severus*, 3:2.
32. Birley, *Septimius Severus*, 53.
33. Barnes, "The Family and Career of Septimius Severus," 92.
34. *Historia Augusta: Severus*, 3:3–4.

Rebbe, however, Severus was well versed in Greek language and culture; most educated Romans were.[35] It is not clear whether Severus viewed Aramaic with the same disdain as did Rebbe; but given his excessive self-esteem, he probably shared with Judah a preference for Greek, the language of the elite, over the language of the masses. No doubt when they finally met, they conversed in Greek, not Aramaic, though each may well have understood the other's Hebrew or Punic.

Severus' posting in Syria represented another major milestone in his career. His command was subordinate to the governor, who was none other than P. Helvius Pertinax, the future emperor. The legion that he commanded was the most prestigious of Rome's legions in Syria, the main Roman force defending the capital, Antioch, from any attack by the Parthians, whose territory was but one hundred miles away.

At around the time that Severus transferred to Syria, Marcus Aurelius died and was succeeded by his son and co-emperor, the eighteen-year-old Commodus. After an initial spurt of popularity with the people and the troops Commodus, fearful of intrigues against him, initiated purges of his leading courtiers and officials both in Rome and abroad, including Syria. Severus was not executed, but he did leave his job in 182 after only two years at his post. It is possible that he was dismissed, since that appears to have been the fate of his superior, Pertinax.

It was either during or just after Severus' service in Syria that he went to Athens, "partly in order to continue his studies."[36] Severus was pursuing what today would be termed "professional military education," which involves taking an extended leave from daily military routines to refresh one's intellect. That Severus, by now a relatively senior officer, chose to further his education rather than merely bide his time in idleness, reflects his single-minded determination to continue moving up the ladder of power and influence.

After a two-year hiatus, Severus returned to a public career, possibly due to the downfall of an enemy, Perennius, the emperor's minister.

---

35. Bruno Rochette, "Language Policies in the Roman Republic and Empire," trans. James Clackson, in *A Companion to the Latin Language* (Oxford: Blackwell, 2011); Strauss, *Ten Caesars*, 178.
36. *Historia Augusta: Severus*, 3:7.

Severus was awarded consular rank, thanks to the support of a one-time slave named Cleander who became the power behind the dissolute Commodus' throne. Cleander got into the business of selling "senatorships, military commands, procuratorships, governorships, and, in a word, everything."[37] In 186, Cleander outdid himself: he appointed twenty-five consuls for one year, and one of them was Severus.

Consuls were nowhere near as powerful then as they had been in the early days of the empire, when they were virtually equal to the emperor himself at local levels; but the position was still highly prestigious. In addition to his appointment as consul, Severus was also granted his first governorship, presumably thanks to Cleander's patronage. As governor of the Gallic province of Lugdunum, he ruled over a major part of what is today France, stretching from the Rhone River to the Atlantic coast and the English Channel.

RISING TO THE VERY TOP

By now Severus was recognized as a capable senior official. He moved swiftly from one office to another, much as talented military officers can climb quickly from one-star to four-star rank in just a few years through a series of increasingly important assignments and commands. In Severus' case, his term as governor ended in 188, and only a few months later, in early 189, he was appointed proconsul of Sicily. He remained studiously apolitical, while making important contacts at the same time, and was therefore able to avoid Commodus' seemingly never-ending series of purges. In 191, through the influence of Quintus Aemilius Laetus, a fellow African who had become prefect of the Praetorian Guard, Severus was made governor of Upper Pannonia, what is now Slovenia and Austria.[38] He now commanded three legions, the largest army that was closest to Italy itself. At roughly the same time his brother Geta, who was also pursuing a successful administrative and military career, took command of two legions in Lower Moesia, along the Danube. Between them the brothers thus controlled a powerful force of nearly thirty thousand crack troops.

---

37. Dio Cassius, *Roman History*, 73:12:3.
38. Birley, *Septimius Severus*, 82–83; Barnes, "Family and Career," 93.

Commodus was assassinated on December 31, 192; Pertinax was proclaimed emperor that same night. Severus may have been part of the plot to eliminate Commodus, despite his publicly apolitical stance.[39] Severus vowed allegiance to the new emperor, but, in one of his many dreams – all of which clearly were expressions of his own ambition – he saw Pertinax unseated by a horse and himself being lifted by the horse upon its back in what had been the new emperor's place.[40] For the moment, however, what was far more important to Severus' career was the fact that Pertinax did not immediately dismiss the bevy of senior Commodus appointees, and certainly not Severus, who a decade earlier had served under him in Syria.

Pertinax was described by his contemporary Dio Cassius as an "excellent and upright man,"[41] but he alienated both the soldiers and the courtiers who had benefited from the corruption that marked Commodus' reign and was murdered on March 28.[42] When Julianus won the throne in a bidding war, Severus was ready soon thereafter to take it for himself. It is not clear when he began to plot his coup. After Pertinax was murdered, he proclaimed his loyalty to the dead emperor and went to work both with kinsmen who were well positioned in Rome and with several fellow-governors of European provinces. Only twelve days after Pertinax's death, he was proclaimed emperor by at least one legion.[43]

Having bribed his way to the throne, Julianus had earned no credibility with anyone. Severus, C. Pescennius Niger, governor of Syria, and D. Clodius Albinus, governor of Britain, each rebelled with a view to becoming emperor in Julianus' place. Severus and his forces quickly moved to the border of Italy even before it became widely known that they had proclaimed him emperor.[44] In order to neutralize his rivals, Severus won over Albinus by promising to make him co-Caesar. Having

---

39. Goldsworthy, *How Rome Fell*, 64.
40. Herodian, *History of the Empire*, 2:9:5–7; see also the comments of Dio Cassius, *Roman History*, 73:23:1–3.
41. Dio Cassius, *Roman History*, 74:1:1.
42. Ibid., 74:5:2–9:3.
43. Birley, *Septimius Severus*, 97
44. Goldsworthy, *How Rome Fell*, 64. The bodyguard consisted of crack cavalrymen organized as *alae* (wings) and chosen from the province's non-Roman auxiliaries.

done so, Severus isolated Niger, who had proclaimed himself emperor at Antioch, and proceeded to march on Rome.

Recognizing the threat to his throne and his life, Julianus had the Senate declare Severus a public enemy and sent legates "ordering his soldiers in the name of the Senate to desert him."[45] Severus was initially "terrified" but soon composed himself, bribed the legates to tell the soldiers to back him, and even got the legates to come over to his side. Julianus, desperate to retain some degree of control, prompted the Senate to decree that he and Severus should share the throne. At the same time he sent assassins to liquidate Severus; they failed in their mission.[46] Julianus then attempted to block the passes to Rome, but his forces offered no resistance to Severus. Julianus also undertook to fortify the city and its suburbs against Severus' impending attack. His fortifications proved useless, even laughable, while the troops meant to defend him defected *en masse* to Severus. The Senate sentenced Julianus to death and proclaimed Severus emperor.[47]

At first blush it is somewhat puzzling that Severus would even have wanted the Senate to validate what his army had already promulgated. Rabbinic literature, in the form of the Tosefta, a tannaitic adjunct to the Mishna, provides an insight into his decision. Pescennius Niger was, to all intents and purposes, emperor in the East, and therefore represented a threat to Severus' legitimacy as supreme ruler of the empire. Proclamation by his own troops could be seen as no more valid than that by Niger's forces. Severus needed something more. A dictum in the Tosefta by Rebbe's student, Rav (more about whom below), explains why the Senate proclamation provided that "something" that Severus so desperately needed.

Rav asserted that the list of days when Jews were prohibited from doing business with heathens (as well as three days before each of the days on the list) included "the day when the ruler was proclaimed emperor." Rav was a younger contemporary of Severus; he clearly was

45. *Historia Augusta: Severus,* 5:5.

46. Ibid., *Severus,* 5:6–10.

47. Dio Cassius provides an eyewitness account; *Roman History,* 74:14:3–17:6.

referring to the latter when he issued his ruling.[48] His point was that only a public proclamation validated the accession of the emperor, as opposed to a private one, such as that by Severus' troops. In the eyes of the rabbis, and presumably most other residents of the Empire, it was only the Senate's proclamation that validated Severus' position. Armed with the Senate's blessing, which Niger had not received, Severus could legitimately call himself Rome's sole emperor. He commanded a force of thirty-three legions, plus a variety of smaller units, naval flotillas, and the Praetorian Guard, which added up to a total of 350,000 men under arms, "all sworn to serve the emperor, and paid and promoted by him. It was not until the French Revolution brought mass conscription that the army of any European state surpassed this total."[49] Indeed, Severus commanded more troops than those serving as active forces in the militaries of any member state in today's NATO alliance apart from Turkey and the United States.[50] The provincial African had made it to the top of the world's most powerful empire.

48. See Saul Lieberman, "Achievements and Aspirations of Modern Jewish Scholarship," *Proceedings of the American Academy for Jewish Research* 46/47, part 1 (1979–80), 370–73.
49. Goldsworthy, *Pax Romana*, 309–10.
50. The International Institute for Strategic Studies, *The Military Balance: The Annual Assessment of Global Military Capabilities and Defence Economics*, 2017 (London: Routledge, 2017), 553–54.

Chapter 4

The Patriarch

> R. Simeon ben Judah said in the name of Rabban Simeon bar Yohai: Beauty, strength, wealth, honor, wisdom, sageness, old age and children are becoming to the righteous and becoming to the world... R. Simeon ben Menasia said: These seven qualities that the Sages enumerated for the righteous were all realized in Rebbe and his sons.
>
> Avot 6:8

ESTABLISHING AUTHORITY: AN OVERVIEW

Rebbe was a "blue blood," a scion of the royal family. In a society that was both highly authoritarian and respectful of dynastic prerogative (exemplified in contemporary times by the hasidic "courts"), Rebbe's leadership as a function of both his office and his royal Davidic ancestry was unassailable. Rebbe's wealth, fabulous by the measure of his times, afforded him a degree of status that simply was out of reach of many of his rabbinical colleagues. He managed a large household and saw to the education of his children, who were raised to assume the mantle of leadership after his passing.

It should come as no surprise that Rebbe was an elitist. He touted his preference for Hebrew and Greek over Aramaic, the language of the street. He and his family dressed differently from most Jews, including his rabbinical colleagues, copying some of the styles of the Roman aristocrats with whom he mixed freely. In that regard it would appear unlikely that he wore tefillin (phylacteries) all day, as did many of the other Sages, given his administrative and diplomatic duties.

Rebbe communicated not just with Romans but with the rulers of Parthia. In both cases he acted as a virtual equal. On the other hand, he openly looked down upon the unschooled *amei haaretz,* until a particular incident, related below, led him to change his views.

Rebbe employed his wealth judiciously to support scholars and students, who became leading rabbis both in Palestine and Babylonia. He could not tolerate *lèse majesté,* however, despite being personally modest, and on occasion clashed sharply with his students. Not all of his colleagues were enamored of him; he had his rivals who chafed at his dominant position in the community.

Whatever his rivals may have felt about him, Rebbe's office and his leadership were officially recognized by the Roman administration. The average Jew may have hated the Romans – though it is not at all clear that most actually did – but he nevertheless could not but respect a people that had conquered not only his land but most of the known world. And that Jew could take pride in the fact that these people accorded so much respect to his own leader.

EARLY YEARS AS PATRIARCH

By the time Septimius Severus asserted his claim to the imperial throne, Rebbe had long been ensconced as patriarch, which meant that he was the officially recognized leader of the Jewish community of Judaea. In practice, he was also the leader of the Jewish community of the Roman Empire. Only the Jews of Babylonia, then a province of the Parthian Empire, and the Jews of Ethiopia and India, of whose existence the rest of world Jewry was totally unaware, lay outside Rebbe's writ.[1]

---

1. For a brief discussion of the Jews of Ethiopia and India, see Dov S. Zakheim, "What Happened to the Ten Lost Tribes?: An Overview from Biblical Times to the Present," in Yamin Levy, ed. *Mishpetei Shalom: A Jublilee Volume In Honor of Rabbi Saul (Shalom) Berman* (New York: Yeshivat Chovevei Torah Rabbinical School, n.d.), 642–47.

Rebbe's early years as patriarch could not have been easy ones. Though he had inherited his position and did not have to claw his way to power as Severus did, he nevertheless could not assume that his authority would remain unchallenged. He had only to recall the attempt to depose his father in order to recognize the imperative of winning over both the rabbinic and economic elites of his community, as well as the Roman authorities.

Little is known about Rebbe's relations with the Roman authorities during the early years of his patriarchate. He may already have succeeded his father during the last stages of the Parthian War (162–166 CE) that Marcus Aurelius had prosecuted. In that case, he would probably have done his utmost not to be identified with any aspect of that war, since he and his fellow-rabbinic scholars were in constant contact with their Babylonian counterparts. To have taken sides would have endangered either those rabbis who lived under Parthian rule or those under Roman rule. Neutrality was the best course to pursue. It is therefore possible, indeed likely, that the rabbis in both communities decided to suspend their communications until the war ended, so as not to appear suspect in the eyes of ruling authorities. However, there is nothing in rabbinic literature that would hint at this development. Indeed, rabbinic literature, which is generally ahistorical, has little to say about the war itself. [2]

It is not certain that Rebbe had assumed the office of patriarch by the time of the war against the Parthians; there is greater certainty that he had done so by 175 CE, when Marcus Aurelius passed through Palestine in the course of crushing the Avidius Cassius rebellion. Roman historians report that the Jews annoyed the emperor with their importunities (even if they did not support Avidius Cassius); if these reports are to be believed, there can be little doubt that Rebbe was the one who either led their delegation or put their case before him on his own. In doing so, he certainly would not have endeared himself to Marcus Aurelius. Nevertheless, he did not anger the emperor sufficiently to bring about any change in the status of either the Jewish community or the patriarchate.

---

2. Jewish leaders did take sides in other wars. For example, during the American Civil War, northern rabbis supported the Union while their southern counterparts supported the Confederacy. Similarly, during World War I, German rabbis supported the Reich, while Russian and Polish rabbis supported the Allies.

In any event, Rebbe was fortunate that he had friendly emperors for much of his tenure as patriarch. As already noted, the Christian leader Jerome would write a century later that Severus and Caracalla "esteemed the Jews very highly."[3] It was not merely that the Roman grip on Palestine eased considerably once Severus came to power; the province benefited from a spate of synagogue construction, as well as road construction. The Jews may have attributed the latter to the beneficence of the Severans, even if road-building was simply a general Roman policy not tied to specific rulers.[4]

The Romans also recognized the favor with which Severus and Caracalla looked upon the Jews. *Historia Augusta* recounts an incident involving Caracalla as a young child: "Once, when a child of seven, hearing that a certain playmate of his had been severely scourged for adopting the religion of the Jews, he long refused to look at either the boy's father or his own because he regarded them as responsible for the scourging."[5]

The story is as apocryphal as many of the talmudic tales about Rebbe and Antoninus, but it reflects the warm feelings that the otherwise-bloodthirsty Caracalla appears to have had for the Jews. Perhaps his attitude derived from the fact that unlike so many others, the Jews posed no threat to his person or his rule. Perhaps he simply inherited his father's fondness for Jews.[6] As for Severus, it may have been that like himself, the Jews were outsiders; he was, after all, an African, not Roman-born. Whatever the reason, the favor with which Severus and his son looked upon the Jews redounded to the benefit of Rebbe, the perceived leader of the Jewish community.

ROMAN HONORS

The Romans did not merely respect Rebbe; they treated him like the prince that he was. Like Nehemiah, to whom Artaxerxes accorded a

---

3. Jerome, *Commentary on Daniel*, 11:34.
4. Smallwood, *Jews under Roman Rule*, 494.
5. *Historia Augusta*, trans. David Magie (Cambridge, MA and London: Harvard University Press, 1924), *Antoninus Caracalla*, 1:6. See also Stern, ed., *Greek and Latin Authors on Jews and Judaism*, 626–27.
6. Severus, though friendly toward the Jews, prohibited conversion to Judaism; see below. The young Caracalla objected both to his father's policies and to his friend's father's flouting of those policies. But he had no problem with his friend being Jewish.

military escort, Rebbe was always accompanied by armed retainers. These troops may well have supported Rebbe courtesy of Rome.[7] It is possible that Rebbe acquired them privately; but neither his father, Rabban Simeon, nor even his imperious grandfather, Rabban Gamaliel, was reported to have such a force at his disposal. It is therefore far more likely that Rebbe's retainers were in fact supplied by senior Roman officials as a special privilege that marked his importance as both communal leader and ally of Rome.

Who these retainers were is a matter of conjecture. The Talmud only specifically identifies retainers of later rabbis, including Rebbe's grandson, R. Yehuda Nesia.[8] These the Talmud terms "Goths," and in one place "Germans," meaning one of the Germanic tribes that Rome had conquered. The talmudic description appears to be accurate: Rebbe's bodyguard would have been similar to that which accompanied Severus on his forced march to Rome. It would have been drawn from the "wings" of the non-Italian auxiliaries, such as the Goths.

The Goths were well known for their military prowess; Rome had encountered considerable difficulty suppressing their rebellions and was ultimately sacked in 410 CE by Alaric, leader of the Visigoths (West Goths). If they indeed were Rebbe's escorts, they were most capable, both as a personal security force and as enforcers of his edicts. The Midrash describes their role: "When a man appeared before Rebbe for a judgment, if he accepted the ruling, all was well; if he did not [Rebbe] would tell his security chief 'hit him on the left side' and would make an imposing gesture with his hand to indicate the left side."[9] In this case, the retainers were acting as marshals or officers of the court, ensuring, by means of violence if necessary, that Rebbe's rulings were neither ignored nor defied.[10]

These support troops were also employed for positive missions. The Talmud recounts that R. Simeon b. Lakish, better known as Resh

7. Berakhot 16b and Rashi, s.v. *ve'af al gav*.
8. *Nesia* is the Aramaic word for *Nasi*, i.e., patriarch. R. Yehuda Nesia succeeded his father, R. Gamaliel III, who was Rebbe's successor.
9. Ecclesiastes Rabba 10:2.
10. It is possible that the Romans also unofficially authorized Rebbe to impose sentences calling for capital punishment. See Oppenheimer, *Rabbi Yehuda HaNasi*, 53–55.

Lakish, ate the juicy and oily fruit of Genosar "until his mind began to wander." R. Yohanan, Resh Lakish's study partner and brother-in-law, informed the patriarch's household what had happened. "And R. Yehuda Nesia sent a band of men for him and they brought him to his house" to recover.[11]

Having retainers was a privilege accorded to nobility and leading personages well into the twentieth century, and indeed the twenty-first. One contemporary equivalent is the motorcycle escort for heads of state, heads of government, and other leading officials. Another is the honor guard, which, like that of the president of Turkey, is decked out in garish uniforms that hark back to the "Ruritanian" guards that were *de rigueur* in 1930s Hollywood movies. Though ostensibly these escorts are meant to allow these personages to move unimpeded through otherwise crowded thoroughfares, they also signal the importance of the individuals for whom they have cleared traffic lanes or even entire highways. In much the same fashion, the fact that Rebbe had his own personal security detachment, provided to him by the Roman leadership, underscored his image and authority as the community's unquestioned leader.[12]

THE ROMANS AND REBBE'S WEALTH

Later rabbis of the Talmud were mesmerized by Rebbe's legendary wealth. The Talmud records in breathless hyperbole that the wedding of his son Simeon cost him 24 million denarii,[13] equivalent to about 75 million dollars today. As if that were not enough, the Talmud also asserts that his wealth was equivalent to that of the Roman emperor: in discussing various kinds of blessings, the Talmud states that "the benediction 'who creates fragrant woods' is said only over the balsam trees of the household of Rebbe and the balsam trees of Caesar's household."[14] Elsewhere the Talmud recounts that the tables of "Antoninus" and Rebbe "never

11. Berakhot 44a.
12. Tosefta Sanhedrin 11:8.
13. Nedarim 50b.
14. Berakhot 43a; see Rashi, s.v. *shel*.

lacked either radish, lettuce, or cucumbers either in summer or winter."[15] At least one Roman source describes wealth in a roughly similar fashion.[16]

It is somewhat unclear how Rebbe amassed a good part of his fortune. The Talmud relates that just one of his ships carried three hundred barrels of fish, indicating that he earned at least part of his fortune through trade.[17] The bulk of Rebbe's wealth derived from his agricultural holdings, however. The family were major landowners; his grandfather R. Gamaliel owned lands in southern Judaea. Nevertheless, Rebbe probably did not inherit much from his father, who, as a fugitive from Roman authority, may have had his properties confiscated. It is unlikely that R. Simeon hid his fortune somewhere, since the greater part of one's assets in those days was in land and livestock. It is possible that the Romans restored Rebbe's grandfather's land either to him or to his father, R. Simeon, when he was permitted to return to Palestine. Rebbe may then have inherited the land, though he never lived in Judaea, residing his entire life in the Galilee.[18] In particular, these restored lands may have included land in the Jordan Valley where "the famous balsam plantations were situated."[19] Alternately, the balsam plantations may have been an outright Roman grant to Rebbe.

Some have asserted that Rebbe married into wealth.[20] While that may have been the case, there is no evidence for it. Of Rebbe's father-in-law, who presumably would have been the source of any wealth Rebbe may have acquired through marriage, there is no mention.

Rebbe owned land in the Galilee which produced high quality wine and balsam. He appears to have had tenant farmers who paid him

---

15. Ibid. 57b.
16. *Historia Augusta, Tacitus* 11:2, speaks of an abundance of lettuce. Cited in Moses Hadas, "Rabbinic Parallels to Scriptores Historiae Augustae," *Classical Philology* 24 (July 1929), 262.
17. Y. Avoda Zara 2:9; Schafer, *History of the Jews in Antiquity*, 168. Schafer erroneously cites Y. Avoda Zara 2:10.
18. See Oppenheimer, *Rabbi Yehuda HaNasi*, 58. However, Oppenheimer does not allow for Roman confiscation of Rabban Gamaliel's land, which was a common practice when dealing with rebellious individuals and subject peoples, as he himself notes in another context (op. cit. 83–84).
19. Schafer, *History of the Jews in Antiquity*, 169.
20. Alon, *Jews in Their Land*, 713.

some percentage of their earnings. Although later patriarchs received gifts from Jews both inside and outside Palestine, Rebbe was not one of them. Donations were not the source of his wealth, nor did they contribute to it. As he testified on his death bed, raising ten fingers upward as he did so, "Master of the Universe, it is revealed and known to you that I have labored in the study of the Torah with my ten fingers and I did not receive any benefits even with my little finger."[21]

On the other hand, while Rebbe may not have taken gifts from his countrymen – again there is a parallel with Nehemiah, who likewise refused to accept offerings that the Jews normally gave to their governors – he does not seem to have scorned gifts from the Romans. The royal prerogative of bestowing land to loyal subjects is one with a pedigree stretching from ancient to near modern times. Augustus Caesar granted land to his troops; in 1664 Britain's Charles II granted all of New England to the Duke of York. There is therefore considerable credibility to the assertion that Rebbe benefited from the generosity of the Severi.[22]

Rebbe, like many wealthy men of our times as well as his own, no doubt drew upon shrewd business instincts to increase his sizable inheritance many times over. His wealth so astounded his countrymen that even centuries later, rabbis of the Babylonian Talmud could assert hyperbolically that Rebbe's house-steward was wealthier than King Shapur of Persia.[23]

REBBE AND ROMAN PLEBEIANS

Rebbe's good relations with the emperors extended to other Roman elites. He inherited from both his father and his teacher, R. Judah bar

21. Ketubot 104a. R. Yosef Hayyim interpreted this statement to mean that Rebbe did not even accept gifts from "Antoninus." See R. Yosef Hayyim, *Ben Yehoyada*, vol. 3, s.v. *velo*.
22. The Talmud (Y. Shevi'it 6:1) asserts that "Antoninus" leased to Rebbe two tracts of fertile land from which he paid rents. The story appears in the context of a discussion as to whether one of the tracts in question was subject to the laws of the Sabbatical year. While the amounts in question may not be accurate, the tradition that the lands were leasehold and not Rebbe's freehold can be taken as accurate, since the question of ownership had a direct halakhic implication and the rabbis were punctilious about attribution when determining halakha, unless they explicitly identified conflicting rabbinical sources. See also Oppenheimer, *Rabbi Yehuda HaNasi*, 59–60.
23. Bava Metzia 85a.

Ila'i, an appreciation for Rome's contribution to civilization. Nevertheless, he recognized that even if many leading Romans shared their emperor's positive attitude toward the Jews, that certainly was not the case with respect to the ordinary Romans who filled the ranks of the legions that occupied Palestine. The Midrash relates:

> When Antoninus came to Caesarea he summoned Rebbe. His son, R. Simeon, and R. Hiyya the Great accompanied him. R. Simeon noticed the handsome, distinguished-looking legionary, whose height reached the capitals of the columns, and he said to R. Hiyya: "See how fat the calves of Esau are." Whereupon R. Hiyya took him to the marketplace and pointed out baskets of grapes and figs covered with flies, and said to him: "These flies and these legionaries are one and the same." When R. Simeon returned to his father, he told him: "This is what I said to R. Hiyya, and this is how he answered me." "R. Hiyya," he replied, "was only partially correct in comparing the legionaries to the flies, for the legionaries are regarded as nothing [before God], while the Holy One, blessed be He, employed flies as His emissaries, as it is stated: 'And it shall come to pass in that day, that the Lord shall hiss for the fly that is in the uppermost parts of the river of Egypt,' and also: 'And I will send the hornet ahead of you' and also the frogs and the vermin. Be aware that at the time when the Holy One, blessed be He, desired to fulfill the promise [of exile in Egypt, namely] 'your seed shall be a stranger,' He selected as His emissary one from the smallest tribe. And so Joseph was sold into Egypt, and later Jacob and his sons went there to fulfill the decree."[24]

Rebbe contrasted his meeting with the emperor, probably Caracalla,[25] with his impression of the ordinary though impressive Roman legionary. By the time Caracalla passed through Palestine in 212 CE, Rebbe was

24. *Midrash Tanḥuma, Parashat Vayeshev* 3.

25. The reference is probably to Caracalla as by the time Caracalla passed through Palestine Rebbe's son would have been a mature adult, while his talented student R. Hiyya would by then have been recognized as "great."

nearing his eighth decade and presumably felt the need to be accompanied by younger men whose counsel he may have sought. Nevertheless, his acuity was as powerful as ever: while he shared R. Hiyya's view of ordinary Romans, he would not apply it to all Romans. The patricians were worthy of respect; and though the plebeians were indeed no better than flies buzzing round some fruit, they did have a role in the Divine plan.

Another account likewise indicates that Rebbe's caution regarding ordinary Romans, especially Roman soldiers, was not unwarranted. The Midrash recounts that when Rebbe had to travel to Rome on some mission, he would look up the biblical verse "And Esau said: 'Let me now leave some of my people with you,' and Jacob demurred: 'For what reason should I find favor in my master's eyes?'"[26] Accordingly, he would refuse any Roman escort, even though in Palestine he did have a permanent troop assigned to him. Indeed, on one occasion Rebbe did not look up the verse and permitted Roman soldiers to accompany him. Sure enough, before he reached Acco he had already been forced to sell his coat, because the Romans had stripped him of all he had with him.[27]

Rebbe ruled that "circumcision performed by a gentile is invalid." While the term "gentile" could have been any one of several non-Jewish nationalities, it certainly included Romans. In this case Rebbe took a harder line than his first teacher, R. Judah bar Ila'i, who held that in a city where no Jew was able to perform the circumcision, a non-Jew (though not a Samaritan) could do so.[28] R. Judah's position was consistent with his relatively positive view of Romans, noted above; he does not appear to have distinguished between the elites and the ordinary folk, as Rebbe clearly did. Nevertheless, despite his comfortable relationships with leading Romans, even Rebbe made no distinction between Roman classes when it came to matters of Jewish ritual.

Finally, and in a similar vein, Rebbe also adopted an equally strict position when it came to sexual relations between Jews and gentiles. Rebbe ruled that a gentile child caused defilement by seminal emission one day after it was born, though in fact no such emission took place.

---

26. Gen. 33:15.
27. Genesis Rabba 78:15.
28. Avoda Zara 26b.

The intent of the ruling was to prevent sexual contact with a heathen of any age. In this case, however, he yielded to the relatively more lenient view of his student R. Hiyya, who held that that it was only at the age of nine years and one day that a heathen child was to be treated as having seminal emission.[29]

Rebbe's distrust of Roman plebeians demonstrated yet again his political acuity. To this day, Western policy makers and analysts are regularly taken in by elites from developing countries who generally are themselves Western educated and tend to speak English and/or French virtually fluently. They present themselves as representing their ordinary countrymen, but rarely do so.[30]

In each of those cases, the local elites had little in common with the people of "the street," who rejected their aspirations to leadership. For his part, Rebbe understood the dichotomy between the attitudes of elites and those of the Roman plebeians, particularly the lower-ranking troops serving as an occupying force in Palestine. He therefore reflected the same degree of caution that, according to rabbinic tradition, his forefather Jacob had displayed when responding to Esau's seemingly kind offer: Even if Esau had been sincere, which was not obviously the case, his men could not be trusted. Neither, for that matter, could those putative descendants of Esau, the Romans who offered to escort him to the imperial capital. And on the one occasion when Rebbe dropped his guard, he paid a price as a result; he should have relied on his usual Visigoth military escort.

---

29. Avoda Zara 36b–37a.

30. Examples include the success that the Iraqi Ahmed Chalabi achieved in convincing Washington elites to launch the attack on Iraq in March 2003, and the assurances that educated young Egyptians gave to those who were all too ready to believe that the "Arab spring" would lead to the emergence of democratic institutions and governance throughout the Middle East. In both cases Western, notably American, elites looked no further than their westernized interlocutors, with results that included resentment of what came to be perceived by the local Iraqi populace as American occupation of their country, as well as civil conflict not only in Iraq, but also in Libya, Syria, and Yemen, while Egypt suffered from the short-lived but traumatic rule of the Muslim Brotherhood.

FINANCING THE PATRIARCHATE: REBBE'S AUTHORITY TO COLLECT TAXES AND OTHER SOURCES OF REVENUE

One of the most important privileges that the Romans granted to Rebbe was the ability to collect taxes from the Jewish community. Tax collection underpins authority; since the reign of Augustus taxes had been collected by Roman officials. That Rebbe was awarded the responsibility for tax collection underpinned his authority within the Jewish community. It also served to underscore the community's autonomy and separate identity within society at large.

It is not clear when exactly Rebbe received the right to collect taxes; it is unlikely that his father, even when restored to power, received such a grant from the emperors who were his contemporaries, Antoninus Pius, Marcus Aurelius, and Commodus. It may well have been when Septimius Severus passed through Palestine and rewarded his supporters in his war with Pescennius Niger, that Rebbe received the authority to tax the community. These taxes maintained Rebbe's household operations,[31] though given the community's generally poor economic state, he may have imposed a heavier burden on the rich (what in modern terms is called a progressive tax).

On the other hand, an inscription in Stobi, Macedonia, that has been dated to 165, states that "anyone who wished to make any alteration in the structure of the synagogue had to pay the sum of 25,000 dinars to the patriarch,"[32] who at this time may still have been Rabban Simeon b. Gamaliel. This was a rather princely sum – equivalent to well over $250,000 in 2021. Evidently the Roman authorities, even during the reign of Marcus Aurelius who showed little sympathy toward the Jews, tolerated such outward transfers of funds for what may have been perceived as religious purposes. In any event, the inscription provides a clear indication that the patriarchate was funded with donations from sources outside Judaea that supplemented whatever taxes the patriarch could impose within the province itself.

31. Schafer, *History of the Jews in Antiquity*, 169.
32. Urbach, "The Rabbinical Laws of Idolatry," 151.

The Limits to Rebbe's Influence

Rebbe's wealth and influence was insufficient when it came to easing the tax burden that the Romans imposed on their Jewish subjects. In particular, he was unable to prevent them from imposing new taxes on the Jewish elites. Nevertheless, as patriarch he was uniquely placed to issue rulings regarding who in the community should be responsible for meeting its tax burden.

The Talmud relates that Rebbe ruled that the government had a claim upon a deceased person's assets for tax purposes prior to their distribution among his heirs. His ruling addressed three different categories of Roman taxes: the levy to support military operations (*arnona militaris*), the poll tax (*tributum capitis*), and the real estate tax (*tributum soli*). The *arnona* was probably the most important of the three. It was originally a monetary tax; but when inflation hit the Empire and the currency was devalued, it was levied on grain, land, and livestock.[33] It amounted to one-fourth of the annual crop yield or its equivalent; the grain was collected in Sidon, where the Romans kept their warehouses to store it.

It was not self-evident that in Jewish law the *arnona* or the other Roman taxes should assume priority over traditional laws of inheritance, but the penalty for avoiding the tax was harsh. It was for this practical reason that Rebbe issued his ruling. In so doing, he drew upon what he considered to be an analogous ruling by the *Tanna* Ben Nannas upholding the claims of a divorcee or a widow to her husband's assets before those of any other claimants.[34] The parallel was not obvious; the obligation to meet the needs of a divorcee or widow was rooted in Jewish law to a far greater degree than the need to pay Roman taxes.[35]

Rebbe's writ extended to other aspects of Rome's system of taxation. The Talmud relates that "the Government once imposed crown money upon Bule and Stratege." The "crown tax" *(aurum coronarium)* originally had been a gift that a grateful public in any given vicinity within the Empire had bestowed on a victorious general. Over time, however, it became a mandatory tax imposed on leading citizens of

33. *Avot DeRabbi Natan* 22:71; Smallwood, *Jews under Roman Rule*, 495.
34. Mishna Ketubot 10:5.
35. See also Oppenheimer, *Rabbi Yehuda HaNasi*, 61.

Roman municipalities. It is not entirely clear how and when the tax actually was imposed. The term *aurum coronarium* may have referred to a tax on the wealthy, a tax to cover the patriarch's own expenses, or a tax for the new emperor,[36] presumably either Septimius Severus or Caracalla (the latter being in constant need of money to feed his outsized spending habits). Similarly, "Bule" and "Stratege" may refer to people from specific places; wealthy elites; officials; or townsmen. From indications in the Talmud,[37] it appears that the difference between the two groups was that the Bule were members of the municipal council, while Stratege were simply the wealthy elites.

Evidently there was some uncertainty as to what per cent of the tax liability fell upon each group. The primary obligation to pay fell upon the city councilors, but wealthy citizens were prepared to contribute funds to ease their financial burden. The Talmud indicates that the Roman officials overseeing tax collection had no objection to such an arrangement.

Both the municipal officials (presumably the Jewish ones) and the wealthy Jews of the municipality in question turned to Rebbe, not to the Romans, for a ruling as to what proportion of the tax burden fell on each group. Rebbe ruled that each group was liable to pay half the tax.[38] It also is noteworthy that the Talmud gives no indication that either side protested the ruling. Nor is there any indication that the Romans overruled Rebbe. Subsequent generations of rabbis considered the ruling to be so significant that it was cited in an entirely different context, namely, the bequest of a man to his wife and her sons, wherein the man did not specify the share the wife and the sons would respectively receive. It was asserted, on the basis of Rebbe's ruling, that the wife and sons should share equally in the bequest. The Talmud ultimately decided that indeed, bequests to two parties should be shared equally if no other proportional division had been specified.[39]

---

36. Smallwood, *Jews under Roman Rule*, 406n46.
37. Bava Batra 143a.
38. Ibid.
39. Ibid. 143b.

REBBE AND HIS COLLEAGUES

Rebbe's toughest challenge probably came from his rabbinic colleagues. They might have been prepared to accept him as their official communal leader and spokesman to the Romans – someone had to engage the country's overlords on an official level – but recognizing his religious authority was an entirely different matter. As far as they were concerned, he had to prove himself. Their watchword was R. Yose's dictum regarding Torah, *she'eina yerusha lakh,* it is not your automatic inheritance.[40]

Rebbe was surely aware of the intrigue and downright rebellion of which his colleagues were capable. It was not only the attempt to unseat his father that must have affected his behavior toward the other leading rabbis. It was also the memory of the actual unseating of a patriarch, namely Rebbe's grandfather, Rabban Gamaliel II. The Talmud relates in detail how this came about.

> Rabban Gamaliel had humiliated R. Joshua several times when, after a disagreement over the nature of the evening (*Arvit*) prayer, Rabban Gamaliel remained sitting and expounding and R. Joshua remained standing, until all the people there began to shout and told Huzpith the translator to stop; and he stopped. They then said: How long is he [R. Gamaliel] to go on insulting him [R. Joshua]? ... now he insults him again! Come, let us depose him! Whom shall we appoint instead? We can hardly appoint R. Joshua, because he is one of the parties involved. We can hardly appoint R. Akiba because perhaps R. Gamaliel will bring a curse on him because he has no ancestral merit. Let us then appoint R. Eleazar b. Azariah, who is wise and rich and the tenth in descent from Ezra. He is wise, so that if anyone puts a question to him he will be able to answer it. He is rich, so that if occasion arises for him to pay court to Caesar he will be able to do so. He is tenth in descent from Ezra, so that he has ancestral merit and he [Rabban Gamaliel] cannot bring a curse on him. They went and said to him [R. Eleazar]: Will your honor consent to become head of the Academy? He replied: I will go and consult the members of my family. And, having consulted

40. Avot 2:17.

> with his wife, R. Eleazar accepted the offer of his colleagues and replaced Rabban Gamaliel as patriarch.[41]

Rebbe knew that his was only one vote on the Sanhedrin and thus formally counted for no more than those of his other colleagues.[42] He therefore recognized that in order to win the support of those colleagues, so as to avoid the fate that befell his grandfather and almost brought down his father, he needed to walk a fine line between demanding respect for his position and working collegially with other rabbinic leaders who commanded wide support within the community. The latter included luminaries such as R. Yishmael b. R. Yose, who was the acknowledged rabbinic leader of Sepphoris; R. Eleazar b. Simeon, whose youthful rivalry with Rebbe was outlined above; R. Pinhas b. Yair, whose adherence to the law was so rigorous that even his donkey refused to eat untithed grain; R. Yose b. Judah, son of Rebbe's teacher R. Judah b. Ila'i; and R. Simeon b. Halafta, a master – and often subject – of rabbinic legend.

Rebbe's approach was therefore never to presume upon rank when the debate was of a halakhic nature. Personally, Rebbe was a modest man – the Talmud explicitly describes him as "exceedingly humble"[43] – and he exhibited this trait when dealing with his

---

41. Berakhot 28a.
42. "Even a patriarch as authoritative as R. Judah Ha-Nasi resorted to the vote when he felt it necessary." Ephraim E. Urbach, *The Halakhah: Its Sources and Development*, trans. Raphael Posner (Tel Aviv: Modan, 1996), 132. The Mishna (Gittin 5:6) addresses the case of *sikorikon*, defined as either property forfeited to, or confiscated by, the Roman government; the holder of confiscated property; or the law dealing with the purchase of such property. At issue was whether in all circumstances, the original owner of the land was automatically to have first rights to repurchase the property from its usurping holder. Rebbe set up a special court, which voted that if the usurping holder possessed the property for twelve months, then anyone could purchase the property; but the buyer should give one-fourth to the original owner from whom the property had been seized. Not all of Rebbe's colleagues approved of his taking votes. For example, R. Yishmael b. R. Yose did not want to participate in an ad hoc vote that Rebbe wished to organize in order to free produce from Ashkelon from tithing requirements. See Tosefta Oholot 18:10 and Urbach, *The Halakhah*, 133.
43. Y. Kilayim 9:3.

colleagues. For example, although by rights he could have been the first among his colleagues to render a civil judgment, he always let the most junior judge pronounce first,[44] and then the others in increasing seniority, so as not to intimidate or influence his colleagues' views of the case.[45] By proceeding in this manner, he recognized the right of even the most junior judge to contradict him, yet when pronouncing judgment he did not exploit his seniority but rather sought to ensure that justice was done.[46]

Rebbe was at times prepared to recognize the authority of his colleagues within their own localities. The Talmud states that "in the place of R. Yose the Galilean they used to eat fowl's flesh cooked in milk." It then goes on to relate that Rebbe's student Levi once visited the house of Joseph, who kept fowl, and was served with a peacock's head cooked in milk. Levi did not eat the dish, but also said nothing about it. When he returned to Rebbe and told him what had happened, Rebbe asked him why he did not place the household under a ban (*shamta*). Levi replied, "It was the place of R. Judah b. Beteira, and I imagine that he must have expounded to them the view of R. Yose the Galilean, who ruled that 'a fowl is excluded since it has no mother's milk.'"[47] Rebbe did not challenge Levi's decision. He recognized that to do so would have undermined both R. Yose's authority and that of R. Judah b. Beteira. This could well have undermined the prestige and authority of all rabbis, including his own.

Rebbe was also not above acknowledging that his position could not always prevail. For example, Rebbe ruled that a certain kind of melon and an Egyptian bean plant could not lean over other plants, because their stalks would get entangled and thereby mix with the other plants even if the latter were planted at a distance that was permissible under the laws of *kilayim* (mixing or grafting different species of plants or

44. Testimony of Rav, Gittin, 59a; Sanhedrin 36a.
45. Sanhedrin 36a.
46. For a discussion see *Ḥazon Ish*, cited at length in Zakheim, *Zvi HaSanhedrin*, vol. 3, 112–13.
47. Ḥullin 116a.

cross-breeding different animal species). Yet he nevertheless accepted the rabbis' more lenient ruling.[48]

Another example of Rebbe's willingness to recede in favor of a contrary position was his reversal of a ruling he gave with respect to storing cold water or food in a cold place on Shabbat. R. Huna was cited as ruling on Rebbe's authority that cold food may not be hidden in a cold place. The Talmud asks: "It was taught: Rebbe permitted cold to be hidden?" And it answers: "There is no difficulty; the initial ruling was issued before he heard otherwise from R. Yishmael son of R. Yose; the other after he heard from R. Yishmael. For when Rebbe declared: Cold may not be hidden, R. Yishmael son of R. Yose replied to him, 'My father permitted cold to be stored in a cold place.' Rebbe thereupon answered, 'In that case the Elder [R. Yose] has already ruled.'"

A similar case involved R. Yishmael son of R. Yose. It seems that Rebbe arrived in the yeshiva during a discussion that his students, among them his son R. Simeon, as well as R. Hiyya and R. Yishmael son of R. Yose, were having among themselves. Seeing the master's entry, they all scrambled to their places – all, that is, except R. Yishmael, who was seriously overweight and could not move quickly. Since the other students were already seated on the ground, R. Yishmael was forced to step over them to get to his place. Another student, Abdan (the nickname of Abba Yudan), called out, "Who is this man, who steps over the heads of the holy people!" R. Yishmael replied: "I am Yishmael son of R. Yose and I have come to learn Torah from Rebbe." The reply did not silence Abdan, however, who cracked: "Are you really qualified to learn Torah from Rebbe?" R. Yishmael, whose tongue could be as sharp as anyone's, gave as good as he received: "Was Moses qualified to learn Torah from the lips of the Almighty?" "So, are you Moses?" Abdan shot back. "And is your teacher a God?" came the reply. "Indeed!" Abdan exclaimed. "Is then your Master a god!" R. Yishmael retorted.

48. Mishna Kilayim 2:8. The Gemara explains that neither of these plants, nor for that matter, the Egyptian gourd, which he also prohibited, spread their stalks as widely as the Greek gourd, which the rabbis did indeed prohibit even at a distance from other plants. Y. Kilayim 2:7.

R. Yishmael's father, R. Yose, clearly was upset at the way Rebbe remained silent while Abdan harassed his son. When R. Yishmael referred to Rebbe as Abdan's master and not his, R. Yose remarked: "Rebbe got what he deserved."[49]

The Talmud then notes that while the heated exchange between Abdan and R. Yishmael was taking place, a young girl whose husband had died came before Rebbe to have him determine whether she was subject to levirate marriage with her brother-in-law and therefore required the *ḥalitza* ceremony. Rebbe told Abdan to check if she was still a minor, in which case she was not bound to the dead husband's brother. After Abdan went out, however, R. Yishmael pointed out that his father had ruled that a woman, regardless of age, qualified for *ḥalizta.* Upon hearing this Rebbe called Abdan back and told him that no examination was needed. Once again, upon hearing R. Yose's decision, Rebbe accepted it without hesitation, stating, "the Elder [R. Yose] has already ruled."[50]

Rebbe's willingness to yield to his colleague was so obviously uncommon that R. Papa commented two generations later: "Come and see how much they [Rebbe and R. Yose] loved each other! For were R. Yose alive, he would have sat submissively before Rebbe since R. Yishmael son of R. Yose, who occupied his father's place, sat submissively before Rebbe yet Rebbe said, 'The Elder has already ruled.'"

R. Halafta, R. Yishmael's grandfather, had been one of the sages of the preceding generation. He had been a contemporary of R. Akiba; his home was in Sepphoris. R. Yose was born there and presumably flourished there as a leading figure in the town's Jewish community until he was forced to flee the Romans. Upon his return he moved to Usha and was one of the five leading students of R. Akiba who convened and legislated in that city during R. Simeon b. Gamaliel's absence. R. Yose

49. Yevamot 105b.

50. The story has a tragic ending. When Abdan returned, R. Yishmael chided him for stepping over the students' heads. Rebbe then told Abdan not to move forward. Abdan immediately developed a case of leprosy, his two sons drowned, and his two minor daughters refused to remain married to their husbands. As if that were not enough, R. Nahman b. Isaac felt compelled to add, "Blessed be the All-Merciful who has put Abdan to shame in this world." Ibid.

was still active at the time that Rebbe became patriarch, and at times they issued conflicting halakhic rulings.

Rebbe did not hesitate to disagree with R. Yose, no doubt in part because as a freshly minted patriarch he had to establish his authority with the older generation of rabbis – a challenge that every young leader faces when taking office and confronting entrenched forces who perceive their interests to be under threat from the newcomer. Rebbe's clashes with R. Yose naturally did not endear him to his son, especially when he succeeded him as leader of the Jewish community of Sepphoris, which had grown markedly as refugees poured in from Judaea after the failed Bar Kokhba rebellion. With the backing of an increasingly large and still loyal community, R. Yishmael represented a major challenge to Rebbe's authority. He once caustically replied to a question put to him by R. Hama regarding a point of law in a matter of menstruation over which his father and Rebbe had disagreed: "Is this [i.e., Rebbe] the purportedly great man? Surely to whom must one listen, the rabbi [that is, R. Yishmael's father, R. Yose] or the student?"

By finally acknowledging the importance of R. Yose b. Halafta, who in reality did not match Rebbe's own stature as a talmudic legislator, Rebbe was able to temper the opposition of R. Yose's son, R. Yishmael, who nominally "sat submissively" before him. Rebbe's successful effort to flatter R. Yishmael, for flattery was what it surely was, was no different from attempts by modern politicians to enlist potential rivals or naysayers to their cause by means of subtle, and sometimes none-too-subtle, blandishments.[51] In Rebbe's case, his advances were both carefully targeted and highly effective; winning R. Yishmael over was no small political triumph.

In yet another instance, R. Nathan the Babylonian asked Rebbe why the Mishna, which Rebbe had edited, sided with R. Yohanan b. Beroka against the majority of rabbis in ruling that a father could designate his inheritance to anyone he wanted. Rebbe flippantly replied that the Mishna was referring to a gift, which of course, was always a father's prerogative. Rebbe later admitted that he regretted his remark, which he termed "rude," and he acknowledged both that the Mishna referred

51. Lyndon Johnson and Ronald Reagan were both masters of this political art form.

to a case of inheritance and that R. Nathan had posed a valid, indeed powerful, challenge, which Rebbe was hard put to answer.

Rebbe sided with the rabbis in their dispute with R. Meir as to whether the apostate Elisha b. Avuya was to have a place in the world to come. The Talmud relates that R. Meir was devoted to his teacher Elisha, even when the latter became an apostate. When Elisha rode a horse in violation of Shabbat, R. Meir followed him to glean his Torah thoughts. When Elisha informed him that he was about to commit a second violation as he approached the two-thousand-cubit Shabbat boundary (*teḥum Shabbat*) R. Meir sought to persuade him to turn back and thereby avoid further sin. R. Meir prevailed upon him to turn back and visit several schoolhouses, where, to R. Meir's chagrin, a child in each one recited a verse that implied that Elisha's fate was sealed. The Talmud goes on to note that when Elisha died, the rabbis did not want him to be judged; because he had been a Torah scholar, they were concerned that he would be forgiven and would be permitted to enter the world to come. So great was R. Meir's devotion to his teacher that he differed with his colleagues, arguing that Elisha should be judged and then allowed to enter the world to come.[52]

Rebbe no doubt was aware of R. Meir's attitude; how could he not have been? Yet he appears to have had little sympathy for R. Meir's late teacher when Elisha's daughter approached him for financial assistance. Upon her approaching him, Rebbe seemed shocked that any of Elisha's progeny had survived.

> "Whose daughter are you?" he asked her. She replied, "I am the daughter of Aher." [In anger] he asked her, "Are any of his children left in the world? But it is written, "He shall have neither son nor grandson among his people, nor any remaining in his dwellings." She answered, "Remember his Torah teachings and don't remember his deeds." Immediately a fire came down and enveloped Rebbe's bench. Rebbe then wept and said, "If this be

52. Ḥagiga 15b.

> what happens regarding those who dishonor her [the Torah] how much more so in the case of those who honor her."[53]

Given the friction between Rebbe's father and R. Meir, and Rebbe's own experience as the man's student, one might put Rebbe's response down to his resentment of R. Meir, and, by extension, R. Meir's beloved teacher. Yet Rebbe was more concerned about the dignity of the Torah and the rabbis who expounded it. In this case, as in his relations with the rabbis, including R. Yishmael, he was underscoring the primacy of the rabbis over all else, since the rabbis considered themselves to be the only rightful interpreters of the laws. By extension, anyone who rejected their interpretation, like Elisha ben Avuya, *ipso facto* also rejected the yoke of Torah. Rebbe's dictum clearly acknowledged the authority of the rabbinate as a collective whole; it placed him within that collective and not as a rival outsider seeking to establish a separate power base from which to challenge their authority in matters of religious law. At the same time, however, he did not send Elisha's daughter away. As zealous as he was about the importance of the rabbis, he was equally compassionate toward those whose misfortune was not of their own making.

By the time Rebbe had settled matters with R. Yishmael, he had developed into a religious scholar of the first rank. His Jewish education had been of the highest caliber; his teachers were the pre-eminent scholars of their own generation. His halakhic rulings, a sampling of which will be outlined below, have stood the test of time; his great work, the Mishna, assumed canonical status. As a leading historian of the era observed, "Judah ben Simeon ben Gamaliel was the patriarch who in his public personality combined most completely the two elements which characterized the office in its classical period – spiritual greatness and scholarly stature, on the one hand; strong political leadership on the other."[54] The

53. Ibid. A variant of this story appears in Y. Ḥagiga 2:1: "Sometime after [his death, Elisha's] daughters approached Rebbe for alms. Rebbe refused, citing 'May he have none who extends kindness, and may no one be gracious to his orphans' (Ps. 109:12). They said to him, 'Do not recall his actions, recall his Torah knowledge.' At that moment Rebbe wept and ordered that they should be supported [financially]. He said, 'If this person, who toiled in Torah but not for the sake of Heaven, yet see whom he produced, how much more so one who toiled in Torah for the sake of Heaven.'"

54. Alon, *Jews in Their Land,* 710.

Talmud goes even further, stating that no one could compare to him in either respect, as it states: "From Moses until Rebbe we do not find sacred learning and [worldly] greatness combined in the one [person]."[55]

REBBE'S RIVAL: R. PINHAS B. YAIR

Even when he was at the apogee of his powers, issuing rulings for the community and for the Diaspora in Rome's territories, enforcing his judgments through his retainers, granting rabbinical ordination, and relating to Rome's leaders, Rebbe still faced internal opposition. This was not a matter of legal disputes per se. Nor was it an issue of a student showing insufficient deference to the patriarch. There was no fundamental disagreement over Rebbe's role as leader of the Jewish community in Palestine, or for that matter, in much of the Diaspora, excluding Babylonia. Rather some rabbis, epitomized by R. Pinhas b. Yair, opposed the very notion of a patriarch who behaved like a prince, especially by maintaining a lavish lifestyle. Despite his personal modesty, Rebbe did have an aura of royalty about him that he did not discourage. Not all his rabbinical colleagues approved.

R. Pinhas was in many ways the polar opposite of Rebbe. He was not a legislator, either religious or secular. He was not a diplomat dealing with the Romans regarding communal matters. He did not grant rabbinical ordination. He does not appear to have led a yeshiva. He was instead a true spiritual leader, concerned as much with the next world as with this one. R. Pinhas was noted for his *ḥasidut,* his piety.[56] He asserted:

> Study leads to precision, precision leads to zeal, zeal leads to cleanliness, cleanliness leads to restraint, restraint leads to purity, purity leads to holiness, holiness leads to meekness, meekness

55. Sanhedrin 36a and see Rashi, s.v. *bemakom.* The author of the talmudic statement is variously given as R. Hillel the son of R. Wallas or Rabba the son of Rava. The Talmud goes on to state that subsequent to Rebbe no one individual embodied both characteristics until R. Ashi. The nineteenth-century talmudist Enoch Zundel b. Joseph explained that what Moses, Rebbe, and R. Ashi all had in common is that through unparalleled leadership and scholarship, each laid a cornerstone of Judaism: Moses produced the Torah, Rebbe, the Mishna, and R. Ashi, the Talmud. Enoch Zundel b. Joseph, *Eitz Yosef,* s.v. *bemakom.*
56. For a brief discussion see Lau, *Ḥakhamim,* vol. 3, 321–24.

> leads to fear of sin, fear of sin leads to saintliness, saintliness leads to [the possession of] the holy spirit, the holy spirit leads to eternal life, but saintliness is greater than any of these, for Scripture says, "Then You spoke in vision to Your saintly ones."[57]

R. Pinhas is perhaps best known for his "religious" mule, which tells as much about his saintliness as about the animal. The Talmud relates as follows:

> Thieves stole R. Pinhas b. Yair's mule. She was with them for three days and did not taste a thing. They said, "She will die soon and we will have to leave our cave [because it will be ritually impure from the dead animal]." So they sent her away and she returned to her master. When she arrived she began to bray. Said he [to his servants], "Open the door to this unfortunate one and give her something to eat since she has not tasted a thing for three days." They gave her barley and she did not taste it. They said, "Rabbi, we gave her barley and she didn't touch it." He asked, "Have you taken the tithe [from the barley]?" They replied in the affirmative. "Did you also take out *demai* [tithe taken as a precaution]?" They replied, "Didn't you teach us that one who takes grain for an animal...is exempt from taking *demai*?" He said, "What can we do? She is personally very strict [in this regard]."[58]

R. Pinhas' piety was so extraordinary that it even affected his mule; he attained a level that Rebbe simply could not match.

Indeed, the Talmud relates a tale of their meeting, which also involves mules, but with a different twist. The story begins with R. Pinhas working a miracle. It seems that R. Pinhas had to cross the river Ginnai in order to redeem Jewish captives. Having no other way to cross, he asked the river to part its waters so he could pass through. There was a man with him who was carrying wheat for Passover and also needed to cross. At R. Pinhas' request, the river parted for him too. And then there

57. Avoda Zara 20b; the verse is Ps. 89:20.

58. Genesis Rabba 60:10.

was a third man, an Arab, who also needed to cross. R. Pinhas told the river to part for him as well, so he would not say "Is this the way to treat a fellow traveler?" That R. Pinhas parted the river once was extraordinary, that he did so three times, including for a non-Jew, demonstrated what a remarkable man he was; R. Yosef noted that in parting the river he rivaled Moses himself.[59]

The story of R. Pinhas' journey does not end there. When he arrived at an inn, his mule again refused to eat the barley that was placed before it. Again it was an issue of untithed produce; the mule was as scrupulous as ever.

When Rebbe heard that R. Pinhas was passing through his neighborhood, he came out to greet him and invite him to dinner. R. Pinhas accepted the invitation, but only after he had returned from redeeming the captives. Having done so, he happened to enter Rebbe's property by a gate near which some white mules were grazing. R. Pinhas believed that the presence of white mules meant that the angel of death was nearby,[60] so he refused to enter Rebbe's house. Rebbe offered to sell the mules; R. Pinhas replied that he would be setting a stumbling block before the blind, in violation of the biblical commandment against doing so.[61] Rebbe offered to abandon them. "You would be spreading danger," was the reply. Rebbe offered to hamstring the animals. R. Pinhas demurred: "You would be causing the animals to suffer." Rebbe then offered to kill them, but once again R. Pinhas disagreed: "You would be violating the law against unnecessary destruction (*bal tashḥit*)." Rebbe, increasingly frustrated, would not give up. Finally a mountain rose between them, and R. Pinhas went on his way. Rebbe wept and said, "If this is [what the righteous can do] in their lifetime, how much more can they do they do after they die" (when the Talmud has asserted they are even more powerful).[62]

59. R. Pinhas' concern for the non-Jewish traveler offers an object lesson for contemporary Jews in their own dealings with Arabs.
60. R. Hanina explained that no one ever recovered from a wound inflicted by a white-legged mule. Ḥullin 7b.
61. Lev. 19:14.
62. Ḥullin 7a.

The "mountain" reflected the fundamental difference between the two men. Rebbe could not subscribe to R. Pinhas' fears, though because of his great respect for the man, he tried his best to accommodate them. R. Pinhas, the austere pietist, disapproved of Rebbe's lifestyle, which was marked by "conspicuous affluence" as represented by the white mules.[63] R. Pinhas chose not to confront Rebbe directly; rather he manifested his disapproval in passive-aggressive fashion by placing Rebbe in a "catch-22" situation. The stand-off was never really resolved: the two men went their separate ways on either side of the "mountain."[64]

REBBE AND THE UNLEARNED

Over the course of his patriarchate Rebbe directed his wealth toward assisting the impoverished. Initially he restricted his alms-giving to poor rabbis and rabbinical students, having disdain for the unlearned, whom he and his colleagues termed *amei haaretz* (literally, people of the land). Talmudic literature variously described these people either as those who did not observe ritual purity, or as those who were not strict about tithing their grain.[65]

The *amei haaretz* constituted a majority of the population. According to some scholars they were the overwhelming majority.[66]

The Babylonian Talmud quotes Rebbe as asserting that "it is the unlearned who bring misfortune to the world."[67] It also has him pronouncing that "an *am haaretz* may not eat the flesh of cattle, for it is said, 'This is the law [Torah] of the beast, and of the fowl';[68] whoever engages in [the study of] the Torah may eat the flesh of beast and fowl, but he

---

63. Alon, *Jews in Their Land*, 723, notes that ownership of white mules was a sign of wealth.
64. The Jerusalem Talmud relates a similar story, but has the two men disagreeing over Rebbe's leniencies regarding *Shemitta*. See below.
65. Tosefta Avoda Zara 3:3. R. Meir defines the *am haaretz* as one who does not observe ritual purity; in the Sages' view he is one who is not strict about tithing.
66. Seth Schwartz, *Imperialism and Jewish Society, 200 BCE to 640 CE* (Princeton: Princeton University Press, 2001), 175–76.
67. Bava Batra 8a.
68. Lev. 11:46

who does not engage in [the study of] the Torah may not eat the flesh of beast and fowl."[69]

Rebbe's rabbinical colleagues were equally if not more hostile to the *amei haaretz*. As the Talmud relates:

> It was taught, R. Eleazar said: "It is permitted to stab an *am haaretz* [even] on the Day of Atonement which falls on the Sabbath." His students queried to him, "Master, do you mean to [ritually] slaughter him?" He replied: "This [ritual slaughter] requires a benediction, whereas that [stabbing] does not require a benediction." R. Eleazar said: "One must not join company with an *am haaretz* on the road, because it is said, for that [the Torah] is thy life, and the length of thy days: [seeing that] he has no care [pity] for his own life [being ignorant of Torah] how much the more for the life of his companions!" R. Samuel b. Nahmani said in R. Yohanan's name: "One may tear an *am haaretz* like a fish! R. Samuel b. Isaac explained: "And [this means] along his back..."[70]

The rabbis were particularly careful not to betroth their children to the children of *amei haaretz*. The Talmud quotes R. Meir: "Whoever marries his daughter to an *am haaretz*, it is as though he bound and laid her before a lion: just as a lion tears [his prey] and devours it and has no shame, so an *am haaretz* strikes and cohabits and has no shame."[71]

All of the foregoing quotations are from the Babylonian Talmud. The Diaspora rabbis took a much harsher view of the *amei haaretz* than did their Palestinian counterparts.[72] In many respects, the attitude of the Babylonian rabbis toward those they perceived to be unlearned and irreligious foreshadowed and no doubt influenced future attitudes on the part of those who strictly adhered to the tenets of rabbinic Judaism

---

69. Pesaḥim 49b.
70. Ibid.
71. Ibid. For a full discussion of the rabbinical attitude to the unlearned, see Urbach, *The Sages*, 630–44.
72. For a discussion of the differing attitudes of Palestinian and Babylonian rabbis toward the unlearned, as expressed in the Jerusalem and Babylonian Talmuds respectively, see Rubenstein, *Culture*, 129–35.

toward movements they considered to be misguided at best and more often simply heretical.[73] For example, such was the attitude of the so-called "rabbanites" toward the Karaites from the ninth century onwards; indeed, many medieval halakhists, among them Maimonides, grappled with the question of whether an adherent of traditional Judaism could marry a Karaite.[74] Kabbalists were particularly hostile to *amei haaretz;* the Zohar, which they attributed to R. Simeon bar Yohai, compared them to slaves and beasts.[75]

---

73. Interestingly, this does not appear to have been the case with respect to at least some of the *Geonim*, notably, R. Sherira Gaon. Ibid., 157.
74. R. Moses Isserles, known as Rema, the ultimate decisor for Ashkenazi Jewry, ruled that one could not marry even a Karaite who had returned to Judaism, because such a person might be the offspring of a banned relationship (*safek mamzer*); see Rema, gloss on *Shulḥan Arukh, Even Ha'ezer* 4:37. This is also the position of a number of contemporary *ḥaredi* decisors. See, for example, R. Ovadya Yosef, *She'elot UTeshuvot Yabia Omer,* vol. 2, 2nd ed.: *Ḥelek Even Ha'ezer* (Jerusalem: n.p, 5746/1986), no. 21. R. Eliezer Yehuda Waldenberg (*She'elot UTeshuvot Tzitz Eliezer,* vol. 4, 2nd ed. [Jerusalem: n.p., 1985], no. 9:6) took a more lenient position, stating that if a Karaite renounced his/her traditions and accepted those of Orthodox Jewry he/she could marry into the community.
75. Similarly, traditional rabbis battled with the Reform movement ever since its emergence in the eighteenth century; not surprisingly, some of Reform's most vociferous opponents, such as R. Moshe Shreiber/Sofer, were heavily influenced by Kabbala. See R. Moshe Schreiber, *Ḥatam Sofer: Oraḥ Ḥayyim* (Bnei Brak: Kodesh Mishor, 1990), no. 36, s.v. *vehaamnam*. For Shreiber's position on Reform, see also R. Eliezer Waldenberg, *She'elot UTeshuvot Tzitz Eliezer,* vol. 5, 2nd. ed. (Jerusalem: n.p., 1985), *Introduction: HaRiformim VeHeikhaleihem BaHalakha,* 1. As with the question of marriage to a Karaite, one of the key issues that the rabbis of the late eighteenth, nineteenth, and early-to-mid-twentieth centuries confronted was whether an Orthodox Jew (as the traditionalists came to be known) could marry a Reform Jew. This issue became especially salient beginning in the late twentieth century, when the American Reform movement declared that Jewish descent in cases of mixed marriage was patrilineal and not matrilineal, thereby reversing centuries of traditional practice that the Talmud had established as normative Jewish law. Although traditional rabbis recognized that Reform leaders were not ignorant of halakha – on the contrary, they were viewed as heretics precisely because they were considered to be aware of traditional practice – in practical terms their concerns about Reform mirrored, and continue to reflect, those regarding Karaites. See, for example, R. Moshe Feinstein, *Igrot Moshe: Oraḥ Ḥayyim* (Hebrew), vol. 2:50 (Brooklyn, NY: Moriah, 1963), 237–38; *Igrot Moshe: Oraḥ Ḥayyim,* vol. 3:21 (Brooklyn, NY: Moriah, 1973), 318; and *Igrot Moshe: Yoreh De'ah,* vol. 2:100, 174–75; Waldenberg, loc. cit.

The *amei haaretz* reciprocated the rabbis' animosity, just as the Reform movement in its early years was hostile to the traditionalists. The Babylonian Talmud relates that R. Akiba, who had only become a learned rabbi later in life, recalled his own hatred of the rabbis: "When I was an *am haaretz* I said: If I had a scholar [before me], I would maul him like an ass." His disciples said to him, "Rabbi, [why not] say 'like a dog!'" He replied, "The former bites and breaks bones, while the latter bites but does not break the bones."[76] Similarly, R. Eliezer said: "But that we are necessary to them for trade, they would kill us."[77]

Still, not all *amei haaretz* hated the rabbis. Many among them may have been ignorant; and both coinage and archeological evidence point to the likelihood that most Jews in Palestine were lax in their religious practice. That is not to imply that they abandoned tradition entirely, however.[78] It may well be that the Greek gods were ubiquitous as symbols employed by the Jewish community, but that does not necessarily indicate the "post-revolt collapse of any normatively Jewish ideological system."[79] For all their abandonment of most practices, many Jews still respected their religious leaders.

Municipal elders, who tended to be more cosmopolitan and thus were more likely to be hellenized, nevertheless appear to have retained a degree of veneration for their religious tradition. For example, the Jerusalem Talmud relates that the people of Simonias requested of Rebbe that he assign to them an individual who would serve as "preacher, judge, capable of leading the community in prayer, school teacher, and fulfilling all our needs."[80] Rebbe assigned one of his students, Levi b. Sisi, to minister to the town. When Levi was unable to answer some technical questions that they posed to him,

> ...the people returned to Rebbe complaining, "Is this the allotment you made for us?" He answered them, "By your lives, I gave

76. Ibid.
77. Ibid.
78. See especially Schwartz, *Imperialism*, 129–61.
79. Ibid., 159.
80. Y. Yevamot 12:6. My translation follows that of R. David Herschel Frankel's commentary known as *Korban Ha'eda.*

> you a man equal to me." He sent for Levi and asked him each of the questions that the people had posed and Levi gave the correct answer. So Rebbe said to him, "Why did you not answer them?" He answered, "They [the townspeople] made a great platform for me and sat me on it, and that made me conceited." Rebbe then applied to him the verse, "If you have been scandalously arrogant, if you have been a schemer, then clap your hand to your mouth,"[81] and [Rebbe then] said, "Who caused you to be arrogant in matters of Torah? [It was] because you elevated yourself though them."[82]

The fact that the townspeople applied to Rebbe for a teacher and then plied the candidate with questions does not necessarily indicate that they all were punctilious in their practice of Judaism; the majority no doubt were indeed *amei haaretz*. What this incident does demonstrate is that ordinary unlearned people nevertheless respected the tradition, as many do to this day, and that when they did engage in religious practice they wanted to be sure that they were doing so properly. No doubt there were some among them who were better versed in the details of Jewish law; they were probably the ones who "examined" the new leader that Rebbe had assigned to them. They were probably a small minority among the populace.

The incident also demonstrates that whatever he thought of *amei haaretz*, Rebbe would not spurn them if they sought religious guidance. On the contrary, his objective was to bring more of the community to accept rabbinical authority, and of course his own authority as both national and religious leader. A Palestinian-based midrash quotes him as stating, "When they [Israel] all stood before Mount Sinai to receive the Torah, all of them were united as one heart to receive the kingship of God with joy. Moreover, they stood surety for each other."[83] Clearly,

81. Prov. 30:32.
82. Genesis Rabba has a slightly different variant, with an agitated Levi coming to Rebbe to recount what had happened; Rebbe's reply is the same as in the talmudic text. See Genesis Rabba 81:2.
83. *Mekhilta DeRabbi Yishmael im Hagahot HaGra zllh"h* (Jerusalem: Sifriati, 5740/1980), *Yitro (Baḥodesh)*, 5, s.v. *anokhi*.

his ideal was to lead a community that was united in observance of the commandments. He could only do so by being responsive to their religious needs and by demonstrating his sensitivity to their concerns.

Uniting the community was one thing; having a positive attitude to the *amei haaretz,* was quite another. A late midrash quotes him as citing passages from Scripture to buttress his assertion that mankind, but particularly the Jews, were "complainers and children of complainers." He then goes on to argue that the complaining will not stop in the future either: "In future I will remove the overlordship of Edom [i.e., Rome], yet she [Israel] continues to complain before Me."[84] Rebbe clearly was not referring to the "righteous," among whom he would have included the community of rabbis of which he was part. Instead, by pointing to a legacy of troubles on the part of those who lived centuries before him, he was also casting aspersions on those who complained about rabbinic dominance of their lives.

Nevertheless, despite his initial dislike of the *amei haaretz,* Rebbe was driven by remorse after an incident that involved a needy rabbi who had always refused to accept charity simply because he was a learned man and for that reason preferred to hide the fact that he was a scholar. As the Babylonian Talmud relates:

> Rebbe would open his storehouse in years of scarcity, proclaiming: "Let those enter who have studied the Scripture, or the Mishna, or the Gemara, or the Halakha, or the Aggada; but the *amei haaretz* should not enter." Once R. Jonathan b. Amram pushed his way in and said, "Master, support me." He said to him, "My son, have you learnt the Scripture?" He replied, "No." "Have you learnt the Mishna?" "No." "If so," he said, "on what basis should I support you [with food]?" He said to him, "Support me as you would a dog and a raven." So he supported him. After he went away, Rebbe was agitated and said: "Woe is me that I have given my bread to an *am haaretz*!" R. Simeon son of Rebbe suggested to him: "Perhaps it is Jonathan b. Amram your pupil, who all his life has avoided deriving benefit from the Torah." Inquiries

84. Solomon Buber, ed., *Peskita DeRav Kahana,* 17 (n.d., n.p.), 130b–131a.

> were made and it was found that it was so; whereupon Rebbe said: *"All may now enter"* [my emphasis].[85]

While Rebbe's final words, like the midrash about the united people accepting the Torah and acting as surety for one another, would indicate that he accepted the importance of feeding the unlearned as well as the knowledgeable, the thrust of the story conforms to the negative view that Babylonians had of the *am haaretz*.[86] Interestingly, Rebbe's remorseful reversal did not sway later generations of rabbis to drop their disdain for the unlearned. Drawing upon an earlier interpretation of R. Yom Tov Asevilli (Ritva), R. Yosef Karo cited Rebbe's initial attitude rather than his final act in determining when one must provide sustainment to an *am haaretz*:

> Rebbe was agitated because he gave his bread to an *am haaretz* because those were years of famine and what the *am haaretz* received would not be available to a scholar, but if this were not the case then one is commanded to sustain him. But if he [the *am haaretz*] appears before us dying of starvation, one is commanded to support him even if it is uncertain whether by doing so there subsequently will be less food available for the scholar.[87]

In other words, R. Karo interpreted the talmudic account of Rebbe's treatment of the impoverished Jonathan b. Amram to indicate that Rebbe's behavior reflected no reversal at all. Rather, as R. Karo saw it, once Rebbe had determined that the scholars had been taken care of he opened the storehouse to all. Subsequent commentators did not challenge R. Karo's position, even though the plain reading of the Talmud would indicate that in times of economic hardship Rebbe no longer initially restricted his support solely to scholars, but instead treated all members of the community equally.

---

85. Bava Batra 8a.
86. Rubenstein, *Culture*, 133–34.
87. R. Yosef Karo, *Shulḥan Arukh: Yoreh De'ah, Hilkhot Tzedaka*, 251:11.

Rebbe certainly was sensitive to the needs of less fortunate fellow-scholars even during less troubling times. Setting an example that many wealthy Jews would follow throughout the ages, Rebbe had regular guests at his table, including his student R. Hiyya.[88] In other words, he was their primary source of financial support. In addition, Rebbe would periodically declare that he was disowning some of his property, rendering it free (*hefker*) for less financially fortunate rabbis to claim it.[89]

Being a rabbi was no guarantee to riches, whether then or today. Rebbe was very much the exception. Most rabbis earned their living through various trades, but their earnings often were meager. The tanner R. Joshua, a contemporary of Rebbe's grandfather, Rabban Gamaliel, was a famous case in point. There is no doubting the purity of Rebbe's motives when he assisted his less-fortunate colleagues. Nevertheless, in so doing he also cemented their political support, even if they were still prepared to challenge his halakhic rulings, as indeed they often did.

REBBE AND SAMARITANS, CHRISTIANS, AND GENTILE SCHOLARS

Rebbe may have been ambivalent about the *amei haaretz*, but he was positively hostile to Samaritans, whom he considered to be non-Jews. The Samaritans were a quasi-Jewish sect who viewed themselves as Jewish but were not accepted by the Jews. The rabbis contended that they were descended from a mixed group of idolaters whom the Assyrians, according to the Book of Kings, had settled in Samaria after their conquest of the kingdom of Israel in the eighth century BCE.[90] Scripture recounts that when these peoples persisted in their idolatrous ways, God sent lions to attack them. They protested to the Assyrian king that they were being unfairly punished, since they were unfamiliar with local religious custom, and the king ordered one of the exiled Jewish priests to instruct them in his religion. The people then proceeded to add Jewish beliefs to their original customs, resulting in a syncretistic form of worship that was anathema to

88. Eiruvin 73a.
89. Ruth Rabba 5:15.
90. L. H. Schiffman, "The Samaritans in Tannaitic Halakhah," *The Jewish Quarterly Review* 75 (April 1985), 325.

the Jews. The Samaritans, as they came to be called, returned the compliment, and from the earliest days of the Second Commonwealth, particularly the governorship of Nehemiah, they were hostile to the growth and expansion of the Jewish community.[91]

Rebbe's stance toward the Samaritans was even harsher than those of some of his rabbinical colleagues. In discussing priestly and levitical gifts offered by non-Jews, the Tosefta, a near-contemporaneous adjunct to the Mishna that was jointly edited by R. Hiyya and R. Oshia, quotes Rebbe as asserting that "a Kuthite (Samaritan) is equivalent to a non-Jew."[92] Interestingly, it was R. Simeon, Rebbe's father, who held the opposite view, at least with regard to priestly gifts. He argued that Samaritans were to be treated as Jews, with all the laws that pertained to the proper transmission of those gifts applying to Samaritans as well.[93]

The Kuthites were responsible for prompting Rebbe to annul previous practice and initiate a number of reforms with respect to proclamation of the new moon. Traditionally, when the rabbinical court in Jerusalem had determined that a new month had begun on what would otherwise have been the thirtieth day of the preceding month (which was now reckoned to have consisted of twenty-nine days), torch-bearing messengers would go forth on the night of the thirtieth day to transmit

---

91. For a discussion of Nehemiah's relations with the Samaritans, see Zakheim, *Nehemiah*, especially 64–68, 113–122. Josephus describes the origins of the Samaritans in much the same terms as the Book of Kings (Josephus, *Antiquities*, 9:14:3; 2 Kings 17:-30). However, modern scholars argue that their origins remain uncertain. See Cohen, *From the Maccabees*, 162–63.

92. Tosefta Terumot 4:12, 13. See also the discussion in *Tosafot*, Menaḥot 67a, s.v. *oved kokhavim*. For a discussion of the place of Samaritan women in rabbinic law, see Charlotte Elisheva Fonrobert, "When Women Walk in the Way of Their Fathers: On Gendering the Rabbinic Claim for Authority," *Journal of the History of Sexuality* 10 (July–October 2011), 405–406. Fonrobert appears to believe that the laws of menstruation were imposed by rabbis seeking to diminish women. Actually, the rabbis' concern was for the preservation of their ritual purity even after the destruction of the Second Temple. Given the biblical dicta that women who bled were ritually unclean, the rabbis' specification of which kinds of blood caused impurity had the effect of exempting women who emitted other kinds of blood.

93. Mishna Nidda 4:1; see also Tosefta Terumot 4:12, 13.

the court's decision that a new moon had been sighted and a new month had begun. The Samaritans, no friends of the Jews, began to light signal torches on the night following that of the actual sighting, i.e., the night following the second day of the newly proclaimed month. Their objective was to distort the Jewish calendar and thus skew the days on which festivals were meant to fall.[94]

To remedy the situation and undermine the Samaritans' subterfuge, Rebbe took the radical step of abolishing the transmission of information by means of torches and instead had messengers personally inform the people that the court had declared the beginning of a new month. Rebbe even allowed murderers, whose testimony normally was invalid, to serve as messengers. Indeed, Rebbe went even further: he accepted second-hand testimony regarding the appearance of the new moon, as long as the accuracy of the sighting could be preserved. Further, in order to ensure that news of the sighting was not delayed, he permitted messengers to leave the night of the sighting, prior to the court's formal proclamation the next day.[95]

Rebbe no doubt also had some contact with Christians, both Jewish and gentile, as the new religion was gaining momentum during the second century despite ongoing persecutions by Roman authorities. There are few accounts of his interactions with Christians, however, either in the Talmud or the various midrashic works. There is one story, however, that appears in the tenth-century *Seder Eliyahu Rabba,*[96] when Christianity was all-powerful in the Western world:

> A priest and Rebbe were once eating and drinking together and when they were feeling relaxed the priest said to Rebbe: "We are more merciful than you people are. When the Lord gave you permission to annihilate us, you left only the women, as it is written, 'For Joab and all of Israel remained [stationed] there for six

94. For a discussion, see Schiffman, "Samaritans," 345–46.
95. Y. Rosh HaShana 2:1, 10b. See also Margolies, *Pnei Moshe*, s.v. *uma kilkul* and ff.
96. *Seder Eliyahu Rabba* is the larger part of the Midrash called *Tana DeVei Eliyahu* that according to the Talmud records dialogues between the Prophet Elijah and R. Anan, an *Amora* who lived in the third century CE. Their relationship is recorded in Ketubot 105b.

> months until he had killed every male in Edom.'" Rebbe remained silent and said nary a word to the priest. [Instead] Rebbe rose, went to the market and relayed these words to his student and returned and sat in his place. Said Rebbe to the priest, "If you are agreeable, let one of my students enter and tell us something pleasing." The priest said, "Let him enter." So that student entered, stood at attention and stated, "The master knows where he places his utensils and when he returns home he brings his utensils into the house." The student repeated this statement twice more until the priest finally understood its meaning [namely, that when God will return his *Shekhina* to Zion, He will gather in all the Jews]. Thereupon the priest rose and lifted his hands to heaven and said, "Blessed is the Holy One, blessed is He, that chose you Israel from all the inhabitants of the earth ... and dispersed you in hundreds of locales, and we considered, 'If we kill those [Jews] in the land of Israel, who will kill those in the north and south? And if we kill those in the north and south, who will kill those in Babylon and in the world?' so our words [about extermination] are meaningless. Of course the master knows where he will place his utensils, and when he returns to his home he will bring his utensils with him."[97]

The story reflects the recognition on the part of later rabbis that Rebbe related well not only to the Romans, but even to "priests," that is, adherents of the upstart religion that would become the cause of so much pain to the Jewish people. It is clear that the midrash is referring to Christianity: the quotation from Kings refers to Edom, and Jewish tradition postulates that Rome and Christianity were descendants of Edom. That Rebbe, despite his rather pointed words, nevertheless was not uncomfortable supping, drinking, and relaxing with a gentile priest, must have come as a shock to many; such behavior was uncommon not only for strictly religious Jews of his time but for those of our days as well.

Rebbe was not only comfortable interacting and even socializing with non-Jews; he was prepared to concede that they at times were

97. *Seder Eliyahu Rabba* 9, s.v. *maaseh*. The priest's lesson is one that Hitler never learned.

more knowledgeable about natural science than his own colleagues. The Talmud relates that the Sages disagreed with gentile scholars regarding the movement of the stars in the heavens and the nature of the sun's rotation around the earth. Jewish scholars postulated that the stars did not move in the heavens, while gentile scholars argued that they did. On the other hand, the Sages believed that the sun revolved in a non-circular orbit around the earth. They asserted that the sun passes below the second layer of the sky (*rakia*) during the day and above it at night. Gentile scholars, reflecting what came to be called the Ptolemaic model, argued that the sun's orbit was regular, passing below the sky in the daytime and below the earth at night. The Talmud then records that Rebbe sided with the rabbis in the first case; on the other hand, with respect to the sun's orbit, "their view is preferable to ours, because during the day wells [that is, springs] are cool but they become warm at night."[98]

In fact, neither Rebbe nor the gentile scholars were correct about the sun's rotation; the fact that springs are cooler in the day than at night is due to the property of specific heat or heat capacity.[99] What matters less than whether Rebbe or the gentile scholars were correct is that Rebbe was so keenly objective and non-ideological that he was prepared to accept the views of gentiles over those of his rabbinical associates if he thought those arguments more compelling. His attitude stands in stark contrast with contemporary figures who refuse to accept the findings of non-Jewish scientists.[100]

WINNING THE SUPPORT OF THE WEALTHY ELITES

The Jewish community's men of wealth constituted an entirely different class of people whose support and trust Rebbe needed to obtain. These individuals represented the hereditary elites of their communities, and they generally took over the governance of local municipalities. Local governance by elites was the norm throughout the Roman Empire – the

98. Pesaḥim 94b.
99. For a discussion, see Jeremy Brown's seminal study of Jews and astronomy, *New Heavens and a New Earth: The Jewish Reception of Copernican Thought* (Oxford and New York: Oxford University Press, 2013), 29–30.
100. Ibid., 254–73.

Severi, the family of Septimius Severus, were a typical example – and indeed throughout Europe up to the early twentieth century. Indeed, it is still the case in certain parts of the United States: Mitch Landrieu, the mayor of New Orleans, Louisiana, is the son of Moon Landrieu, who also was mayor of New Orleans and the brother of Louisiana Senator Mary Landrieu; Congressman Joseph P. Kennedy III bears the name of a royal American political family.[101]

As might have been expected, the local Jewish elites often had their own independent contacts among the Roman rulers; they could have undermined Rebbe's standing with Rome should they have wished to do so. On the other hand, their support reinforced Rebbe's own position as spokesman to the Romans on behalf of the Jewish community. Therefore, as with his rabbinical colleagues, Rebbe went to great lengths to cultivate the wealthy by showing them the honor they no doubt thought they deserved. As the Talmud observed, "Rebbe showed respect to rich men… in agreement with the statement by Rab b. Mari: *May he be enthroned before God forever; appoint mercy and truth that they may preserve him.*[102] When 'may he be enthroned before God forever'? When he 'appoints mercy and truth that they may preserve him.'"[103]

The Talmud also relates that when a man named Ben Bunais appeared in Rebbe's court, the latter told his retainers to "make way for a man worth 100 maneh," the equivalent today of some $25,000. When someone else came in, Rebbe announced, "Make way for one worth 200 maneh" ($50,000). Though not insubstantial in an agrarian economy, these were not especially large sums. It is not surprising therefore, that when R. Yishmael b. R. Yose remarked to him that the second man's father had "a thousand ships at sea and owns a thousand villages on land," that is, was truly a rich man, Rebbe replied, "When you next see his father tell him not to send his son to me so improperly dressed." In other words, Rebbe was seeking to protect the wealthy

101. Of course the Bush family has produced father and son as presidents of the United States.

102. Ps. 61:8.

103. Ibid. It is the wealthy who are in a position to show mercy and uphold truth. Eiruvin 86a, and see Rashi, s.v. *eimatai.*

father's public image, something that the father certainly would have appreciated.[104]

When speaking of Rebbe's respect for the wealthy, the Talmud notes that R. Akiba likewise honored them. The Talmud does not indicate when R. Akiba did so; he was initially very poor but became rich after becoming a leading scholar. Yet while R. Akiba was not officially recognized as the leader of his people – on the contrary, the Romans considered him a subversive – he did command a large and loyal following and was regarded as the most influential rabbi of his generation. Perhaps he showed honor to the rich precisely in order to enlist their support against the Romans; his calculus was highly political. In that respect, he was setting an example of what it took to be a successful leader. It was a lesson that was not lost upon his students, several of whom became Rebbe's teachers and, recognizing his future as patriarch, may well have transmitted that lesson to him.

REBBE'S GENEROSITY

Wealthy as he was, and much as he cultivated the rich, Rebbe was equally generous to the less fortunate with his time and his resources. The Talmud and Midrash recount several tales to underline his commitment of each. As with other stories about him, these tales probably were either completely imaginary or exaggerations of actual occurrences, but their import no doubt was real. Two such stories offer examples of his diligence in responding to the material needs of others.

The Midrash relates that Rebbe would deal regularly with the needs of the common folk. On one occasion he emerged from the bathhouse and proceeded to deal with matters that the people had brought before him. While he was doing so, his servant poured him a cup of wine, but Rebbe was so engrossed in addressing the matters before him that he had no time to imbibe the drink. In the meantime, the servant dozed off and fell asleep. Rebbe looked at him and remarked, quoting Ecclesiastes, that "we who are immersed in the needs of humanity are not even permitted to sleep."[105]

---

104. The incident is related in Eiruvin 85b–86a.

105. Eccl. 5:11.

On another occasion, Rebbe had to deal with then financial consequences of a dreadful family tragedy. Twelve of thirteen brothers, all of them married, had died childless. The twelve widows faced penury unless they could be married to the surviving brother; but while they hoped he would support them, they realized that he probably did not have the wherewithal to do so. They therefore came to Rebbe asking that he authorize them all to marry him in accordance with the law of levirate marriage (*yibum*), but recognizing that the financial burden on the prospective husband was onerous, they asked Rebbe to support them. Rebbe declined; it was a tall order even for a man of his wealth to support the equivalent of twelve families in perpetuity. The women, clearly desperate, offered to divide the household expenses among themselves, so that each would receive one month's maintenance. The prospective husband then asked who would cover the costs of the extra month of the leap year, which normally occurs every third year. This Rebbe was prepared to do; he prayed for each of them to have children, and they departed.

After three years they returned to Rebbe along with thirty-six children; each had given birth to a child every year of the intervening period. That year was a leap year, and they came to ask Rebbe to finance the families during the extra month of Adar. Upon spying the approaching women, Rebbe's attendants informed him that "a village of infants has come to inquire after your welfare." Rebbe looked out the window and spotted the oncoming crowd. He asked the women, "What brings you here?" And they responded, "We request that you finance the thirteenth month of this year." And so he did.[106]

REBBE'S RELATIONS WITH THE BABYLONIAN DIASPORA

By the time Rebbe assumed the patriarchate, Diaspora Jewry had begun to recover from Trajan's crushing of the revolt of 115–17. Jews had fought Roman forces in Egypt, Cyrenaica, and Cyprus, and one outcome of their defeat was the decimation of Egyptian Jewry and of

106. Y. Yevamot 4:12.

their main center, Alexandria.[107] And as has been noted, the Jews had also fought the Romans in Mesopotamia, which Trajan had recently annexed, and were "among the most powerful and loyal supporters of the Parthian cause,"[108] though in this case they joined non-Jews in what was a general uprising.

Initially, the Alexandrian Greeks had called in the Roman army in late 115, and the city's Jews had been subdued. But then the revolt spread throughout North Africa. Trajan sent one of his leading generals, Q. Marcius Turbo, to put down the uprising. Despite leading a joint land and naval force, Turbo had to fight several battles to restore order; tens of thousands of Jews died in the conflict.

The uprising in Mesopotamia took place "sometime after midsummer 116."[109] Trajan dispatched the Moorish Roman general Lusius Quietus, who successfully crushed the rebellion. Trajan then named Quietus to be legate of Palestine. There he singled out the Jews for retribution and perpetrated a major massacre that left thousands dead. The Talmud included this massacre as one of the great tragedies of Jewish history: "During the war of Quietus they abolished the bridal crown."[110]

Though Trajan's eastern conquests had brought the largest Diaspora Jewish communities under Roman control, Hadrian's subsequent withdrawal from the east (he also removed Quietus from Palestine) brought the Jews back under Parthian control. The community had thrived in Babylonia under the Parthians, even to the point of being entirely self-governing for a brief period.[111] Unlike other parts of the Diaspora, the community boasted its own Davidic leader, the exilarch, who exerted local control with the king's blessing. Babylonian Jewish authorities, presumably under the exilarch's ultimate leadership, appear to have "enjoyed the prerogative of a retinue of horses, possessed influence with the government so that they might

107. Orosius uses the term "annihilated." *Seven Books,* 344.
108. Neusner, *Economic and Political Life,* 175.
109. Smallwood, *Jews under Roman Rule,* 397.
110. Mishna Sota 9:14.
111. Smallwood, *Jews under Roman Rule,* 415.

issue sentences of imprisonment and death, bore Parthian military names … wore Parthian equestrian dress and were endowed by [the government] with the prerogatives of the nobility."[112]

The community also was led by first-rate scholars like the *Tanna* R. Judah ben Beteira.[113] Moreover, after the Bar Kokhba rebellion, Babylonia benefited from an influx of Palestinian refugees, including sages, who sought to live beyond the boundaries of the Roman Empire. In many ways, Babylonia was, as a leading scholar has termed it, the Jewish world's "America" of its day.[114]

The Babylonian community included some very wealthy traders, who, like R. Hiyya, imported silk from China into Babylonia, shipped it to Palestine for weaving, "and sold it to Tyre for export to Rome."[115] Although the Parthian government not only heavily regulated and taxed the silk trade, but also limited the presence of foreign merchants, it permitted the Jews to be commercial intermediaries between China and Rome. It was therefore as traders that the Parthian Jews accumulated their wealth.

Rebbe's relations with this large, relatively prosperous, self-governing, and religiously observant community therefore called forth his considerable skills and generally required him not to vent his true feelings about the Babylonian Jews. Indeed, the presence of R. Hiyya and his sons at Rebbe's court, which could be taken as a sign of the exilarch's influence,[116] certainly called for discretion on Rebbe's part. Every so often, however, Rebbe could not restrain himself and his emotions ran away from him.

Rebbe's attitude to the exilarch has already been noted: he blanched when R. Hiyya told him the exilarch was arriving in Palestine (without mentioning that he had arrived in a coffin!) because he

112. Neusner, "Economic and Political Life," 179.

113. Ibid., 416, citing, *inter alia*, Pesaḥim 3b and Kiddushin 10b. See also Sanhedrin 32b. Oppenheimer (*Rabbi Yehuda HaNasi*, 143) considers that R. Judah b. Beteira arrived in Babylonia as a refugee from the Bar Kokhba rebellion. The Talmud supports Smallwood; see *Jews under Roman Rule*, 416.

114. Oppenheimer, *Rabbi Yehuda HaNasi*, 143.

115. Neusner, "Economic and Political Life," 170.

116. Ibid., 171.

recognized that the exilarch, as a direct descendant of the Davidic line, outranked him at least in terms of protocol. And Rebbe, confidant of emperors, was very sensitive to issues of protocol, perhaps overly so.

Another example of Rebbe's sensitivity regarding his status, especially vis-à-vis Babylonian Jewry, was his refusal to give rabbinic ordination to Hanina bar Hama, a product of the Babylonian academies. The fact was that Rebbe simply did not consider Babylonian scholarship on a par with his own or that of his Palestinian colleagues. Nevertheless, he thought it politic to maintain decent relations with the Babylonian community (unlike, some would say, the attitude of many Israelis to their American "cousins").

Rebbe's concern about his status may have been a reason why he never traveled to Babylonia. He would not have wanted to play second fiddle to the exilarch. Instead, his contacts with the community were managed via rabbis and acolytes whom he dispatched to its leaders, as well as through written communications, as can be seen in the case of his dispute with Hananiah the nephew of R. Joshua.

The incident with Hananiah actually was an example of the limits to Rebbe's willingness to cooperate with the Babylonian community. Rebbe would not tolerate any effort on its part to be independently responsible for setting the calendar. The Talmud reports that when Hananiah attempted to intercalate the calendar outside Palestine, Rebbe sent R. Isaac and R. Nathan to him bearing three notes. The first note was meant to flatter Hananiah by noting that he was a distinguished scholar. The second note was a veiled effort to cut him down to size by pointing out that the two emissaries were themselves distinguished scholars. The third note was blunt: employing the imagery of Yotam son of Yerubaal's censure of Abimelech's attempt to rule over Israel, the letter from Rebbe rebuked him by suggesting that if he wished to be a leader he should repair to the desert and there rule over brambles. When Hananiah protested to R. Judah ben Beteira, Babylonia's leading scholar, the latter upheld Rebbe's position.[117]

---

117. Y. Nedarim 6:8; see also the comments of both Frankel, *Korban Ha'eda,* and R. Moshe Margolies, *Pnei Moshe,* s.v. *kadmita* ff. The biblical reference is to Judges 9:6–21. The Jerusalem Talmud goes on to relate that R. Judah ben Beteira mounted

Rebbe also deeply disapproved of the Diaspora community's reluctance to live in Judaea. A midrash recounts a debate between R. Eliezer and Rebbe when they saw a casket that had been brought from an unspecified location in the Diaspora for burial in Judaea:

> Said Rebbe to R. Eliezer, "What is the point of this individual, who passed away in the Diaspora, coming to be buried in the Land of Israel? Of him I say, 'You have rendered my heritage an abomination. In your lives you did not make *aliya* and in your death you have come and defiled the land.'" R. Eliezer said to him, "Since he was buried in the Land of Israel, the Holy One, blessed be He, forgives him, as it is written, 'And the land shall cleanse His people.'"[118]

Rebbe, the fierce nationalist, simply could not countenance the reluctance of his co-religionists to return to their ancestral land. R. Eliezer, more tolerant of their situation, gave them credit for their desire to be buried in the Holy Land. R. Eliezer's attitude has prevailed over the centuries and millennia. Especially since the creation of the State of Israel, an increasing number of observant Jews who have lived out their lives in the Diaspora are seeking burial in Israel in general and in Jerusalem in particular.

Just as Rebbe regarded his status and that of his community as superior to that of Babylonia, the Jews of that region likewise felt that they, not the Palestinian Jews, were the true elite. The Babylonian Jews were especially particular about the purity of their lineage. They were scrupulous about accepting proselytes, demanding that conversions be fully in compliance with halakha. Non-Jews whose

---

his horse and, somewhat like Paul Revere, announced to all the towns he was able to reach that they should follow Rebbe's ruling. Those towns that he did not reach continued to follow Hananiah's calendar. The Babylonian Talmud (Berakhot 63a) relates a similar story but does not mention Rebbe *by name*, referring only to an anonymous "they," and names the messengers as R. Yose b. Kippar and the grandson of R. Zechariah b. Kebutal.

118. Deut. 32:43. R. Eliezer gave a positive spin to the passage, since its translation actually reads, "and cleanse the land of His people."

conversions were suspect were not accepted into the community. Nor were the children of priests who had married divorcees in defiance of halakhic norms. Slaves whose manumission had not been conducted according to strict halakhic terms were likewise excluded from the community, as, not surprisingly, were *mamzerim*, children born of illicit relations.

The Babylonians contrasted their scrupulousness not only with other Diaspora communities, but even with that of Palestine, which they grudgingly acknowledged was superior to that of all communities but their own. In contrast, Rebbe in particular seemed less averse to accepting proselytes, observing on the basis of a passage in Isaiah:[119]

> There is a kind of dove that is fed and her companions smell her and come to her dove-cote; similarly when a sage sits and expounds [Torah] many proselytes are converted at that time. Thus Jethro heard [Torah] and converted, thus Rahab heard and converted, even in the case of Hananiah, Mishael, and Azariah, many proselytes converted at that time.[120]

The Babylonian tradition held that Ezra had ensured the purity of Babylonian Jewry before leaving for Judaea in 458 BCE. In Judaea, as his book makes clear, he was unable to prevent intermarriage with the indigenous non-Jewish peoples. It was for this reason that the Babylonians saw themselves as superior; indeed, they felt that they, rather than the Palestinian Jews, were the more authentic upholders of Jewish tradition. It was a classic case of intra-Jewish snobbery, akin to that displayed by West European Jews to those from Eastern Europe throughout much of the nineteenth and twentieth centuries and even after the Holocaust, which did not discriminate among Jews regardless of their countries of origin. On the other hand, the fact that to this day subsequent generations accord greater importance to the Babylonian Talmud rather than the Jerusalem Talmud, would appear

119. Is. 29:23.
120. Song of Songs Rabba 4:1; see also Urbach, *The Sages*, 545–54.

to justify the claims to superiority that Babylonian Jews asserted for themselves eighteen centuries ago.

Rebbe did not accept Babylonian claims, however. As he lay dying, he revealed his true feelings about their snobbishness:

> When Rebbe was on the verge of death, he stated: There is a place in Babylonia called Humania; its residents are all Ammonites. There is a place in Babylonia called Misgaria; they are all *mamzerim*. There is a place called Birka in Babylonia; two brothers live there who wife-swap. There is a place in Babylonia called Birta Desatya; today they have turned away from the Almighty. A pond overflowed on Shabbat and these people went and caught fish on Shabbat. And when R. Ahi b. R. Josiah banned them, they become apostates.[121]

It is noteworthy that the original Aramaic appears to indicate that Rebbe was playing on words, matching the names of places to sins of various kinds. His real intention was to assert his role as the ultimate Jewish authority by demonstrating that the Babylonian community had no basis for claiming superiority over that of Palestine, whether with regard to family genealogy or anything else.[122]

Indeed, some of the communities that bordered the Babylonian Jewish centers looked to Rebbe, rather than to the geographically more proximate Babylonian rabbis, for halakhic guidance. They may have done so because as geographic outliers they found that the Babylonian Jewish leadership called their ethnic purity into question. One such community

---

121. Kiddushin 72a.

122. Oppenheimer, *Rabbi Yehuda HaNasi*, 149–50. Oppenheimer notes that the stories about Rebbe's attitude to the Babylonians appear only in the Babylonian Talmud. He argues that these stories reflect the speculations of later generations of Babylonian rabbis as to how the great Palestinian *Tanna'im* viewed them. One might add that such speculation may well have reflected an inferiority complex on the part of the Babylonians. See also R. Yose's assertion that the Palestinian rabbis "hated" the Babylonians (Menaḥot 100a).

was that of Meishan (Masene), located in the marsh country of what is today southern Iraq.[123]

Perhaps because they resented the Babylonian religious leadership, the Jewish community of Meishan turned to Rebbe with an important economic question that they hoped he could resolve. With Septimius Severus' capture of Palmyra, Meishan, because of its location near the Arabian Gulf, had become a key way station on the trading route from India and the Far East to Rome. The Jews of Meishan naturally wanted to capitalize on the economic opportunities that lay before them. They were hamstrung, however, by an ancestral tradition of not sailing on the Indian Ocean. They hoped that Rebbe would release them from that tradition.[124]

Rebbe disappointed them; he told them that the tradition must stand. The reasoning behind his decision is not entirely clear. One scholar speculates that perhaps he feared that the Jews would be inordinately exposed to pagan influences. Living in the marshlands, on the far outskirts of the Babylonian Jewish community, the people of Meishan were already familiar with the religious practices of the heathen Parthians. Another possibility is that Rebbe feared the traders of Meishan would violate the Sabbath. If this were the case, however, he should have issued a ban on all Jews putting to sea. There is no clear evidence that he ever did so. In any event, the fact that the people of Meishan approached Rebbe to resolve their dilemma illustrates the extent to which his halakhic writ extended far beyond Palestine to the very borders of Babylonia.

Finally, although Rebbe never met the Parthian emperor, as he did Severus and Caracalla, he did exchange gifts with Artabanus the Fifth. Artabanus did not succeed to the throne until 208; at the time Rebbe was over seventy years old. The Talmud records that Artabanus

123. See statement by R. Papa, Kiddushin 71a. For an extended discussion, see Yakir Paz, "'Meishan Is Dead': On the Historical Contexts of the Bavli's Representations of the Jews in Southern Mesopotamia," in Geoffrey Herman and Jeffrey L. Rubenstein, eds., *The Aggada of the Bavli and its Cultural World* (Providence, RI: Brown University Press, 2018), 47–55, 96–99.

124. Y. Pesaḥim 4:1.

sent Rebbe a priceless gem. Artabanus then told Rebbe, "Send me something equal in value."

> So [Rebbe] sent him a single mezuza. He replied: I sent you something priceless and you sent me something worth a penny? [Rebbe] replied: Your items and mine are not equal; moreover, you sent me something that I guard, while I sent you something that guards you even when you sleep, as it is written, "When you travel it will lead you [and when you sleep it will guard over you]."[125]

The exchange of gifts, which was common among rulers, again demonstrated – at least to the rabbis who recorded the event centuries after they believed it took place – Rebbe's near-imperial stature.

Several years later, having passed through Palestine, Caracalla attacked Parthia. If the exchange of gifts with Artabanus took place subsequent to the Roman invasion, it would have placed Judah and the Jewish community of Palestine in an awkward position; they might have suffered from Roman suspicion of their ties to the Babylonian community, as had happened in Hadrian's time. On the other hand, if the exchange with Artabanus took place prior to Caracalla's decision to launch his operation, the Romans would have been unlikely to give it much notice.[126] Fortunately, Caracalla

---

125. Y. Pe'ah 1:1. The passage is from Prov. 6:22. The eighteenth-century commentator R. Moshe Margolies stated that Artabanus was a wealthy Jew (Y. ibid., s.v. *Artaban*). Perhaps he shared the opinion of other leading decisors that one could not give a mezuza to a non-Jew, and therefore the man had to be Jewish. As R. Adin Steinsaltz points out, not only is it clear that the Artaban of this story, and throughout the Talmud, is most certainly the Parthian king, but it is from this very story that the sixteenth/seventeenth-century decisor R. Issakhar Ber Eilenburg ruled that one may indeed present a mezuza to a non-Jew. See *Talmud Yerushalmi: Pe'ah*, ed. R. Adin Steinsaltz (Jerusalem: Israel Institute for Talmudic Publications, 1987), 31, *Iyunim*, s.v. *shalaḥ*.
126. Oppenheimer, *Rabbi Yehuda HaNasi*, 153–54. Oppenheimer is unsure whether the Artabanus is the Fourth or the Fifth. As has already been noted, Artabanus the Fourth died nearly a half century before Rebbe was born.

never returned to Palestine, as he was assassinated in 217 CE while still fighting the Parthians.[127]

PERSONAL LIFE: REBBE'S HEALTH AND HIS HOUSEHOLD

Rebbe's Health

Tradition has it that Rebbe was both handsome and powerfully built.[128] We do not know much more about his physical appearance; the Talmud rarely offers any details about what individual rabbis may have looked like. We do know, however, that Rebbe suffered from some serious and chronic physical ailments. Later traditions asserted that these ailments included scurvy, kidney stones, eye infections – possibly pinkeye – and dental problems. Rebbe was fortunate in that Mar Samuel, his much younger contemporary and perhaps his student, was also a doctor. Samuel provided him with an eye ointment that cured his eye infections. Rebbe was unable to find cures for his other ailments, however.

Rebbe's chronic intestinal problems were exceedingly serious, and he appears to have found no cure for them, other than perhaps eggs and apple cider. Regarding eggs he was reputed to have said, "An egg is superior [in food value] to the same quantity of any other kind of food."[129] As for apple cider, the Talmud reported that on one occasion when he was seeking a cure for a disorder of his bowels, Rebbe inquired as to whether he might be permitted to drink apple cider produced by gentiles, which was understood to be a curative. His student R. Yishmael b. R. Yose, who as previously noted became the leading rabbi of Sepphoris, advised him that his own father, Rebbe's childhood friend R. Yose, had been cured when he drank seventy-year-old apple cider that had been produced by gentiles. A frustrated Rebbe scolded him: "You had this information all this time and you let me suffer?" His attendants checked and found a certain heathen who owned three hundred jars of seventy-year-old apple cider. Rebbe drank and was cured and, recognizing

127. See below, pp. 287–88.
128. Dictum of R. Simeon b. Menassia, *Kalla Rabbati* 8:6.
129. Stated by R. Yannai in Rebbe's name. Berakhot 44b.

his good fortune in finding cider that had been preserved for such a great length of time, exclaimed, "Blessed be the All-Present who delivered His world to guardians."[130]

Rebbe's health issues never left him. They caused him such agony that the Talmud reports that when Rebbe's steward would feed the livestock, he timed the feeding to Rebbe's need to relieve himself, so that Rebbe's cries of anguish would be drowned out by the mooing and braying of the animals. Nevertheless, Rebbe's cries of pain were louder even than the noises the animals made and "were heard even by sailors."[131]

The Babylonian Talmud states that Rebbe believed that "suffering is dear"[132] and that he deliberately undertook to accept the pain that his ailments caused him. It explains that his sicknesses were brought upon him as punishment for his display of cruelty. The Talmud relates that once a terrified calf that was being led to slaughter had broken away and hidden under his clothes. Rebbe had harshly told the calf, "Go, because you were created for this." Immediately, "they said [in Heaven], 'Since he has no pity let inflictions come upon him.'"[133]

The Jerusalem Talmud offers a different version regarding Rebbe's physical difficulties. It also asserts that Rebbe's dental problems were due to his harshness to the calf, but it adds that he was cured after he showed mercy to some mice. It makes no mention of Rebbe's willing dental troubles upon himself. Moreover, in the Jerusalem Talmud the tale continues:

> One day Rebbe's maidservant was sweeping the house; she saw some young weasels lying there and was about to sweep them away. "Leave them," Rebbe said. "It is written 'And His tender

---

130. Avoda Zara 40b.
131. Bava Metzia 85a.
132. Ibid.
133. Ibid.

> mercies are over all His works.'"[134] They said [in Heaven], "Since he is compassionate, let us be compassionate to him."[135]

Both Talmuds have Rebbe suffering for the same amount of time – thirteen years – though the Babylonian Talmud cannot even determine how many of those years he suffered from scurvy and how many from kidney stones.[136] Moreover, there is no agreement as to the effects of his suffering: the Jerusalem Talmud asserts that during the thirteen years he suffered from dental pains, no woman died of childbirth or had any miscarriages, while the Babylonian Talmud states that during his years of suffering, "the world needed no rain" and plants grew anyway because there was plenty of ground water. This was considered a blessing because the rabbis considered rain a necessary evil. In addition, whereas the Jerusalem Talmud indicates that Rebbe was finally cured, the Babylonian Talmud, as will be shown, has him suffering virtually until he breathed his last.[137]

Late in life Rebbe moved his residence, court, and yeshiva from Beit She'arim to Sepphoris, where he spent the final seventeen years of his life.[138] Rebbe's move was reportedly facilitated by Septimius Severus, who granted him a large tract of land there.[139] Sepphoris was a mixed city. Most of the town's Jews lived near the top of the hill, well above the *cardo* (the main Roman thoroughfare). Their neighborhood was in the shadow of what today are the remains of a Crusader fortress, which was itself built on what was probably a Roman military building, since the location offers a commanding view of the entire region. If Rebbe,

134. Ps. 145:9.
135. Bava Metzia 85a. A variant in the Jerusalem Talmud has Rebbe's thirteen years of suffering from dental troubles coming to an end when, quoting the same verse, he saved some mice from being exterminated in their hole. Y. Kilayim 9:3; Y. Ketubot 12:3.
136. Bava Metzia 85a.
137. Bava Batra 104a.
138. Y. Kilayim 9:3.
139. Aviva Bar Am, "Ancient Tzipori," *The Jerusalem Post* (January 25, 2010), http://www.jpost.com/Israel-Guide/Top-Tours/Ancient-Tzipori.

as was likely, lived among his brethren, he would have had but a short walk between his home and the Roman fort, which may have been a way station for visiting dignitaries, including Severus and Caracalla, when they passed through the region.

The Crusader fortress, built on what was probably an earlier Roman fort. The outer boundary of the Jewish area began about fifty yards from the Roman building. Right: the view from the fortress. (Photo: Dov Zakheim)

Rebbe's move to Sepphoris was prompted by his concern that the atmosphere in Beit She'arim, lower down in the Jezreel Valley, was affecting his health. Rebbe felt that the air in Sepphoris, which is located in the upper Galilee some 950 feet above sea level, was more salubrious than that of Beit She'arim, which is about 500 feet lower.[140] Sepphoris is the Greek form of the Hebrew name Tzipori (from *tzipor*, or bird). As the Talmud puts it, "Ze'ira said... why is it called Tzipori? Because it is perched on the top of a mountain like a bird."[141] Of course, if

140. Ketubot 103b–104a: "Rebbe was living at Beit She'arim but when he fell ill he was brought to Tzipori because it was situated on higher ground and its air was salubrious."

141. Megilla 6a.

Rebbe's intention was to suffer for the common good, then the move is somewhat puzzling.

The conflicting stories about Rebbe's poor health – that suffering was "dear" to him in order to protect the community from tragedy,[142] or alternately, that he sought to improve his condition by moving to a more hygienic location – indicate that the actual details regarding Rebbe's health, not to mention their implications for society at large, were lost over time. Certainly, later rabbis felt that there had to be something miraculous about Rebbe's illnesses, since they had also asserted that he was unusually strong. In a society where miscarriages and death in childbirth were common, their absence would have been no less a miracle than plants growing without rain. The tales would seem to indicate, however, that Rebbe suffered from chronic ailments of some sort, and that they hounded him for a considerable time.

As might be expected of a prince in ancient as in modern times, Judah had a large household including servants and retainers. At the same time, he held himself somewhat aloof from others outside that household. He certainly welcomed students and friends to his home, yet the Talmud records him as saying: "A man should not invite too many friends to his house, as it says, *There are friends that one has to his own detriment*."[143]

Rebbe's Children

Rebbe had two sons and at least two daughters. Although both sons appear often in the Talmud, we know far less about them than about their father. Both were rabbis. Gamaliel, the older son, eventually succeeded his father, but Simeon was the wiser.[144]

The Talmud relates that Simeon would turn to his father when he was distressed. Thus, when "a daughter was born to R. Simeon the son of Rebbe, he felt disappointed. His father said to him: Increase has

142. Bava Metzia 85a.
143. Berakhot 63a; the quote is from Prov. 18:24.
144. Ketubot 103b.

come to the world," meaning that she would soon bear his grandchildren.[145] Unfortunately, Bar Kappara, who was something of a spoiler, said to him:

> Your father has given you an empty consolation. The world cannot do without either males or females. Yet happy is he whose children are males, and alas for him whose children are females. The world cannot do without either a spice-seller or a tanner. Yet happy is he whose occupation is that of a spice-seller, and alas for him whose occupation is that of a tanner.

On occasion, R. Simeon would also engage his father when the latter issued a ruling, whether of halakhic or non-halakhic nature. As has already been recounted, it was R. Simeon who prompted his father to reconsider his antipathy to the *amei haaretz*. On other occasions, however, Rebbe displayed considerable impatience with his son, rebuking him for his intervention.

> A folded [deed] was once brought before Rebbe, who said, "There is no date on this." R. Simeon said to Rebbe, "It might be hidden between its folds." He [Rebbe] opened it and he saw the date. [But] Rebbe then turned around and looked at him with annoyance. "I did not write it," said his son. "R. Judah the tailor wrote it." "Stay away from such slander (*lashon hara*)," his father said to him.[146]

Shortly before recounting this incident, the Talmud relates that Rebbe was not an expert regarding the laws that applied to folded deeds. What he did know about them – which may not have been all that much – he learned from his administrator, a fellow with the Greek name of Zunin. As an administrator, Zunin was familiar with folded deeds to a degree that Rebbe was not. Rebbe also seems to have disapproved of these documents because they tended to cause

145. Bava Batra 16b; Rashbam, s.v. *rivya*.
146. Bava Batra 164b.

people to err regarding their contents, as indeed Rebbe had done, assuming it was undated.

Because R. Simeon recommended that he tear open the deed to see the date, Rebbe assumed that his son had written the deed. When R. Simeon denied that he had done so, Rebbe remained annoyed at him for implicating R. Judah. He should have merely stated that he was not the deed's author. Perhaps Rebbe's annoyance was due to his frustration at his own lack of expertise regarding folded deeds. Yet it appears that there was more to it than that.

Rebbe was a forceful advocate for the commandment to respect one's parents. He equated the honor due to parents with the honor due to God.[147] And he was a demanding father, even when his son was not only a grownup but an ordained rabbi. The Talmud follows the story of the folded deed with another example of Rebbe's annoyance at his son: "Once R. Simeon was sitting in Rebbe's presence reading sections of the Book of Psalms. 'How fine is this script?' said Rebbe. 'I did not write it', replied his son, 'Judah the tailor wrote it'. 'Keep away from this slander,' Rebbe said to him." The Talmud then asks: "In the former case one can well understand Rebbe's rebuke, since slander was involved; but in this case, what slander was there?" The Talmud then explains Rebbe's position based on the dictum of R. Dimi: "For R. Dimi, brother of R. Safra, taught: A man should never speak in praise of his friend, because in the course of praising him he lapses into something bad" and ultimately slanders him.[148]

Rebbe may have been on solid ground in both cases, but it does appear that he had little patience for his son, who meant nothing wrong in the latter case, and probably didn't intend to slander R. Judah the tailor in the former case either. We do not know what kind of father Rebbe was when his children were young; but if the talmudic record

147. Rebbe stated: "How precious is the honoring of father and mother before He who spoke and the world came into being, for He equated their honor to His own.... It is written 'Honor your Father and your Mother' (Ex. 20:12) and it is written 'Honor the Lord with your wealth' (Prov. 3:9). He equated the honoring of parents to the honoring of God." *Mekhilta DeRabbi Yishmael, Yitro (BaḤodesh)* 8, s.v. *kabed*.

148. Ibid.

is any indication, he preferred to offer his sons "tough love" when they had matured into adulthood.

Like most families at that time and for centuries thereafter, Rebbe managed the betrothal of his children. The Talmud[149] relates:

> Rebbe was engaged in the arrangements for the marriage of his son into the family [i.e., the daughter] of R. Hiyya but she died just when the *ketuba* was about to be written. Rebbe asked, "Is there, God forbid, any taint [in the proposed union]?" They looked into [the genealogy of the two] families and found that Rebbe descended from Shephatiah the son of Avital [a wife of King David] while R. Hiyya descended from Shimi, one of David's brothers.[150]

The Talmud does not indicate which son Rebbe sought to marry off to R. Hiyya's daughter. In any event, whichever son it might have been, since R. Hiyya was a leading rabbinic scholar, Rebbe's outstanding student, and a scion of a prominent line from the tribe of Judah, on its face the betrothal made considerable sense. Evidently, for all his qualities and heritage, however, R. Hiyya was not a suitable in-law for Rebbe. It was not fitting for a direct descendant of King David to marry someone who was only indirectly related to the royal house.[151]

When the betrothal collapsed, Rebbe then determined to do the next best thing: in place of a royal marriage, he sought to marry his son

149. Ketubot 62b.

150. Rashi, s.v. *i'asuk*.

151. Rubenstein considers this story, which attributes the "death of an innocent girl" to her inferior lineage, to be a "Babylonian fiction. There is not one hint of this event in Palestinian sources, and the putative genealogies contradict those given in the Yerushalmi." He goes on to assert that "the story's focus is a quintessential concern of Babylonian sages: lineage." Rubenstein, *Culture*, 81. While it may well be that the Babylonian rabbis garbled or embellished the story, as did others, the importance of lineage should not be downplayed. Though Rubenstein compares Rebbe's behavior to that of "eighteenth-century European nobility," the fact is that the marriage of a royal – which is what Judah considered himself to be – to someone not of royal blood, i.e., to a commoner, is actually a twentieth-century phenomenon. Moreover, while there may be no extant reference to this story in the Jerusalem Talmud, only

off to a daughter of another prominent rabbi. Having related the failed match with R. Hiyya's daughter, the Talmud goes on to recount:

> Rebbe was engaged in preparations for the marriage of his son into the family of R. Yose b. Zimra. It was agreed that his son should spend twelve years at Rav's academy [in Babylon]. When the girl was led before him, he said to them, "Let it be six years." When they made her pass before him again, he said, "I would rather marry first and then go off to study." He felt embarrassed before his father, however, but Rebbe said to him, "My son, you have the mind of your creator; for it is first written, 'You bring them and plant them,'[152] and later on it is written, 'And they shall make Me a sanctuary that I may dwell among them.'"[153]

Rebbe's son clearly had fallen in love with his betrothed, something with which Rebbe, by then perhaps having failed to marry the woman he had pursued, fully empathized. As if to justify his agreeing that his son put off his studies, Rebbe cited biblical passages to prove his point. Just as the Israelites were first to settle in Palestine and only then to build the Temple, so too was it proper for his son and his new wife to establish their household and only then for him to go off to pursue his studies in the yeshiva, an equivalent, however pale, of the Sanctuary.

The story does not end there, however. It appeared that the couple might not live "happily ever after." Having married the woman he loved, Rebbe's son departed and spent twelve years at Rav's yeshiva. By the time he returned, his wife had lost the power to give birth. "'What shall we do?' said Rebbe. 'If we order him to divorce her, it would be said: This poor soul waited in vain! Were he to marry another woman, it would be said: The latter is his wife and the other his mistress.' So Rebbe prayed for mercy to be shown to her, and she recovered."[154]

---

portions of that work have survived; missing are the entire order of Kodashim and several tractates in Teharot. The story may well have appeared in one of the missing tractates. For further observations regarding his thesis, see Appendix 2.

152. Ex. 15:17.
153. Ibid. 25:8.
154. Ketubot 62.

Having shown considerable sympathy toward his son's wishes during the betrothal, Rebbe again demonstrated his generosity of spirit when tragedy struck the young couple. He could have applied the law in its strictest manner: halakha states that if a woman cannot bear a child after ten years of marriage, her husband should divorce her.[155] A heartless man would have applied a strict interpretation of the law and demanded that his son obtain a divorce and marry another woman. But Rebbe was not heartless. And he recognized that halakha is sufficiently flexible to be variously applied as circumstances require. In this case he ruled that the there were extenuating circumstances: perhaps if his son had not trundled off to a Babylonian yeshiva for more than a decade, leaving his wife to fend for herself in Palestine, she might have borne him children. That the Talmud looked approvingly upon his decision can be inferred from its happy conclusion that the woman miraculously gave birth to a child.

Rebbe appears to have been less consistent about the character he sought in his sons-in-law than that of his sons. The Talmud relates that he was prepared to marry off one of his daughters – neither is ever named – to a grandson of R. Tarfon. The latter was one of R. Simeon ben Gamaliel's contemporaries. R. Tarfon had served as a priest in the Temple and had survived the revolt after the fall of Betar. Despite the misfortunes that befell the Judaean population after the Roman victory, Tarfon nevertheless remained, or perhaps became, a wealthy man. He was also a leading scholar of his generation, flourishing in Yavneh and perhaps serving as an interim *Nasi* in R. Simeon ben Gamaliel's absence.[156] A devoted family man, he also was extremely generous to the poor, providing them with resources in good times and bad.

The young man did not appear to have inherited any of his grandfather's good traits, however. His character resembled that of R. Eliezer ben R. Simeon's son prior to the latter's coming under his uncle's tutelage. For when Rebbe traveled to Yavneh to enquire if R. Tarfon had a

155. Karo, *Shulḥan Arukh: Even Ha'ezer, Hilkhot Gittin*, 154:10; but see R. Moses Isserles (Rema), ad loc., who states that this law is no longer enforced.
156. Oppenheimer, *Rabbi Yehuda HaNasi*, 24.

son to whom he could betroth his daughter he received some shocking news. As the Talmud recounts:[157]

> Rebbe happened to visit the town of R. Tarfon. Said he to [the townspeople]: "Has that righteous man, who used to swear by the life of his children [i.e., if he were lying he should bury his children] left a son?" They replied: "He has no son, but he has a grandson by his daughter, and every harlot who charges two [*zuz*] hires him for eight."

This time, Rebbe did not assign the young man to anyone's tutelage. Instead, he had the fellow brought before him, and told him, "If you repent, I will give you my daughter's hand in marriage." The marriage did not work out well, however. Relating the story centuries after it was said to have taken place, the Talmud is not sure what went wrong. It offers two versions of what happened. One version has it that the man repented, married Rebbe's daughter, and later divorced her. Another version also has him repenting, but then not marrying the girl because he did not want it to be said that he had repented on her account – a strange explanation if ever there was one.

The Talmud asks the obvious question: Why should Rebbe, perhaps the community's most prominent personality, make enquiries as to whether various rabbis had sons, and then choose young men who had to transform themselves through Torah study? Surely the offers of betrothal must have been pouring in; who would not want Rebbe as a *meḥutan*? Because, answers the Talmud, citing various sages,

> He who teaches Torah to his neighbor's son will be privileged to sit in the Heavenly Academy, as it is written, "If you will cause [Israel] to repent, then I bring you back and you will stand before me."[158] And he who teaches Torah to the son of an *am haaretz,* even if the Holy One, blessed be He, issues a decree, He annuls

157. Bava Metzia 85a.
158. Jer. 15:19.

> it for his sake, as it is written, "And if you will extract the precious from the vile, you shall be as my mouth."[159]

It appears that having changed his attitude to the *amei haaretz,* Rebbe was ready not only to undertake to educate them, but even to use the prospect of marrying into his immediate family as an incentive for them to do so. In fact, Rebbe went on successfully to marry off one of his daughters to an unreformed but exceedingly wealthy ignoramus named Ben Eleasa, whom the Talmud describes as spending large sums of money at the hairdresser's![160] It hints its disapproval of Rebbe's willingness to let his daughter marry below her station. Yet in one important respect Ben Eleasa was far from unrefined: he felt strongly about preserving his father-in-law's honor. As will be discussed in detail below, he was especially put off by the behavior of one of Rebbe's closest students, Bar Kappara, at R. Simeon's wedding. Together with his wife, Rebbe's daughter, Ben Eleasa rose and left the festivities. Perhaps he was not as much a boor as the later rabbis of the Gemara wished to imply.

Rebbe's Household Staff

Rebbe claimed never to have had an administrator supporting his household and advised others against having one, asserting that "had not Potiphar appointed Joseph as steward over his house, he would not have fallen into such trouble as he did."[161] Nevertheless, Rebbe did have a steward, Zunin, who was immensely wealthy in his own right. Indeed, the Talmud claims in exaggerated fashion that he was wealthier than King Shapur the Great, the Sassanid emperor.[162]

In addition, there was another important member of Rebbe's household whose name, unlike that of the steward, the Talmud never identifies. This was Rebbe's maidservant, a woman who was so well

---

159. Ibid.
160. Nedarim 51a and Sanhedrin 22b. Alon, *Jews in Their Land*, 713, surprisingly misreads the Hebrew/Aramaic word for son-in-law *(ḥatan)* as *ḥoten* (father-in-law).
161. Berakhot 63a.
162. Bava Metzia 85a.

versed in Jewish matters that she could confidently discuss them with Rebbe's colleagues – this despite a marked rabbinical reluctance to discuss anything with a woman, even one's own wife. As the *Tanna* Yose son of Yohanan was recorded as saying, "Do not chat excessively with a woman," and the rabbis amplified: "This was said about one's own wife, and certainly his counterpart's wife...whoever chats excessively with a woman causes grief for himself, neglects the study of Torah, and will eventually inherit Gehenna."[163]

An illustration of the maidservant's ability to draw upon her knowledge of Jewish law is the Talmud's description of her successful effort to repel a man's unwanted advances. She told him, "If my mistress is not immersing herself in the ritual bath (*mikve*), then neither am I [and being therefore ritually impure, you cannot sleep with me]." He replied, "[Since you are a non-Jewess] are you no better than an animal [and therefore do not require ritual immersion]?" To which the quick-witted maidservant retorted, "Are you not aware that one who mates with a beast is subject to stoning?" As it is written, "Whoever lies with an animal shall be put to death."[164] The man backed off.

That the housemaid also had a well-developed knowledge of Hebrew is evident from a series of talmudic reports regarding the inability of Rebbe's students, themselves rabbis,[165] to understand the meaning of several unusual words until they heard the maidservant using them in their proper context. The rabbis did not understand the meaning of the word *serugin,* which the Mishna employs as one of several cases where flaws in a Megilla scroll do not render it invalid if read on the holiday of Purim. It was only when Rebbe's maidservant saw them entering his house at intervals, and exclaimed, "How long will you continue to enter in *serugin*?" that they understood that the word meant "breaks," that is, ellipses in the Megilla.

On another occasion the rabbis did not know the meaning of *ḥaluglugot,* a term that appeared in various *mishnayot* and *baraitot,* until the rabbis overhead her asking a man who was peeling vegetables, "How

163. Avot 1:5.

164. Y. Berakhot, 3:4, 23b; Ex. 22:18.

165. See Rashi, Megilla 18a, s.v. *rabbanan.*

long will you continue to peel *ḥaluglugot*?" Again, the rabbis did not know what was meant by the passage in Proverbs, "*Salseleha* and it shall exalt you."[166] It was only when they heard the housemaid say to a man who was curling his hair, "How long will you continue to *mesalsel* your hair," that they understood the word to mean "turn about and about," and that the passage in Proverbs inspired the statement of Ben Bag Bag: "Turn it [the Torah] over and over, for everything is in it."[167]

The rabbis had trouble understanding the words *vetetetiha bematateh hashemad*.[168] Once again it was the maidservant's use of the word that clarified matters for them. They overheard her telling one of her fellows, "Grab the broom (*matateh*) and sweep the house." They then understood that the phrase means "And I will sweep her with the broom of destruction."

At least two of the words that stumped the rabbis were Hebrew words appearing in Scriptures. It is unclear whether the other two words were Hebrew; but the language of the Mishna, where these words appear, is usually Hebrew as well. In any event, those words were clearly uncommon, otherwise the rabbis would not have had a problem understanding their meaning. It is unlikely that the maidservant was not aware that the rabbis were listening to her conversations. That the maidservant used these words indicates that she was cognizant of the rabbis' difficulties, and that she was able to afford them an opportunity to understand them easily and do so discreetly.

The maidservant was so knowledgeable that the rabbis respected the bans she placed on wayward Jews.[169] When the Babylonian *Amora'im* considered a case of removing a ban that R. Judah had placed on a rabbi whose reputation was unsuitable for his position, they upheld his ban on the grounds that it was no less valid than that of the maidservant, and "the Rabbis did not belittle a three-year ban that the maidservant of the House of Rebbe would impose."[170] Bans were not thrown about lightly; that the maidservant's bans not only were respected, but were

166. Prov. 4:8.
167. Avot 5:25.
168. Is. 14:23.
169. Mo'ed Katan 17a. A ban (*niddui*) is a milder, usually temporary, form of excommunication.
170. Ibid.

not removed for three years, indicates just how seriously the rabbis took her judgments.

The Talmud relates yet another case of the maidservant's cleverness. Rebbe would host his students at his table, but it was the maidservant who decided whether it was time for them to depart or to linger a bit longer. She would indulge in what the Talmud called *lashon ḥokhma* (the language of wisdom, i.e., code words), saying things like "The ladle strikes against the jar and let the eagles fly to their nests," meaning that there was no wine left to ladle from the jug and that it was time for Rebbe's students to make their way home.[171] Similarly, when she wanted the students to remain at Rebbe's table, she would say, "The crown of her friend will be removed and the ladle will float in the jar like a ship that sails in the sea," meaning "Let us remove the bung from another jug and pour some more wine."[172]

The maidservant's elliptical language was not really some sort of game she played. Her intention was to ensure that no one other than Rebbe's students would understand her. Many of those students were prominent rabbis themselves; otherwise, they may not have understood her intent. Indeed, the Talmud immediately goes on to relate that R. Yose son of Assyan and R. Abbahu, the latter one of the more frequently cited *Amora'im,* also employed "language of wisdom" in certain circumstances. Clearly, the maidservant was in excellent company. The stories about the maidservant, like so many of the Talmud's other stories, are a mixture of fact and fantasy. Perhaps that is why the Talmud never mentions the maidservant's name; it was forgotten due to both the passage of time and the tale's constant embellishment. Or perhaps it was simply that the rabbis found it embarrassing that an ordinary maid could hold her own with them.[173] Whatever the reason, she was manifestly a formidable individual. The incident regarding the broom would indicates that the maid was the senior servant in Rebbe's

171. Eiruvin 53b, per Rashi, s.v. *alat, nikfat bekad, yidun nishra.*
172. Ibid., per Rashi, s.v. *yaadei.*
173. For a discussion see Leonard Swidler, *Biblical Affirmations of Woman* (Philadelphia: Westminster, 1979), 106–110. Swidler offers a somewhat different view of the maidservant's intellectual prowess.

household, along the lines of senior servants in the stately homes of the British aristocracy, such as those made famous in "Downton Abbey," and was equally as influential.

Rebbe's household servants were devoted to him. Unlike many leaders, both in his days and in ours, Rebbe believed that loyalty was a two-way street. He demonstrated his conviction in this regard with one of his last pronouncements before passing on. His household had included two long-time servants, Joseph of Haifa and Simeon of Efrat. Accordingly, when on his deathbed Rebbe ordered that just as they had served him in life so they should do in death. Observers presumed that he meant that they should attend to his burial. As matters transpired, however, they passed away before him and were buried first. Clearly, service in this world was not Rebbe's intent; he must have meant service in the world to come. And the reason he had issued this rather unusual injunction was to ensure that they would not be victims of nasty gossip that they had sinned in some way and that it was only due to Rebbe's merits that they had survived as long as they had. For Rebbe, loyalty to those loyal to him extended even beyond the grave.[174]

REBBE'S STUDENTS AND JUDICIAL COLLEAGUES

Based on his encyclopedic knowledge of the Talmud, Maimonides lists eleven rabbis who were Rebbe's leading students and served as members of his court.[175] Two were his sons, Simeon and Gamaliel; and among his other leading students were R. Afes, R. Hanina bar Hama, R. Hiyya, Rav, Bar Kappara, and possibly Rav's great counterpart in Babylonia, "Mar" Samuel.[176] Rebbe's students spread the word of Torah throughout Palestine and the Diaspora to a far greater degree than ever before.

174. Ketubot 103a.
175. Maimonides, *Mishneh Torah*, Introduction (Hebrew).
176. Maimonides (ibid.) also includes R. Yohanan, R. Hoshaya, R. Yannai. These were younger students; R. Yohanan, for one, admitted that he did not really understand what Rebbe was teaching (see Ḥullin 137b). While he does not challenge Maimonides' list, R. Abraham of Posquieres (Raavad) argues that Samuel, R. Yohanan, R. Hoshaya, R. Yannai, and Bar Kappara were not members of the court. Instead, Raavad identifies Levi, R. Bisa and his son R. Hama, R. Yishmael b. R. Yose, and

R. Hiyya

Of Rebbe's students, the best known are probably R. Hiyya, Levi, Rav, and Samuel. R. Hiyya b. Abba[177] was more than just a student of Rebbe. He was one his most prominent colleagues, both in the academy and on Rebbe's judicial bench. He was referred to as R. Hiyya the Great; even Rebbe sometimes applied that epithet to him.[178] His father, Abba Karsala, hailed from Kafri, a town about 160 miles south of Baghdad, now known as Najaf, one of the two cities in modern Iraq that are holy to Shi'a Muslims. Kafri was the seat of both the high court for the Jewish community of Babylonia and, for a time, of its exilarch; since both Hiyya and the exilarch claimed to be descended from King David, they may have been related.[179] Kafri was also located near the town of Sura, where R. Hiyya's nephew, Abba Arikha, better known as Rav, would later found a great yeshiva.

Hiyya had a rather unhappy personal life. He had two twin daughters named Pazi and Tavi, one of whom died after being betrothed to Rebbe's son.[180] R. Hiyya then had two sons, Judah and Hezekiah, whom the Talmud calls twins, though one appears to have been born after seven months while the other was carried to term. Apparently Hiyya's wife Judith had a very difficult pregnancy and was determined to bear no more children. The Talmud relates two different stories in that regard. One version states that she told her husband that her mother told her that she had been betrothed to someone else when she was a child. Hiyya dismissed her story with the remark that her mother could not be relied upon in order to prevent them from having marital relations.[181] The second story,

---

R. Yose b. Lekunia. Based on estimates of the dates of their birth and the Talmud's assertions regarding their teachers, Raavad's critique appears accurate, with the exception of Samuel, whom the Talmud records as curing Rebbe of an eye disease.

177. R. Hiyya's father was named Abba, but the Talmud refers to him solely as R. Hiyya. He is not to be confused with the later *Amora* to whom the Talmud always refers as R. Hiyya b. Abba.

178. Y. Kilayim 9:2; Y. Ketubot 12:3; Genesis Rabba 33:3.

179. Neusner, "Economic and Political Life," 183.

180. Yevamot 63a.

181. Kiddushin 12b.

which would appear to follow naturally upon the first, relates that she donned a disguise and approached her husband with the question as to whether a woman was subject to the same commandment to have children as was a man. When he told her that a woman was exempt from the commandment, she drank a contraceptive potion and some time later told him what she had done. His response was that he hoped the potion would not be effective and that they could have another child.[182]

Perhaps because she felt that her husband seemed indifferent to her pain, perhaps because she was suffering from post-partum depression, Judith became an embittered woman. It did not help matters that though his two sons became great rabbis in their own right, one of them died young.[183] Judith became an extremely difficult person to live with; she constantly tormented him. He nevertheless possessed a good nature and took his difficulties in stride. His motto could well have been "happy wife, happy life." He continued to ply her with expensive gifts, on the grounds that she was a good religious mother and prevented him from immoral entanglements.

At some point R. Hiyya and his sons emigrated to Judaea. He established himself as a silk merchant and evidently made a success of his trade.[184] His business travels may have taken him to Edesa, which had a Jewish community, and which also was the birthplace of Julia Domna, Septimius Severus' second wife. Hiyya's earnings were not just from the silk trade, however. Whether before or after arriving in Judaea, he seems to have come into possession of "large tracts of land in the Galilee, particularly around Tiberias."[185]

Having established roots in the Galilee, Hiyya soon found his way to Rebbe's court and became a key member of Rebbe's circle. Rebbe recognized his vast knowledge of Torah and treated him as virtually an equal rather than as a mere student, though Hiyya was considerably younger. He became a close and trusted aide.

182. Yevamot 65b.
183. Ibid., 63a.
184. Genesis Rabba 79:2.
185. Neusner, "Economic and Political Life," 169.

R. Hiyya's twin sons, Judah and Hezekiah, were also part of Rebbe's circle, and he would have them dine at his table. On one such occasion, Rebbe sought to test their Torah knowledge in the manner that centuries later, a dean of a Lithuanian yeshiva often would test a student (called *fahrherung*), except that they sat silently at the table. Rebbe then told his attendant to ply them with strong wine so as to loosen their tongues. Once they were inebriated, they said: "The son of David [the Messiah] cannot come until the two major houses of Israel are terminated, these being the exilarch in Babylonia and the patriarch in the Land of Israel, as it is written, *He will be a Sanctuary, a stone for stumbling, and a rock that entraps for the two houses of Israel.*"[186] Rebbe, clearly shaken that they were foretelling the extinction of his dynasty, exclaimed, "My sons, are you throwing thorns in my eyes?" R. Hiyya sought to mollify his agitated teacher: "My rabbi," he said, "don't be offended: the *gematria* [numerical value of Hebrew letters] for both wine (*yayin*) and a secret (*sod*) is identical and amounts to seventy for both. When wine goes in, secrets come out." The Talmud does not record whether Rebbe calmed down.[187]

The relationship between the two men was not without friction, as might be expected when two exceedingly talented individuals work closely together under sometimes stressful conditions. For one thing, while R. Hiyya accorded Rebbe the respect due his official position, he was somewhat disdainful of Rebbe's scholarship. When Rav put a question to Rebbe from a tractate that the academy was not reviewing at the time, R. Hiyya admonished him, "Have I not told you that when Rebbe is engaged on one tractate you must not question him about another, lest he be not conversant with it. For if Rebbe were not a great man, you would have put him to shame, for he might have answered you incorrectly."[188] The implication was clear: the breadth of Rebbe's knowledge was limited to the subject matter at hand, and there were others who were more proficient in the "sea of the Talmud."

186. Is. 8:14.
187. Sanhedrin 38a.
188. Berakhot 57a. See also Neusner, "Economic and Political Life," 187–88.

In another instance, the Babylonian Talmud relates that Rebbe was opposed to teaching Torah in public, but R. Hiyya defied him and taught his two nephews, Rav and Rabba bar Bar Hana "in the marketplace."[189] Rebbe was exceedingly annoyed and banned R. Hiyya for thirty days. Once the ban was over, Rebbe asked him why he had contravened his order. R. Hiyya replied with a quotation from Proverbs: "Wisdom cries aloud in the street... at the entrance of the gates."[190] But Rebbe chided him saying:

> If you have read Holy Scripture, you have not read it a second time; if you have read it a second time, you have not read it a third time; and if you have read it a third time, they [who taught you] have not explained it to you. "Wisdom cries aloud in the streets" is in the sense in which Rava [explained it]; for Rava said: "If one studies the Torah indoors, the Torah proclaims his merit abroad."

The reference to Rava, who lived decades after Rebbe, indicates that the tale may have been fashioned, or at least heavily edited, by the Babylonian rabbis. In any event, it is clear that they preferred that their studies be closed to the general public, despite the fact that tradition beginning with Scripture itself mandated the study of Torah by all of Israel. It was the Babylonian rabbis' disdain for the unlearned that motivated their attribution to Rebbe of behavior that so clearly contradicted tradition passed down from Sinai.[191]

The Jerusalem Talmud and *Midrash Rabba* attribute Rebbe's ban to an entirely different and far more plausible incident. Rebbe was exceedingly sensitive about his status because he was only descended from King David through his mother, rather than through his father, as was the Babylonian exilarch.[192] While Rebbe was prepared to yield his patriarchate to the exilarch if ever they should come into contact, it was

---

189. Mo'ed Katan 16a–b.
190. Prov. 1:20–21.
191. Rubenstein, *Culture*, 137–30.
192. Y. Kilayim 9:3.

clearly a circumstance that he preferred to avoid. Thus Rebbe was not amused when R. Hiyya informed him that R. Huna the exilarch had arrived in Palestine, but only explained that he had arrived in a coffin after he saw Rebbe's consternation at the potential challenge to his status – a reaction common to senior government officials from his day to ours. Outraged, Rebbe banished R. Hiyya for thirty days.

The Talmud then recounts that it was only after Elijah the Prophet assumed R. Hiyya's identity and healed Rebbe's long-standing toothache that Rebbe and R. Hiyya reconciled.[193] The story is a charming one and reflects the Talmud's association of Elijah with all sorts of miracles, in this case serving as a dental surgeon to restore R. Hiyya's place at Rebbe's court. That Rebbe believed it actually was R. Hiyya was due to the fact that R. Hiyya did indeed practice what was then considered to be the art of medicine. At bottom, the story also offers another insight into Rebbe's character: though deeply concerned about his image and status, to the point of having a short temper, he could be won over through an act of kindness. It was not that he did not bear grudges, for he did, but he only did so if he was not offered any opportunity for reconciliation with the perceived offending party.

Another talmudic tale involving Elijah, Rebbe, and R. Hiyya also deserves mention.

> Elijah used to frequent Rebbe's academy. One day – it was New Moon – he was waiting for him, but he did not appear. [The next day Rebbe] said to him: "Why were you delayed?" He replied: "[I had to wait] until I awoke Abraham, washed his hands, and he prayed and I put him to rest again; and similarly for Isaac and similarly for Jacob." "But why not awake them together?" – "I worried that they would pray so powerfully that [if all pray together][194] they would bring Messiah ahead of his time." "And is there anyone like them in this world?" – "There are R. Hiyya and his sons." Rebbe then decreed a fast, and they brought R. Hiyya and his sons down to the *ḥazzan*'s

193. Y. Kilayim 9:3; Genesis Rabba 33:3.

194. Thus Rashi, Bava Metzia 85b, s.v. *umaytai.*

> stand. When [R. Hiyya] pronounced, "He causes the wind to blow," a wind blew; when he said, "He brings down the rain," the rain came. When he was about to say, "He resurrects the dead," the universe trembled, [and] in Heaven it was asked, "Who revealed our secret to the world?" They said, "Elijah." So they brought Elijah and subjected him to sixty flaming lashes; Elijah then went off and disguised himself as a fiery bear, entered among them and scattered them.[195]

These stories of Elijah not only demonstrate what a distinguished teacher Rebbe was – after all, not everyone had the honor of lecturing to the great prophet – but also indicate the esteem in which later generations held R. Hiyya. Indeed, the miracles recounted in this story were not the only ones with which R. Hiyya was later associated. The Talmud credited his arrival in Palestine as the reason storms no longer occurred and no wine soured during the remainder of his lifetime.[196] His prayers were credited with bringing rain and driving off a lion that had wrought havoc on Palestine's roads.[197]

When R. Hiyya spoke of his accomplishments, he did not talk of miracles. He appears to have been proudest of the fact that he spread Torah knowledge throughout the community. As he once put it in a debate with his colleague R. Hanina:

> I guarantee that the Torah shall not be forgotten in Israel. I bring flax seed, sow it, and weave nets [from the plant]. [With the nets] I hunt stags with whose flesh I feed orphans and from whose skins I prepare scrolls, and then proceed to a town where there are no teachers of young children, and write out the five Books of the Pentateuch for five children and teach another six children respectively the six orders of the Mishna, and then tell each one: "Teach your section to your colleagues."[198]

195. Bava Metzia 85b.
196. Ḥullin 36a.
197. Genesis Rabba 31:18.
198. Bava Metzia 85b.

Rebbe was deeply appreciative of R. Hiyya's commitment to spreading the word of Torah. He exclaimed, "How great are the deeds of Hiyya!" and when his son Simeon asked, "Are they greater even than yours?" Rebbe replied in the affirmative.[199] It is noteworthy however, that when Rebbe was asked the same question with relation to R. Yose, he replied, "God forbid, let no such thing be [mentioned] in Israel!"[200]

Hiyya ultimately came to be called R. Hiyya the Great. He was intimately familiar with those elements of law and tradition that Rebbe chose to omit when he edited the Mishna. R. Hiyya proceeded to edit that body of non-mishnaic laws into what became called "the *baraitot* of R. Hiyya." Tradition also ascribed to him the compilation of non-mishnaic elements called "Tosefta (addition)" which became almost as critical a source of talmudic legal precedent as the Mishna itself. His greatness as a scholar was underscored by another legend according to which stones of fire fell from the skies at his passing.[201]

Rav

Rav's name was actually Abba b. Aivo; and he went by the nickname Abba Arikha (Abba the long one), because he was very tall. Born in 175, Rav's maternal uncle was R. Hiyya, whose daughter's hand Rebbe had initially sought for his son. Rav was thus a scion of the same prominent Babylonian family that claimed descent from King David's brother Shimi.

Rebbe ordained Rav, though he set a precedent still followed to this day by not empowering him to rule on every issue brought before him. The Talmud relates: "When Rav went there [to Babylonia], R. Hiyya said to Rebbe: 'My sister's son is going to Babylon. May he rule (*yoreh*) on matters of ritual law?' 'He may so rule (*yoreh*).' 'May he rule (*yadin*) on [monetary] cases?' 'He may so rule (*yadin*).' 'May he declare first-born animals permissible for slaughter?' 'He may not.'"[202]

---

199. Ketubot 103b; Bava Metzia 85b records a variant in which it is R. Yishmael b. R. Yose who asks the question.
200. Ketubot 103b.
201. Mo'ed Katan 25b.
202. Sanhedrin 5a.

The ability to ordain – to confer *semikha,* or *minui* as it was called in Palestine, was a powerful tool in Rebbe's hands that he guarded jealously. Prior to his taking office, the patriarch had no special authority to ordain. In acquiring that right, apparently through a concession granted him by his colleagues on the Sanhedrin,[203] Rebbe was able to ensure that virtually all religious judges were beholden to him. This may not have been the Sanhedrin's intention; for his part, however, Rebbe – no mean politician – understood exactly the ultimate consequence of their granting him that authority.

It is also noteworthy that Rebbe's grant of *semikha* was also recognized as authoritative in Babylonia. One might have expected ordination of Babylonian rabbis to be a privilege held exclusively by, or perhaps jointly with, the exilarch. Clearly, the example of Rav illustrates that this was not the case.[204]

The Talmud asks why Rebbe did not grant Rav permission to rule on the third category. Permission to slaughter a first-born animal depended on a determination that a blemish in the animal was permanent. If it was determined that the blemish was temporary, nothing could be done and it could not be slaughtered, since there was no longer a Temple wherein it could be eaten by the Priests. Since Rav was an acknowledged expert in all matters relating to Rebbe's teachings, his mandate would have been expected to extend to this area as well.

The Talmud offers two explanations. It speculates that indeed Rav was a noted expert in the matter of blemishes, and precisely because he was, he would have overshadowed another of R. Hiyya's nephews, Rabba the son of his brother, Bar Hana, who also returned to Babylonia. Rabba bar Bar Hana has been called "the Munchausen of the Talmud" because of his many tall tales, but he was more than just a story-teller. He was a genuine scholar, though not of the same rank as Rav. Rebbe, sensitive to the fact that Rabba bar Bar Hana's expertise would be dismissed

203. This is the view of classical commentators and modern historians. Alon, *Jews in Their Land*, 708, argues that Rebbe was granted this right *de facto* but not *de jure*. On the other hand, the twelfth/thirteenth-century scholar R. Meir ben Todros Halevi Abulafia appears to accept that Rebbe obtained *de jure* authority as well. *Yad Rama*, Sanhedrin 5a, s.v. *veha*.

204. See also Alon, *Jews in Their Land*, 10; Urbach, *The Halakhah*, 295.

by those who would merely see him as a raconteur, judged that Rav's reputation was sufficiently secure that he need not have the additional designation as a judge of ritual blemishes.

The second talmudic explanation focuses specifically on Rav's expertise. The Talmud asserts that Rav's sophistication in matters of blemishes was so great that he might permit certain blemishes and this would lead non-experts to conclude, erroneously, that blemishes similar to these were permanent when they were actually transitory, so that the animal was forbidden from being slaughtered. Better, therefore, that he not treat of blemishes at all.[205]

Each explanation offers an insight into the way later generations of talmudists viewed Rebbe. The first demonstrates his extreme sensitivity toward the feelings of his students, based no doubt on his own unhappy experiences both in the yeshiva of R. Eleazar b. Shammua, where he had been harassed by his fellow-students ("like the cocks of Beit Bukia"), and in the yeshiva of R. Meir, who ignored him. Rebbe knew that Rav was the superior student and would overshadow Rabba bar Bar Hana. Indeed, Rav went on to found the first major yeshiva in Babylonia and to devise the method of interpreting the Mishna that became the template for all talmudic analysis of that work. Nevertheless, Rebbe also recognized that Rabba too was talented and deserved the respect of the Babylonian community and its rabbis. Recognizing that Rav's reputation would remain intact, he afforded an extra honor to the son of Bar Hana.

Nowadays, not every student who earns the designation "rabbi" is granted the same level of authority to render halakhic decisions. Some students receive a diploma that simply names them *rav beYisrael* (a rabbi in Israel), with no specific authority to rule at all. Others are given "permission to rule" (*heter horaa*). More talented students are granted the formulation that Rebbe used for ruling on ritual matters, *yoreh,* to include issues of what is permitted and forbidden in matters of *kashrut,* centered on the portion of *Shulḥan Arukh* known as *Yoreh De'ah* (and in some yeshivas additionally on the section called *Oraḥ Ḥayyim*). The term itself incorporates both R. Hiyya's request to Rebbe

205. Sanhedrin 5b.

and Rebbe's reply. Finally, in order to obtain the license to rule on monetary matters, termed *yadin* (again borrowing R. Hiyya's request and Rebbe's response), a student must pursue advanced legal studies, primarily involving the rulings in the part of the *Shulḥan Arukh* known as *Ḥoshen Mishpat.*

The second explanation for Rebbe's refusal to grant Rav the same license as Rabba reflects his concern that exceedingly sophisticated rulings would mislead the pious masses. The Talmud is noted for its casuistry, an approach that has persisted throughout the ages as a way of addressing the many complications that arise from that body of work. While Rebbe was not above employing that methodology himself on occasion, he did not want it to distort what he considered to be a straightforward approach to Jewish law that ordinary Jews could understand and follow. He recognized that an excess of rabbinical cleverness could lead either to unwitting transgression or, worse, to cynicism about the law and the rabbis who promulgated it.

In practice, there was a third reason as well. Not every scholar was granted – or needed – the highest level of ordination. Not every ordained rabbi was, or needed to be, a scholar of the first rank; many were appointed to fill the needs of their communities. In that respect, little has changed from Rebbe's days to ours. The most famous leader of Ashkenazi Jewry in the mid-twentieth century, Abraham Yeshaya Karelitz, known as the Hazon Ish, was never formally ordained. On the other hand, many lesser lights have become communal rabbis both in Israel and throughout the Diaspora. In any event, despite his lack of the highest level of ordination, Rav was acknowledged as a leading decisor: the Talmud records that the citizens of both Babylon and its environs adhered to his rulings.[206]

Rav appears to have commuted between Babylonia and Palestine. He was sufficiently active in Rebbe's court that the Talmud records him challenging not only rulings of the *Tanna'im*, a privilege not accorded to the *Amora'im*, among whom Rav was otherwise counted, but even anonymous rulings in the Mishna. As a general principle, when the Mishna recorded a decision without attribution to any rabbi, the assumption

206. Ketubot 54a.

was that the decision had been reached unanimously.[207] According to talmudic rules of jurisprudence, however, if a member of the *beit din* had not been available to make his case when it reached a decision, he could still argue a contrary position afterwards, because the biblical injunction of following the majority (*aḥarei rabim lehatot*)[208] had not been fulfilled. Rav's commitments in Babylonia must at times have prevented his participation in the court's deliberations; he could only articulate his dissenting views after a decision had already been taken. It was when he had done so that the biblical standard was met, and Rebbe recorded the opinion in the Mishna without attribution, because Rav had made his case after the actual decision had been reached.[209]

In 219, near the end of Rebbe's life, Rav moved permanently to Babylonia, and founded the great yeshiva at Sura, a town located near the branching of the Euphrates. The yeshiva lasted into the eleventh century, under the leadership of *Amora'im* and then *Geonim*, of whom the most notable was the tenth-century Rav Saadia Gaon. Its fortunes fluctuated during its eight-hundred-year existence: it was at times overshadowed by rival academies at Nehardea, when that academy was led by Rav's younger contemporary Samuel, and later at Pumpeditha. It also closed on several occasions only to reopen and continue to function. Whatever its vicissitudes, the yeshiva at Sura was one of Rav's greatest legacies, second only to his many dicta that have enriched halakha for nearly two thousand years.

Levi

Levi bar Sisi was nowhere near as prominent as R. Hiyya; indeed, Maimonides does not even list him among those of Rebbe's leading students

207. There were cases when Rebbe recorded a ruling without attribution that was actually the view of an individual *Tanna*. He did so in order to create the impression that the ruling in question represented a majority view rather than that of an individual. See Rashi, Beitza 2b, s.v. *man satam*. I am indebted to R. Brahm Weinberg for pointing me to this source.

208. Ex. 23:2.

209. For a discussion, see Rabbi Micah Segelman, "The Status of Minority Opinions in Halacha," *The Journal of Halacha and Contemporary Society* 71 (Pesach 5776/Spring 2106), 66n12.

who transmitted his teachings to the next generation. Moreover, Levi (the Talmud rarely mentioned his father's name, presuming that he was so famous that all knew who *that* Levi was) never received ordination. Unlike Rav, who was permitted to issue rulings on ritual matters and judgments on financial ones, Levi received no such permissions. Yet Levi was recognized as a leading scholar, and in his relationship with Rebbe he was described as "those who sit before the wise," a phrase which became a code word for Levi whenever his name was not mentioned explicitly.[210]

Perhaps precisely because Levi was an intimate of Rebbe's, he at times found himself on the receiving end of his master's taunts. When Levi questioned Rebbe why he listed only fifteen cases that exempted a childless woman from having to either marry her late husband's brother or be subject to the *ḥalitza* ceremony, when in fact there were other cases where the exemption applied, Rebbe slapped him down with the remark "He seems to have no brains in his head."[211] Rebbe used the same gibe when he was told that Levi claimed he had found a solution to a complicated question regarding the confusion that arose when a cow was designated as a replacement for another that had been meant to serve as a sacrifice, only to have one of the two cows die without there being a clear indication as to which cow had died – the one originally identified as a sacrifice or its replacement.[212] It is possible that Rebbe simply was acting impatiently toward a subordinate, as many superiors do, for he certainly did not consider Levi to be anything but brilliant. Or Rebbe may have been under great stress. Because the Talmud is not written in any chronological order and is not a historical record even in the Greek and Roman sense of the word, there is no way to know what other concerns might have been on Rebbe's mind that led him to snap at one of his favorite students. Whatever the reason, the rebuke must have hurt.[213]

---

210. Sanhedrin 17b.
211. Yevamot 9a.
212. Menaḥot 80b has Rebbe replying, "It seems to me this man has no brains in his head."
213. Rebbe generally had no patience for questions or comments that he considered foolish. The Talmud (Menaḥot 37a) reports that one Polemo asked him upon which head a two-headed man should place his tefillin. Rebbe responded brusquely by telling him to leave the academy or be excommunicated. The Talmud clearly did

Levi was described by his contemporaries as great, tall, and lame.[214] He also appears to have been rather shy; he was most comfortable in the academy. Like many outstanding graduates of contemporary yeshivas, he was ill-suited to leading a congregation, evidently because of a lack of people skills.

It has already been noted that when Rebbe was passing through Simonias, in the lower Galilee, he responded to the townspeople's request for a religious functionary – lecturer, judge, superintendent of the synagogue, public scribe, and teacher[215] – by dispatching Levi to Simonias to serve in what would today be termed the local community rabbi. The townspeople erected a large podium and upon his arrival placed him on it. Those in the community who were more educated then put three rather abstruse questions to him, two of which related to the *ḥalitza* ceremony, which requires a childless widow to remove her brother-in-law's shoe and spit at him in order to avoid marrying him. In order to gauge Levi's expertise, they asked him whether the ceremony would be valid, first, if it involved an armless woman, and second, if the widow spat blood rather than saliva. Finally they asked him to interpret the statement by Daniel "I will tell you that which is inscribed in the Writing of Truth." Was one to infer that there existed divine writing that was not true?

When Levi was unable to answer even one of the three queries, the community of Simonias rejected him as their spiritual guide. The rejection of Levi reflected badly on Rebbe, who had chosen Levi to lead that community. The people accused him of sending someone unfit to

---

not approve of Rebbe's behavior, for it immediately cites a case similar to that which Polemo had raised. The question in this matter was how much the father of a two-headed firstborn should give the priest after thirty days – five shekels, as was the normal case, or ten. The Talmud's ruling: ten.

214. Shabbat 59b.

215. Schwartz (*Imperialism*, 122) argues that the fact that it was the townspeople who approached Rebbe demonstrates that Rebbe had "something less than formal administrative authority" but rather was petitioned because of his personal prestige. Schwartz's argument is hardly airtight, however. Since Rebbe was passing through the town, it was natural that he was asked to name a functionary. That does not mean that if he had not been in the vicinity but had learned of the need for a community leader, he would not have been in a position to appoint one.

lead. Naturally stung by this accusation, Rebbe insisted to the people of Simonias that Levi was eminently qualified, and that indeed Levi was as qualified as he was. Luckily, the people did not respond that perhaps Rebbe also was unqualified; they had implicitly challenged his competence and therefore the legitimacy of his authority. Puzzled as to why Levi had muffed his first interview, Rebbe summoned him and put the same three questions to him. Levi answered them all, saying that the Torah did not explicitly require that the woman use her hand, or spit spittle, while the passage in Daniel referred to a case where the writing was accompanied by a divine oath and therefore could never be reversed, while writing unaccompanied by an oath was reversible.

Levi's correct replies only added to Rebbe's confusion. He asked Levi why he did not offer the correct answers to the people of Simonias. Levi answered that he had developed cold feet; he simply did not see himself as a communal leader. He was purely a scholar at heart.[216]

When Rebbe was dying, he ordered that Levi's great friend, R. Hanina bar Hama, should preside over the yeshiva. R. Hanina ceded the post to Rebbe's secretary, R. Afes, who was a few years older than he. Nevertheless, R. Hanina could not bring himself to attend R. Afes' lectures, because he considered himself to be the more capable scholar. When R. Hanina removed himself from the yeshiva, Levi opted to join his friend. Upon R. Afes' passing, R. Hanina succeeded him and Levi, having lost his study partner, migrated to Babylonia. His reputation preceded him, thanks in part to Rav's endorsement, and he became a lecturer at the yeshiva in Nehardea.[217]

Upon his arrival in Nehardea, Levi befriended Abba bar Abba, better known as "the father of Samuel." (Samuel was Levi's most famous student, who later assumed the presidency of the yeshiva.) The two older men would travel together; they would rise early, say the morning prayers, and later in the morning recite the *Shema* at the appropriate time.[218] They would occasionally issue a joint ruling:

216. Y. Yevamot 12:6. The Babylonian Talmud, Yevamot 105a, has the members of Rebbe's academy providing the correct responses.
217. Shabbat 59a; Ketubot 103b.
218. Berakhot 30a.

as when they prohibited a lentil drink because it might be mixed with non-kosher vinegar.[219] Levi predeceased both Samuel and his father; at his passing he was eulogized as being worth as much as all of humanity.[220]

R. Hanina bar Hama

R. Hanina spent most of his days in Palestine, though he did visit Babylonia. Originally a student of Rebbe's students R. Hiyya and Bar Kappara, he eventually became attached to Rebbe's academy and to Rebbe himself. Under Rebbe's tutelage he became accomplished and self-confident to the point of arrogance. In a dispute over a point of law, he challenged his former master R. Hiyya: "Do you dispute with me? Were the Torah, God forbid, to be forgotten in Israel, I would restore it by means of my dialectical arguments." R. Hiyya, older and wiser, responded calmly by noting his exertions, outlined above, to foster Torah education and thereby preserve it for future generations.[221]

R. Hanina was several decades younger than Rebbe, and the older man took to him; he became Rebbe's intimate, much as R. Hiyya had been some time earlier. Unfortunately, R. Hanina did not intuit that intimacy is not the same thing as excessive familiarity, and that this was especially the case with Rebbe, who did not tolerate *lèse majesté*. Thus when R. Hanina publicly corrected Rebbe when he mispronounced a word in a passage from Ezekiel, and then compounded his error by announcing that he had learned his Bible from R. Hamnuna of Babylonia, Rebbe became annoyed. Rebbe did not consider R. Hamnuna his equal in scholarship, so he snapped: "When you go to Babylonia, tell him to ordain you as a *ḥakham*." R. Hanina recognized that he had fallen out of favor; and indeed, he was never ordained by his master.[222]

R. Hanina had two sons and two daughters; one son and one daughter both died young.[223] A physician, he explained that he shed

219. Avoda Zara 38b.
220. Y. Berakhot 2:8.
221. Ketubot 103b.
222. Avoda Zara 10b.
223. Bava Kamma 91b and Shabbat 151b.

no tears for the loss of his daughter because he felt they were bad for his eyesight. His surviving son, Hama, who carried the same name as his grandfather, became a major scholar in his own right. His surviving daughter married a scholar, R. Samuel b. Nadav.[224]

As a physician, R. Hanina advocated wellness, especially the prevention of colds. Despite his qualifications, he was heartily disliked by the people of Sepphoris, where he was attached to Rebbe's household. He tended to blame the townspeople for whatever misfortune that happened to them. Thus when they blamed him for failing to stop a plague, he promptly blamed *them* for committing adultery and bringing the plague on themselves.[225] When he was unable to end a drought, even when he prayed alongside R. Joshua b. Levi, who had ended a drought in the south, he again blamed the townspeople for failing to submit to the Law, unlike the southerners who had done so and thus merited rain.

Clearly, Rebbe was not alone in finding that R. Hanina could be annoying. Nevertheless, Rebbe was not one to overlook a young talent. He also considered him to be a miracle worker, who could bring the dead back to life.[226] On his own deathbed Rebbe announced that R. Hanina should serve as head of the yeshiva, though the latter chose not do so until the more senior R. Afes passed away.

R. Hanina lived to a ripe and vigorous old age. He had the pleasure of seeing his students become leading scholars. Ever the physician, he attributed his good health to the hot baths and oil that his mother had given him when he was a child.

Samuel

Traditional commentators disagree as to whether Samuel bar Abba, known also as "Mar Samuel" and "Samuel Yarkhina'a," actually studied under Rebbe. There is no disagreement, however, that he did interact with the patriarch, curing him of a chronic eye disease. Samuel was not only a leading talmudic scholar and head of the yeshiva at

224. Arakhin 16b.
225. Bava Metzia 107b.
226. See below, p. 219.

Nehardea, but also a physician, an astronomer, and a veterinarian; he had non-Jewish friends; according to the Talmud, he had a strong personal relationship with the Persian emperor Shapur I. In other words, whether or not he actually studied under Rebbe, his broad exposure to and knowledge of worldly matters were very much in the patriarch's mold.

Samuel's father, Abba bar Abba, was the leading scholar in Babylonia prior to Rav's arrival.[227] Initially he did not teach his son himself but instead hired a tutor for him. Samuel was a prodigy, however, and the tutor was no match for the young boy. As the Talmud records:

> Samuel's father found Samuel crying. He asked him, "Why are you crying?"
> "Because my teacher beat me."
> "But why?" [his father asked].
> "Because he [the teacher] said to me, 'You fed my son and didn't first [ritually] wash your hands.'"
> "And why didn't you wash them?"
> He replied: "He [the teacher's son] should eat and I should wash?"
> Said [his father]: "It's not enough that [your teacher] is not knowledgeable but he has to beat you as well?"[228]

Recognizing that the tutor had beaten his son for all the wrong reasons – one need not wash when feeding another if one is not eating as well – Abba bar Abba decided to teach Samuel himself. He later sent Samuel to study under Levi, when the latter returned to Babylonia upon R. Hanina's elevation to the deanship of Rebbe's yeshiva.

Samuel then moved on to Palestine, where he distinguished himself as a first-rate scholar.

He returned to Babylonia, where he initially appears to have served as a judge alongside his friend Karna. The two developed a reputation for high standards; whenever the Talmud referred to "the judges

227. He did not get along well with Rav, whose students actually beat him on one occasion (Y. Yevamot 15:4). For a discussion of this incident, see Lau, *Ḥakhamim*, vol. 4, 159–60.
228. Ḥullin 107b.

of Babylon" it meant them.[229] Samuel then went on to lead the academy at Nehardea after Rav had rejected the position. Together Rav and Samuel were termed "our rabbis in Babylon"[230] because of their outsized influence over the interpretation of the Mishna and the development of halakha. Indeed, Samuel was so confident of the academic excellence of the Babylonian yeshivas that R. Judah reported him as saying, "Just as it is forbidden to depart the Land of Israel for Babylonia, so it is forbidden to leave Babylonia for other lands."[231] Like Rav, Samuel's rulings held sway in the vicinity of his yeshiva: "Nehardea and all its environs followed Samuel."

Though the Talmud mentions only one meeting between Samuel and Rebbe (Samuel provided Rebbe with an ointment that healed his chronic eye infection), it seems unlikely that a scholar of Samuel's stature would not have interacted with the patriarch while he was in Palestine. Perhaps he was not Rebbe's student in a formal sense; but it is possible that Samuel, who was proficient in Rebbe's great work, the Mishna, also adopted some of Rebbe's progressive views.

Like Rebbe, Samuel held no biases against non-Jews. He made his views clear on numerous occasions, such as when he became angry at his attendant for paying a ferryman with an inferior product. On the basis of this incident, the Talmud attributed to Samuel the maxim that "it is forbidden to deceive anyone, even an idolater," a principle that has been incorporated into halakha but that to this day is far too often honored in the breach.[232]

Just as his views about non-Jews might be seen as progressive for his time, given the persecutions that his co-religionists had suffered at the hands of gentiles, so too were his views about medicine. The Talmud has numerous tales and statements relating to the "evil eye." Indeed, Rav was so convinced that the biblical statement "The Lord shall remove all sickness from you"[233] referred to the evil eye that he visited a cemetery, and

229. Sanhedrin 17b lists only Karna, but Rashi (Bava Batra 70b, s.v. *shtar kis*) lists them both.

230. Sanhedrin 17b.

231. Ketubot, 111a, Rashi, s.v. *kakh assur*. See also Maharsha, *Aggadot*, s.v. *kakh assur*.

232. Ḥullin 94a; Karo, *Shulḥan Arukh: Ḥoshen Mishpat, Hilkhot Onaa*, 228:5.

233. Deut. 7:15.

he asserted by means of incantations that he could determine who had died a natural death and who from the evil eye. As he put it: "Ninety-nine [have died] from an evil eye, and one from natural causes."[234] Samuel, a trained physician, would have none of it. The passage, he said, refers to the wind, because "all illness is caused by the wind," in other words, is airborne. In light of his milieu, and the superstition that was rampant among his colleagues – even one as distinguished as Rav – his observation, and willingness to state it openly, was nothing short of remarkable.

Again like Rebbe, Samuel befriended his emperor, in his case Shapur of Persia (*Shvor Malka* in talmudic Aramaic), known as Shapur the Great. Shapur was the second of the Sassanian line of Persian kings; his father Ardeshir had defeated the Parthians, established a Persian ruling house, and restored the ancient Zoroastrian religion of Persia. Unlike the Parthians, who had adopted a hands-off attitude to minorities' management of their internal affairs, Ardeshir, like the present-day rulers of Iran, saw religion and state as a single unit. Ardeshir's son, Shapur, was a great warrior; his most famous victory was his defeat and capture of the entire Roman army, including the emperor Valerian, at Edessa in 260 CE.

Rav seemed unable to accommodate to the new state of Persian politico-religious affairs. He had been on good terms with Artabanus V, the last king of Parthia, whom Ardeshir defeated in 224.[235] The Talmud relates that when Artabanus died, Rav borrowed the words of Rebbe's lament over the passing of Severus. Rav was probably fortunate in that all he suffered was alienation from the royal court; as one who was identified with the *ancien régime*, his fate could have been much more tragic.

Samuel had an entirely different relationship with the new ruling dynasty. He probably was acquainted with Ardeshir, but there is little record of their interaction. His relationship with Shapur was quite another matter; the many stories of his conversations with Samuel parallel those of Rebbe with Septimius Severus and/or Caracalla.

---

234. Bava Metzia 107b, see Rashi, s.v. *kol* and s.v. *avad.*

235. Some say Rav was friendly with Artabanus IV. (See Soncino commentary on Avoda Zara 10b.) This is unlikely, however, since Artabanus IV reigned over a century before Rav returned to Babylonia.

Samuel's close ties to the Sassanids may have contributed to one of his signal dicta, namely the well-known principle of *dina demalkhuta dina* (the law of the land is the law), which has governed Jewish behavior ever since.[236]

The Special Case of Bar Kappara

The Talmud is not short of people we would today call "characters." One of them, R. Jeremiah, was fond of asking abstruse, pointless questions. When he seemed to be poking fun at an assertion that a bird could only hop fifty cubits – he asked what if it had one foot over the fifty cubit line – that was too much for his colleagues, and they expelled him from the Tiberias academy. He was only readmitted after he displayed exceptional modesty in replying to halakhic questions that had been put to him.[237]

Perhaps the most prominent character of them all, however, was a brilliant scholar named Bar Kappara, whom we saw adding to R. Simeon b. Rebbe's distress about having sired a daughter. As his name implies, he was the son of R. Eleazar HaKapor, a leading *Tanna* whose twin dicta regarding man's fate are familiar to all who have perused the end of the fourth chapter of *Pirkei Avot* (Ethics of the Fathers). R. Eleazar was one of the most fatalistic individuals in all of rabbinic literature, as his final words in the fourth chapter of Avot make clear: "Without your consent you were formed, without your consent you were born, without your consent you live, without your consent you will die, and without your consent you will in the future have to give an account and reckoning before the Supreme King of kings, the Holy One, blessed be He."[238]

236. Samuel's dictum has not always been adopted by contemporary Jews, including Orthodox Jews. Indeed, a leading *ḥaredi* decisor actually was able to reason that Samuel's ruling did not apply to the laws of the United States. See Rabbi Menashe Klein, *Mishneh Halakhot: Mador HaTeshuvot: Mahadura Kamma*, vol. 6 (Brooklyn, NY: Mishne Halachoth Gedoloth Institute, 5758/1998), no. 277. He argues (s.v. *vegam*) that as democracies are not kingdoms, Samuel's dictum no longer applies!
237. Bava Batra 23b, 165b.
238. Avot 4:29; translation from *The Authorized Daily Prayer Book of the United Hebrew Congregations of the Commonwealth*, 4th ed., trans. with commentary Chief Rabbi Sir Jonathan Sacks (London: Collins, 2007), 552.

Bar Kappara – his full name was Eleazar ben Eleazar HaKapor – studied under Rebbe as well as in the academies of R. Nathan the Babylonian[239] and R. Jeremiah ben Eleazar, not to be confused with R. Jeremiah of the pointless questions, though the latter and Bar Kappara were kindred spirits. Bar Kappara's relationship with Rebbe was awkward at best, however, and not merely because of his remarks regarding the birth of R. Simeon's daughter. Several unpleasant incidents ultimately led Bar Kappara to leave Rebbe's circle and move south. He later founded his own yeshiva at Caesarea; among his students was the great aggadist R. Joshua b. Levi.

Despite his erudition, Bar Kappara never received ordination; Rebbe refused to ordain him because of his flippant attitude. Bar Kappara had previously annoyed Rebbe and his family at the marriage of Rebbe's son Simeon. The Talmud relates:

> Bar Kappara (once) said to Rebbe's daughter: "Tomorrow I will drink wine to your father's dancing and your mother's singing." Now Ben Eleasa, a very wealthy man, was...invited to the wedding of R. Simeon b. Rebbe. (At the wedding) Bar Kappara asked Rebbe, "What is meant by *to'eva* (the biblical term for abomination)?" He then refuted every explanation that Rebbe offered. Rebbe then said to him, "Explain it yourself." He replied, "Let your housewife come and fill a cup (of wine) for me." She did so, upon which he said to Rebbe, "Get up and dance for me, and I will tell you." This is what the Torah meant: *to'eva* is an acronym for *to'eh atta ba* – he leaves his actual wife and cohabits with a man instead.[240]

Rebbe, like most monarchs both in his days and in ours, always conducted himself publicly in an exceedingly dignified manner. Bar Kappara

239. *Midrash Tehillim* 12:4.

240. Nedarim 51a; see also R. Nissim Gerondi (Ran), s.v. *mai* and s.v. *to'eh*. Rashi, s.v. *to'eh*, interprets the retort as meaning a harlot. Maharsha, *Aggadot*, s.v. *mai to'eva*, notes the various sins to which the word *to'eva* applies; see also the following s.v. *umishum hakhi*.

was determined to get Rebbe to let his hair down. Not only did he get Rebbe to dance and Rebbe's wife to serve him, as he promised an obviously uneasy R. Simeon, he also made a lewd inference about Rebbe's marital relations, citing one of the biblical passages on forbidden liaisons.[241]

But that was not enough for Bar Kappara. The Talmud continues the story by noting that Bar Kappara asked Rebbe a second time, "What is meant by *tevel,* the biblical term for bestiality?" Once more Bar Kappara refuted all of Rebbe's explanations; and when a frustrated Rebbe again said, "You explain it," he again asked Rebbe to dance and have his wife bring him another cup of wine. When Rebbe complied a second time, Bar Kappara played on words again, stating that the biblical *tevel hu* stood for *tavlin yesh bah* (is there perfume in the animal?). Bar Kappara's reply implied the question "Is this form of sex sweeter than all other intimacies, that prompt a woman to leave her husband for an animal?"

Bar Kappara was venturing further into forbidden territory. Not only did he once again provoke Rebbe into dancing, and once again get Rebbe's wife to serve him, he seemed to be casting crude aspersions on her. Bar Kappara should have stopped taunting Rebbe, but he had abandoned any sense of propriety. He posed yet another lewd question: What is meant by *zimma,* the biblical term applied to incest? Again he refuted all of Rebbe's replies. Again he asked Rebbe to dance and asked for his wife to pour him a third cup of wine. At that point he said, *zimma* stands for three words, *zu mah hi* (who is this). Bar Kappara's point was that where there is widespread promiscuity, a man sires children from various wives, while a woman gives birth to children from different fathers. No one knows whose child belongs to whom, with the result that fathers marry daughters and brothers marry sisters.

Was Bar Kappara implying something nefarious about Rebbe and his wife? Rebbe's son-in-law, Ben Eleasa, decided he didn't want to find out: Bar Kappara's crudeness had proved too much for him. Ben Eleasa may have been unschooled in matters of Torah, but he did have a strong sense of right and wrong. He may have been aware of R. Eleazar ben Azariah's famous dictum recorded in *Ethics of the Fathers,* "If there is

241. Lev. 20:13.

no respect, there is no Torah."[242] Ben Eleasa knew how civilized people should behave. No doubt he also felt for his wife, Rebbe's daughter, who must have been shocked and embarrassed by her parents' humiliation at Bar Kappara's hands. As has already been noted, the Talmud relates that Ben Eleasa and his wife left the wedding in disgust.

Rebbe took no action to punish his student. Perhaps he realized that he should have been a bit more relaxed about the entire situation because it was an occasion for merriment. Even Bar Kappara's double entendres may not have been entirely out of line. To this day, many hasidic weddings will feature a professional jokester, known as a *badḥan*, whose Yiddish wisecracks can border on the risqué. Rebbe may have blamed himself for allowing Bar Kappara to provoke him.

> Bar Kappara tested Rebbe on another occasion. This incident also involved R. Simeon. R. Simeon, Rebbe's son, and Bar Kappara were once sitting and studying together when a difficulty arose about a certain passage. R. Simeon said to Bar Kappara, "This needs Rebbe's explanation." But Bar Kappara answered R. Simeon, "What could Rebbe say about this matter?" He went and told his father [what Bar Kappara had said]. Rebbe was annoyed. Bar Kappara went to Rebbe to visit him because he was unwell, but he said: "Bar Kappara, I have never known you!" Bar Kappara recognized that Rebbe had taken the matter to heart and submitted himself to reproof for thirty days.[243]

Given Bar Kappara's behavior at R. Simeon's wedding, it should come as no surprise that when R. Simeon married off his own daughter, Bar Kappara was not on the invitation list. The Midrash relates that Bar Kappara, never to be outdone, defaced the banquet hall gate with the inscription "After rejoicing comes death, so there is no point to rejoicing." While the phrase could have been his father's in Avot, it was not exactly what one would inscribe in a wedding book.

242. Avot 3:21.

243. Mo'ed Katan 16a, and Rashi s.v. *le'itḥazuyai.*

R. Simeon asked who had scribbled on the wall, and when told it was Bar Kappara, he decided to invite him. R. Simeon did this not because he had any regrets or change of heart at previously excluding Bar Kappara. Instead, recognizing that Bar Kappara could be uncontrollable, he decided that it was better that he not become an enemy. Bar Kappara, evidently delighted, regaled the wedding guests with "three hundred fox fables." Whether he knew these stories because he had been exposed to Hellenistic literature, such as Aesop's fables, or the stories were the product of a hyperactive mind, is not clear. He may have learned them from R. Meir, who, R. Yohanan later reported, also was able to relate three hundred fox stories, though only three had survived the passage of time.[244] Whatever the case, Bar Kappara was the hit of the wedding. The guests were so enraptured by his storytelling that they forgot to eat their dinner and all the food was returned to the kitchen.[245]

Bar Kappara's irrepressible behavior eventually brought down Rebbe's wrath upon him. What finally caused a rupture between the two men was another incident involving Ben Eleasa. It seems that Rebbe had told his son-in-law not to interrupt him while he was replying to

244. Sanhedrin 38b–39a. The three stories that R. Yohanan spoke of related to three different biblical passages, Ezek. 18:2, Lev. 19:36, and Prov. 11:8. Rashi combined the stories into one: The fox outsmarted the wolf first by slyly suggesting that the wolf help the Jews prepare their Shabbat meals, which resulted in the wolf getting beaten. When the wolf wanted to attack the fox, the fox, quoting a passage in Ezekiel said, "It's not my fault – your father helped the Jews prepare their meal and ate all the best bits." The fox then suggested that there was meat and cheese in a well which had a beam across it and had a bucket at either end of the beam (the "cheese" actually was a reflection of the moon). The fox jumped into the upper bucket and lowered himself to the water, while the second bucket rose to the top. The fox called the wolf to join him, and the greedy wolf jumped into the second bucket, causing the fox to rise and leave, quoting passages in Leviticus and Proverbs while the wolf struggled in the well. Rashi's stories may well have been influenced by Aesop's very different fable of a clever fox, an arrogant and foolish wolf, and a lion. Visotzky, ever eager to prove that rabbinic Judaism was, in his words, "a Roman religion," naturally assumes that Bar Kappara was influenced by Hellenistic fox fables. That the Jews may have developed fox fables of their own – as did the African Tswana, the ancient Dogon mythology, and Finnish mythology – seems beyond Visotzky's comprehension. Visotzky, *Aphrodite and the Rabbis*, 23.

245. Leviticus Rabba 28:2.

questions relating to Torah matters. Bar Kappara, always disruptive, whispered a complex riddle to Ben Eleasa and urged him to repeat it to Rebbe. Ben Eleasa, not realizing that he was being set up, did so. Rebbe, annoyed at the interruption, looked around, saw Bar Kappara smiling, and realized that it was he who had prompted Ben Eleasa. Rebbe had enough and informed Bar Kappara, "I do not recognize you as an elder or a sage." It was the ultimate rebuke, because it meant that Rebbe would never ordain Bar Kappara. Brilliant as he may have been, and great teacher that he was, Bar Kappara never was able to call himself "rabbi." His immature behavior finally had done him in.

REBBE AS EDUCATOR

Rebbe was exceedingly sensitive to his students' feelings, perhaps because of his own unhappy experience in the yeshiva of R. Eleazar b. Shammua. He had a small side door installed near his seat at the academy so that his students would not have to rise when he entered the hall. The Talmud relates that because the door was exclusively for Rebbe's use, it did not require a mezuza. Indeed, the Talmud subsequently exempted all doors used in similar fashion from the requirement for a mezuza.[246]

Rebbe's basic educational philosophy no doubt endeared him to his students. "Train the youth according to his way"[247] was his educational watchword. Rather than forcing his students to engage with matters that were of little interest them, he instead was inclined to let them focus on those subjects within the Jewish canon that most excited them. The Talmud relates:

> Levi and R. Simeon b. Rebbe were once sitting before Rebbe and expounded portions of Scripture. When they concluded that particular book, Levi said, "Now bring in the Book of Proverbs." But R. Simeon b. Rebbe said, "Bring the Book of Psalms." They overruled Levi and brought in the Psalms. When they came to the verse "but the Torah of God is his desire,"[248] Rebbe interpreted

246. Menaḥot 33a.
247. Prov. 22:6.
248. Ps. 1:2.

> the passage and remarked: "One can only learn well that part of the Torah which his heart desires." At which point Levi said, "My Rabbi, you have given us permission to leave."[249]

Levi had been overruled, perhaps because of Simeon's seniority, perhaps because Simeon was the patriarch's son. In ultimately allowing Levi to focus on those portions of Scripture that most interested him, Rebbe offered a model for the education of young students. He clearly believed that a student must be encouraged to enjoy the subject at hand and not be force-fed material that was of no interest to him. Perhaps he recalled his own unhappy experiences at some of the academies he had attended.

Rebbe's great student Rav, founder of the Babylonian yeshiva at Sura, interpreted the passage in Psalms in identical terms and applied the same principle to the teaching of both Torah and tradition.[250] It is a lesson well worth recalling in the context of modern curricula in Jewish day schools, for Rebbe's and Rav's approach stands in stark contrast to contemporary teaching methods. Sadly, all too often schoolchildren and young adults have found their Jewish studies to be stultifying and boring. Too many young people are turned off by mindless forms of teaching, rather than drawn to one or another aspect of the wealth of Jewish experience that could be made available to them. In particular, not everyone finds the identical degree of intellectual stimulus in studying Talmud, the staple of yeshiva education for centuries. Rebbe and Rav both understood this, and recognized that only by offering a variety of approaches to *limudei kodesh* (sacred studies) could they nourish their acolytes' fascination with their subject matter and thus lay the groundwork for a lifetime of commitment to Torah study. Thus they would be inspired to continue their studies and, hopefully, to maintain Jewish law and tradition.

Rebbe found other ways to keep his audiences interested in their studies. A midrash relates that once Rebbe was publicly teaching a Torah lesson when

249. Avoda Zara 19a.
250. See Rashi, s.v. *mimakom*.

> the audience began to doze off. He sought to wake them and said, "A young woman in Egypt gave birth to six hundred thousand souls in a single batch." There was in attendance a student named R. Yishmael b. R. Yose who asked, "Who was this?" Said Rebbe: "This was Jokhebed who gave birth to Moses, who was equal to sixty thousand, that is, all of Israel, as it is written: Then sang Moses and the children of Israel;[251] and the children of Israel did all that God commanded Moses,[252] and no prophet arose in Israel like Moses."[253]

Even if he was not always the most exciting of lecturers, at times putting his audience to sleep, most of Rebbe's students were completely in awe of their teacher. They considered him a miracle worker. It was related that two mutes who lived in his neighborhood would always attend his lectures in the *beit midrash*, and would nod and move their lips the entire time. Rebbe prayed for them and they were healed, and it transpired that they were experts in halakha, Midrash and the entire Talmud.[254]

Rebbe not only was respected but venerated. He was after all a man of more parts than most of them could comprehend. He was not only a scholar but an administrator, a statesman, and a wealthy landowner; and he was schooled in a language, Greek, that most of them did not understand. In short, he was a towering figure of almost mythical proportions.

The attitude of Rebbe's students prefigured the awe with which students at Yeshiva University continue to hold Rabbi Joseph Soloveitchik decades after his death. This level of reverence, exemplified by their referring to him as "the Rav" – that is, *the* rabbi – calls to mind what the Soviets used to term "cult of personality"; it has in no small part been due to his students' inability to absorb fully his mastery of either Talmud, or of philosophy, or of both. Much the same could be said of the degree to which Lubavitch Hasidim venerate their late rebbe,

251. Ex. 15:1.
252. Ibid. 39:32.
253. Deut. 34:10; the entire story appears in Song of Songs Rabba 4:2.
254. Ḥagiga 3a.

Rabbi Menachem Mendel Schneerson. He too was a man of remarkable breadth, a talmudic scholar, steeped in mysticism, yet in possession of strong academic credentials. It is perhaps no wonder, therefore, that just as some of Rebbe's students thought he might actually be the Messiah,[255] some of the Lubavitcher Rebbe's followers have continued to see him as the Messiah incarnate years after his passing.

Just as his students venerated him, so Rebbe demonstrated the greatest respect for them. As he put it, "I have learned much Torah from my teachers, and even more from my colleagues, but from my students more than all the rest."[256] The mutual admiration between the teacher and his students, as well as his colleagues, reflected the great degree to which Rebbe exemplified Ben Zoma's dictum: "Who is wise? Who learns from everyone."[257]

Rebbe's students went on to establish Torah centers throughout Palestine and in the Diaspora. At least three headed yeshivot: Bar Kappara in Caesarea and then Lod,[258] Rav in Sura, and Samuel in Nehardea. As a contemporary scholar has put it, Rebbe "expanded the reach of the rabbis into cities, in tune with the greater urbanization of Palestine. Tzipori (Sepphoris), Lod (Lydda), Tiberias, and other cities became centers for Jewish study."[259] A teacher's most important legacy is to be found in the activities of his or her students; by that measure alone, Rebbe must be ranked among Judaism's greatest educators.

REBBE AND NIGER'S REBELLION

Rebbe had held his office for at least two decades when Pescennius Niger, the governor of Syria, rebelled in the aftermath of the demise of both Commodus and Pertinax and laid claim to the imperial throne. The Jewish community of Roman Palestine had little sympathy for

255. Discussed below.
256. Horayot 10a.
257. Avot 4:1.
258. Ben Zion Rosenfeld demonstrates that Bar Kappara also led a yeshiva in Lod. See Ben Zion Rosenfeld, *Torah Centers and Rabbinic Activity in Palestine 70–400 CE: History and Geographic Distribution*, trans. Chava Cassell (Leiden and Boston, MA: Brill, 2010), 45–46 and 46n14.
259. Barry W. Holtz, *Rabbi Akiva: Sage of the Talmud* (New Haven and London: Yale University Press, 2017), 34.

rebellion and even less for the prospect that Pescennius Niger might be the next Caesar.

Niger appears to have been the scion of an Italian equestrian family; he himself served in the army as an equestrian. He was a man of no special talents, but that did not prevent him from moving up the military/administrative ladder, including a term as consul.[260] He may have seen service as Procurator of Palestine in the late 170s or early 180s, and Rebbe may have come into contact with him at that time.

In 191 Commodus appointed him governor of Syria and commander of its armies; Syria's boundaries included the province of Palestine. Commodus may have assigned Niger to Syria "precisely because of his mediocrity."[261] An alternate though not inconsistent version explains his appointment as being on the recommendation of "the athlete with whom he was accustomed to exercise."[262] This was not an unusual process during the reign of Commodus, "for so, at that time, were all appointments made."[263] In our time too, a similar process has not been "unusual" either: several decades ago, a former car salesman was appointed Secretary of the U.S. Air Force, because he was the president's long-time associate.[264]

However he may have obtained his position, as governor of Syria Niger now held the most important military office in the empire, since Syria bordered on Rome's greatest adversary, the Parthian Empire. Niger appears to have pursued an especially harsh policy toward the Jews. Perhaps he did so because he saw them as a "fifth column" for the Parthians, in whose territories the largest Jewish community was flourishing.

When the legions in Syria proclaimed him emperor in 193 CE, he won the "widespread if not universal support from the other eastern provinces from Bithynia [modern-day northwestern Turkey] to Egypt."[265]

---

260. Herodian, *History of the Empire,* 2:7:4. Many modern bureaucrats have likewise risen to positions for reasons other than their talent.
261. Birley, *Septimius Severus,* 85.
262. *Historia Augusta: Commodus Antoninus,* 17:1; *Pescennius Niger,* 1:1.
263. *Historia Augusta: Pescennius Niger,* 1:1.
264. Verne Orr, Secretary of the Air Force in 1981–85, had previously worked in his family's car dealership. https://en.wikipedia.org/wiki/Verne_Orr.
265. Smallwood, *Jews under Roman Rule,* 487.

Not surprisingly, the Jews were a notable exception. According to the fourth-century *Historia Augusta*, Niger imposed a particularly onerous taxation regime on the Jewish community. His behavior may not have surprised Rebbe; no doubt Niger's attitude to Jews was known to him from the days of the Roman's procuratorship. Rebbe therefore doubtless led the community's protests against Niger's tax policies, and would certainly have been disconcerted by Niger's response, as *Historia Augusta* recorded it: "You wish me to lighten the tax on your lands, verily, if I had my way I would tax your air."[266]

Most contemporary historians dismiss much of the *Historia Augusta* as nothing more than fantasy; this is especially the case with regard to the biography of Niger. On the other hand, its assertion does correspond to other evidence that the Jews in Judaea "paid a capitation tax higher than that levied on the Empire's subjects in neighboring territories."[267] Moreover, it is commonly understood that most of the Jews supported Septimius Severus when he clashed with Niger, but that most of the Samaritans supported the governor of Syria.[268] In this regard, there appears to be little reason to doubt Spartanius' claim that "the citizens of Neapolis in Palestine... had long been in arms on Niger's side."[269] Neapolis is modern-day Nablus, or Shechem, in the Samaria region of the West Bank; it has always been a major Samaritan center and still is.

If Niger did not single out the Jews for higher taxes or other forms of discrimination, one would wonder why they did not support him. It could not have been that they opposed him simply because the Samaritans supported him. Some Samaritans had supported Bar Kokhba in his rebellion; some Samaritans also supported Severus.[270]

---

266. *Historia Augusta: Pescennius Niger*, 7:9. Aelius Spartanius, the author of Niger's biography in *Historia Augusta*, may well be a fictional name. Computer-based analysis appears to indicate that all six of the supposed authors of the *Historia Augusta* were actually one person. See Ian Marriott, "The Authorship of the *Historia Augusta*: Two Computer Studies," *The Journal of Roman Studies* 69 (1979), 65–77.
267. Alon, *Jews in Their Land*, 64, citing Appianos of Alexandria.
268. Ibid., 683; Graetz, IV, 206. See also A. Buchler, "Der Patriarch R. Jehuda I und die Griechish-Romichen Stadte Palastinas," *Jewish Quarterly Review* 13 (July 1901), 715–16.
269. *Historia Augusta*: *Severus*, 9:5.
270. Smallwood, *Jews under Roman Rule*, 489.

The Jews had previously supported a local general in his quest for the imperial throne: the Talmud records that R. Yohanan b. Zakkai predicted to Vespasian, the general who was besieging Jerusalem, that he would soon be acclaimed as Caesar.[271] Sure enough, Vespasian succeeded Galba to the imperial purple. Clearly, the Jews harbored some resentment against Niger that motivated their opposition to his becoming ruler of the empire.

At the same time, there must also have been some reason why they supported Severus. The community could have remained neutral and awaited the outcome of the generals' war for the throne. Moreover, Rebbe, as custodian of his community's interests, surely should have counseled them not to get involved. The community was only just recovering from Bar Kokhba's disastrous rebellion. Why risk more depredations on the part of a vengeful Niger, should he prevail over Severus?

It is therefore arguable that Rebbe had reason actively to promote Severus' cause, and the community followed his lead. As patriarch, with good ties to the Romans, Rebbe must have become aware of the chaos that engulfed Rome after the death of Commodus and Pertinax. The news of Severus' march on Rome and his acclamation by the Senate as emperor – reminiscent of a similar march by Julius Caesar, with similar results – must have reached Rebbe not long after Severus ascended to the throne. Why then did he support the African general against Niger?

Severus, like Niger, had also served as governor of Syria. Rebbe probably had not met him during that period; but as leader of the community, he would have been aware, possibly from Roman sources but certainly from Jews living in Syria, of anything that was being done in Antioch, Rome's capital in Syria, that might have affected his community. Severus left no record, either in the Roman histories or rabbinical writings, of any discriminatory behavior toward the Jews. On the contrary, Jerome, writing some two centuries later, stated that Severus and Caracalla "were very fond of the Jews."[272]

An inscription in Kaisun, in northeastern Galilee, provides support for Jerome's assertion. The inscription, which records a prayer for

271. Gittin 56a–b.

272. Jerome, *Commentary on Daniel*, 11:34.

the welfare of Severus and his sons, has been dated between spring 196 and January 198, the latter date being several months before Severus, Caracalla, and Geta first arrived in Palestine after having successfully prosecuted the Second Parthian War (discussed below) but not long after Severus was formally proclaimed emperor of Rome. It is possible that the prayer was for their success in that war. Or it may merely have been in the tradition of the Prophet Jeremiah's injunction: "Seek the peace of the city to which I have carried you in exile. Pray to the Lord for it, because in its peace you shall find peace."[273] But the Jews of Kaisun were not in exile! Most likely, therefore, the prayer reflected the Jews' recognition that this man was a long-time friend who deserved their blessings and prayers. It therefore should come as no surprise that three years earlier, Severus would certainly have been preferred by Rebbe and his followers as Rome's next emperor.

273. Jer. 29:7.

Chapter 5
Emperors

> The voice is the voice of Jacob, but the hands are the hands of Esau.
>
> Gen. 27:22

SEVERUS DEFEATS NIGER

Severus did not linger in Rome after being crowned emperor. In fact, he remained there for fewer than thirty days. Recognizing that virtually all of Asia Minor supported Niger, he strengthened his own forces by means of a recruiting drive throughout Italy. In the meantime he ordered the forces stationed in Illyricum (present-day northern Albania, Bosnia, coastal Croatia, and Montenegro) to march through Thrace to meet up with his troops.[1] In addition, he fitted out a naval force, complete with troops that today would be termed marines.

During his brief time in Rome in June-July 193, however, Severus took several steps to strengthen his position, enrich his family and friends, and issue several rulings based on his adjudication of Roman law. First, after appearing before the Senate to justify his assumption of imperial power, he secured passage of a senatorial decree that the emperor could not put any senator to death without first consulting the Senate. As Dio

---

1. *Corpus Inscriptionem Latinarum* vi, 1408 cited in G. A. Harrer, "The Chronology of the Revolt of Pescennius Niger," *Journal of Roman Studies* 10 (1920), 157.

Cassius, himself a senator, pointed out, Severus violated the decree almost immediately by murdering the very man who had proposed the law at his request.[2] He then freed his friends from debt, married off his daughters, and enriched his new sons-in-law. He undertook the administration of Rome's grain supply, which he was to manage so well during his reign that upon his passing he left the Romans a large surplus equivalent to "seven years' tribute."[3] He also was ruthless in punishing corrupt magistrates "whenever the accusations against them were proved."[4] He then set off to deal with Pescennius Niger.

Niger reportedly panicked when he heard the news of Severus' large invading force.[5] Although he was able to muster the three Syrian legions, he apparently was unable to win the support of the two legions stationed in Palestine. He was able to conquer Byzantium, but his forces then suffered multiple defeats at the hands of Severus' forces. Niger fled first to Antioch and then to the Parthians, but he was caught and beheaded. Severus was now in full control of the eastern portion of the Empire.

Now that he was fully in charge, Severus began to repay his supporters. Among them were the Jews. *Historia Augusta* records that "he revoked the punishment which had been imposed upon the people of Palestine on Niger's account."[6] Since it was the Jews that Niger tormented, the reference must be to them. Rebbe's decision to support Severus had proved to be politically astute.

The war between the rebellious Niger and Severus prompted a talmudic ruling regarding the validity of bartered coins. In general, the payment of money could not finalize a sale until the purchaser took hold of the actual article that had been purchased. On the other hand, if goods were bartered, the transaction was final as soon as one of the parties took possession of the article bartered for. Resh Lakish treated the exchange of monies as barter. On the other hand, R. Aha argued that such an exchange was only barter in the case of canceled, that is,

---

2. Dio Cassius, *Roman History*, 75:2:1–2; see also *Historia Augusta: Severus*, 7:4–6.
3. Ibid., 8:5.
4. *Historia Augusta: Severus*, 8:3–5.
5. Herodian, *History*, 3:1:1
6. *Historia Augusta*: *Severus*, 14:6.

invalidated, monies, and he used as an example coins struck by Niger and canceled after his defeat. R. Aha posited that if Niger's coins, which would have been valid elsewhere except in his former domains, were exchanged for coins of conquered territories that Severus had subsequently invalidated, but which might still be in clandestine circulation, the exchange was to be treated as a valid form of barter.[7]

THE SAD END OF R. ELEAZAR B. R. SIMEON

Severus' and Niger's forces did not confront each other in Palestine. Nevertheless, "the general uncertainty and confusion which inevitably accompanied the Roman civil war"[8] resulted in the conditions that continue to accompany Middle Eastern civil wars to this day: the creation of thousands of internally displaced persons. In the case of Niger's rebellion, so many Jews found themselves homeless and destitute that a state of lawlessness seems to have characterized significant parts of the province. In particular, thievery had become so rampant in Palestine that the Roman authorities seemed incapable of maintaining law and order.

The Talmud relates that R. Eleazar b. Simeon, Rebbe's old rival, bragged to a Roman officer that he had a foolproof method of identifying thieves who hid among the general population. The Roman authorities quickly responded by commissioning him as a senior security officer. R. Eleazar proceeded to round up and incarcerate many thieves, all of them Jewish. As a result, he became a target of opprobrium on the part of his co-religionists and rabbinical colleagues, who argued that he should have left the job of arresting thieves to the Romans, and who compared him unfavorably with his father, who defied Roman authority.[9]

The rebuke that must have hurt him the most came from his now-aged former teacher R. Joshua b. Korha, who called him "vinegar son of wine." R. Eleazar defended himself, but the attack hit home; after

---

7. Bava Metzia 46b; the halakha follows R. Aha's position.
8. Smallwood, *Jews under Roman Rule,* 488.
9. Smallwood (*Jews under Roman Rule,* 489), misreading the talmudic report, claims that "the Jewish governing class appears in its typical second-century role, appreciating both the inevitability and the benefits of Roman rule and taking open, if unpopular, action against...hot-headed troublemakers."

all, R. Eleazar had no love for his employers. When a fuller[10] hurled the "vinegar son of wine" epithet at him, R. Eleazar overreacted and had the man arrested. When he finally cooled down and regretted what he had done, he tried to have the fuller released, but it was too late to save him. The authorities hanged the man, while R. Eleazar stood under the gallows and wept.

R. Eleazar subsequently learned that the fuller was indeed a criminal, having been guilty of the capital crime of seducing a betrothed maiden on Yom Kippur. R. Eleazar was not placated, however, and he inflicted upon himself a variety of pains and sores as penance for what he had done. His colleagues were not mollified, and he therefore avoided joining them in the *beit midrash*, while he continued to pursue Jewish thieves. His family life also fell apart; his wife and daughter both left him.

As a result of these developments, R. Eleazar must have suffered from extreme stress. His condition was complicated by the fact that he was also seriously overweight. The Talmud relates that he and his colleague R. Yose, Rebbe's childhood friend, were both so fat that a yoke of oxen could pass through the space below their bellies without touching either of them.[11] Though the story is an exaggeration, it is clear that R. Eleazar had a weight problem. Indeed, a Roman matron asked him how he could have relations with his wife, a rather plump woman built along the lines of those ladies who posed for a painting by Peter Paul Rubens; the implication was that their children were not really his. R. Eleazar, who was not one to laugh at himself, retorted that he and his wife managed quite well.

The combination of stress from his work for the Romans, his colleagues' opprobrium, and his weight problem contributed to what must have been a massive heart attack. Recognizing that death was imminent and that the rabbis would not attend to him, he asked his wife, with whom he seems to have been reconciled, to place him in an upper chamber, where he fell into a prolonged coma. After eighteen or

10. In ancient Rome, fullers, who usually were slaves, washed and whitened wool cloth.
11. Bava Metzia 84a.

twenty-two years – his estranged wife had lost track of how long it had been – his relatively short and unhappy life came to an end.[12]

SEVERUS TAKES FULL CONTROL

Having defeated Pescennius Niger, Severus initially planned to attack Hatra and Parthia in retaliation for their having supported Niger. In 195, Severus launched an operation into Parthia, where many of Niger's remaining forces had fled. He then annexed the territory he had conquered and established Mesopotamia as another Roman province.[13] Severus later claimed that he annexed the territory to make it "a bulwark or shield for Syria making that province more secure."[14] The historian Dio Cassius pointed out, however, that "on the contrary, it is shown by the facts themselves that this conquest has been a source of constant wars and great expense to us. For it yields very little and uses up vast sums."[15] He could have been writing about America's quagmire in Iraq, which into the early twentieth century was called Mesopotamia.

Instead of pressing onward to take on Parthia's forces, Severus turned his attention to his nominal co-emperor, Clodius Albinus, whom he now considered to be "a nuisance for whom he had no further use."[16] Albinus had spent much of his career in the military, however, and the legateship of Britain, which he now held, was an exceedingly important one, given the constant challenges that the various island tribes posed to Roman rule. In addition, Albinus was highly popular with the legions of the Empire's western provinces, the Senate, and the people.[17] His challenge to Severus was therefore at least as serious as Niger's had been.

After some preliminary skirmishing, on 19 February 197 the two armies clashed at Lugdunum (present-day Lyon), where Albinus had taken refuge. The fighting was fierce, but Albinus' troops broke and were

12. For a discussion, see Daniel Boyarin, "Literary Fat Rabbis: On the Historical Origins of the Grotesque Body," *Journal of the History of* Sexuality (April 1991), 553–57.
13. Goldsworthy, *Pax Romana,* 174. See also Strauss, *Ten Caesars,* 245.
14. Goldsworthy, *Pax Romana,* 184.
15. Dio Cassius, *Roman History,* 75:3:2–3.
16. Herodian, *History,* 3:5:2.
17. Hammond, "Septimius Severus," 164–65.

massacred. Lugdunum was burned to the ground; Albinus was executed and his head brought to Severus.

The victorious emperor then reorganized the administration of both Britain and Gaul and at the same time wiped out all of Albinus' supporters. He proceeded post-haste to Rome, lavishly rewarding his generals and troops, avenging himself on Albinus' generals and troops, and enriching himself at the expense of actual or conjured-up enemies.[18] Severus' behavior was not unusual for his times, or for ours. Contemporary authoritarian strongmen have adopted the same approach to enriching themselves, by conjuring up all manner of accusations against those whose wealth they covet.

Having eliminated his rivals and their supporters, Severus decided to resume the military expedition against Parthia that he had postponed in order to deal with Albinus. And it was in the course of his operations in the east that he passed through Palestine and at that time coud have met with Rebbe.

FAMILY LIFE

Paccia Marciana died while Severus was governor of Lugdunum, and "wishing to take another [wife], he made enquiries about the horoscopes of marriageable women, being himself no mean astrologer; and when he learned that there was a woman in Syria whose horoscope predicted that she would wed a king… he sought her for a wife."[19] Thus it was that in the summer of 187 he married the beautiful and formidable Julia Domna.

Julia was the daughter of Julius Bassanius, a priest of the cult of Elagabal or Elagabalus (the Latinized form of the Semitic appellation meaning "god of the mountain") in the wealthy Syrian city of Emesa.[20] It is likely that the couple conversed in Greek, the lingua franca of the eastern Roman world, just as Severus once probably did with the Jews of his native Lepcist, though Julia's Aramaic – also spoken on the Jewish

18. Herodian, *History of the Empire,* 3:8:6–7.
19. *Historia Augusta: Severus,* 3:9.
20. Julia Domna was exceedingly proud of her native city; she probably influenced Severus to declare Phoenice, the area within which Emesa was located, a separate Roman province. See G. W. Bowersock, "Rootless Cosmopolitans," *The New York Review of Books* (June 28, 2018), 77.

"street" – was close enough to Severus' Punic tongue to enable them to communicate in that language as well.[21]

Julia conceived quickly after the marriage; their first son, Bassianus, named after his grandfather, was born on 4 April 188 at Lugdunum. History would remember him as Caracalla, initially Severus' co-emperor and upon Severus' passing, emperor in his own right. Julia would play a critical role as queen while Severus was alive and became even more powerful as queen mother after his passing.

Julia and Severus had three other children. P. Septimius Geta was born within a year of his brother, in early 189. He was named for Severus' father and brother. Like many men of his time, Severus focused primarily on his sons and their future as potential leaders of the Empire.

Septimius Severus had great plans for his children – and for himself. Shortly after having chalked up three victories across the Euphrates, and prior to launching his operation against Albinus, Severus proclaimed himself to be the adopted son of Marcus Aurelius. His wife Julia became *mater castrorum* ("mother of the military"), a title that had been granted to Faustina, Marcus Aurelius' empress. Having asserted that he was therefore a legitimate successor to that emperor, and in the midst of his struggle with Albinus for sole rulership of Rome, Severus in 194 also renamed his six-year-old son M. Aurelius Antoninus,[22] which became the latter's official name. In so doing Severus sought to establish a dynasty of his own that he could claim was actually an extension of the Antonines.

Even as he renamed his son, he also bestowed upon him the title of Caesar, possibly at the urging of the exceedingly ambitious Julia.[23] By granting the imperial title to Caracalla, Severus sought to refute any claims that Caracalla's uncle, also named Antoninus, might have to the throne. Just to be "safe" as it were, Severus also named his younger son, the five-year-old Geta, Antoninus, so that he too could lay claim to the

21. See Strauss, *Ten Caesars*, 241–42, who notes that Domna "also spoke Latin, although probably not as well."
22. The exact date is unclear; see Herodian, *History*, ed. Whitaker, 287n2.
23. Grant, *The Severans*, 46.

succession should anything happen to Caracalla.[24] The proliferation of names in the family could be confusing, but it is noteworthy that Rebbe's family was not much different: Rebbe's grandfather and oldest son bore the same name, as did his father and his second son.

SEVERUS ATTACKS PARTHIA

Having disposed of Albinus and his supporters, Severus led an expeditionary force eastward against Parthia in 197. He took his sons with him, and Julia accompanied him as well, as did Plautianus, the Prefect of the Guard and a relative. As Severus' forces made their progress, they found that the towns that lay along their planned route had been abandoned by the Parthians. When Severus reached Ctesiphon, the Parthian capital, he encountered little resistance. His forces plundered the city and took a huge number of prisoners.[25] Perhaps because he had already achieved his objectives, Severus chose not to occupy Ctesiphon nor to pursue Vologaesus, the Parthian king.

Running out of provisions, Severus led his men out of Parthia and besieged Hatra in western Iraq. The siege failed, however, and he lost many men and much equipment. After twenty days Severus left Iraq and moved on to Palestine late in the year 198. Severus and his sons remained in Palestine until spring of the following year, when they went on to Egypt. In all likelihood it was during this short stay in Palestine that Severus and his sons, and perhaps his wife too, first met the patriarch of the Jews, Rabbi Judah the Prince.

It was also during this period, probably in the early months of 199, that Severus established two new cities: Lucia Septimia Eleutheropolis and Lucia Septimia Severa Diospolis. Eleutheropolis was built on the site of Beit Guvrin (Beth Gabra), a town located between Jerusalem and Gaza. Established during the Second Temple period, it was captured by Vespasian during the great revolt and may have suffered considerable damage.[26] The town began to issue its own coins while Severus was

---

24. *Historia Augusta: Severus,* 10:4–5.
25. Dio Cassius asserts that he took 100,000 prisoners, surely an exaggeration. Dio Cassius, *Roman History,* 76:9:4.
26. Josephus, *The Jewish War* 4:8:1 and note 445(d), ad loc., 297.

in the region. It came to be considered one of the most beautiful and important in Palestine.[27]

Diospolis had previously been known as Lod (Lydda), a major Jewish center (though not a large one) in what was considered to be "the South" of Judaea. It occupied a strategic location between the interior lowlands and the coastal plain. Several major roads, including a branch of the coastal road, the Via Maris, passed through it.[28] While Hadrian may have changed the city's name, it was Severus who granted it city status and established it as a regional capital with administrative authority over two toparchies, or districts.[29] His action was a reward for a town that had supported him in the operations against Niger that took place in Palestine.[30] The city may have issued its own coins at the time of its establishment; it certainly did so within a few years thereafter. Importantly, the coins, like those of Eleutheropolis, had pagan symbols; the city, once mostly Jewish, had become mixed, with Roman culture clearly predominating on an official level.

The rabbis continued to call the city by its original Hebrew name, akin to Eastern European Jews referring to their towns and villages by their Yiddish rather than Polish, Russian, or German names.[31] Its location at the southern edge of what the rabbis considered to be the territory of the Land of Israel raised some questions as to whether its Jewish residents were committed to fulfilling commandments that applied only in the Holy Land. Rebbe was among the rabbis who ruled that its ambiguous status as a border town freed residents from the economically onerous obligation to tithe annually. The rationale behind his decision was similar to his ruling, discussed in detail below, that exempted these towns from the septennial *shemitta* obligation to leave the land to lie fallow. For Jewish farmers to have to set aside an additional ten percent of their annual yield for ritual purposes, and to forgo all produce every

27. Alon, *Jews in Their Land,* 141, and Smallwood, *Jews under Roman Rule,* 491, both citing Ammiannus Marcellinus.
28. Joshua Schwartz, "The Morphology of Roman Lydda," *Jewish History* 2 (Spring 1987), 33.
29. Smallwood, loc. cit.; Lau, *Ḥakhamim,* vol. 3, 56.
30. Schwartz, "Morphology," 36.
31. For example "Brisk," rather than Brest-Litovsk.

seven years, would have wrecked their livelihoods. Just as he could not get the Romans to restore the waiver on the tax, so Rebbe was unable to eliminate the tithe and *shemitta* on territory that clearly was inside the boundaries of the Holy Land. But Rebbe was ready to exploit more ambiguous situations, such as the status of the border towns, and he did so, even if his rulings did not go unchallenged.[32]

Despite the change in its status and the influx of pagans that came with that change, Lod was also a center of Jewish learning, with a yeshiva jointly led by Bar Kappara and R. Hana bar Bizna.[33] Though Bar Kappara had been a member of Rebbe's circle, once he left Sepphoris and moved south, he adopted what appears already to have been a partially different set of laws and traditions that prevailed in that part of the country. Moreover, Bar Kappara was unafraid to challenge the rulings of the patriarchate openly, as seen in the following talmudic report:

> R. Simeon son of Rebbe was annoyed at the southerners who disparaged the second tithe [by redeeming it at nominal, rather than actual value]. So Bar Kappara took fruit [meant to be tithed] and chopped them up before R. Simeon. He said: "Are these fruit worth anything? Before this they were chopped up and not worth anything to you [as valid tithe]; now are they worth anything?"[34]

In other words, if R. Simeon persisted with his demands, the southerners would not even redeem fruit at a nominal value.

True to his independent character, Bar Kappara would not back down in the face of anyone, not Rebbe, not his son. Of course, none of these Jewish ritual issues rose to the level of the Roman emperor; by the time Bar Kappara had established himself in Lod, Severus was long gone from Palestine, never to return.

While Severus was conducting his operations in the East, violence appears to have erupted between the Jews and Samaritans of Palestine.

32. Tosefta Oholot 18:18; see discussion in Smallwood, *Jews under Roman Rule*, 495; see Y. Demai 2:1.

33. Rosenfeld, *Torah Centers*, 46.

34. Y. Maaser Sheni 4:1.

The details are unclear; nor is there conclusive evidence that Severus and Caracalla intervened to restore tranquility. In any event, given Severus' favorable attitude toward the Jews, any intervention on his part would likely have been to the Jews' advantage.[35]

Severus also appears to have contracted a mild form of smallpox while he was in Egypt. He also suffered from bad feet, which limited his physical activity to some degree. Nevertheless, he did not permit his ailments to prevent him from acting out his ambitions.

As noted, Rebbe also suffered from various ailments, not only the eye infection that Samuel had cured, but especially serious intestinal trouble that may have been a form of dysentery. Neither eggs nor apple cider nor any other remedy brought his troubles to an end, any more than Severus' ailments were ever completely cured. Nevertheless, neither man permitted any of his ailments to stand in the way of his many and varied activities.

ADMINISTERING THE EMPIRE

Managing the Military

Severus' predecessor Julianus had reached the pinnacle of Roman power by promising bribes to the Praetorian Guard. When he failed to deliver, the troops stood aside as the Senate condemned him to death. Severus recognized that his tenure was not assured unless he had the support of the military. "He was ... a man who had won power through military force and feared that someone else might follow his example. His insecurity guided his decisions at all levels,"[36] most particularly with respect to the troops.

Accordingly, Severus doubled the size of the Praetorian Guard by expanding the recruiting pool for the Praetorian Guard, accepting soldiers from non-Italian units on the basis of merit.

He also increased the Guard's pay by 40 percent and approved pay increases and more avenues for promotion for ordinary legionnaires as well. Finally, he recognized their marriages as legally valid. accepting the reality that, as with volunteer militaries in the United States and

35. See discussion in Birley, *Septimius Severus*, 135.
36. Goldsworthy, *How Rome Fell*, 68.

elsewhere in the West, service in the military involved families, not just individuals.

Downgrading the Senate

Upon arriving in Rome following his defeat of Clodius Albinus at Lugdunum, Severus placed sixty-four of the Senate's six hundred members under arrest; twenty-nine were executed. He also proceeded systematically to reduce that body's already diminished status by formally concentrating all power in his hands and those of his imperial successors. The Senate had been a locus of support for Albinus; it also was an exceedingly conservative body that Severus knew would resist his attempts at reform.[37] In that regard he was no different from kings, emperors, kaisers, and chief executives who in days past and indeed in contemporary times have resented the fact that legislatures could frustrate their plans, usually through their control of public expenditures.

Severus also reduced the status of Italy, which previously was placed on a pedestal above all other Roman territories. Instead Italy was to be treated as just another Roman province. This reform was an attempt at efficiency; it put an end to a cumbersome bifurcated management system. Severus also changed the provincial administrative structure by replacing senators with military officers as local governors. By installing military men beholden to him, he minimized the likelihood of provincial rebellions similar to that of Pescennius Niger.[38]

Daily Routine in Peacetime

Severus was an exceedingly efficient administrator. An early riser, he was "sure to be doing something before dawn" and would then walk while discussing the management of the empire with his senior staff. Next, he would "hold court" until noon, dealing with legal issues as

37. Hammond, "Septimius Severus," 168–69. Severus' tribulations with the Senate may have been the basis for one of the dialogues between Rebbe and "Antoninus." See below, pp. 205–207.

38. In contemporary times, Vladimir Putin restructured Russia's provincial government structures by replacing elected officials with his own henchmen. See Fiona Hill and Clifford Gaddy, *Mr. Putin: Operative in the Kremlin* (Washington, DC: Brookings, 2013), 233–34.

they presented themselves, listening at length to litigants and giving his advisers "full liberty to speak." He then would ride, exercise, bathe, have a "plentiful luncheon" and nap. Upon waking he would complete the day's government business and engage in various discussions in both Greek and Latin, though evidently not in his native Punic.[39] He would also engage sophists to give oratorical displays before his court.[40] Toward evening he would bathe again and dine with his close associates. He was not in the habit of inviting guests to dinner – as, for example, was Rebbe – and would only host banquets "when it was quite unavoidable."[41]

Among his priority projects was the honoring and beautification of his native Lepcis, a practice continued by autocrats to this day: witness Saddam Hussein's favors to his native Tikrit, or Vladimir Putin's beautification of St. Petersburg. Severus granted Lepcis the *ius Italicum*, awarding it the status of a city on Italian soil. Beginning in 202, roughly the tenth anniversary of Severus' rule, the citizens of Lepcis began to style themselves "Lepcitani Septimiani." Severus adorned the city with both a new harbor and magnificent buildings "unparalleled elsewhere in Africa." Finally, the emperor built a temple to the city's divinities.[42]

PLAUTIANUS

By the time Niger had been defeated, C. Fulvius Plautianus, a member of Severus' grandmother's family, had become the emperor's most powerful ally. Plautianus had a checkered background, but found his main chance when he accompanied Severus on his expedition against Niger. Like many ambitious underlings then and now, he made it his business to be at the emperor's side as much as possible.[43] Severus rewarded Plautianus with a series of offices and titles, including Prefect of the powerful Praetorian Guard. By then he had been at Severus'

---

39. Dio Cassius, one of Severus' advisors, outlined the details of his daily routine. Dio Cassius, *Roman History*, 77:17:1–4.
40. Philostratus, as noted in Barnes, "Family and Career," 92n47.
41. Dio Cassius, *Roman History*, 77:17:3.
42. For a discussion, see Barnes, "Family and Career," 105.
43. Ibid., 107.

side for four years and presumably was seen by the emperor as virtually indispensable.[44]

Plautianus' promotion to Prefect of the Guard offered him the opportunity to consolidate his power to the point that he appeared to be even more powerful than Severus himself.[45] He successfully eliminated all who might have vied for the emperor's favor. As in virtually every nation's capital nowadays, power resided with those who possessed information that was available to no one else, and Plautianus had that power: "He knew virtually everything that Severus said or did, whereas no one was acquainted with any of Plautianus' secrets."[46] Indeed, Severus virtually turned all power over to him, much to the disgust of other leading Romans. Like many such men, however, Plautianus was soon to fall from power at the hands of one as vicious and conniving as he was.

CARACALLA

In 202, at the age of fourteen, Caracalla had married Plautilla, Plautianus' pampered daughter.

The marriage was not a success; Caracalla, who had developed into a young tyrant, despised both his wife and his father-in-law. For this reason, historians have speculated that the marriage was never consummated.[47]

Caracalla soon found an opportunity to eliminate Plautianus. Severus' brother Geta denounced Plautianus while on his deathbed; he alleged that Plautianus was plotting to take over the throne.[48] There appears to have been some truth to the accusation, as Plautianus had asked his loyal subordinate Saturninus to assassinate both Severus and his two sons.[49] That was all that Caracalla needed. Just three years after his marriage, the seventeen-year-old Caracalla managed to get three

44. Ibid., 128.
45. Dio Cassius, *Roman History,* 76:15:1 ff.
46. Ibid., 76:15:1.
47. Birley, *Septimius Severus,* 161.
48. Another version has Plautianus ordering a tribune to kill the two emperors, but instead the man denounced Plautianus when he came before them. Herodian, *History,* 3:11:1–12.
49. Herodian, *History,* 2:4–12.

centurions to denounce Plautianus to Severus, accusing Plautianus of plotting to murder both him and Caracalla. Caracalla's mother Julia Domna may well have been in on the plot, since she detested Plautianus for abusing her and torturing her noble female friends to gather evidence that she was promiscuous.[50] And she was one of the very few people that Caracalla actually trusted.[51]

In any event, influenced by yet another of his dreams, Severus summoned Plautianus, who – like Haman before Ahasuerus – tried to explain himself. Caracalla physically attacked him and finally ordered one of his attendants to finish him off. Plautilla was banished to an offshore island, as was her brother.[52] They died during Caracalla's reign.

Not long before Plautianus met his fate, Septimius Severus designated both his sons for the consulship beginning in 205. It was at that point that Geta no longer was called Antoninus like his brother, but officially took the name of Publius. Caracalla, on the other hand, retained the name Antoninus, by which he remained known for the rest of his life. That he was known by that name was not insignificant in terms of talmudic memory; for by the time he was married, Caracalla had already accompanied his father to Palestine, which Severus crossed on his way to Egypt in 199–200 CE. It was there that the father and son likely met the Prince of the Jewish community, R. Judah. And it was that encounter that probably gave rise not only to the many stories about Rebbe's relationship with "Antoninus," Caracalla's preferred – and later official – name, but also to the remarkable decision that the two men made years later to grant Roman citizenship to the Jews, which may well have contributed to the evolution of those stories, which will be discussed in detail below.

Upon the death of Plautianus, Caracalla and his brother literally went wild: "They outraged women and abused boys, they embezzled money." Like Shakespeare's Prince Hal, they befriended rough and ready

50. Dio Cassius, *Roman History,* 76:15:6; Birley, *Septimius Severus,* 168; Grant, *The Severans,* 46.

51. Grant, *The Severans,* ibid.

52. Ibid., 77:6:3.

types: "They made gladiators and charioteers their boon companions."[53] And they became bitter rivals.

Severus was "upset by his sons' way of life" and wanted to get them out of Rome and expose them to the rigors of military operations.[54] He was concerned as well that his legions had not been engaged in military operations for some time. Accordingly, responding to a request from Britain's governor that either "the garrison should be strengthened to give the province protection or that the emperor should come in person" because the Britons had revolted, "laying waste to the countryside, carrying off plunder and wrecking almost everything," Severus invaded the island.[55] By now Severus was old and suffering from gout, and he knew he was unlikely to return to Rome alive. Having pacified the southern portion of the island, he placed his son Geta in charge and took Caracalla with him to attack the northern tribes.

Caracalla was much less interested in conducting operations than in replacing his father, whom "he regarded ... as a troublesome nuisance."[56] As Severus was preparing yet another military operation, "his sickness carried him off on the fourth of February, not without some help, they say, from Antoninus."[57]

Caracalla and his brother Geta were both in Britain with Severus when the emperor finally passed on. Caracalla wasted little time plotting to seize power and to eliminate all whom he considered loyal to his father or brother. His initial attempts to bribe the Roman officer corps that was operating in what is now Scotland to kill Geta, fell on deaf ears. Evidently, for the time being their loyalty to the departed emperor prevented them from harming his younger son, who, it is reported, resembled Severus.[58] Once back in Rome, however, the rivalry was renewed, as the two brothers, now both emperors, lived apart in the same palace and "led separate existences."[59]

53. Ibid.
54. Herodian, *History,* 3:13:14.
55. Ibid., 3:14:1.
56. Dio Cassius, *Roman History,* 77:15:2.
57. Herodian, *History* 3:14:2.
58. Dio Cassius, *Roman History,* 78:1:3; Birley, *Septimius Severus,* 188.
59. Ibid.

Geta seems to have been more popular in the Senate than his brother, but that only encouraged Caracalla to eliminate him as quickly as possible. On 26 December 211, Geta was stabbed to death in his mother's arms. Caracalla promptly claimed that he too was the target of an assassination attempt.

Caracalla sought to purchase the loyalty of the Praetorian Guard, evidently with some success. The following day he proclaimed an amnesty in the Senate and then proceeded to oversee the murder of some 20,000 of Geta's supporters, including one of his cousins. Then, in the manner of Stalin centuries later, he oversaw the complete obliteration of Geta's memory; all inscriptions that mentioned his brother were systematically erased.

Caracalla – the name was the Celtic word for a hooded cloak that he wore – was a soldier's soldier; he won the support of the army because he was willing to work alongside them, eat the same food, and generally share their burdens. He was not, however, physically strong. He suffered from some unknown ailment; it has been speculated that he was impotent, having contracted syphilis while conducting operations in the east.[60] In any event, not long after he had Geta eliminated he issued the edict for which history has made him famous: he granted Roman citizenship to all free inhabitants of the Empire. For the Jews the edict meant that for the first time since the Bar Kokhba revolt, and perhaps since the destruction of the Temple 142 years earlier, they were now to be reckoned fully the equals of their long-time Roman overlords.

Caracalla's motives were not entirely, or even mostly, altruistic. Determined to follow in his father's martial footsteps and to maintain the loyalty of a military that expected monetary rewards, Caracalla had to increase the sources of his revenues. By expanding Roman citizenship, he was also expanding his tax base, since it was citizens' taxes that funded the military budget. Moreover, Caracalla did not only add to the taxpayer rolls, he doubled the taxes that supported his military expenditures.

Whatever the financial implications of Caracalla's edict, there was no denying that it had a major impact on the fortunes of the Jews in the Roman Empire. Perhaps it was the issuance of this edict, more than anything else, that gave Rebbe the sense that the Jews had turned

60. Grant, *The Severans*, 19 and 95 fn 3:7.

a corner in their recently sad history, and that the level of mourning for the loss of the Temple could be considerably toned down if not entirely eliminated. That Caracalla was known to share his father's favorable view of the Jews could only have reinforced Rebbe's optimism about the Jewish future.

Caracalla followed in his father's footsteps as a supporter of major civil works. Severus had restored many ancient buildings and built several new temples.[61] Caracalla, for his part, sponsored "the largest set of public baths then built in Rome, whose towering brick walls still provide the impressive backdrop for a summer, open-air opera season."[62] Caracalla also shared his father's warlike tendencies and soon was leading his forces into battle. In 213 he led his forces in operations on the upper Danube, while during the following years he led his forces in the east, intending to mount yet another assault on Parthia. Having passed through Alexandria, Caracalla headed north through Palestine in 215, at which point he may well have met Rebbe. He had encountered the prince nearly two decades earlier, when he was a boy accompanying his father and Rebbe was at the height of his power and influence. Now Caracalla was the sole leader of the Roman Empire; and while Rebbe's authority had not waned, he was being overtaken by old age. Still, with the impact of Caracalla's edict still very much in the air, Rebbe could only have been pleased to meet once again with the Roman emperor. And this meeting with the man whose formal name was Marcus Aurelius Antoninus, perhaps even more than Rebbe's earlier encounter with Septimius Severus, gave rise to the many talmudic stories, some perhaps based in reality and others complete fantasies, of the friendship between the Prince of the Jews and the emperor of the Romans.

---

61. Dio Cassius points out that Severus used other people's money to restore the buildings, but put his name on them as if he had drawn upon his own funds. Dio also did not think much of Severus' new construction, calling the expenditures "useless." Dio Cassius, *Roman History,* 77:16:2–3. The analogous contemporary practice is for wealthy people to take credit for giving funds to charity that actually are not their own. See, for example, John Cassidy, "Trump and the Truth: His Charitable Giving," *The New Yorker* (September 24, 2016), https://www.newyorker.com/news/john-cassidy/trump-and-the-truth-his-charitable-giving.
62. Beard, *SPQR,* 528.

Chapter 6

The Prince and the Emperors

Antoninus attended on Rebbe.

Avoda Zara 10b

WHEN THE PRINCE MET THE EMPERORS

We have no idea of the first impression that each of the interlocutors made on the other when they first met or when their paths crossed again years later. The Talmud records that Rebbe was an imposing figure, a handsome man with a princely air about him, who was the scion of a royal family that had been established more than a millennium earlier. Moreover, as the leader of the Sanhedrin, he exhibited all the qualities that the Talmud attributed to that august body: stature, wisdom, a good but also imposing appearance, mature age, knowledge of sorcery, and knowledge of all the seventy languages of mankind.[1]

Severus, on the other hand, was a tough soldier, relatively short, swarthy, and barrel-chested.[2] His family was prominent, but neither

---

1. Dictum of R. Yohanan, Sanhedrin 17a. "Seventy languages" was a phrase that the Talmud employed to indicate the need to be multilingual. Rashi, s.v. *baalei,* states that judges needed an imposing appearance so as to intimidate the public.
2. Dio Cassius, *Roman History,* 77:16:1.

as ancient nor as noble as Rebbe's. How did the soldier react when he encountered the Jewish prince? He certainly considered it important to converse with Rebbe, as would have been befitting his dealings with a local leader. But if there is even a germ of truth to the talmudic tales of their friendship, Severus saw in Rebbe something that caused him to engage in conversations that went far beyond what protocol required of him. The men were about the same age; both commanded respect and devotion from their followers; both were rich; both were politically astute. Severus was obsessed by his dreams; Rebbe was familiar with the occult. Severus spoke Greek, Latin, and Punic; Rebbe was conversant in Greek and probably in Latin and may have understood Punic because it was spoken in nearby Phoenicia.[3] Finally, Severus, who since his youth had always respected men of wisdom, could not have failed to see that Rebbe was himself a fount of wisdom.

What about Caracalla? His personality was entirely different from that of his father. He had inherited the throne after a failed attempt to kill his own father. He commanded little respect and had good reason to be paranoid about those around him. Nevertheless, his paranoia would not have extended to Rebbe, an old man who had no designs at all upon Caracalla's position. For that very reason, Caracalla may well have felt it safe to confide in the Jewish leader. He was already well disposed toward the Jews. Moreover, he may have retained a favorable impression of Rebbe that derived from his father's meeting with him many years earlier, when he accompanied Severus on his Middle Eastern operations.

Caracalla therefore did not see Rebbe as a threat, but rather as a source of counsel. He was unlikely to have have engaged in philosophical discussion with the Prince. Caracalla had what is today termed "street smarts," but he was no deep thinker. Instead, he probably looked to Rebbe for political advice, and some of the talmudic stories about Rebbe providing such advice to "Antoninus" may well have been based on a tradition deriving from Rebbe's meeting with Caracalla.

Although the rabbis could only embellish the conversations between Rebbe and either of the emperors when they reported those talks centuries later, it is reasonable to assume that those talks may have

3. Punic continued to be spoken until about the fifth century CE.

been lengthy even if the meetings themselves took place over a relatively brief period. For example, President Franklin Roosevelt and Prime Minister Winston Churchill were known to have engaged in long late-night conversations during Churchill's visits to the White House. Churchill loved to stay awake and talk into the wee hours of the morning "about the world and its history," and Roosevelt accommodated him; but no one else appears to have been present. As with Rebbe and the emperors, one can only speculate as to what the two great Western leaders actually discussed.[4]

ADDRESSING THE EMPERORS

The Talmud accords many wonderful attributes to Rebbe. One attribute that served him especially well during his entire term as patriarch was his political acuity, something that distinguished him from many of his rabbinical colleagues, whose cloistered lives rendered them naïve when it came to dealing with those outside the "four ells of halakha." The Midrash highlights the distinction between Rebbe's political sensibilities and those of one of his students and junior colleagues, R. Afes, who was an important scholar in his own right.

> Our teacher instructed R. Afes: "Write a single letter in my name to our lord the Emperor Antoninus." Thereupon he rose and wrote, "From Rabbi Judah the Prince to the Emperor Antoninus [greetings]." Rebbe took it, and read it, and tore it up. He said to him [R. Afes], "This is what you should write: 'From your servant Judah to our lord the Emperor Antoninus.'" He protested to him, "My master, why do you abuse your honor?" He [Rebbe] replied, "Am I better than my ancestor? Didn't Jacob say in this manner, 'Thus says your servant Jacob'?"[5]

The reference is to Jacob when he was on his way to meet Esau and sought to placate his brother, who had initially sought to kill him, by means of a

4. See, for example, Elliott Roosevelt and James Brough, *The Roosevelts of the White House: A Rendezvous with Destiny* (New York: G. P. Putnam's Sons, 1975), 306.
5. Genesis Rabba 77:5.

generous gift – in other words, a bribe. Because rabbinic tradition identified Rome with Esau's descendants, Rebbe expected that his comparing Jacob's behavior toward Esau with his own conduct toward the Roman emperor would be understood by his less politically astute acolyte.

While his biblically based explanation was all that was needed to convince R. Afes to revise the letter, it does not fully explain why such a revision was necessary. Rebbe understood that he could not address the emperor, most likely in this case the murderous Caracalla, as he would an equal. Normally, letters among equals began with "From so-and-so" (the sender) "to so and so (the recipient) greeting."[6] On the other hand, a letter to the emperor opened with "My lord."[7] Moreover, ever since the reign of Augustus, who revised the Law of Treason, great care had to be taken not to be guilty of *lèse majesté,* which the emperors had left vague in order to employ it as a weapon to terrorize opponents. Rebbe fully understood the risks of any sort of misstep in his relations with the paranoid Roman emperor.

REBBE AND THE POLITICS OF ROME

The talmudic stories about Rebbe's relationship with the emperors focus on the dialogues that supposedly took place between them. Some are philosophical, which led later historians to assume that Antoninus was Marcus Aurelius; but others, as noted, were political; and virtually all were fanciful, the products of rabbinical imagination centuries later. There is, however, at least one instance where the Talmud refers to "Antoninus" in a context other than that of his discussions with Rebbe, and that reference points to Rebbe's first interaction with Severus when the latter passed through Palestine in 198/99 CE.

The talmudic chapter of Tractate Sanhedrin called "*Ḥelek,*" which perhaps is the greatest single repository of rabbinic legends, recounts: "R. Hama bar Hanina stated: Joseph buried three treasures in Egypt. One was revealed to Korah, one was revealed to *Antoninus son of Severus,* and

6. See, for example, letter from Pliny in *Letters* II:11, quoted in Naphtali Lewis and Meyer Reinhold, eds., *Roman Civilization vol. II: The Empire* (New York: Harper&Row, 1966), 120.
7. Pliny, *Letters* X:1–4; quoted ibid., 134.

one is hidden [and preserved] for the righteous in the world to come."[8] The Talmud does not indicate what those treasures were or how Joseph obtained them. Later commentators could only speculate.[9] In any event, it is significant that the Talmud identifies Severus as the father of Antoninus, which, as has been noted, was Caracalla's actual name.

Three times in the course of the same general discussion, Tractate Avoda Zara reverses the order of succession outlined in Sanhedrin, and identifies Antoninus as the father and Severus as the son. In the first of these cases, the Talmud puzzles over the meaning of the mishnaic term *genosia* and concludes that it means the accession to the throne of a new ruler – and of his son as co-ruler, if the father so desires. As evidence, the Talmud points to "Asverus son of Antoninus," which would identify Asverus, that is, Severus, as the son of the emperor named Antoninus.[10]

In the second instance, what appears to have been a frustrated emperor once said to Rebbe:

> "I wish that my son Asverus succeed me and that Tiberias be declared a *colonia*.[11] But if I put one of these requests [to the Senate], the other will not be granted." Rebbe then had a man

8. Sanhedrin 110a.
9. The contemporary scholar R. Adin Steinsaltz writes that Joseph used the monies he received from selling grain to the Egyptians during the seven-year famine to create the three treasures (R. Adin Steinsaltz, ed., *Talmud Bavli: Sanhedrin* vol. 1 [Jerusalem: Israel Institute for Talmudic Publications, 1989], 479). The nineteenth-century scholar R. Yosef Hayyim of Baghdad somewhat fancifully posits that Joseph sold the grain to three different elements of Egyptian society: idol worshipers, bandits, and those who kept the seven commandments given to the sons of Noah. The funds from the first group, which constituted the first treasure, were obtained by Korah, who was evil like the men whose funds these were, and who perished when the earth swallowed him up together with his associates. The funds collected from those who engaged in banditry were obtained by Severus, whose nation robbed the Jews of their homeland. The third treasure, consisting of funds collected from righteous gentiles, is naturally reserved for the righteous in Messianic times. See R. Yosef Hayyim, *Ben Yehoyada,* vol. 3, Sanhedrin 110a, s.v. *shalosh.*
10. Avoda Zara 10a.
11. During Rebbe's time a *colonia* was the highest rank that a community could attain; presumably, the emperor wished to honor Rebbe. See R. Dr. I. Epstein, ed., *Hebrew-English Translation of the Babylonian Talmud: Abodah Zara,* trans. A. Mishcon

> ride upon another's shoulders, placed a dove in his hands, and asked the man doing the carrying to tell the man on top to free the dove. Said [the emperor]: "This is what he [Rebbe] meant: Ask [the Senate] to grant permission for Severus to rule in my stead, and tell Severus to establish Tiberias as a *colonia*."[12]

Finally, again in the course of the same discussion, the Talmud relates a third case:

> Antoninus said to Rebbe: "Prominent men of Rome are causing me grief."[13] Rebbe [thereupon] took him into the garden. Every day, in his presence, he would pick some radishes, one at a time. Said [the emperor]: "This is what he means to tell me: You should eliminate them one at a time, but do not attack them all simultaneously."[14]

Some scholars assume that the Antoninus in all three of these passages is Caracalla and that it is his son Severus Alexander to whom they refer. It is arguable, however, that only the third passage actually refers to Caracalla, while it is Severus who is the "Antoninus" of the other two stories. In the instances that address the emperor's desire to abdicate in favor of his son, the notion that Caracalla would have sought to designate Alexander as his successor simply is not credible. To begin with, Caracalla's temperament rendered it unlikely that he would designate anyone as his successor while he was still early in his reign. Moreover, Severus Alexander was not his son, but rather his great-nephew.

It is equally improbable that Caracalla was prepared to accept anyone as his co-ruler. After all, he had gone to great lengths to eliminate

---

(London: Soncino, 1983), 10a fn. c5. Rashi (Avoda Zara 10a, s.v. *colonia*) notes that citizens of a *colonia* were exempt from taxes and that the honor paid to Rebbe meant that scholars would no longer be taxed. See also Alon, *Jews in Their Land*, 139.

12. Avoda Zara 10a.
13. Caracalla may have been referring to the Senate, which he had downgraded. On the other hand, the Senators were not alone. "He had many enemies. Who could trust a man who ordered the murder of his brother?" (Strauss, *Ten Caesars*, 254).
14. Avoda Zara 10a.

his brother Geta, whom his father actually had designated as co-ruler. Accordingly, the names in the first two instances appearing in Avoda Zara only make sense if they are reversed; reference in both is to Severus' designation of Caracalla as co-emperor. The first case would explain the talmudic explanation of the meaning of *genosia*. The second case would indicate that while Severus had already decimated the Senate, and had cowed those who served in that body, he may nevertheless have felt that simultaneously proclaiming his son as emperor and designating a city in Palestine as a *colonia* might have fomented new opposition to his rule.

It is only logical that something along the lines of both events took place either just before or during Severus' stay in Palestine in 198/99 CE. Indeed, one Roman historian explicitly states that Severus "turned his steps toward Alexandria, and while on the way thither, he conferred numerous rights upon the communities of Palestine."[15] Moreover, a midrash appears to place the creation of colonies in Palestine at that time: "The people of a locality... sought of a king that he constitute the locality a colony. Once he had two enemies [Pescennius Niger and Clodius Albinus] and they fell before him. They said, 'This is the time that we should seek of the king that he make our locality a colony.'"[16] All of the foregoing would explain why the *Amora'im* of the Talmud would have focused on Caracalla's promotion to co-emperor during the same time frame. Those rabbis living in Palestine, many of whom commuted to Babylonia, would have been attuned to the fact that many centuries earlier the emperor had designated his son as co-ruler while he was in the Holy Land.

The third passage, on the other hand, could well refer to Caracalla. The man was exceedingly unpopular in Rome; he appears to have trusted only his mother, Julia Domna, and even then "in a warped sort of way."[17] "As for his own people," recounts the historian Dio Cassius, "he dismissed some... and killed others,"[18] including his brother Geta.

15. *Historia Augusta: Severus*, 17:1.
16. Rabbeinu Shimon HaDarshan, *Yalkut Shimoni: Va'etḥanan*, 811; R. David B. Amram Ha'edni, *Midrash Hagadol: Devarim*, ed. R. Shlomo Fish (Jerusalem: Mossad Harav Kook, 5757/1997), 59, s.v. *ba'et*. See Hadas, "Rabbinic Parallels," 259.
17. Grant, *The Severans*, 46.
18. Dio Cassius, *Roman History*, 78:1:1.

Caracalla passed through Palestine in 215 CE. His itinerary included Sycamina (near present-day Haifa), Caesarea, Betaro (near the present town of Afek, southeast of Netanya), Disopolis (Lod), and Jamnia (Yavneh).[19] As he proceeded southward, generally along the coastal plain, he would have had numerous opportunities to meet with Rebbe, who was then based in Sepphoris.

Caracalla had already been emperor in his own right for four years, and had never ceased his murderous ways. As has already been noted, he was certainly paranoid and he had good reason to be. Moreover, he was especially haunted by his failed attempt to kill his father and his successful murder of his brother. Again, Dio Cassius: "He was sick not only in body...but in mind as well, suffering from certain distressing visions and often thought he was being pursued by his father and by his brother, armed with swords."[20] Herodian adds that like contemporary American presidents, Caracalla preferred travel abroad to facing political opposition at home. "He...loathed the life in Rome and preferred to get away from the city, no doubt in order to deal with the military administration and to inspect the provincial territories."[21] Caracalla asked "no one's advice"; not merely "because of the obstinacy with which he clung to his own opinions,"[22] but because he could never be sure that those advising him were not seeking his undoing.

Rebbe, however, was someone Caracalla could trust. The great and aging rabbi was unlikely to join any plot against the emperor. Over the course of his patriarchate he owed too much to the Romans in general and to the Severi in particular. Moreover, it appears that Rebbe had few if any contacts in Rome; he lived far from the capital and focused on his own community, not on Roman political intrigue. If there was anyone in whom Caracalla could confide, far from the city he detested, it was Rebbe.

19. "Itinerarium Antonini Augusti," in Stern, ed., *Greek and Latin Authors on Jews and Judaism*, 488.
20. Dio Cassius, *Roman History*, 78:15:3–4.
21. Herodian, *History of the Empire*, 4:6:7.
22. Dio Cassius, *Roman History*, 78:11:5.

The talmudic analysis of the story about Antoninus' troubles with the Senate also highlights his paranoia. Having related the exchange between Rebbe and the emperor regarding the emperor's political troubles, the Talmud asks why Rebbe replied in riddles and not explicitly. It answers, "He thought his words might reach the ears of those prominent Romans who would persecute him [Caracalla]." The Talmud then asks, "Why then did he not say it in a whisper? – Because it is written: 'For the bird of the air will carry the voice.'"[23] Rebbe, understanding Caracalla's psychological shortcomings and not wanting to exacerbate the emperor's precarious political standing, chose to convey his message elliptically. And indeed, Caracalla appears to have followed Rebbe's advice, carefully choosing among those he allowed to remain alive for a variety of reasons, and those whom he put to death.[24]

The rabbis recounted yet another instance of Rebbe's proffering political advice to the emperor, again with reference to Rebbe's garden, but in this case probably addressing Septimius Severus. Severus' unquenchable lust for riches appears to have been well known throughout the empire, as he seized the fortunes not only of those who supported Albinus in the west, but also of Niger's supporters as well.[25] The Midrash records that Antoninus inquired of Rebbe:

> "As our Treasury is deficient, what shall we do to fill it?" Thereupon he [Rebbe] took his [Antoninus'] messenger, led him into his garden, and began uprooting the large radishes and planting small ones in their place. The messenger asked, "Give me a written answer." "You don't need one," was Rebbe's reply. [Antoninus asked the messenger:] "What did he say to you?" "Nothing at all, but he led me into his garden and began to uproot the large radishes and to plant small ones." At that he [Antoninus] began dismissing officers and replacing them with others until his treasury was filled.[26]

23. Avoda Zara 10b; Eccl. 10:20.
24. Dio Cassius, *Roman History*, 78:5:1-6:1.
25. Herodian, *History of the Empire*, 4:6:6.
26. Genesis Rabba 67:6.

The rabbis of the Talmud and Midrash of course had no idea whether such a dialogue took place, any more than they did about others they recorded. Indeed, Severus had seized the wealth of his enemies before he embarked on the eastern operation that led him through Palestine. But the rabbis no doubt were aware of a long-standing tradition of what a contemporary scholar terms "enigmatic counsel," a practice that dated back to both Greek and early Roman sources.[27]

Perhaps the earliest example of "enigmatic counsel" appears in Herodotus' history of the Persian Wars. The Greek historian recounted the messenger that Periander, who inherited his father's place as ruler of Corinth, sent to Thrasybulus with the request that he identify "what mode of government it was safest to set up in order to rule with honour." Thrasybulus took the messenger to a field where he proceeded to break off and throw away all the ears of corn that were taller than the rest. "In this way he went through the whole field and destroyed all the best and richest part of the crop; then without a word he sent the messenger back." The messenger was confused, but Periander understood "that Thrasybulus advised the destruction of all the leading citizens."[28] Tales involving similar "enigmatic advice" appear in other Greek sources as well as in Livy's *History of Rome,*[29] while the image of "the uncomprehending messenger" parallels a motif in the story of David and Jonathan: "And Jonathan called after the lad, 'Quickly, hasten, do not stand!' And Jonathan's lad gathered up the arrows and came to his master. And the lad knew not anything; only Jonathan and David knew the matter."[30]

For their part, the rabbis never could pass up an opportunity to credit the worldly patriarch with instigating whatever successful policy the Roman emperor – actually the two emperors – was able to implement. Since it suited their purpose, they employed the device of Rebbe's supposed "enigmatic counsel," as they also did when relating the above-noted exchange between Rebbe and "Antoninus" regarding the Romans

27. D. Felton, "Advice to Tyrants: The Motif of 'Engimatic Counsel' in Greek and Roman Texts," *Phoenix* 52 (Spring-Summer 1998), 42–43.
28. Herodotus, *The Persian Wars*, trans. George Rawlinson (New York: Random House, 1942), 5:92.
29. Felton, "Advice," 42–44.
30. I Sam. 20:38–39.

who were causing him grief.[31] There was, however, one significant difference between the accounts given by the gentile historians and those of the rabbis. Herodotus and others had their protagonists advise that the opposition be killed. In contrast, the rabbis tended to advise "rather than kill, replace" and "kill only intermittently," implying that Rebbe was both more clever and more humane than his Greek predecessors.[32]

With the benefit of hindsight, the rabbis of the Talmud were well aware of the reality that the position of the Jews had declined sharply since Rebbe's lifetime. They had "Antoninus" foretell the deterioration of Jewish relations with Rome in yet another dialogue between the two men:

> Every day [Antoninus] would send Rebbe a leather bag of gold dust covered with wheat, telling his servants, "Carry the wheat to Rebbe." Rebbe would reply to him, "I don't need it; I have much of my own." [Antoninus] would answer, "Leave it to those who will come after you so that they give it to those who come after me, for your descendants and their descendants will give it to them."[33]

In other words, it was "an ironical allusion to the Jews always having to purchase their freedom with gold from their Roman masters."[34]

The Midrash recounts, in Rebbe's own name, the emperor's practice of personally escorting his children when darkness fell. As *Mekhilta* puts it:

> Rebbe said: "When Antoninus was holding court upon the dais and it would get dark while his children were still with him, when he left the dais, he would take a torch and light the way for his children. And the leading members of the Imperial Court would approach him and say, 'We will carry the torch to light the way

31. Felton, "Advice," 51.
32. Ibid., 52.
33. Avoda Zara 10b.
34. Epstein, ed., *Hebrew-English Translation of the Babylonian Talmud: Abodah Zara*, 10b fn. b2.

> for your children,' but he would say to them, 'It is not that I have no one to carry the torch and light the way for my children, but I am herewith informing you of my affection for my children – so that you should treat them with honor.' Thus did the Holy One, blessed be He, proclaim His affection for Israel to the nations of the world, in that He Himself went before them, so they would treat them with honor."[35]

The Midrash relates Rebbe's dictum in relation to the passage in Exodus that speaks of the Lord leading the Israelites with pillars of smoke and fire. In this case it was not offering a "record" of a dialogue that took place between what it hoped to convey as between two equals, but rather Rebbe's homiletical use of an incident involving the emperor.

Nevertheless, while Rebbe was imparting a biblical homily to his students, he was at the same time shedding some light on the emperor's concern for the safety of his offspring. Severus was, after all, a usurper, even if he was a relatively popular one. He wanted to ensure that his sons Caracalla and Geta, who did indeed accompany him in the course of his official duties, would be in no danger at nightfall, when assassinations were easier to carry out. Having downgraded the Senate, and being still uncertain that there were no rivals plotting against him, he naturally preferred personally to accompany his children at night with the support of his imperial escorts. That Rebbe could relate this story was in fact an indication that there appears to have been a significant degree of intimacy between himself and the emperor.

The rabbis offered one other example of Rebbe's intimacy with Severus: his advice regarding a daughter of Severus who had gone astray, presumably by committing adultery. As in the case of the radishes, the two men were reported to have communicated with a secret code. Severus sent Rebbe "a rocket-herb, and Rebbe in return sent him coriander. The emperor then sent some leeks and he sent lettuce in return."[36] The code was a talmudic invention, because it only made sense if one spoke Aramaic. Thus, the Aramaic word for rocket-herb was *gargilla*,

35. "Introduction," *Mekhilta DeRabbi Yishmael, Parashat Beshallaḥ*, s.v. *veHashem*.
36. Avoda Zara 10b.

which, when broken into two words, *gar* and *gilla,* meant that "Gilla has been seduced by adulterers."[37] Coriander in Aramaic is *kusbarata,* which, when broken into two words, *kus* and *barta,* means execute the daughter.[38] *Karti* in Aramaic is leeks. It is also a cognate of *karet,* extermination; Severus was concerned that should he follow Rebbe's advice, he would exterminate his own progeny.[39] Rebbe finally responded by sending lettuce (*ḥasa* in Aramaic and Hebrew) to the emperor. *Ḥasa* is a cognate of *ḥas,* to have mercy; Severus should take mercy on his wayward daughter.

Severus, according to the *Historia Augusta,* had two daughters by his first wife Paccia Marciana; upon becoming emperor he married them off and named his new sons-in-law consuls. Although Roman historians relished reporting gossip, there are no extant reports that either woman committed adultery. Moreover, it is only the less-than-trustworthy *Historia Augusta* that records that Severus had any daughters.[40] The talmudic story is clearly fanciful; but it does reveal that the rabbis viewed Rebbe as tolerant of human foibles, even one as serious as adultery.

All of these tales presume that a king would ask an unbiased stranger with no pretensions to power for political or personal advice. That has been the case throughout history. In America such advisors to the president, who almost invariably are personal friends, have often been termed "the president's kitchen cabinet." It was not unreasonable to assume that Septimius Severus, who was after all something of a usurper and distrusted the Senate, and Caracalla, who had plotted the murder of his brother and had even less reason to trust Roman politicians, would confide in a wise and unbiased outsider. Did these emperors discuss their personal and political concerns with the leader of the Jewish community? Perhaps not in detail, and most certainly not in the details outlined by rabbis who lived centuries later and, being overwhelmingly residents of Babylonia, had no real idea of what Rome was really all about. Yet

37. Rashi, loc. cit., s.v. *shadar* (1).
38. Ibid., s.v. *shadar* (2).
39. Ibid., s.v. *hadar*.
40. *Historia Augusta: Severus,* 8:1–3.

the claim that Rome's great leaders sought some sort of advice from the prince of the Jews, and that such advice was proffered, should not be as easily dismissed out of hand as some critics have done.

REBBE AND THE CONVERSION OF "ANTONINUS"

Ever since they became a distinct people, Jews have continuously added proselytes to their numbers. The Torah refers frequently to the stranger (*ger*) and mandates that he/she should be treated as an equal with other Jews. Recognizing that strangers are never fully welcome in what at the outset was an extended family that had developed into twelve tribes, each with its own identity, the Torah warned against tormenting strangers. The rabbis applied the term to proselytes and interpreted the Torah's commandment as mandating that a Jew should love the proselyte "as you would yourself."[41]

That was certainly the case with respect to Ruth, as highlighted in her eponymous biblical book. Her famous promise to her mother-in-law Naomi, "Whither you go I will go…"[42] became the basis for later rabbinical rules regarding the induction of a proselyte into the Israelite community. Moreover, the fact that it was through her that the royal Davidic line was descended underscored the degree to which the proselyte was meant to be viewed as a full-fledged member of the Jewish people.

Biblical injunctions and the story of Ruth notwithstanding, talmudic discussions regarding proselytes did not consistently reflect that love. The Babylonian Talmud related three incidents that highlighted the rabbis' ambivalence toward the proselyte, exemplified by the respective attitudes of the two great leaders, Hillel and Shammai, toward gentiles who sought to convert to Judaism. In each of the three cases, a gentile approached Shammai seeking to convert to Judaism, but only if Shammai were willing to grant an outlandish condition. The first gentile was only willing to accept the Written Law, not the Oral one. The second gentile would only convert if he could be taught the Torah while standing on one leg. The third gentile wanted to be converted so he could be a High Priest. In each case, a furious Shammai

41. Lev. 19:34.
42. Ruth 1:16.

chased away the non-Jew while wielding a measuring stick. But Hillel found a way to convert all three. In this case the Talmud sided with Hillel. It related that when all three gentiles, now converted to Judaism, met and discussed their experiences, they agreed that Shammai would have driven them "from the world," but Hillel brought them "under the wings of the *Shekhina*."[43]

Hillel and Shammai flourished in the latter part of the first century BCE, while the Temple still stood in Jerusalem. The Jewish War of 68–70, and even more so, the great rebellion of 132–135 prompted the Romans to reconsider their previous indifference toward Jewish proselytizing of gentiles.

The Talmud's discussion of the rules of conversion begins with the phrase *bazman hazeh* – "at present" or "nowadays." Beginning in the mid-second century BCE, and especially during the first and second centuries, despite the great Jewish rebellions of 68–70, 117, and 132–35, many Romans converted to Judaism, while a larger number adopted some but not all Jewish practices. The latter group were called sympathizers, fearers of Heaven, God-fearers, or Judaizers. Many of these people kept Shabbat, attended synagogue, and observed the dietary laws, but the men did not undergo circumcision.[44] The rabbis of the Talmud termed God-fearers living in Palestine who rejected idolatry *gerei toshav* – literally resident aliens.[45] Taken together, these groups reflected the hold that Judaism had on the imaginations of a not-insignificant slice of the Roman population.

---

43. Shabbat 31a.
44. See Cohen, *From the Maccabees*, 47–49; Smallwood, *Jews under Roman Rule*, 205–206. Smallwood considers the term "God-fearers" to be a mistranslation of the Greek term.
45. The Talmud discusses the nature of a *ger toshav* in Avoda Zara 64b. R. Meir stated that a *ger toshav* is one who renounces idolatry before three *ḥaverim* (members of the rabbinical class, even if not rabbis themselves). The Sages considered anyone who accepted the seven commandments of the sons of Noah to be a *ger toshav*. "Others" (*aḥerim*) asserted that a *ger toshav* was one who ate meat that was not ritually slaughtered. Rashi (ad loc., s.v. *harei*) notes that in all three cases, such a person did not undergo circumcision. Halakha follows the opinion of the Sages that *gerei toshav* can only be accepted when the Jubilee Year is in force. For an extended discussion, see *Encyclopedia Talmudit*, vol. 6, 289–304.

Roman fascination with Judaism was not limited to the plebeians. Prominent patricians flirted with Jewish practices or converted outright. Among them were Fulvia, the wife of Emperor Tiberius' close friend Saturninus; Emperor Vespasian's granddaughter, Flavia Domitilla; and her husband – and Vespasian's nephew – the consul Titus Flavius Clemens. As has been noted, Vespasian's son, the Emperor Domitian, expanded the *fiscus Judaicus* tax to include non-practicing Jews and converts during the first decade of his rule. He also put to death a number of Romans, among them Flavius Clemens who either converted or adopted Jewish practices.[46] Flavia Domitilla escaped death but was sent into exile.

Roman official policy in the reign of Antoninus Pius was to ban conversion to both Judaism and Christianity. The ban on conversion to Christianity appears to have been enforced with greater rigor than that relating to Judaism. Ironically, Septimius Severus, for all his friendliness toward the Jews, reconfirmed the prohibition against conversion to Judaism.[47] Severus, as has been noted, was highly superstitious and seems to have truly believed in Rome's pagan gods. Like his predecessors, he had no problem tolerating Judaism as practiced by the Jews themselves. But tolerance had its limits; conversion, even "partial" conversion to Judaism, was simply unacceptable and could not be tolerated.

Nonetheless, the reports of Dio Cassius and others indicate that gentiles continued to convert to Judaism well into the reign of Caracalla. However, the rabbis had to maintain at least the pretense that they discouraged conversion, especially as they did not want to fall out of favor with Severus and his son. Moreover, some felt strongly that converts adulterated the purity of the Jewish people. In this vein the Talmud records that R. Helbo asserted that "converts are worse than a skin disease."[48]

Rebbe does not appear to have shared R. Helbo's view. On the contrary, his requirements for conversion seem to have been less demanding than those outlined above. For a non-Jew to convert, in Rebbe's view, he needed to be circumcised, to immerse himself in the

---

46. Smallwood, *Jews under Roman Rule,* 378–79.
47. *Historia Augusta: Severus,* 17:1; see also Smallwood, *Jews under Roman Rule,* 500–501.
48. Yevamot 47b.

mikve, and to bring a sacrifice.[49] Obviously, the first requirement was not applicable to a female convert. Moreover, once the Temple was destroyed, the need for a sacrifice also was obviated.[50]

Rebbe's view of converts was rather complex. While his requirements for conversion appeared to be lenient, he apparently placed them in a somewhat different category from Jews by birth. The Mishna ruled that a convert could not recite the formula that was associated with the bringing of the firstfruits on Shavuot, because it began with the words "An Aramean [Laban] sought to exterminate my father [Jacob]," and a proselyte was not descended from Jacob.[51] Since the Talmud linked that recitation with the opening prayer of the *Amida,* which speaks of the "God of Abraham, Isaac, and Jacob," presumably Rebbe would have ruled against a convert reciting those words as well.[52] The Talmud did not uphold Rebbe's ruling, however. Instead it supported the position of his teacher, R. Judah b. Ila'i, who held that a convert could recite both sets of passages.[53] Normative halakha is not definitive on the issue; some decisors rule according to the Mishna, while others follow R. Judah.[54]

Whatever their attitude to conversion, the rabbis lay claim to one prominent proselyte; not surprisingly, the conversion involved Rebbe. The Talmud relates:

> There are indications that Antoninus converted to Judaism and there are indications that Antoninus did not convert. They saw him

---

49. Keritot 9a.
50. Immediately after the destruction of the Temple, the rabbis substituted the contribution of a dinar for the sacrifice. Because he feared the funds would be misappropriated, Rabban Yohanan b. Zakai dropped this requirement (ibid.).
51. Y. Bikkurim 1:4. The mishna is anonymous, meaning it is likely to have reflected the view of R. Meir. The biblical passage is from Deut. 26:5. See also David Ellenson and Daniel Gordis, *Pledges of Jewish Allegiance: Conversion, Law and Policymaking in Nineteenth- and Twentieth-Century Orthodox Responsa* (Stanford, CA: Stanford University Press, 2012), 13–14, 23.
52. Y. Bikkurim, loc. cit.
53. Ibid.
54. For a discussion see the entry for *Ger* in *Encyclopedia Talmudit*, vol. 6, 257–259. Maimonides, Nahmanides, the anonymous author of *Sefer HaḤinukh*, and R. Moses of Coucy support R. Judah. *Tosafot* supports the Mishna.

> go out on Yom Kippur with a broken shoe [since wearing of leather is prohibited]. But that is no proof since even Fearers of Heaven do the same. Antoninus ... was circumcised. He went back to Rebbe and said, "Look at my circumcision." Rebbe replied, "I have never looked at mine, would I look at yours?"... He was called Rabbeinu HaKadosh [our Holy Rabbi] because he never looked at his circumcision...so conclude that Antoninus converted; indeed the rabbis state that he converted; for as R. Hezekiah observed, R. Abbahu said in the name of R. Lazar [i.e., R. Eliezer], "If converts (*gerei tzedek*) arrive at the world to come, Antoninus will lead them."[55]

Were the rabbis aware that the emperor who they asserted converted to Judaism actually had come out strongly against such conversions? Probably not, though they could not but have been cognizant of long-standing Roman opposition to Jewish proselytizing.

This tale appeared in the Jerusalem Talmud, which was edited in approximately 350 CE. By then Christianity had become the official religion of the Empire. Indeed, it may well have been Constantine's conversion that inspired the rabbis to create the myth of an earlier emperor converting to Judaism.

The myth of Antoninus' conversion to Judaism notwithstanding, the rabbis doubled down on discouraging converts, since, as a result of the Edict of Constantine, the Roman ban on conversion to Judaism took on much greater force. Indeed, it remained a capital offense in much of Christendom until the nineteenth century. Ironically, even in modern Israel, where there are no non-Jewish strictures against conversion, there are those who would still apply R. Eliezer's dictum as a governing principle.[56]

---

55. Y. Megilla 1:11; for a variant of the story see Y. Sanhedrin 10:5, which asserts that he circumcised himself; Leviticus Rabba 3:2. The fifteenth-century scholar R. Abraham Zacuto, basing himself on a possible misreading of *Mekhilta DeRabbi Yishmael,* wrote that "Antoninus" was even a rabbi! See Marc Shapiro, "Rabbi Joseph Hertz, Women and Mitzvot, Antoninus, The New RCA Sddur and Rabbis Who Apostasized Part I" in *The Seforim Blog,* https: //seforimblog.com/2–19/05/rabbi-joseph-hertz-women-and-mitzvot-antoninus-the-new-rca-siddur-and-rabbis-who-apostasized-part-1/.
56. Speaking to an international conference in 2009, R. Avraham-Chaim Sherman, a member of the the Israeli Supreme Rabbinical Court of Appeals, asserted: "There

ANTONINUS' FEALTY TO REBBE

Consistent with the rabbinical fantasy that the Roman emperor converted to Judaism is an extended tale that reflects the rabbis' amazement at Rebbe's relationship with a leading Roman, much less the emperor himself. The story, which deserves to be quoted in full, appears after the Talmud records Rebbe's political advice to Severus or Caracalla.[57]

> Antoninus had a cave which led from his house to the house of Rebbe. Every day, when he visited Rebbe [to study Torah],[58] he brought two slaves, one of whom he killed at the entrance to Rebbe's house and the other he killed at the door of his own house [in order to keep the visits secret]. He told Rebbe, "When I arrive, no other person should be with you." One day he found R. Hanina bar Hama sitting there, so he said: "Didn't I tell you that no one should be with you when I visit?" Rebbe replied, "This is no human." "Then," said Antoninus, "let him tell that servant who is sleeping at the gate to get up and come in." R. Hanina bar Hama found that the slave had been killed. He said to himself, "What should I do? If I go and say that the man is dead, one is not meant to spread bad news. If I go off and leave him, I would be slighting the king." So he prayed for mercy for the man, revived him and sent him inside. Antoninus replied: "I am well aware that the least one among you can bring the dead to life; still, when I come round you should be alone." Every time [Antoninus would come] he would attend to Rebbe and serve him food or drink. When Rebbe wanted to get on his bed Antoninus crouched in front of it saying, "Get on to your bed by stepping on me." Rebbe said, "It is not the proper

is no logic to telling tens of thousands of goyim (non-Jews) who grew up on heresy, hate of religion, liberalism, communism, socialism, that suddenly they can undergo a revolution deep in their souls. There is no such reality." See Rabbi Avraham-Chaim Sherman, "Bedika Ḥozeret Shel Giyur BeVeit Din Aḥer" (Repeat Investigation of [a] Conversion in Another Rabbinical Court), *Teḥumin* 31 (5771/2011), 234–35.

57. Avoda Zara 10b.
58. Thus Rashi, ad loc., s.v. *lebeitei*.

> thing to treat a monarch so disrespectfully." Antoninus replied: "If only I could serve as your mattress in the world to come!"[59]

The first part of the story has Rebbe teaching the emperor Torah, despite the fact that the rabbis frowned upon such acts, unless, of course, Antoninus either had already converted or was in the process of doing so (!). The myth of the emperor's studying Torah could therefore be seen as an adjunct to the story of his conversion.

It is unclear, however, why the story focused on Antoninus' cruel and shocking murder of the two slaves; in any event, R. Hanina's "miracle" affected only one of them. Later commentators, groping for an explanation, postulated that important people normally had two servants accompany them. They asserted that "Antoninus" intended to kill both slaves in order to maintain secrecy regarding his study of laws that Romans such as Tacitus had ridiculed for decades. He was concerned not to kill one slave, however, when the murder could be witnessed by the other who would perhaps report the crime before he too was killed.[60] One wonders whether those who "explained" the tale really believed it.

As incredible as the first part of the story may be, it pales before the latter tale of Antoninus' acting as Rebbe's footstool. To suggest that any leading Roman official, much less the emperor, would prostrate himself before anyone, let alone a Jew, is preposterous. Surely the rabbis were aware that only the most gullible would accept their story at face value. Why then, did they bother to tell that tale at all?

---

59. Avoda Zara 10b.

60. Maharsha, Avoda Zara 10b, s.v. *ḥad*. Maharsha offers an additional explanation, namely, that one servant was stationed at the entrance to the emperor's palace and the other before Rebbe's door. The emperor had the first servant killed upon leaving Rebbe's home, and upon arrival at the palace killed the second servant. In part, this interpretation might be consistent with the tale – the emperor would have wanted to leave the palace via a secret door and would therefore have stationed a slave there. Nevertheless, it falls flat, since the story has R. Hanina bar Hama already at Rebbe's home when the emperor arrives, and then reviving the slave while the emperor is still at Rebbe's home, whereas Maharsha has the slave killed only upon the emperor's departure.

THE ULTIMATE FATE OF A CRUEL EMPEROR

The rabbis of the Talmud were certainly aware of the murderous ruthlessness that was characteristic of so many Roman emperors. How then, were they to reconcile an emperor's viciousness with his positive attitude toward the Jews? Their answer was to fashion yet another exchange between Rebbe and Antoninus, in which the emperor marshals his knowledge of Torah that he had "studied" under Rebbe's tutelage, and accepts, with obvious relief, Rebbe's exposition of the relevant biblical texts:

> Once he [Antoninus] asked him: "Shall I enter the world to come?" "Yes!" said Rebbe. "But," said Antoninus, "is it not written, 'There will be no remnant to the house of Esau'? "That," he replied, "applies only to those whose evil deeds are like to those of Esau. Indeed we have learned: 'There will be no remnant to the house of Esau' might have been taken to apply to all [Esau's descendants]; therefore Scripture says distinctly – 'To the *house* of Esau,' so as to make it apply only to those who act as Esau did." "But," said Antoninus, "is it not also written: 'There [in the nether world] is Edom, her kings, and all her princes'?" "There, too," Rebbe explained, "[it says:] 'her kings,' it does not say all her kings; 'all her princes,' but not all her officers! This is indeed what has been taught: 'Her kings' but not all her kings; 'All her princes,' but not all her officers'; 'Her kings', but not all her kings – excludes Antoninus the son of Asverus."[61]

The story may well refer to a conscience-stricken Caracalla, "Antoninus the son of Asverus," whose cruelty was well documented; hence the emperor's reported uncertainty as to whether he would have a place in the world to come. The tale highlights Rebbe's spiritual influence on and superiority to the emperor. Rebbe is said to have taught the emperor Torah. Doing so was consistent with the notion that Antoninus had converted to Judaism. It is striking that the emperor's tuition is said to have taken place in Rebbe's home, in contrast to the practice throughout the

61. Avoda Zara 10b.

centuries whereby royals young and old were tutored in their palaces. Finally, nothing could be more uplifting for Jews who were subservient to the Roman Empire than to have their leader receive homage – literally to be served hand and foot – from the emperor himself at a time when their overlords enabled Jews to live in peace and prosperity.

Centuries later, a variant of this fantasy was recounted in an entirely different context, namely in the recorded travels of the twelfth-century Spanish Jew, Benjamin of Tudela. Benjamin's description of the exalted position of the exilarch is worth quoting at length. Describing his passage through Baghdad, the capital of the Muslim caliph, Benjamin wrote:

> About 40,000 Jews…dwell in security, prosperity and honor under the great Caliph, and amongst them are great sages, the heads of the Academies engaged in the study of the law.… At the head of them all is Daniel the son of Hisdai, who is styled "Our Lord the Head of the Captivity of all Israel." He possesses a book of pedigrees going back as far as David, King of Israel… the Mohammedans call him "Saidna ben Daoud" [the Lord son of David] and he has been invested with authority over all the congregations of Israel at the hands of the Emir al Muminin [Commander of the Faithful – a title currently held by King Mohammed VI of Morocco] the Lord of Islam. For thus Mohammed commanded…that every one, Mohammedan or Jew, or belonging to any other nation in his dominion, should rise up before…the exilarch and salute him, and that anyone who should refuse to rise up should receive one hundred stripes.… And every fifth day when he goes to pay a visit to the great Caliph, horsemen, as well as Jews, escort him, and heralds proclaim in advance, "Make way before our Lord, the son of David, as is due unto him".… He is mounted on a horse, and is attired in robes of silk…from [his] turban is suspended a long white cloth adorned with a chain upon which the cipher of Mohammed is engraved. Then he appears before the Caliph and kisses his hand, and the Caliph rises and places him on a throne which Mohammed had ordered to be made for him,

> and all the mohammedan princes who attend the court of the Caliph rise up before him.[62]

Arabic records confirm that the exilarch did command the respect of Muslims, who indeed regarded him as a direct descendant of King David. The Caliph granted him considerable authority over the Jewish community, including the power to inflict corporal punishment on those transgressing his edicts. Perhaps he never sat alongside the Caliph or was adorned with Mohammed's cipher, but the fact that a good part of what Benjamin asserted was true could well indicate that the same could apply to the essence of the Talmud's accounts of Rebbe's interaction with the emperor of Rome.

The story of Caracalla's obeisance to Rebbe offers one other important lesson, especially for contemporary times. The report that not all descendants of Esau were excluded from the world to come flies in the face of historic Jewish enmity toward Christians, those inheritors of Rome, or some of the invective that is bandied about far too freely in contemporary Israel, where political enemies are dubbed "Amalekites," descendants of that most evil of Esau's grandchildren. As Rebbe – and the talmudic report of his statement – would have it, the children of Esau were not intrinsically evil, though many of them did commit egregious crimes. It is a sentiment that deserves far more recognition in contemporary times, whether with reference to Christians or adherents of other religions.

DISCUSSIONS ON PRINCIPLES OF JUDAISM

Though not entirely consistent with the notion that the Roman emperor was a convert to Judaism, the Talmud and Midrash offer extensive dialogues between Rebbe and his interlocutor that highlight basic Jewish concepts. These supposed dialogues fulfilled several other functions as well. They impressed upon both students in the yeshivas and the common people Rebbe's exalted status as virtually an equal to the great Roman emperor. More broadly, they underscored the principle that rabbis

62. Marcus Nathan Adler, ed. and trans., *The Itinerary of Benjamin of Tudela* (London: Oxford University Press, 1907), 38–39.

deserved the utmost respect. As throughout the subsequent centuries, and perhaps especially since the Enlightenment and the Emancipation, the rabbis were forever expressing their concern about the extent of their influence on the ordinary Jewish populace. Typical of such expressions was Rava's comment: "How stupid are most people who would stand up for the Scroll of the Torah but do not stand up before a great [rabbinic] individual, for in the Torah it is written [that a man receives] forty lashes, but the Rabbis came and [by interpretation] reduced them by one."[63] Others went even further, comparing rabbis to kings and to angels.[64]

Several examples can serve to demonstrate the educational value of these stories. In the context of a long discussion on God's blessing of Shabbat, the Midrash records:

> Our teacher [Rebbe] made a meal for Antoninus on Shabbat. He set cold dishes before him; he [the emperor] ate them and found them tasty. He made a meal for him during the week and brought hot dishes before him. Antoninus said to him: "I enjoyed the others more." Rebbe replied, "They are lacking a particular condiment." He said to him, "Do the royal pantries lack anything?" Said he [Rebbe], "They lack Shabbat; do you possess Shabbat?"[65]

The rabbis, in the spirit of Isaiah who urged the people to "call the Shabbat a delight,"[66] wanted to impress upon the larger Jewish public the importance of venerating Shabbat beyond mechanically obeying its ordinances. What better way to do so than to have Rebbe explaining the spiritual value of Shabbat to the leader of the greatest empire the ancient world had ever known?

Similarly, the Midrash records:

> Antoninus asked our holy Rabbi [i.e., Rebbe]: "What if a man should pray every hour?" He replied: "It is forbidden." "Why?"

---

63. Makkot 22b.
64. Nedarim 20b: "Amemar said: Who are the 'Ministering Angels'? The Rabbis."
65. Genesis Rabba 11:4.
66. Is. 58:13.

> he asked. "So as not to act irreverently towards the Mighty One," Rebbe replied. Antoninus rejected this answer. What did Rebbe do? He arose early [the next morning], went to him and said: "O master, O ruler." After an hour later he visited him again, and said: "O emperor." After another hour, he said to him: "Peace be unto you, O king." The king said to him: "Why are you demeaning the throne?" Rebbe replied: "Let your ears hear what your lips are saying. If you, who are a mere mortal, considers the man who greets you every hour is guilty of *lèse majesté*; how much more so, should the King of kings, not be annoyed every hour."[67]

Once again, the intended audience for this midrash was the Jewish community at large. As the Talmud notes, "I might say that a man should pray the whole day? Daniel already made it explicit: *And three times a day he kneeled on his knees and prayed and offered thanks before his God just as he had done prior to this*."[68] The notion that one prayed three times a day, no more, no less, was one that the Talmud sought to imbue upon the Jewish public. "Antoninus" simply provided a vehicle for the rabbinic message. In this case the rabbis, through the mouth of Rebbe, were making an additional point as well: There was a time for prayer and a time for other activities, whether they be earning a living or studying Torah. In economists' terms, the opportunity cost of excessive prayer is high; or as the Talmud says of one who prays excessively, "His gain is outweighed by his loss."[69]

The nature of prayer was the subject of another dialogue between Rebbe and the emperor:

> Antoninus came before Rebbe and said to him: "Pray for me." He replied to him: "May it be (the Lord's) will that you may be protected from the cold." He [Antoninus] responded to him: "Rabbi, this is no prayer; just add a garment and the cold disappears." So he said to him: "May it be that you are protected from excessive

67. *Midrash Tanḥuma: Miketz* 9:2.
68. Dan. 6:11.
69. Avot 5:15.

> heat." He replied: "Now that is a truly a prayer, may it be that your prayer is answered, as it is written, 'There is no protection from its [the sun's] heat.'"[70]

The rabbinical message in this instance was that if one uttered a special prayer, it should not be trivial. The rabbis frowned upon those who prayed for heavenly assistance when one could address the issue on one's own. In common parlance, "God helps those who help themselves."

THE VALUE OF SECULAR KNOWLEDGE: REBBE CONCEDES TO ANTONINUS

Ever since the era of the Sages, rabbis have debated whether there is knowledge external to Scripture. Those who argue that there is no need to look elsewhere for knowledge echo Ben Bag Bag's aforementioned dictum in *Pirkei Avot* (Ethics of the Fathers): "Turn it [the Torah] over and over, for everything is in it."[71] On the other hand, the Sages not only recognized that there are wise men among the nations, but even mandated a blessing upon seeing the "sages of the nations": "Blessed be He who imparted wisdom to His creatures."[72] Two colloquies between Rebbe and Antoninus demonstrated, however, that while non-Jewish wisdom may have been derived from factors external to Scripture, it actually was supportable by Scripture.[73] In other words, the findings of non-Jewish sages could shed light on aspects of Scripture that Jewish sages may not have discovered on their own.

> Antoninus also said to Rebbe, "When is the soul placed in man; as soon as it is decreed [for example, that the sperm shall be male or female], or when [the embryo] is actually formed?" Rebbe replied, "From the moment of formation." Antoninus objected: "Can a piece of meat be unsalted for three days without becoming putrid [i.e., the sperm cell would become putrid and not function]?

70. Y. Sanhedrin 10:5. The quote is from Ps. 19:7.
71. Avot 6:25.
72. Berakhot 58a.
73. Sanhedrin 91b.

> On the contrary, it must be from the moment that [God] decrees [its destiny]." Rebbe said, "This thing Antoninus taught me, and *Scripture supports him* [my emphasis], for it is written, 'And Your decree has preserved my spirit [i.e., my soul].'"[74]

Rebbe initially believed that the soul entered a human being only upon formation of the embryo. When Antoninus argued that logically it should enter even earlier, Rebbe acknowledged the emperor's point, and then found a passage in Scripture that confirmed it.

Antoninus and Rebbe both reversed themselves regarding the nature of the fetus prior to birth, and once again Antoninus had the better of the argument:

> Antoninus also enquired of Rebbe, "From what time does the Evil Inclination hold sway over man; from the formation [of the embryo], or from [its] issuing forth [into the light of the world]?" – "From the formation," he replied. "If so," he objected, "it would rebel in its mother's womb and go forth. But, on the contrary, it is from when it emerges [from the womb]." Rebbe said: "This thing Antoninus taught me, and Scripture supports him, for it is said, 'At the door [i.e., when a child emerges into the world] sin lies in wait.'"[75]

In this case as well, Rebbe acknowledged that Antoninus had the more persuasive case; but once again he was able to find a basis in Scripture for the emperor's assertion. Based on these two incidents, one might reinterpret Ben Bag Bag's dictum as meaning that all indeed may be found in Scripture, but there is at times a need for secular knowledge and findings to identify previously unidentified Scriptural observations about the world in which we live.

ADDRESSING DUALISM

The Babylonian rabbis functioned in an environment in which dualism was the predominant underpinning of the Zoroastrian faith. The

---

74. Job 10:12.
75. Gen. 4:7.

Talmud has numerous examples of rabbinic debates with Persian magi, but it also has Antoninus and Rebbe addressing the question of dualism:

> Antoninus said to Rebbe: "The body and the soul can both free themselves from judgment. How so? The body can say: 'The soul has sinned, since from the day it left me I lie like a dumb stone in the grave.' And the soul says: 'The body has sinned, since from the day I departed from it I fly about in the air like a bird.'" He replied, "I will tell you a parable. To what may this be compared? To a human king who owned a beautiful orchard that contained splendid figs. Now, he placed two watchmen in it, one lame and the other blind. The lame man said to the blind, 'I see beautiful figs in the orchard. Come put me on your shoulder, so that we can get them and eat them.' So the lame man rode the blind one, obtained them and ate them. Some time after, the owner of the orchard came and asked, 'Where are those beautiful figs?' The lame man replied, 'Do I have feet to walk with?' The blind man replied, 'Do I have eyes to see with?' What did he do? He placed the lame upon the blind and judged them as one. So will the Holy One, blessed be He, bring the soul, install it in the body, and judge them as one, as it is written, 'He shall call to the heavens from above, and to the earth, that He may judge His people.'[76] He shall call to the heavens from above – that is the soul; and to the earth, that He may judge His people – that is the body."[77]

The rabbis placed in the mouth of the emperor a challenge to the rabbinical beliefs that man was accountable for his deeds and that the body would come to life to be judged. Dualism, in this case, involved a complete separation of body and soul; it therefore both rendered judgment impossible and meant that body and soul could never be reunited. The

76. Ps. 50:4.
77. Sanhedrin 91a–b. This story also appears in somewhat different form in *Mekhilta DeRabbi Yishmael, Parashat Beshallaḥ* (*HaShira*): 2, s.v. *sus* (3). See also the discussion in Reuven Hammer, trans., intro., and commentaries, *The Classic Midrash: Tannaitic Commentaries on the Bible* (New York and Mahwah, NJ: Paulist Press, 1995), 102.

rabbis then had Rebbe refute Antoninus with a passage from Psalms. Since the emperor was Rebbe's acolyte and had studied Torah under him, he accepted the reply as conclusive.[78]

This tale does not appear in the Jerusalem Talmud. Roman paganism was not structured around a premise of dualism, though it did incorporate some dualistic elements, and gnostic sects had earlier existed in Palestine.[79] By the time the Jerusalem Talmud appeared in the fourth century, Christianity, which was the official Roman religion from Theodosius' reign onward, rejected dualism as it was expressed in the form of gnostic heresies.[80] On the other hand, dualism was central to Persian belief. It was therefore the Babylonian rabbis who, despite their generally cordial relations with their non-Jewish neighbors, nevertheless sought to refute Zoroastrianism's premises as forcefully as possible. To that end they co-opted and embellished the centuries-old reports of Rebbe's relationship with powerful Romans and created a new dialogue with "Antoninus" to address their contemporary concerns.

---

78. For a discussion of rabbinic attitude toward dualism/Zoroastrianism, see Aharun Agus, "Some Early Rabbinic Thinking on Gnosticism," *The Jewish Quarterly Review* 71 (July 1980), 18–30. He refers to Rebbe and Antoninus' dialogue on pp. 29–30. See also Shai Secunda, *The Iranian Talmud: Reading the Bavli in Its Sassanian Context* (Philadelphia: University of Pennsylvania Press, 2014), chapter 3, especially 70–71. See also Urbach, *The Sages*, 222ff.
79. H. W. Basser, "Allusions to Christian and Gnostic Practices in Talmudic Tradition," *Journal for the Study of Judaism in the Persian, Hellenistic, and Roman Period* 12:1 (1981), 88.
80. The second-century Bishop of Lugdunum, Irenaeus, was perhaps the first Christian leader to brand Gnosticism as a heresy.

Chapter 7

Rebbe, Leader of His People

> Rabba the son of Rava, or as some say R. Hillel the son of R. Volas, also said: Between Moses and Rebbe we do not find an individual who was supreme both in Torah and in worldly affairs.
>
> Gittin 59a

A PATRIARCHATE TRANSFORMED

Rebbe's predecessors as patriarchs, as well as their rabbinical colleagues, appear to have had limited influence over the Jewish community as a whole. To begin with, Roman hostility, which endured through the civil war between Severus and Pescennius Niger, circumscribed the degree to which they could impose their authority beyond their immediate environs. In addition, they appear to have focused their concerns on their own economic class, which consisted primarily of "well-to-do landowners who lived in villages and small towns."[1]

It was during Rebbe's era that the patriarchate was transformed into an institution of leadership for the entire community. In part this

1. Cohen, *From the Maccabees,* 214.

was due to the favorable attitude of the Severans, who were well disposed toward Rebbe in particular and backed his authority. In part it derived from the fact that the "rabbinic estate came to include the poor, who depended on charity and public employment for their survival, and became increasingly urban with centers in Caesarea, Tiberias and Sepphoris."[2] But it is doubtful that even with Roman support and societal change, the patriarchate would have developed into a powerful institution without Rebbe's unique combination of legal expertise, political acumen, and impeccable character.[3] As shown below, Rebbe introduced numerous legal initiatives, often based on his keen understanding of human nature and the economic necessities of the times. But his greatest contribution to Jewish life, both then and subsequently, was the book that remains a cornerstone of Jewish law and practice to this day: the Mishna.

THE MISHNA

Rebbe Compiles the Mishna

Septimius Severus left a major legal legacy to generations that followed him. Some 150 rescripts found their way into the sixth-century Code of the Emperor Justinian.[4] Rebbe's legal legacy, the Mishna, was both more extensive and longer lived. It was sometime around when his meetings with Severus and Caracalla would likely have taken place that Rebbe threw himself into committing to paper the many laws and traditions that had preoccupied him and his rabbinical colleagues throughout their lives and whose structure (according to rabbinical tradition) had been set by R. Akiba. Scholars estimate that the Mishna was completed around 200 CE.[5] It was a time when Rebbe was at the zenith of his powers.

---

2. Ibid.
3. As a historian of halakha has pointed out, "it was ... intellectual and moral stature which was decisive in the teaching and clarification of *Halakhah*. It was only thanks to such stature that patriarchs such as Rabban Gamaliel, his son, Rabban Simeon, and his son, R. Judah ha-Nasi, achieved recognition and admiration" (Urbach, *The Halakhah*, 275).
4. Birley, *Septimius Severus*, 106.
5. Cohen, *From the Maccabees*, 206.

The rabbis had traditionally resisted transcribing the Oral Law and its accompanying traditions. Ever since the Torah had first been handed down to Moses, no one had presumed to alter the practice of publicly teaching the law orally to the people, much as Ezra had done in the years after the construction of the Second Temple. Indeed, according to Maimonides,

> in every generation the Chief Judge or the prophet of those times would transcribe for himself the lessons he had learned from his own masters and would then orally transmit those to the public. And every one of those leaders would interpret the Torah and its laws to the best of his ability to comprehend what he had been taught. Moreover, there were provisions that were initiated in every generation that had not been transmitted from Moses onward but rather were derived from [R. Yishmael's] thirteen exegetical principles and that had been approved by the Great Court [in Jerusalem].[6]

Tradition, as expressed by Maimonides, had it that Rebbe collected all the oral laws, explications, and interpretations that had been passed down the generations from Moses onward. These included the rulings of individual courts throughout the generations that addressed the entirety of Torah and the various collections of *mishnayot* such as those of his father Rabban Simeon and his teacher R. Judah b. Ila'i.[7] Rebbe synthesized them all into the Mishna.

Nowhere does the Mishna actually speak of an author.[8] Nor does it have an explanatory preface, or a justification for why, after so many centuries, its contents had been committed to writing. Nevertheless, R. Yohanan, who was one of Rebbe's most junior students,[9] explicitly

6. Maimonides, "Introduction," *Mishneh Torah,* 3–4.
7. Urbach, *The Halakhah,* 292–93.
8. The Mishna does cite Rebbe; see, for example, Menaḥot 66b, as well as the discussion below regarding gentile oil.
9. Ḥullin 137b. R. Yohanan admitted that when he sat in the back of the Academy, he hardly understood the dialogues between Rebbe and Rav, who sat seventeen rows in front of him.

attributed authorship of the Mishna to his master. So too did his own student, the Babylonian *Amora* R. Hiyya b. Abba several decades later.[10]

Centuries later, Maimonides wrote that Rebbe's authority was beyond questioning:

> He was unique in his generation and in his time, a man who embodied all that was beloved and [possessed] all the right character traits so that he merited that his contemporaries would refer to him as our Holy Rabbi, his name being Judah. He was the essence of wisdom and greatness... as well as piety, modesty, and abstinence... he was a fluent [writer] and unequalled in his mastery of the Holy Tongue to the point that the Sages, blessed be they, would learn from his slaves and servants the meaning of confusing Scriptural passages.... He possessed great wealth and power to the point that his steward was wealthier than King Shapur [of Persia]... and he likewise was dominant among men of wisdom and those who sought it, and promulgated Torah in Israel and [in that vein] gathered the legal rulings, the words of the Sages, and the disputes that had been passed down from the days of Moses until his time... and when he had gathered all the opinions and positions, he commenced to produce the Mishna which incorporates the explication of all of the Torah's commandments, be they ones that were received directly from Moses blessed be he; or those derived from tradition that won unanimous acceptance; or those involving conflicting traditions, wherein he would write "So-and-so supports this tradition, and so-and-so that one"; or those involving an individual taking a position in conflict with the majority, in which case he listed both the individual proponent and the majority that disagreed with him.[11]

Rabbi Shmuel HaNagid, who preceded Maimonides by about a century, explained why Rebbe chose to include in the Mishna minority

10. Ibid., 85a.
11. Maimonides, Commentary on Mishna, introduction to Order Zera'im (Hebrew), in standard version of Vilna *Shas* (Talmud), s.v. *vekaasher meit.*

opinions that were not validated halakhically. Rebbe's objective, he argued, was to prevent someone who had received a halakhically rejected position to assert that it was a received tradition from his rabbis. Quoting the Mishna itself, R. Shmuel pointed out that "if one should assert 'I have learned this from tradition,' he may be told, 'You heard it according to the [rejected] opinion of that individual.'"[12]

The aforementioned R. Hiyya b. Abba figured in a talmudic discussion regarding one of Rebbe's halakhic decisions that revealed not only how, in at least one case, conflicting opinions in the Mishna were subsequently dealt with, but also how the Oral Law was transmitted and how Rebbe played a key role in the chain of transmission.

Although conflicting opinions on legal issues that the Mishna cited generally were resolved by later generations of Sages, the Talmud addressed a case where it was Rebbe himself who resolved a dispute that he had recorded in the Mishna without comment. The issue in question was whether one could slaughter an animal whose dam or calf had been slaughtered that day by a deaf person, a mentally ill person, or a child. R. Meir had ruled that if the first slaughtering had taken place with no witnesses, there was no sanction against the subsequent slaughter. The rabbis ruled that slaughtering the dam or calf would in fact violate the biblical prohibition against slaughtering "it and its offspring."[13] The Talmud records that "Rebbe decided a case according to the view of R. Meir, and Rebbe also decided a case according to the view of the Sages" and then asks, "Which was the later [and therefore determinative] decision?" [14] In the course of attempting to establish which of Rebbe's rulings was determinative, the Talmud related an incident that, *inter alia*, demonstrated the way in which the Oral Law was transmitted from master to student.

> R. Abba the son of R. Hiyya b. Abba and R. Zera were standing in the open square in Caesarea at the entrance of the House of Study (*beit midrash*). R. Ammi came out and found them standing there and said, "Have I not told you that during sessions at the

12. R. Shmuel HaNagid, *Mevo HaTalmud*, s.v. *amar*. The citation is from Eduyot 6.
13. Lev. 22:28.
14. Ḥullin 86b.

> *beit midrash* you should not stand outside? There may be someone within who is in difficulty about a matter and there might be a disturbance" [and if you were inside, you could resolve the issue]. Thereupon R. Zera went in, but R. Abba did not. [In the *beit midrash*] they were sitting and trying to determine which was Rebbe's later decision. R. Zera said to them, "[What a pity] you did not let me ask that old man [R. Abba] about this. He might have heard something about this from his father [R. Hiyya b. Abba] and his father [R. Hiyya b. Abba] from R. Yohanan, for R. Hiyya b. Abba used to review his studies in the presence of R. Yohanan every thirty days."[15]

Ultimately, though they never did get R. Hiyya b. Abba's view of the matter, the students in the Babylonian *beit midrash* received a message from R. Eleazar in Judaea that in the end Rebbe ruled like R. Meir, even though his was the minority opinion. The message appears to have been verbal; normative halakha follows Rebbe's decision.[16]

In light of the long-standing rabbinical emphasis on preserving the laws orally, there can be little doubt that when Rebbe undertook to write them down he must have encountered resistance from the more conservative of his colleagues. Maimonides, who, like R. Shmuel, resembled Rebbe in so many respects – as a scholar, a compiler of traditional laws, a master of the Hebrew language, and a renowned statesman who was held in awe by most of his contemporaries – clearly empathized with Rebbe. Like Rebbe, he faced opposition, both from the *Geonim* of Babylonia and from communities in northern Europe, primarily because, like Rebbe, he sought to consolidate all preceding rulings into one comprehensive work. Perhaps he glossed over the opposition to Rebbe's effort because he did not wish to draw attention to the criticism that confronted him in his time.

Whatever opposition Rebbe may have faced did not deter him from proceeding with his project. He had good reason to conclude

15. See also R. Hiyya b. Abba's dictum in Ḥullin 85a, referring to the Mishna in Ḥullin 81b.
16. Karo, *Shulḥan Arukh: Yoreh De'ah* 17:9.

both that there was an urgent need to commit the Law to paper, and that if ever there was a time when the Oral Law could safely be edited, it was then.

For the first time in decades, the Jews could be more relaxed about the Roman occupation. Already as early as when Septimius Severus and his forces transited through Palestine in 197–98, there had been a renewed burst of synagogue construction. Synagogues had now replaced the Temple *in toto* as the focus of Jewish religious ritual; and the rabbis had identified the synagogue as a *mikdash me'at,* a micro-sanctuary. Construction was especially concentrated in the Galilee district, where much of the Jewish population of Palestine lived.

An additional factor was the more relaxed Roman attitude toward Jewish entry into Jerusalem. Hadrian had banned Jews from the city, which he viewed as a symbol around which Jews could rally and revolt a third time. Antoninus' officials appear to have looked the other way if individual Jews occasionally entered the city on days other than Tisha B'Av, when the community was permitted to enter its environs to mourn the Temple's destruction.[17] Under Severus and Commodus, however, Jews were able to enter the city "openly and freely."[18] It was likely due to these favorable circumstances, as well as to his own secure position with the Romans, that Rebbe deemed that he could safely commit the Mishna to writing.

Maimonides had a different explanation. He wrote:

> And why did our Holy Rabbi do all of this and not leave well enough alone? Because he saw that there were ever fewer students and that the troubles were re-emerging, and the Roman Empire continued to expand throughout the world and gain strength. And the Jews were continuing to disperse to the edges of the Empire. So he composed a single work that would be available to all so that they could quickly consume it and it would not be

17. Smallwood, *Jews under Roman Rule,* 478. See also Simon Sebag Montefiore, *Jerusalem: The Biography* (London: Phoenix, 2012), 184.
18. Smallwood, *Jews under Roman Rule,* 500.

> forgotten. So he and his colleagues on the court spent their entire lifetimes teaching the Mishna publicly.[19]

At first glance, this view of why Rebbe composed the Mishna appears entirely at odds with the description of Rebbe's relations with the Romans during his years as patriarch. The state of Jewish life in Palestine was so much improved since the Bar Kokhba rebellion that Rebbe actually entertained the notion of abolishing Tisha B'Av. This hardly would have been the case if "troubles were re-emerging." Moreover, there is no evidence that the number of students declined during Rebbe's patriarchate; if anything, the peace that reigned over the country allowed for an increase rather than a decrease in the number of students applying themselves to knowledge of the Oral Law. Indeed, R. Sherira Gaon, leader of the yeshiva at Pumpeditha in Babylonia, who flourished two centuries before Maimonides, explicitly linked the tranquility of the times to the compilation of the Mishna. As he put it, "the Rabbis relaxed and avoided persecution during Rebbe's time because of the cordiality that existed between Antoninus and Rebbe, and he agreed to compile the halakha that the rabbis studied into one uniform version, so that each would not study his own variant."[20]

On the other hand, there can be little doubt that the Jews continued to create new communities that reached to the outskirts of the Empire. Jews had spread throughout the Middle East well before the region came to be dominated by Rome. Jews may have settled in Spain as early as the middle of the first century CE. But many settlements were of much older vintage. Writing early in the first century CE, Philo recorded that

> The metropolis [Jerusalem is] not only of the one country of Judaea but also of many [i.e., Jewish communities] because of the colonies which it has sent out from time to time into the

19. Maimonides, "Introduction," *Mishneh Torah*. For a discussion of how and why Maimonides linked the troubles that led to the writing of the Mishna to his decision to write the *Mishneh Torah*, see Moshe Halbertal, *Maimonides: Life and Thought*, trans. Joel Linsider (Princeton, NJ and Oxford: Princeton University Press, 2014), 168–71.
20. Dr. Binyamin Menashe Levin, ed., *Iggeret Rav Sherira Gaon: Nusaḥ Sefarad VeNusaḥ Tzorfat* (Haifa: Itzkovski, 1921), 21–22.

> bordering districts of Egypt, Phoenicia, Syria in general… and also with those more distant regions of Pamphylia, Cilicia, the greater part of Asia Minor as far as Bythinia and the furthermost corners of Pontus [all regions of present-day Turkey]. And in the same manner into Europe, into Thessaly, and Boeotia, and Macedonia, and Aetolia, and Attica, and Argos, and Corinth and all the most fertile and wealthiest districts of Peloponnesus [all regions of Greece]. And not only are the continents full of Jewish colonies, but also all the most celebrated islands are so too; such as Euboea, and Cyprus, and Crete.[21]

In addition, there were Jewish colonies in Malta, Aquitania (present-day southwest France), Moesia (Balkans/south bank of Danube), Lycia, and Phrygia (Anatolian Turkey).[22]

The Jewish settlements throughout the Empire, and particularly those on its outskirts, had to rely heavily on the rabbinical leadership in Judaea for spiritual guidance. There were no yeshivas or academies in any of these places, even in Rome itself, though Rome did produce some leading scholars. What Philo had written about in the first century CE applied 150 years later: the Roman Diaspora looked to Rebbe for guidance. So, to some extent, did the Jews of Babylonia, though they did have established centers of learning and their own leader, Huna the exilarch. Ultimately, the Mishna came to be canonized, occupying a place second only to Scripture itself. As Maimonides observed, "The rabbis taught it all publicly everywhere so that the Jewish people would not forget the Oral Law."[23]

The Mishna's Structure and Taxonomy

The Mishna was far more than a code of law. It incorporated "anecdotes, maxims, exhortations, scriptural exegesis, and descriptions of the rituals of the Jerusalem Temple," and it did so with considerable

21. "On the Embassy to Gaius," in *The Works of Philo*, trans. C. D. Yonge (Peabody, MA: Hendrickson, 1993), 782–83.
22. Smallwood, *Jews under Roman Rule*, 122–23 and fn. 13.
23. Maimonides, "Introduction," *Mishneh Torah*.

brevity.[24] Nevertheless, even if it was not a legal code, it was replete with legal material, virtually all of it dating from the century when Yavneh and then Usha were the centers of rabbinic activity (80–180 CE). Rebbe, who had spent his early years in Usha, inherited these legal traditions, many of which were in conflict with one another. He organized the Mishna on the basis of six major divisions or "orders": Zera'im (seeds), Mo'ed (festival or season), Nashim (women), Nezikin (damages or torts), Kodashim (sanctified objects), and Teharot (ritual purity).

The six orders had been initially established by Rebbe's great-great-great grandfather Hillel and modified extensively by R. Akiba, the greatest scholar of his generation and perhaps of all the *Tanna'im*. Rebbe openly acknowledged his debt to R. Akiba. He described him as "a well-stocked storehouse" of Torah and compared him to

> a worker who went out with his basket; when he found wheat he placed it inside; barley, the same; spelt the same; beans, the same; lentils, the same. When he returned home he sorted them out, separating the wheat, the barley, the spelt, the beans and the lentils. Such was the practice of R. Akiba; he sorted the Torah into rings and rings, that is, every item individually into separate compartments.[25]

Zera'im actually opens with the tractate of Berakhot ("blessings"), which deals primarily with the liturgy, much of which still forms the principal content of modern prayer books. The remainder of this order addresses ritual observance of agricultural laws. Mo'ed addresses the various laws of Shabbat, festivals (including Purim, which was rabbinically ordained), fasts, and the funding of Temple operations and maintenance. Nashim addresses matters of family life, marriage (including levirate marriage and the laws of *sota* – the wife suspected of adultery), divorce, vows, and laws pertaining to the nazirite. Nezikin deals with civil and criminal law, governance, idolatry, and the treatment of erroneous decisions or rulings

24. Cohen, *From the Maccabees*, 206. See also Urbach, *The Halakhah*, 346–47.
25. *Avot DeRabbi Natan* 18: 1. See Barry Holtz, *Rabbi Akiva*, 180–81.

issued by a court. Kodashim deals with matters pertaining to sacrifices, the Temple and its contents, the priests who officiate over rituals, the slaughtering of animals and birds for normal consumption, and all the dietary laws. Finally, Teharot deals with laws of ritual purity and defilement both with respect to people and to objects.

While the first four orders of the Mishna dealt with practical realities confronting the Jewish people, the last two addressed matters that had long been overtaken by events. There was no Temple, and therefore no sacrifices, no rituals over which priests would officiate; there was no immediate reason to record the dimensions of the Temple[26] nor the requirements for purity upon entering the Temple precincts.

Traditional scholars have argued that the inclusion of these reflected the "unquenchable" hope that the Third Temple would be rebuilt sometime soon, which would call for "the restoration of the sacrificial cult, so that the knowledge of its laws would once again become essential."[27] In addition, as the Talmud indicated, the rabbis believed that "the study of the sacrificial laws could serve as a surrogate for the Temple cult and was no less efficacious than the actual offering of the sacrifice itself."[28] This latter reason is articulated in the preliminary morning prayers of the hasidic prayer book (*Nusaḥ Sefarad*), wherein after reciting each portion of the Mishna dealing with a particular sacrifice, the congregant inserts a brief sentence that reads "May it be Thy will that it be as if I sacrificed (name of sacrifice just recited)."

Modern scholars offer yet another, equally plausible and related reason for the inclusion of these two orders. Because the laws they contain are no longer practiced but only taught and studied, and the rabbis are in charge of teaching and study, they establish the rabbis as the pinnacle of Jewish society in place of the priests, who held that position when the Temple was still standing. Moreover, the expansion of ritual purity from the Temple and its priests to society at large, as reflected in

---

26. These are described in great detail in Tractate Middot.
27. I. Epstein, "Introduction to Seder Kodashim," in Rabbi Dr. I. Epstein, ed., *Zebahim*, trans. Rabbi Dr. H. Freedman (London: Soncino, 1988), 2.
28. Ibid.; see also Menaḥot 110a; Taanit 27b; Exodus Rabba 38:4.

the order Teharot, underscored the role of the rabbis as "official upholders and guarantors of purity and holiness."[29]

THE MISHNA AND HALAKHA: SETTING THE RULES

In editing the Mishna, Rebbe took care to offer the views of rabbis that often contradicted each other, as well as minority opinions and opinions that were not adopted as normative halakha. Of course, the Mishna identified positions that it intended to be treated as normative – certainly the *Amora'im* considered that to be its intention – by citing minority and dissenting opinions. But it fulfilled an additional function by providing a basis for study of the range of opinions on a given issue, even if those did not ultimately prevail as binding law.[30] For example, in most cases when Beit Shammai and Beit Hillel disputed an issue, halakha generally followed Beit Hillel. Nevertheless, Rebbe and his co-editors took care to present both views. He also made it clear that both were the words of Heaven. Moreover, the Mishna explicitly added that "although one [Beit Shammai] prohibited and the other [Beit Hillel] permitted, one invalidated and the other declared valid, Beit Shammai did not refrain from marrying the women of Beit Hillel, nor did Beit Hillel refrain from marrying the women of Beit Shammai."[31]

In addition to ruling most often in favor of Beit Hillel in opposition to Beit Shammai, the Talmud adopted an additional set of rules that governed the resolution of legal disagreements cited in the Mishna. The Jerusalem Talmud ruled that Rebbe's view prevailed in all disputes, even if his view was contradicted by the majority.[32] That was not the fully accepted view of the Babylonian Talmud, which records that *Amora'im* were divided over the extent to which Rebbe's opinion was meant to be followed. Rabba bar Bar Hana asserted in the name of Rebbe's great student R. Hiyya that

29. Schafer, *History of the Jews in Antiquity*, 166.
30. For a discussion, see Richard Hidary, *Dispute for the Sake of Heaven: Legal Pluralism in the Talmud* (Providence, RI: Brown, 2010), 44–46.
31. Y. Yevamot 1:4.
32. Y. Terumot 3:1.

> if one acted according to Rebbe, he acted [legitimately]; if one acted according to the rabbis [who were in dispute with Rebbe], he too acted [legitimately]. [The reason being that] he [i.e., R. Hiyya] was uncertain whether the halakha followed Rebbe [only] when he disagreed with a colleague, but not when he disagreed with [multiple] colleagues, or whether the halakha followed Rebbe even when he disagreed with [several] colleagues.[33]

R. Hiyya's dictum appears to apply both *ab initio* and *post factum*. That, however, is not the case in Rava's view. Rava, who was not a student of Rebbe, acknowledged his authority in a more restricted fashion. He stated that "one is forbidden to act according to Rebbe; but if he did so, it was acceptable. He was of the opinion that [regarding Rebbe and the sages] one inclined [toward the latter]."[34] In other words, unlike R. Hiyya, who was prepared to accept the possibility that halakha could indeed follow Rebbe's position, Rava would not do so, but only validated an action that had already been taken based on Rebbe's opinion. Indeed, as seen below, the rabbis did overrule some of Rebbe's most ambitious proposals, and halakha has confirmed their view.

As has been noted, if no rabbi was mentioned at all in a given mishna, it reflected a unanimous opinion, or one that Rebbe wished to present as unanimous.[35] Alternately, a mishna that cited a legal position without attribution, or simply did so in the name of "the Sages," reflected an opinion that was consistently held by a majority that – as Maimonides put it – reached to Moses himself.[36] In either case, the Mishna was attributable to R. Meir, who was the recipient of that unanimous or majority tradition. In addition, in a number of limited cases discussed at varying points in the Talmud, the undisputed opinion in a mishna was actually that of someone other than R. Meir.[37]

---

33. Bava Batra 124a–b.
34. Ibid.
35. See chap. 4, "The Patriarch," pp. 160–61.
36. Maimonides, *Hakdamat HaRambam MiSeder Zera'im*, published together with Berakhot 56a, s.v. *haperek hashishi.*
37. Ibid.

It should also be noted Rebbe had never forgotten R. Meir's attempted coup against his father; he referred to him in the Mishna as *aḥerim omrim*, "others say." Similarly, he would cite R. Nathan, who joined R. Meir in the plot, as *yesh omrim*, "there are those who say."[38] Rebbe did not limit his code words to those who had wished his father ill, however. For example, when he would cite "the Sages" he sometimes meant a group of rabbis and sometimes individual rabbi whom the Talmud later identified and whose opinion was accepted by many others. When Rebbe would cite Beit Shammai and Beit Hillel, he was referring to the scholars who adopted the opinion of one or the other of the great leaders, without mentioning any one of them individually by name.[39] When Rebbe would cite R. Eliezer without a patronymic, he always meant R. Eliezer b. Hyrkanos. When he cited R. Joshua, he meant R. Joshua b. Hananiah. R. Judah always denoted his teacher R. Judah b. Ila'i. R. Eleazar was always R. Eleazar b. Shammua, in whose academy Rebbe had suffered various indignities. R. Simeon always denoted R. Simeon bar Yohai, that implacable enemy of the Romans.

Rebbe generally referred to some rabbis only by their patronymic. Thus Ben Azzai, Ben Zoma, and Ben Nannus all were named Simeon, while Ben Beteira was actually Judah b. Beteira. On the other hand, Ben Bag Bag, whose name appears in Avot,[40] was actually R. Yohanan, while references to R. Yohanan the High Priest denoted the father of Matityahu, who initiated the Maccabean revolt.[41]

As noted above, the two Talmuds adopted somewhat different views of the halakhic outcome when Rebbe disagreed with his colleagues. The Talmuds also differed when the Mishna outlined disagreements

38. R. Samson ben Isaac of Chinon, a fourteenth-century Tosafist, asserted in *Sefer Keritot* that R. Meir was only called *aḥerim* when he was quoting his teacher Elisha ben Avuya, the heretic who was known as *aḥer*. Cited in a gloss on Maimonides, ibid., s.v. *uvesefer*, by R. Samuel Freund, a nineteenth-century *dayan* of Prague. R. Freund also pointed out that there are occasions when *aḥerim* are mentioned alongside R. Meir, suggesting either that he was not the only one who received the appellation, or alternately, that a scribal error had crept into the text at some point during its transmission.
39. Maimonides, loc. cit.
40. Avot 3:27.
41. Maimonides, loc. cit.

between other rabbis. The same passage in the Jerusalem Talmud that codifies the law in accordance with Rebbe's opinion also notes that the halakha follows R. Yose's opinion in any dispute other than one with Rebbe; that it follows R. Simeon's opinion when he disagrees with R. Meir; but that if he disagrees with R. Judah it follows the latter, and "it goes without saying" that where R. Meir and R. Judah disagree the halakha follows R. Judah.[42]

In contrast, the Babylonian Talmud outlines several views, none of them entirely in accord with its Jerusalem counterpart. R. Jacob and R. Zerika held that the halakha always follows R. Akiba when he disagrees with another rabbi and that the same holds true for Rebbe, and that it also holds for R. Yose even if he disagrees with more than one rabbi. Several other rabbis disagreed among themselves, however, as to what R. Jacob and R. Zerika really meant. R. Asi took their statement literally: the halakha follows the rules they have laid out. R. Hiyya bar Abba – Rebbe's great student, who therefore should have had a much better idea of what the Mishna meant to say – argued that these rules are really guidelines, determining where one should "incline." Finally, R. Hanina, another of Rebbe's students, took a slightly softer view. He argued that R. Jacob and R. Zerika merely identified what "appeared preferable."

R. Jacob b. Idi, in R. Yohanan's name, then noted – as did the Jerusalem Talmud – that in a dispute between R. Meir and R. Judah, or between R. Yose and R. Meir, the halakha followed R. Meir. R. Yohanan took issue with R. Jacob and R. Zerika, and instead was in agreement with the Jerusalem Talmud that halakha followed R. Judah when he disagreed with R. Yose. R. Asi then clarified that the halakha follows R. Yose when he disagrees with R. Simeon; and R. Abba said the same in R. Yohanan's name. After this entire discussion, however, R. Mesharshiya initially rejected all of these rules of thumb. After all the discussion, however, the Talmud stated that "what he meant to say" was that these rules were not universally accepted, since Rav – another of Rebbe's great students – rejected them.[43]

---

42. Y. Terumot 3:1.
43. Eiruvin 46b–47b. For an extended discussion see Hidary, *Dispute*, 44–77.

The foregoing outlines only some of the disagreements as to whose views prevailed as normative halakha. Both Talmuds outline disputes among the *Amora'im* as to whose opinions are to be followed in a given case and whether those opinions apply only when they take a lenient, or alternately, a stringent position. Clearly, the Mishna hardly settled matters regarding halakha, which is why it also served as an important heuristic tool, in addition to preserving minority views that at some future time, and in special circumstances, might provide a basis for ruling contrary to what had been adopted as normative halakha.

REBBE'S IMPACT ON JEWISH LAW

Rebbe's influence can be felt throughout the Talmud, not only because he edited the Mishna, upon which both the Babylonian and Jerusalem Talmuds are based, but because of his many dicta that addressed every aspect of Jewish law and practice. His legal positions appear throughout the two Talmuds: the *baraitot*; Tosefta; and the halakhic midrashim (*midreshei halakha*), which include the *Mekhiltas* on Exodus of R. Yishmael and R. Simeon bar Yohai respectively, *Sifra* (also known as *Torat Kohanim*) on Leviticus, and *Sifrei* on Numbers.[44]

Many more of his views were transmitted by his students, who hailed from both Palestine and Babylonia, and who became the most prominent jurists of their generation. Some were even circulated by common folk who witnessed his rulings.[45] Some of his views fit well into the mainstream of rabbinical thought. Others, however, could only be termed radical, if not revolutionary.

The following brief sections offer a mere sampling of his legal rulings, not all of which were accepted by his colleagues and incorporated into normative halakha. These sections represent his positions regarding daily practices such as prayers and benedictions; then turn to rulings

44. He also makes frequent appearances in all the aggadic midrashim, just as he does in the aggadic portions of the two Talmuds.

45. For example, the testimony of the man who was "in charge of the assemblies," possibly the janitor (!), who saw Rebbe rule that an animal which had a needle stuck in the thick wall of the reticulum (*beit hakosot*) and protruding only on one side, was defective and forbidden to be eaten (*treifa*). Ḥullin 51a; see *Hullin*, trans. Eli Cashdan (London: Soncino, 1989), 51a fn. a4.

relating to key dates on the Jewish calendar, which included some of his more controversial opinions; then discuss some marital issues; and finally outline his attempts at reform, primarily motivated by economic considerations, whether with regard to the Sabbatical year, to usury, or foods that were forbidden to Jews.

PRAYER

Recital of the *Shema*

The *Shema* consists of three distinct sections from the Torah and opens with "Hear O Israel, the Lord is our God, the Lord is One." This verse from Deuteronomy is the ultimate expression of a Jew's "allegiance to the One GOD, sovereign of the universe, to whose authority all earthly powers are answerable."[46] It is recited twice daily, in morning and evening prayers, as well as at bedtime. It represents the cornerstone of a Jew's faith and comprises the last words that he or she hopes to utter before departing from this world.

The Talmud discusses in great detail when the *Shema* is to be recited, in what language, under what conditions, and whether it must be verbalized or can be uttered in silence. Rebbe held that one could only recite the *Shema* in Hebrew; in contrast, the rabbis accepted that the prayer could be recited in any language. Rebbe's position may well have derived from his outspoken view that Hebrew, and secondarily Greek, were far superior to other languages, particularly Aramaic. When, on the other hand, the rabbis allowed the *Shema* to be recited in any language, they no doubt had Aramaic, the language of the common people, in mind. The rabbis' opinion prevailed, and recitation of the *Shema* in any language remains acceptable, though the Hebrew original is preferred.

Rebbe also argued that the *Shema* had to be recited audibly, so that one's ears hear what one's mouth enunciates. Again, the rabbis rejected his position. Instead they ruled that one could recite the verses silently. The rabbis' position prevailed.

Rebbe's ruling that one fulfills the commandment to recite *Shema* merely by uttering the first verse surprised the rabbis of the Talmud. In

46. *The Authorized Daily Prayer Book*, 67.

this case, however, they accepted his view that by covering one's eyes when reciting the verse, one submits to "the yoke of Heaven."[47] Indeed, such is the normative practice to this day.[48]

Rebbe's disciples could not agree as to whether or not he would complete the *Shema* when he was free to do so. Bar Kappara argued that he did not, and that he would take pains to recite a lesson with the third part of *Shema*, which relates to the Exodus, so as to have recited that portion of the prayer. Rebbe's son R. Simeon argued that he did indeed complete the *Shema* when he could, and presumably recited the passages relating to the Exodus at that time, but he nevertheless would also recite a lesson of the Exodus together with the first verse of *Shema* so that both would be recited at the proper time.[49]

Later commentators assumed that Rebbe could not initially recite the entire *Shema* because he did not wish to interrupt his lectures in the academy. This may well have been the case and indeed this interpretation led some decisors to rule that one does not interrupt Torah study to say the *Shema*, other than its first verse.[50] It is also arguable, however, that Rebbe adopted the shorter version because he had pressing duties that could not be postponed, such as meetings with Roman officials or court cases, whose delay is prohibited.[51]

An Introductory Prayer

The Talmud relates that a number of prayers uttered by individual rabbis were incorporated into the order of service. As has already been noted, Rebbe always was accompanied by a military escort that Severus had designated as his personal guard.[52] It is in the context of the retainers'

47. Berakhot 13b.
48. Karo, *Shulḥan Arukh: Oraḥ Ḥayyim: Hilkhot Keriat Shema*, 61:5.
49. Berakhot 13b.
50. R. Menahem ben Shlomo Meiri, *Beit HaBeḥira: Berakhot*, ed. Shmuel Dickman (Jerusalem: Makhon HaTalmud HaYisraeli HaShalem, 5725/1965), 43.
51. His practice does not appear to have been accepted as halakha, although if it was indeed due to official government responsibilities, it would fall under the general rabbinic exemption for those in government.
52. Rashi, Berakhot 16b, asserts that "Antoninus" assigned the guards to him. This is quite plausible, given that guards were an indication of recognized authority. In

role as Rebbe's security detachment that the Talmud records a prayer that he uttered and that has since been incorporated in the initial portion of the morning service:

> Rebbe on concluding his prayer added the following: "May it be Thy will, O Lord our God, and God of our fathers, to deliver us from the impudent and from impudence, from an evil man, from the evil impulse, from an evil companion, from an evil neighbor, and from the destructive Accuser, from a hard lawsuit and from a hard opponent, whether he is a son of the covenant or not a son of the covenant."

The Talmud then adds that he prayed in this manner "although guards were appointed to protect" him.[53] Much as the Secret Service and its counterparts in other countries ensure that unsavory persons are unable to come near the person of the American president and other leading officials, so too did Rebbe's security detachment prevent "evil" men, companions, neighbors and the like from getting physically too close to the patriarch.

It is not clear why the rabbis who formatted the prayerbook moved Rebbe's prayer from the end of the service, when Rebbe introduced it, to its present position immediately after the fourteen blessings that open the service. Possibly those rabbis felt that it was appropriate to open the daily prayer regimen with a recognition that "we are social beings, influenced by our environment, therefore we pray to be protected from harmful people, events and temptations. The prayer reflects the 'social fabric of faith.'"[54]

Why then did Rebbe recite the prayer *after* the morning service? Perhaps because he was now beginning his administrative day,

---

this case "Antoninus" was probably Septimius Severus, rather than Caracalla, since Rebbe's authority would likely have been recognized by Rome well before Caracalla became emperor in his own right.

53. Berakhot 16b.
54. Chief Rabbi Lord Immanuel Jakobovits, "The Social Fabric of Faith," in *The Authorised Daily Prayer Book of the United Hebrew Congregations of the Commonwealth:* Revised and Enlarged Centenary Edition (London: Kuperard, 1998), 17.

during which he did not want to be placed in the position of having to order his guards to punish someone for disobeying his rulings, although he would have been entirely within his rights in doing so. Though he was known to be close to the Romans and protective of his own authority, he did not want the populace to view him as they did their foreign overlords, that is, with respect but with an undercurrent of hostility. Instead, he wished to be identified by his own people with his own people. Having his non-Jewish guards lash out at Jews, even if they were malefactors, would have made him look rather too much like the Romans themselves. Hence he placed this prayer not at the outset of his morning service, but rather at the beginning of his administrative day.

If Rebbe's prayer was geared to his workaday responsibilities, this would explain the tradition of the Lithuanian Brisk dynasty not to recite the prayer on Shabbat and holidays. On those days Rebbe did not conduct his daily business and therefore was unlikely to confront persons who would challenge his authority. The prayer was superfluous, indeed inappropriate, for days when all forms of work were forbidden.[55]

Treatment of Tefillin

Tefillin (phylacteries) are holy ritual objects; they contain passages from the Torah, written on parchment. Tefillin must be treated with care and respect. Indeed, one modern rabbinic leader is reported to have been careful to return them to their bag prior to reciting the supplementary service for the New Moon, rather than leaving them uncovered until the service was done.[56]

The definition of "respect," however, is both fluid and subjective. The Talmud therefore devoted considerable discussion as to how tefillin should be treated, in particular, whether they should be treated with the same degree of respect as that accorded to a

55. For a discussion of the omission of this prayer by Rabbis Hayyim Brisker and Joseph Ber Soloveitchik, see Hershel Schachter, *Nefesh HaRav* (Hebrew) (Jerusalem: Reishit Yerushalayim, 5755/1994), 107.
56. Ascribed to R. Joseph Ber Soloveitchik.

Torah scroll. R. Hanina, one of Rebbe's leading students, reported that he had witnessed his teacher hanging up his tefillin, a practice that not only was impermissible if done to a Torah scroll, but about which the rabbis asserted, "If one hangs up his tefillin, his life will be suspended." It quickly became clear that Rebbe was not hanging the tefillin by their straps or boxes, but had first placed them in a bag. His innovation was that while tefillin were holy, they did not carry with them the same sanctity as a Torah scroll, which cannot be hung up in any manner.[57] Rebbe's ruling was incorporated into normative halakha.[58]

Sneezing and Other Bodily Functions

R. Hanina also witnessed Rebbe sneezing, spitting, yawning, belching, and feeling his prayer shawl to remove insects all while in the midst of reciting the *Amida*, the Eighteen Benedictions that are the core of each service. R. Hanina did not specify the circumstances in which Rebbe seemed to act in an undignified manner, but the Talmud explained them all as in no way acting disrespectfully during prayer. Rebbe suffered from serious intestinal maladies and it was therefore not surprising that he would involuntarily belch on occasion, but he always covered his mouth when he felt he was about to do so. He likewise always covered his chin and mouth when he yawned; his yawning and sneezing also were involuntary. Indeed the Talmud quoted the school of R. Hamnuna that "if one sneezes in his prayer it is a good sign for him, that as they give him relief below [on earth] so they give him relief above [in heaven]."[59] As for his spitting, which also might have been a result of his intestinal troubles, Rebbe always took care to bring his scarf to his mouth when he felt the spittle beginning to collect there. Finally, in feeling for insects, Rebbe made certain that his tallit would

57. Berakhot 24a.
58. Karo, *Shulḥan Arukh: Oraḥ Ḥayyim, Hilkhot Keriat Shema*, 40:1. The same ruling applies to holy books, such as the Talmud; see R. Israel Meir Kagan, *Mishna Berura*, loc. cit., 40:1:3.
59. Berakhot 24b.

not fall down, but if it did, he did not interrupt his prayer to put it back on.[60] Once again, Rebbe's practices became normative halakha.[61]

Importance of Responding with Amen

The word "amen" appears frequently in Scripture, most notably when the Israelites were commanded to respond amen to a series of blessings and curses that would be uttered on Mount Gerizim and Mount Eval, respectively. The Talmud and Midrash state that the word is actually an acronym for *El Melekh Ne'eman*, that is, God is a faithful king.[62] A number of leading rabbis, both *Tanna'im* and *Amora'im*, outlined the rewards for responding with amen after a blessing. R. Joshua b. Levi asserted that replying amen "with all one's strength" would annul an evil decree. R. Hiyya bar Abba, citing R. Yohanan, goes even further: doing so would even erase the taint of idolatry.[63]

These statements appear to indicate that saying amen is a meritorious act with great rewards, rather than the fulfillment of an obligation. Rebbe, however, viewed amen as a mandatory response to a blessing. Juxtaposing a passage in Proverbs that states "The mention of the righteous is for a blessing,"[64] and one in Psalms that proclaims "The Lord is righteous in all his ways,"[65] Rebbe decreed, "Render unto him a blessing by saying amen."[66] Of course, as is the case with respect to all positive commandments, whether biblical or rabbinic, one is rewarded for their fulfillment. Nevertheless, it was Rebbe who clearly pointed out that responding to a blessing with amen is not merely a "nice to have."

60. Ibid., per Rashi, s.v. *aval lo*.
61. Karo, *Shulḥan Arukh: Oraḥ Ḥayyim, Hilkhot Tefilla*, 97:1–4. R. Jacob ben Asher and R. Isaac Alfasi both emphasized that in stifling a yawn one should not simply put one's hand on the chin (presumably to close the mouth), since doing so appeared arrogant while one recited the *Amida* (Gloss of R. Moses Isserles, loc. cit. 97:1).
62. Dictum of R. Hanina, Shabbat 119b.
63. Ibid.
64. Prov. 10:7.
65. Ps. 145:17.
66. *Mekhilta DeRabbi Yishmael, Parashat Bo* 17, s.v. *vayomer*. See also Hammer, *The Classic Midrash*, 66, whose translation is followed here. The translation is slightly more expansive than the text.

Concentrating One's Prayer

The rabbis taught that if a person was riding on an ass and the time arrived for saying the *Amida*, he[67] should dismount and pray if an attendant was present who could hold the animal. Otherwise he should pray while sitting on his mount. Rebbe disagreed. He argued that in either case the person could pray while mounted on the animal. He reasoned that even if a servant were present, the rider would be concerned about delaying his journey.[68] Rebbe always traveled with a retinue that could have held his mount; nevertheless, he clearly placed great value on punctuality, perhaps because it was important that he not be late for official functions, perhaps because his punctuality set the proper example for others.

Although he was in the minority, it was Rebbe's opinion that became normative halakha.[69] The later decisors added several provisos, however. If one subsequently has occasion to dismount, one should repeat the *Amida* if the time for its recitation has not yet passed.[70] Even if one cannot dismount, the rider should attempt to get his mount to back up three steps, so that in effect he would be doing so.[71] These rulings initially were important for riders on a ship or a wagon who may have been unable to stand. They are also of special significance to contemporary long-term air travelers, who often cannot leave their seats in order to recite the *Amida* while standing. In a seminal ruling, R. Moshe Feinstein, the leading decisor for Ashkenazi Jewry since the mid-twentieth century, wrote that "one who prays in an airplane need not repeat the *Amida* afterwards, and even ab initio, if it is difficult to stand in the plane and doing so would be a cause for upset, it is better to sit and merely stand immediately prior to the point when one is meant to bow."[72]

67. One might add "or she."
68. Berakhot 30a, and Rashi, s.v. *she'ein daato*.
69. Karo, *Shulḥan Arukh: Oraḥ Ḥayyim, Hilkhot Tefilla*, 94:4.
70. Ibid., 94:9, and Kagan, *Mishna Berura*, 94:9:26.
71. Gloss of R. Moses Isserles, *Shulḥan Arukh: Oraḥ Ḥayyim, Hilkhot Tefilla*, 94:5.
72. R. Moshe Feinstein, *Igrot Moshe: Oraḥ Ḥayyim* (Hebrew), vol. 4:20 (Bnei Brak: Yeshivat Ohel Yosef, 5741/1981), 32.

Grace after Meals (*Birkat HaMazon*)

According to tradition, not only must one wash one's hands prior to commencing a meal, but also at its conclusion immediately preceding *Birkat HaMazon*. The reason given for what are termed *mayim aḥaronim* (final water) is that one's hands have been soiled by salt originating in Sodom. While such salt is not available in most places, the practice of cleaning one's fingers persists. Indeed, it is not unique to practicing Jews; many formal dinners include a finger bowl for rinsing one's hands after each dinner course.

Rebbe linked *mayim aḥaronim* to *Birkat HaMazon* in another way as well: He ruled that whoever was first to wash his hands would lead the call to saying grace if three or more persons were eating together (*zimmun*). The Talmud relates that "Rav and R. Hiyya were once sitting before Rebbe at dinner. Rebbe said to Rav: Get up and wash your hands. He [R. Hiyya] saw him [Rav] trembling. R. Hiyya said to him: Son of Princes! He is telling you to think over the Grace after Meals."[73] Rav apparently had thought that Rebbe was chiding him for having dirtied his hands; R. Hiyya said he actually was honoring him. By asking Rav to wash his hands first, R. Hiyya was also telling him to prepare himself for leading the Grace. Tradition still follows Rebbe's practice.[74]

Rebbe was exceedingly punctilious regarding the wording of the *zimmun* itself. With respect to the phrase "Blessed be the One from whose food we have eaten, and by His goodness we live," Rebbe said that if the leader "says 'and by His goodness,' he is a scholar; if he says 'and from His goodness,' he shows himself an ignoramus."[75] "From His goodness" in Rebbe's view, would seem to imply that it was a small thing that we live by His goodness.[76] Rebbe's view has prevailed.

Rebbe also issued another ruling relating to the Grace after Meals. The third blessing of *Birkat HaMazon* opens with a request for mercy for the Jewish people and for Jerusalem. The rabbis differed as to

73. Berakhot 43a.
74. Meiri, *Beit HaBeḥira: Berakhot*,158.
75. Ibid., 50a.
76. Rashi, loc. cit., s.v. *umituvo*.

whether the conclusion of this blessing should emphasize Israel, Jerusalem, or both. The exilarch would always conclude with reference to both. Rebbe, on the other hand, argued for reference to only one. His view was sustained, and the blessing states "who in His compassion will rebuild Jerusalem."[77]

THE CYCLE OF JEWISH HOLIDAYS

Yom Kippur

Jews and even non-Jews universally recognize Yom Kippur, the Day of Atonement, as the holiest day of the Jewish year. As its name implies, it is the day when men and women can atone for their sins of the previous year and receive divine forgiveness. The Talmud asks whether the day itself is sufficient for the granting of atonement, or whether the act of repentance is necessary as well. Rebbe asserted that the day was sufficient in itself, with the exception of one who rejects the Torah, interprets it unlawfully, or breaks the covenant of Abraham, that is, forgoes circumcision. In those cases, full repentance would be necessary as well. Rebbe recognized that not everyone was of a sufficiently elevated moral and ethical stature to repent for every sin. If a person observed Yom Kippur and submitted to the five strictures of Yom Kippur – abstaining from food, drink, bathing with oil, sex, and the wearing of leather – then that was enough to absolve him/her of past transgressions. Indeed, adopting these restrictions could produce miraculous results. The Talmud recounts:

> Once a pregnant woman smelled [food that she craved]; when people came to Rebbe [for his ruling] he replied, "Go and whisper to her that it is the Day of Atonement." They whispered to her and she was dissuaded [from eating]. Thereupon Rebbe applied the verse to her "Before I formed you in your womb I knew you,"[78] and she gave birth to [the great scholar] R. Yohanan.[79]

77. Ibid., 49b. Translation is from Sacks, *The Authorized Daily Prayer Book*, 765.
78. Jer. 1:2.
79. Yoma 82b; see the discussion in Urbach, *The Sages*, 244.

But Rebbe added a proviso: while Yom Kippur need not be accompanied by repentance, "repentance requires the Day of Atonement."[80] One not only had to regret one's past deeds, but also actively to submit to the rigors of Yom Kippur if that regret was to be accepted as sincere. As Rebbe saw it, saying "I regret" was nothing more than uttering a platitude. As a politician, he understood the value of words, or lack thereof. One had to act upon one's words, and Yom Kippur was the appropriate vehicle for action.

As noted, Rebbe states that "Yom Kippur atones for all the sins of the Torah, whether an individual repented or not, apart from one who rejects the yoke of Torah, interprets the Torah unlawfully, and breaks the covenant of Abraham. In these cases, if he repented, Yom Kippur atones, if not, not."[81] It is interesting that Rebbe did not list idolatry, adultery, and murder, the three sins to be avoided even at the cost of martyrdom, for which repentance would be mandatory in order to obtain atonement on Yom Kippur. Instead, he identified repentance as a necessary condition for obtaining atonement in the case where one rejected the Torah's laws, or when one had interpreted the Torah unlawfully, in other words, who challenged the rabbinical interpretation of Torah.

Finally, a version of the early sixth-century midrash *Pesikta DeRav Kahana* attributes to Rebbe a notion that rabbis have long included in their sermons on the Shabbat that falls between Rosh Hashana and Yom Kippur, known as *Shabbat Shuva,* which opens with the prophet Hosea's words *Shuva Yisrael* (Return O Israel).[82] After having cited Scriptural proof-texts in support of the principle that the completely righteous are inscribed in the Book of Life[83] while the completely evil are blotted out of the book,[84] Rebbe asserts: "To those neither completely righteous nor completely wicked, the Holy One gives ten days between New Year's Day and the Day of Atonement: if they resolve to repent, they are inscribed with the righteous; but if they do not resolve

80. Yoma 85b; *Mekhilta DeRabbi Yishmael, BaḤodesh,* 197.

81. Yoma 85b.

82. Hos. 14:2.

83. Dan. 12:2.

84. Ps. 69:29.

to repent, they are inscribed with the wicked. Therefore Hosea, admonishing Israel, says to them: Return O Israel."[85] Rebbe argued that even without repentance, with but a very few exceptions, apart from Yom Kippur, "the day of death effects atonement";[86] still, repentance was most certainly to be preferred.

Rebbe had an extremely positive view of those who repented. When told of the strange case of R. Eleazar b. Dordai, who was addicted to frequenting brothels, but, when chastised by no less than a prostitute, "placed his head between his knees and wept until his soul departed," Rebbe wept and exclaimed: "One may acquire eternal life after many years, but one can also acquire eternal life in but an hour." He went on to say, "It is not only that repentants are accepted, they are even called 'Rabbi.'"[87]

Hanukkah

The Mishna barely mentions Hanukkah, a rather surprising fact, since it devotes an entire tractate to the holiday of Purim. In fact, the Mishna discusses the holiday at length only once, in Tractate Bava Kamma:

> If a camel loaded with flax was passing through a public thoroughfare and the flax penetrated a shop, caught fire from the shopkeeper's [lit] candle and burned the whole building, the owner of the camel is liable. If the shopkeeper left his candle on the street, he is liable. R. Judah says: If it was a Hanukkah candle the shopkeeper is not liable.[88]

The Gemara then debates what might be the appropriate height of the menora in order to exempt the shopkeeper. Ravina, in the name of Rava, argues that it is ten handbreadths, which is relatively low to the ground. Others take the view that it can be higher, though all agree

85. *Pesikta DeRab Kahana: R. Kahana's Compilation of Discourses for Sabbaths and Festal Days*, trans. William G. (Gershon Zev) Braude and Israel J. Kapstein (Philadelphia: Jewish Publication Society of America, 1975), 367.
86. *Mekhilta DeRabbi Yishmael, BaḤodesh*, 196–97; for a discussion see Urbach, *The Sages*, 431–34.
87. Avoda Zara 17a.
88. Bava Kamma 62b. Examples of brief references are Megilla 3:4, 6.

that the menora can be placed no higher than thirty-five feet, the limitation that is imposed on the height of a sukka. Apart from this reference to Hanukkah, however, and certainly regarding the historical basis for the holiday, the miracles identified with it, or even how the holiday should be celebrated, the Mishna has little to say. For that reason, some later commentators simply asserted that the Mishna *never* mentions Hanukkah.[89]

The Talmud does not address Hanukkah at great length either. There is no tractate for Hanukkah as there is for Purim (Tractate Megilla). Moreover, the Jerusalem Talmud says virtually nothing about Hanukkah. The holiday is only discussed in detail in the Babylonian Talmud, primarily, and relatively briefly, in Tractate Shabbat. Apart from citing the case of the menora candles that burned the camel's flax which in turn set a building on fire, the passage mostly deals with lighting the Hanukkah candles: who is to light, how many candles to light each day, and where to place the lamp.

In contrast to the Mishna, the Babylonian Talmud does discuss the reasons for celebrating the holiday, and in so doing makes minimal mention of the Maccabees' victory over the Syrian Greeks.

> What is the reason for Hanukkah? For our Rabbis taught: On the 25th of Kislev begin the days of Hanukkah, which are eight, during which lamentation for the dead and fasting are forbidden. For when the Greeks entered the Temple, they defiled all the oils in it, and when the Hasmonean dynasty prevailed against and defeated them, they [the Hasmoneans] searched and found only one cruse of oil which possessed the seal of the High Priest, but which contained sufficient oil for only one day's lighting; yet a miracle occurred there and they lit [the lamp] for eight days. The following year these days were appointed a Festival with the recitation of *Hallel* and thanksgiving.[90]

---

89. See, for example, Abraham Isaac Sperling, *Taamei HaMinḥagim UMekorei HaDinim* no. 847 (Jerusalem: Eshkol, 5732/1972), 365.
90. Shabbat 21b.

In fact, the military victory is mentioned only in the apocryphal books of Maccabees I and II, both of which discuss the battles at some length, as does Josephus' *Antiquities*.[91]

It is clear that the rabbis deliberately sought to obscure the military aspects of the holiday. One theory postulates that they did so to avoid creating the impression that they were fomenting yet another insurrection against the Romans; after all, the Hanukkah story is about a revolt against a foreign overlord. Instead the rabbis elected to focus on the miracle of the oil and to mention the Greeks only in passing, in order to provide a context for the miracle.[92]

While at first blush this theory seems plausible, particularly in light of increasing Roman persecution of Jews in the two centuries after Constantine converted to Christianity, the theory does not account for the fact that it is not the Palestine-based Jerusalem Talmud that discussed the holiday, but rather the Babylonian Talmud. Babylonia's Jews may have suffered from some persecution, but it was neither as sustained nor as intense as that which was directed at their counterparts in the Roman Empire. Moreover, there never was anything like a Jewish revolt against the Parthians or the Persians who ruled Babylonia along the lines of the revolts of 68–70, the Bar Kokhba revolt, or the insurrection against Trajan that was sandwiched between the two Judaean rebellions. Finally, this theory does not explain why the Mishna does not mention the miracle of the oil either.

About a century ago, R. Aryeh Leib Feinstein posited an entirely different argument, namely that Rebbe did not believe in the miracle of the oil. R. Feinstein argued that Rebbe sided with R. Yose in his disagreement with R. Judah as to whether any miracles involved the oil that was used to anoint the High Priest and kings. R. Yose argued that there was no miracle; R. Judah countered that there were many miracles. As he put it:

> With the anointing oil which Moses prepared in the wilderness there occurred many miracles from the beginning to the end. Originally

91. Maccabees I: 1:1–23; 41–50; 2:1–6; 15–28; Maccabees II: 1:1–9 and 10:1–8; Flavius Josephus, *Antiquities of the Jews*, 12:7:3–6.
92. Malka Z. Simkovich, "Uncovering the Truth About Chanukah," *TheTorah.com* (November 27, 2013), http://thetorah.com/uncovering-the-truth-about-chanukah/.

> it only measured twelve logs. Now, consider how much the pot absorbed, how much the roots absorbed, and how much the fire burned, and yet it sufficed for the anointing of the Tabernacle and its furniture, and Aaron and his sons, throughout the seven days of consecration; and High Priests and kings also were anointed with it.[93]

Because Rebbe sided with R. Yose, there was no need to mention the Hanukkah miracle of oil in the Mishna, as there was no miracle.[94]

R. Feinstein's argument begs the question of why Rebbe did not mention the other Hanukkah miracle, namely, the victory of the Maccabees. It has been asserted that Rebbe omitted any mention of Hanukkah because the Hasmoneans displaced the House of David, from which he was descended, and ruled in its stead. "This upset our holy Rebbe and when he wrote the Mishna through the medium of the Holy Spirit (*ruaḥ hakodesh*), he omitted the miracle in his treatise."[95]

This view would certainly explain why the battlefield victory was not mentioned. Yet its basis is highly problematical. To begin with, it first was outlined more than fifteen hundred years after Rebbe's passing. One wonders why there was no reference to this particular concern of Rebbe's prior to the mid-nineteenth century. Moreover, this theory presupposes that Rebbe was so petty that he would omit discussion of a holiday on the Jewish calendar simply because of personal pique. Finally, when the Hasmoneans took power, there were no real claimants to David's throne. Though Rebbe claimed royal blood through his maternal line, and R. Huna and his predecessors as *Resh Galuta* claimed patrilineal descent from the House of David, the Book of Maccabees, which records the Hasmonean victory, does not mention any descendant of David's house who, as a contemporary of the Hasmonean rulers, might have launched a competing claim to the throne. Nor, for that matter, does the vast talmudic literature identify any such claimant.

---

93. Horayot 11b.
94. Aryeh Leib Feinstein, *Elef HaMagen*, 35b, cited in Marc B. Shapiro, "The Hanukkah Miracle," *The Seforim Blog* (April 27, 2017), http://seforim.blogspot.com/2017/04/the-hanukkah-miracle.html.
95. Sperling, *Taamei HaMinhagim*, no. 847, quoting *Ḥatam Sofer*, 365.

The *Al HaNissim* prayer that is included in the *Amida,* which is central to every Hanukkah service, does mention the victory of "the few over the many." While the rabbis were certainly predisposed to emphasize the miracle of the oil, they evidently were not prepared to eradicate the memory of the military victory. Why then did Rebbe omit to mention Hanukkah in the Mishna?

Like the nineteenth-century commentators, one can only speculate regarding Rebbe's motives. Perhaps, despite his excellent relations with the Romans, Rebbe did not want to resuscitate images of rebellious Jews. The Bar Kokhba rebellion was not a distant memory, nor indeed was the revolt against Trajan. The Jews were hardly universally popular: Domitian had planned to kill many of them, Marcus Aurelius held them in low regard, and Pescennius Niger treated them harshly. It was one thing for the rabbis to mention very briefly, and submerged in a prayer, that there had been a battle with an enemy. It was quite another thing to stress that battle or to link it to the menora, as Israelis do today. Rebbe, as an astute politician, recognized that there was far more to be lost than to be gained by highlighting a portion of Jewish history that could antagonize the Romans. He decided that discretion was the better part of valor, and successor generations of rabbis, especially the Babylonian *Amora'im,* followed his example.

Rebbe's Attempt to Abolish Tisha B'Av

Apart from Yom Kippur, the Jewish calendar features several other fast days, four of which commemorate various aspects relating to the destruction of the two Temples. The prophet Zechariah referred to all four of these fasts, mentioning the months in which they fell, but omitting specific dates.[96] R. Akiba provided the dates for each fast:

> [Scripture] states, "Thus says the Lord of hosts: The fast of the fourth month, and the fast of the fifth, and the fast of the seventh, and the fast of the tenth shall be joy and gladness for the house of Judah, and cheerful seasons; therefore love truth and peace.…

96. Zech. 8:19: "Thus says the Lord of hosts: The fast of the fourth month, and the fast of the fifth, and the fast of the seventh, and the fast of the tenth, shall become times of joy and gladness, and cheerful feasts for the house of Judah."

> The fast of the fourth month" refers to the Seventeenth of Tammuz, when the city was breached.... The "fast of the fifth" is Tisha B'Av, the day upon which the *Beit HaMikdash* was burned.... The "fast of the seventh" is the day upon which Gedalya ben Akhikam was murdered by Yishmael ben Netanya. This is to teach you that, before God, the death of the righteous is equal to the destruction of the Temple.... The "fast of the tenth" is the Tenth of Tevet, when the king of Babylon laid siege to Jerusalem.[97]

The rabbis disagreed among themselves as to whether the fifth or the tenth of Tevet should be observed as a fast. The fifth was when the news of the First Temple's destruction reached the Jews in Babylon;[98] the tenth was when the siege commenced. The rabbis opted for the tenth. They also shifted the fast of Tammuz from the ninth to the seventeenth of that month to commemorate Titus' breach of the city walls on that day, which in turn led to the destruction of the Second Temple three weeks later.

When R. Judah edited the Mishna, he included a multiplicity of reasons for the dating of two of the fasts. Regarding the Seventeenth of Tammuz, the Mishna states: "On the seventeenth of Tammuz, the Tablets [with the Ten Commandments] were broken, the daily [burnt] offering was stopped, the city was breached, Apostamos burned the Torah and placed an idol in the Temple." The Mishna then continues with respect to the Ninth of Av: "It was decreed that our fathers should not enter the Promised Land; the Temple was destroyed the first and second time; Betar was captured and the city [of Jerusalem] was ploughed up."[99] It is therefore especially surprising that the Babylonian Talmud records R. Eleazar

97. Tosefta Sota 6:10. A variant reading of the Tosefta, which appears in Rosh HaShana 18b, has the breach of the city on the ninth of Tevet (per Jer. 16:1–2). A version of the Tosefta has the siege beginning on the fifth of Tevet, but that is clearly erroneous since Jeremiah records the siege beginning on the tenth (II Kings 25:1, Jer. 52:4–6), while R. Simeon, who advocated for the fifth being the fast day, did so because it was on that day that the community in Babylon learned of the tragedy in Jerusalem.
98. Ezek. 33:21–22: "And it came to pass in the twelfth year of our captivity, in the tenth month, in the fifth day of the month that one that had escaped out of Jerusalem came unto me, saying: 'The city is smitten.'"
99. Taanit 28b.

as saying in the name of R. Hanina that Rebbe "planted a sapling on the seventeenth of Tammuz and wanted to uproot Tisha B'av."[100] It would appear that Rebbe had concluded that these two fasts, and by extension, the other two fast days related to the destruction of one or both of the Temples, were no longer necessary. The Jerusalem Talmud, which was compiled about one hundred years after the Mishna and more than two centuries before its Babylonian counterpart, has a different variant which omits any mention of Tisha B'Av: "Rebbe would conduct himself in public twice a year. He would bathe on the seventeenth of Tammuz and plant saplings on Purim."[101] It has been asserted that this variant indicates that the Babylonian Talmud's version may not have been accurate.[102]

It is arguable that the reason the Jerusalem Talmud made no mention of Tisha B'Av was that the Talmud was actually addressing a different matter, namely, whether work was permitted on the holiday of Purim. In the course of citing Rebbe's practice, which clearly indicated that work was indeed permitted, the Talmud recounted another of Rebbe's major leniencies. In this case, he was dealing with the question of whether all of the five prohibitions that were in force on Tisha B'Av (and Yom Kippur), namely eating or drinking, wearing footwear made of leather, bathing or washing, applying ointments or lotions, and abstinence from marital relations, applied to the other Temple-related fasts as well. The Talmud cited Rebbe's decision to bathe publicly on the seventeenth of Tammuz to indicate that on that day, as well as on the third of Tishrei and the tenth of Tevet, only abstinence from food and drink was mandated.

The question of abolishing Tisha B'Av was therefore not at all relevant to the Jerusalem Talmud's discussion. Indeed, whereas Jews still observe all five restrictions on Tisha B'Av, as well as several others unique to that day, notably the study of Torah, Rebbe's view with respect to the seventeenth of Tammuz has been accepted as normative halakha;

100. Megilla 5a–b.
101. Y. Megilla 1:1.
102. David Golinkin, "Should we continue to fast on Tisha B'Av and the other three fasts which commemorate the destruction of the Temple?" (June 17, 2010), http://www.schechter.edu/should-we-continue-to-fast-on-tisha-bav-and-the-other-three-fasts-which-commemorate-the-destruction-of-the-temple-1/.

only eating and drinking are forbidden on that day, as they are on the tenth of Tevet or the third of Tishrei.[103] Similarly, halakha technically permits work on Purim, though over the centuries it became customary in many communities to avoid working on that day if at all possible.

It is also noteworthy that the Babylonian version cites R. Hanina, who, as has been shown, was a student of Rebbe. R. Eleazar, R. Hanina's student, often spoke in his teacher's name, presumably with some accuracy. Moreover, since the rabbis were constantly traveling back and forth from Palestine to Babylonia, they were equally capable of preserving traditions in either place. The Babylonian version therefore appears to be authoritative: Rebbe concluded that fasts related to the destruction of the Temples, as opposed to either Yom Kippur on the one hand, or the far less stringent Fast of Esther on the other, no longer should remain in force. What, then, led Rebbe to conclude that "times had changed," to the point where he could justify doing away with a series of national fast days?

Several scholars have noted that a messianic atmosphere prevailed in Rebbe's court. They speculate that Rebbe may even have perceived himself as a nascent messiah, in which case he may have reasoned that the time had come to abolish the fasts.[104] The Babylonian Talmud cites an instance when Rebbe instructed R. Hiyya, perhaps his most talented student, to report to him on sanctifying the new moon using the password "David King of Israel is alive and vigorous."[105] Strictly speaking, one could interpret the phrase as simply noting that the moon is "alive and vigorous," in other words, that "the moon is reborn."[106] Rebbe's choice of that particular password is nevertheless somewhat unusual; the phrase could be construed as referring as much to himself as to the new moon.[107]

---

103. *Shulḥan Arukh, Oraḥ Ḥayyim,* 549:2.
104. Alon, *Jews in Their Land,* 717; David Golinkin, "Should we continue"; Moshe Aberbach, "Hizkiyah Melekh Yehuda VeRabbi Yehuda HaNasi: Heksherim Meshiḥiyim" (Hezekiah King of Judah and Rabbi Judah the Patriarch – Messianic Aspects) (Hebrew), *Tarbiz* 53:3 (5744/1984), 353–71.
105. Rosh HaShana 25a.
106. Thus Maurice Simon's commentary on the passage in Rabbi Dr. I. Epstein, ed., *Hebrew-English Translation of the Babylonian Talmud: Rosh HaShana,* trans. Maurice Simon (London: Soncino, 1990), 25a fn. c6.
107. Thus Golinkin, "Should we continue," loc. cit.

There is some additional and stronger evidence for this conjecture elsewhere in the Talmud. In an extended discussion regarding the personality of the Messiah, Rav, another of Rebbe's students, asserted, "If he [the Messiah] is of the living, it would be our holy teacher (*Rabbeinu HaKadosh* – i.e., Rebbe), if of the dead, it would have been Daniel the most desirable man."[108] Rebbe exhibited two of the critical characteristics that the rabbis attributed to the Messiah: he was the epitome of piety (*Ḥasid gamur*) and also suffered from a variety of infirmities.[109] Rav therefore speculated that Rebbe, his uncle R. Hiyya's teacher, could well be the Messiah; if not, he was the equivalent of Daniel. It was not an unflattering comparison.[110]

In editing the Mishna, Rebbe had inserted a passage that treated a prince (*Nasi*) as equivalent to a king, who had no superior other than God Himself.[111] The Babylonian Talmud then relates that Rebbe inquired of R. Hiyya whether, given his stature, had he lived during the Temple era he would have been biblically mandated to bring the king's sin offering.[112] Rebbe clearly viewed himself as effectively king of Israel. R. Hiyya disappointed him somewhat by replying that he was outranked by the exilarch. Unlike Rebbe, who claimed maternal descent from the House of David, the exilarch claimed paternal descent.

Despite this minor putdown, R. Hiyya was prepared to acknowledge Rebbe's special status. The Jerusalem Talmud relates that Rebbe once injured his finger on his way home from studying the Book of Lamentations on the eve of Tisha B'Av. He reacted by exclaiming, "Many are the torments of the wicked."[113] R. Hiyya replied, "It is for our sins that this befell you, for it is written, '*The breath of our lives,* the Lord's anointed, *was captured in their traps.*'"[114] Clearly, those around Rebbe

---

108. Sanhedrin 98b.
109. Rashi, s.v. *ee min ḥayya.*
110. The Talmud then relates that according to the rabbis, the Messiah's name would be "the leper from the house of Rebbe," since they had previously stated that the Messiah was to be found among the lepers of Rome. Rashi, loc. cit., s.v. *hivra.*
111. Mishna Horayot 3:2.
112. Horayot 11b, Rashi, loc. cit., s.v. *mah.*
113. Ps. 32:10.
114. Lam. 4:20. The emphasis is mine.

shared his view that he was more than just a religious leader; he embodied the national revival of his people.

The sense that Rebbe represented a positive turning point in the status of Palestinian Jewry no doubt was reinforced by the positive attitudes that both Septimius Severus and Caracalla displayed toward the Jews. When Severus was conducting his second expedition against Parthia in the autumn of 198 CE, he redeployed the VI Legion Ferrata from Palestine to the Parthian front. He could only have done so if, as a leading historian has pointed out, "by 198 the province of Palestine was sufficiently peaceful that half its garrison could safely be removed, and that it was the legion from the Galilee, not the one from the more strongly gentile south, that was chosen for the expedition."[115] From the Jewish perspective generally, and from Rebbe's specifically, the withdrawal of Roman occupying forces could only be taken as a sign of a more relaxed environment in which Jews could more easily carry on with their lives. The withdrawal proved temporary; still, the very fact that it took place at all must have been a basis for optimism about the Jewish future.

This sense of optimism reached its apogee when Jews, like all free subjects of the Roman Empire, were declared to be Roman citizens in the edict that Caracalla issued in 212. The key passages of the emperor's proclamation, formally known as the *Constitutio Antoniana,* stated: "I grant Roman citizenship to all aliens throughout the world, with no one remaining outside the citizen bodies…for it is proper that the multitude should not only help carry all the burdens but should also now be included in my victory."[116]

The rabbis in particular were sensitive to the fact that becoming a Roman citizen did not make them Romans. They never saw themselves as "Romans of the Jewish faith,"[117] unlike many German Jews, particularly Reform Jews, from the nineteenth century until the Nazis rose to power. Moreover, by the time citizenship was granted to most of Rome's

115. Smallwood, *Jews under Roman Rule,* 498.

116. Giessen Papyrus No. 40, in Lewis and Reinhold, eds., *Roman Civilization,* vol. II, 417–18. For a brief discussion see Goodman, *Rome and Jerusalem,* 157–58.

117. Ibid., 483.

subjects, it meant far less in terms of privileges than it had centuries before. Nevertheless, the status it conferred was not to be sneered at; and it did underscore, for the Jews at least, what seemed to be a further step toward reconciliation with their overlords.

It is not at all clear why Caracalla chose to issue the edict at that precise time, or at all, even if by then "the legal advantages of the status were already being eroded."[118] No matter. For the first time since Pompey the Great had set foot in Judaea during the reign of the Hasmoneans, Jews were considered to be on a par with other Roman citizens, indeed with the Romans themselves. For Rebbe, his followers, and the Jewish community as a whole, the edict may well have appeared as the end of the darkest era of their history. It is therefore possible, if not likely, that the proclamation of the Edict of Caracalla prompted Rebbe to conclude that there was no longer any reason to observe the four fasts commemorating the Temple's destruction.

It was no doubt in light of these developments that Rebbe felt he could ignore the widely accepted rabbinic dictum that "he who eats and drinks on Tisha B'Av will not witness the consolation of Jerusalem."[119] From his perspective, Jerusalem's consolation had already begun; he and the Jewish community of Palestine were witnesses to that fact. Tisha B'Av had been, to use a modern phrase, overtaken by events.

Rebbe was an old man when the Edict of Caracalla was proclaimed throughout the empire; he was probably in his late seventies. If he indeed passed away in Kislev 217, as the Talmud relates, his attempt to abolish Tisha B'Av most probably took place between 212 and 217, possibly in 215, when Caracalla visited Palestine for a second time and most likely met with Rebbe. As the Talmud also makes clear, Rebbe maintained his authority even on his deathbed, and any pronouncement that he issued was taken with the utmost seriousness. Nevertheless, his views did not go unchallenged, either then or throughout his reign as patriarch.

The Babylonian Talmud notes that in this case Rebbe indeed did not prevail; his colleagues refused to abolish Tisha B'Av. Moreover,

118. Goldsworthy, *Pax Romana*, 297; Beard, *SPQR*, 528.
119. Taanit 30b, see also *Tosafot,* Megilla 5b, s.v. *uvikesh.*

medieval commentators were puzzled by his even having presumed to suggest that Tisha B'Av be abolished. It was not merely that his position flew in the face of the principle that "whoever eats and drinks on Tisha B'Av will not see the consolation of Jerusalem."[120] As noted, he could have explained away that prohibition. There was, however, a second restriction that stood in the face of his proposed reform: the principle that no court could vacate a prior judgment unless it both outnumbered and was more expert than its predecessor.

The medieval commentators who compiled the *Tosafot* therefore speculated that Rebbe was not trying to abolish the fast, merely to loosen its restrictions so that only eating and drinking would be prohibited. Alternately, *Tosafot* speculated, Rebbe was seeking to move the fast day to the tenth of Av, consistent with a view expressed by other sages.[121] The fact that two explanations are offered is an indication that the authors of *Tosafot* themselves were unsure as to what Rebbe was proposing. Moreover, the talmudic statement regarding Rebbe's intentions is unequivocal; only one *Amora*, R. Abba bar Zavda, a student of Rav and R. Huna who lived later in the third century, attempted to reinterpret Rebbe's proposal by speculating that it was made in a year that Tisha B'Av fell on Shabbat and Rebbe merely sought to move the fast to Sunday.[122] The fact that the talmudic report of Rebbe's activities also indicates that he bathed on the seventeenth of Tammuz, which clearly was not intended to be a one-time affair, argues for taking his attempt to abolish Tisha B'Av at face value. This indeed was the position of the English Tosafists, who flourished prior to Edward I's edict of expulsion in 1290. As they put it, Rebbe sought "to abolish it entirely (*laakor mikol vakol*) and no longer make it a fast day."[123]

Notwithstanding the concerns that *Tosafot* outlined regarding the validity of Rebbe's ruling, as well as the talmudic principle that when a single view is contradicted by a majority the halakha follows

120. Taanit 30b.
121. Tosafot, Megilla 5b, s.v. *uvikesh.*
122. Megilla 5b.
123. Abraham Sofer/Schreiber, *Tosafot Ḥakhmei Anglia Al Masekhtot Beitza, Megilla, Kiddushin* (Jerusalem: n.p., 1970), 45, s.v. *uvikesh.*

the majority (*yaḥid verabbim, halakha kerabbim*), the decision to overrule Rebbe was not as open-and-shut as might have been expected. For despite Rebbe's willingness to defer to the view of a colleague, all the more so to a majority, he commanded a degree of authority that was unique to him. The Talmud relates:

> Rabba b. Hana said in the name of R. Hiyya, "He who acts in accordance with the opinion of Rebbe is acting correctly, [and] he who acts in accordance with the opinion of the Sages is acting correctly."[For] he was in doubt as to whether the *Halakha* is in accordance with Rebbe's ruling [when it is in opposition to that] of his colleague, but not [when it is opposed to that] of several of his colleagues, or whether the *Halakha* is in accordance [with] Rebbe [when in opposition to] his colleague and even [when he is opposed to] his [more than one of his] colleagues. R. Nahman said in the name of Rav, "It is forbidden to act in accordance with the decision of Rebbe, for he [Rav] is of the opinion [that] the *Halakha* is in accordance [with] Rebbe, [when in opposition to] his colleague, but not [when he is opposed to] his colleagues." R. Nahman stated in his own name, however, that "It is permitted to act in accordance with the decision of Rebbe"; for he holds the opinion [that] the *Halakha* is in accordance [with] Rebbe [when in opposition to] his colleague and even [when opposed to] his colleagues. Raba said, "It is forbidden to act in accordance with the decision of Rebbe, but if one did act [accordingly], his action is legally valid"; for he is of the opinion [that at the yeshiva] it was said [that they were] inclined [toward the opinion of the Rabbis].[124]

Clearly, the *Amora'im* were not at all certain that the ordinary determination regarding a solitary halakhic viewpoint, or that regarding the ability of a later court to reverse legal precedent, applied to Rebbe. Ultimately, however, they did rule in accordance with the view of the majority who did not concede Rebbe's argument. In effect, both Rebbe's interlocutors and later generations of talmudic sages reasoned that the "end of history"

124. Bava Batra 124a–b.

had not yet arrived.[125] And they were every bit as correct in presuming that the Edict of Caracalla was more a respite than a sea-change in Jewish history, just as, more than a millennium later, predictions that the end of the Cold War signaled the "end of history" and the triumph of liberalism proved equally short-lived.

While Rebbe's attempt to terminate Tisha B'Av did not succeed,[126] it does appear to have generated an important ruling regarding the fate of its three sister fasts, which, in his view, would *a fortiori* have been eliminated if Tisha B'Av no longer was a fast day. R. Hana b. Bizna, in the name of R. Simeon the Hasid, noted that the fact that the abovementioned passage in Zechariah spoke of the seventeenth of Tammuz, the ninth of Av, the third of Tevet, and the third of Tishrei as both days of fasting and days of joy, signified that

> when there is peace they shall be for joy and gladness, but if there is not peace they shall be fast days. R. Papa replied: What it means is this: When there is peace they shall be for joy and gladness; if there is persecution, they shall be fast days; if there is no persecution but yet not peace, then those who desire may fast and those who desire need not fast.[127]

R. Papa posited that, as is currently the case with respect to the State of Israel's security, if there is no persecution but no peace the three fasts other than Tisha B'Av would become optional rather than mandatory.[128]

---

125. As noted in the text, an effort was made to explain that Rebbe issued his ruling only in the context of Tisha B'Av falling on Shabbat; he proposed to abolish the deferred fast. While this explanation seems forced, the fact remains that the rabbis overruled him even in such circumstances. Megilla 5b.
126. R. Moshe Schreiber, better known by the title of his books as Ḥatam Sofer, citing the speculation that Rebbe was trying to move the fast to the tenth of Av and that his effort failed, argued that the Temple lost its sanctity immediately upon it being set on fire, and that it was to commemorate that loss that the fast takes place on the ninth. Schreiber, *Ḥatam Sofer: Oraḥ Ḥayyim*, no. 233.
127. Rosh HaShana 18b.
128. Indeed it is arguable that with respect to the vast majority of Jews living in the Diaspora, Jews are not being persecuted either, though it is questionable whether those living in Europe truly feel at peace.

Rebbe's desire to abolish Tisha B'Av was never realized. Indeed, given the many tragedies that subsequently befell the Jewish people, several of which, like the expulsion of the Jews from Spain, fell on that day,[129] the rabbis were justified in overruling Rebbe. Moreover, in light of the recrudescence of anti-Semitism in Europe some seventy years after the liberation of the concentration camps, Tisha B'Av will command an important place in the Jewish calendar as long as Jews anywhere, including in the State of Israel, are insecure. Only when "Jacob will sit in peace and quiet without fear"[130] will Tisha B'Av be a thing of the past.

On the other hand, the basic principle that underlay Rebbe's desire for change, his sense that Israel was at peace, was also reflected in R. Papa's dictum. Moreover, the Talmud's uncertainty regarding Rebbe's authority vis-à-vis his colleagues may have contributed to R. Papa's ruling, since there was no clear indication that the rabbis necessarily disagreed with him regarding the three other fasts. Nowadays, when outright persecution is minimal, while Jews have their own independent state and Jerusalem is under Jewish sovereignty, neither of which was the case when Rebbe made his revolutionary proposal, some rabbis have argued that, apart from Tisha B'Av, Jews can opt to suspend the other Temple-related fasts.[131] Until now this view has not been adopted, but perhaps if Rebbe were alive today, he might have advocated for its adoption.

MARITAL RELATIONSHIPS

Sympathy for Those Affected by Unusual Circumstances

Rebbe could be exceedingly sensitive to the impact of the law upon those who found themselves in difficult and unusual circumstances. As has already been noted, Rebbe permitted a woman who had been held in

---

129. Tisha B'Av fell on 8 August 1492. While the edict of expulsion initially required all Jews to leave Spain by July 31 (see *Edict of the Expulsion of the Jews (1492)*, trans. Edward Peters, http://sephardicstudies.org/decree.html), Ferdinand and Isabella extended the date of expulsion by as much as ten days, so that Tisha B'Av fell near the end of the extended deadline.
130. Jer. 30:10.
131. See Golinkin, "Should we continue."

captivity by gentiles to marry a Kohen on the basis of her minor child's testimony that she had not been violated.

In another case, Rebbe permitted a man to remain married to a woman even though she had shown no blood when they first had intercourse, thereby creating doubt as to whether she was a virgin. The Talmud recounts Rebbe's sensitivity to the unfortunate and unhappy couple's situation:

> A certain man came before Rebbe and said, "My master, I had intercourse [with my new wife] and found no blood." The woman said, "My master, I am still a virgin, and these were times of famine." Rebbe discerned that their faces were dark because of starvation and he ordered that they be brought to the bath, and he fed them, gave them drink, and brought them to the bridal chamber, and he [the husband] had intercourse with her and found blood. Rebbe [then] said to him, "Go, be happy with thy bargain." Rebbe applied to them the verse: "Their skin is shriveled on their bodies, it is dried up like a stick" (Lam. 4:8).[132]

Both cases demonstrate Rebbe's humanity and his belief that context is a critical factor when issuing a legal ruling. In the case of the captive woman, Rebbe was prepared to accept the testimony of a minor – normally considered to be invalid – because the child's credibility was borne out by his innocence; this, combined with the uncertainty that anything had been done to the woman, militated for a lenient ruling. In the case of the impoverished newlyweds, Rebbe recognized the validity of the woman's assertion that she could not bleed due to her near starvation.

A Case Involving an *Aguna*

Still another of Rebbe's rulings related to a case involving uncertainty about the death of an individual whose wife, if his death could not be confirmed, would suffer as a "chained woman" (*aguna*). Rebbe related the following story:

---

132. Ketubot 10b.

> Once when two men were casting their nets in the river Jordan, one of them entered a subterranean fish pond, and when the sun had set he could not find the entrance to the pond. His partner waited long enough until [it was safe to assume that] the man was dead and informed [the man's] household [of what had occurred]. The following day, when the sun rose [the man in the cave] found the entrance and returned to find his...household deep in mourning. Upon which Rebbe remarked, "How great are the words of the Sages, who ruled that if a man fell into water all of whose shores are visible to someone standing on its edge, his wife is permitted to remarry [since if he were alive he would have been seen by someone], but if he fell into "water without end" [i.e., with no visible boundary], his wife cannot remarry.[133]

Rebbe related this incident to make the case that one must account for the possible existence of a subterranean cave when a man disappears underwater, and in such circumstances his wife may not remarry.

The Talmud upheld Rebbe's ruling in cases where the water had no boundaries.[134] It then debated and seemingly rejected the notion that an exception might be made for the wife of a scholar, about whom there might be no concern that he survived in a subterranean cave, for had he survived, he would have been recognized. In this case too, the rabbis would not permit her *ab initio* to remarry (though if she went ahead and did so, she could remain with her new husband).

Over the centuries, however, the issue emerged in a somewhat different form, namely, the case of a scholar who fell through the ice of a frozen lake, all of whose shores were not visible. Despite the Talmud's ruling seemingly to the contrary, the sixteenth-century scholars, R. Samuel Edels, better known by his acronym Maharsha, and R. Joel Sirkis, better known as Baḥ (an abbreviation of his best-known work,

133. Yevamot 121a.

134. Such ponds are rare in small enclosed lakes or streams where a person standing onshore could see the entire body of water.

Bayit Ḥadash), both permitted the scholar's wife to remarry.[135] Some two centuries later, in the winter of 1813, when a man – not a scholar – drowned in the icebound Vistula River outside Warsaw, R. Yehezkel Landau, the chief rabbi of Prague, ruled that despite the fact that the river had to be considered "water without end," as long as there was a witness who remained on the river banks for two hours and saw no one emerge, and the wife subsequently was able to identify her husband's body, one need not take into account Rebbe's possibility of a subterranean cave.[136]

The nineteenth-century chief rabbi of Jerusalem, R. Shmuel Salant, wrote a brief responsum upholding the three rulings; a number of other decisors rejected his position.[137] To this day, there is little rabbinical consensus on how, and in what circumstances, an *aguna* might be freed to remarry. Rebbe's ruling was but one aspect of this seemingly never-ending debate, which until fully resolved, will continue to result in tragic outcomes for far too many unfortunate Jewish women.

Overruled by the Rabbis

Some of Rebbe's rulings were more problematical, however, despite the fact that he could cite biblical law in support of his positions. For example, he ruled that a husband could "legally betroth a married woman on the condition that she became his wife after the death of her husband." He issued a similar ruling if a man wished to betroth his wife's sister after his wife's passing. Biblical law supported him. Nevertheless, the rabbis overruled him, arguing that accepting the betrothal would create unwanted stress between the husband and his current wife.[138]

Another especially vexing case involved a husband's decision to revoke a writ of divorce (*get*) – which only a male could issue – without his wife's knowledge. On the one hand, revoking the *get* could

---

135. See R. David Halevi Segal, *Turei Zahav,* s.v. *afilu tava,* in Karo, *Shulḥan Arukh: Even Ha'ezer, Hilkhot Ishut,* 17:32.

136. R. Yehezkel Landau, *She'elot UTeshuvot Noda BiYehuda HaShalem, Even Ha'ezer,* vol. 1 (Jerusalem: Machon Yerushalayim 5754/1994), *Mahadura Tinyana,* no. 58.

137. See R. Yosef Hayim Sonenfeld, *Torat Hayim: Teshuvot Rabbi Yosef Hayim Sonnenfeld,* 3rd ed. (Jerusalem: Machon Re'em, 5765/2005), no. 119.

138. Kiddushin 63a; Eliezer Berkovits, *Not in Heaven* (Jerusalem and New York: Shalem Press, 2010), 38.

create a situation where the woman, upon receiving the document, and unaware that it was not worth the paper it was written on, might remarry. In doing so, she would be unwittingly committing adultery and any offspring from that marriage would be deemed illegitimate. On the other hand, it was possible that the first husband had issued the document out of spite, or as a result of a bitter argument, subsequently had remorse and wished to remain married. Should the marriage be dissolved in such a case?

Three generations of Rebbe's own family debated the issue. Rebbe's ancestor, Rabban Gamaliel the Elder, who lived while the Second Temple was still intact, worried about the implications of adultery, and therefore forbade the revocation of a *get*. Rebbe took the opposite view, especially since the Torah permitted a man to revoke the writ at any time before it was delivered. Presumably Rebbe was concerned about the rupture of a marriage that both sides wished to preserve. Rebbe's son, also named Gamaliel, disagreed with his father, however, and sided with his ancestral namesake.

Rebbe proved to be on the losing side of this argument as well, even though his position was backed by no less than the authority of the Torah itself. The rabbis ruled that such a marriage would be retroactively annulled, possibly because if the couple chose to resume their marriage they could still do so if the woman had not yet married another man. Interestingly, the rabbis' rationale for upholding the rulings of the two Rabban Gamaliels was based upon the fact that "the legal basis of the marriage is the law as perceived by the rabbis." In other words, it was not out of concern for the woman's situation, which had underpinned R. Gamaliel the Elder's ruling. Rather, it was concern for their own authority that led them to decide as they did.[139]

REFORMS DERIVING FROM ECONOMIC CONSIDERATIONS

Waiving *Shemitta* Restrictions

In accordance with biblical mandate to observe *shemitta*, the Sabbatical year, Jews did not harvest crops and let the land lie fallow every seventh

139. See Gittin 33a; for a brief but excellent discussion, see Berkovits, *Not in Heaven*, 65–67. Berkovits seems to favor the position that the rabbis ultimately took.

year. The Torah also commanded that all debts be forgiven upon the commencement of the Sabbatical year. During the Second Temple period, the latter rule proved increasingly impractical: despite the biblical commandment to continue to lend money to the poor until the *shemitta* year, those with available resources were unwilling to part with them as the Sabbatical year drew near. As a result, not only were they violating a biblical precept, they were also creating very real difficulties for the poor, or even more fortunate farmers, who needed cash to carry them through the Sabbatical year when they could not sell their produce.

To resolve this very real challenge, which undermined both the social and economic fabric of society, Hillel the Elder devised a legal workaround called the *pruzbul*. Reasoning that the Torah had only addressed the question of forfeiture of private debts, Hillel had lenders place the loan in the hands of a court prior to the Sabbatical year. As a public entity, the court was entitled to collect the funds, acting in effect as a "pass-through" for the creditor. The *pruzbul* was the document that codified this transaction and that enabled the lenders to collect their funds from court distributions. It stated, "I (the creditor) hand (my bonds) over to you (the names of the judges) in (their location), so that I may be able to recover any money owing to me from (the debtor) at any time I shall desire."[140] Hillel further justified his circumvention of biblical law by asserting that after the destruction of the First Temple, the law was no longer biblical, since the Jubilee Year was no longer operative. Instead the rabbis had preserved *shemitta* for reasons of tradition, and it could therefore be adjusted in time of extreme necessity.[141]

It was some two centuries after Hillel had introduced his legal fiction to circumvent the strictures of *shemitta* that Rebbe confronted a new challenge relating to the Sabbatical year. During the Temple period the Romans had exempted the Jews from the *arnona* tax on produce during the *shemitta* year. This exemption was removed by the time Rebbe assumed the patriarchate.[142] It seems that even those Jews who were lax

140. Gittin 36a–b.

141. Per the dictum of Abaye, Gittin 36a.

142. Louis H. Feldman, *Studies in Hellenistic Judaism* (Leiden and New York: E. J. Brill, 1996), 475.

about other aspects of religious practice, as they once had been about lending funds prior to the *shemitta* year, adhered to the laws regulating *shemitta*'s agricultural aspects. Rebbe therefore had to address the implications of the loss of the *shemitta* exemption.

Since he was unable to get the Romans to restore the waiver – good relations never stood in the way of raising funds for the military and other Roman needs – he sought to exempt the farmers from any requirement to leave their lands to lie fallow. Rebbe's approach, like that of Hillel before him, was rooted in practicality. He too wanted to maintain a stable economic system that was not disrupted by the Sabbatical year. Furthermore, he, like Hillel, recognized the reality that some Jews would sin unless they were offered a solution to their concerns. Hillel's *pruzbul* had effectively obviated the likelihood that wealthier Jews would violate Scripture's commandment by refusing to lend to their less fortunate brethren. Rebbe's initiative removed the taint of sin from those Jews who out of desperation to feed their families found themselves violating the strictures associated with the Sabbatical year. The Talmud records that "a certain schoolteacher was suspected of violating the laws of *shemitta*. He was hauled before Rebbe [to be punished]. But Rebbe told [his accusers], 'What should this unfortunate one do, he does this [works the land] for his survival.'"[143] Indeed, based on Rebbe's teaching, R. Ze'ira went so far as to argue that the shofar would be sounded for a fast during the Sabbatical year to protect the produce of people who were suspected of violating *shemitta* due to economic necessity.[144]

Rebbe not only sought to follow Hillel in modifying the impact of *shemitta* on the Jews' economic activities, he also drew upon the principle that underlay Hillel's initiative, namely, that the biblical prohibition against farming the land in the Sabbatical year had lapsed with the destruction of the First Temple. As he put it, "The [biblical] text indicates two kinds of release, one the release of land and the other the release of monies [i.e., debts]. When the release of land is operative so is the release of money, and when the release of land is not operative neither is the release

143. Y. Taanit 3:1.

144. Ibid. See also the comments of R. Eliezer Berkovits in *Not in Heaven*, 149.

of money."[145] Therefore, just as Hillel had effectively terminated *shemitta*'s monetary impact by means of the *pruzbul,* Rebbe sought permanently to suspend the injunction to leave the land fallow and instead leave as much of it arable as was needed for the farmers to subsist.[146]

Rebbe's rationale, while firmly grounded in precedent, was nevertheless rejected by the rabbis. The leader of the opposition was none other than R. Pinhas b. Yair, who, according one version of the abovementioned story regarding his reaction to seeing Rebbe's white mules, had actually come to Rebbe to object to his ruling and to convince other rabbis likewise to oppose his proposal.[147] R. Pinhas took the view that there simply was no basis for overriding the original rabbinic rationale for preserving the tradition of *shemitta*. Moreover, whereas Rebbe was constantly seeking economic stability and was concerned for the welfare of a diminishing agricultural population, R. Pinhas attached greater importance to sustaining the tradition, even if it resulted in economic hardship for the poor.

It is ironic that Rebbe, one of the wealthiest men in Palestine, was more sympathetic to the plight of the impoverished than R. Pinhas b. Yair, who does not appear to have been particularly prosperous. R. Pinhas was a *Ḥasid* in the ancient sense of the word, a rather otherworldly, stringent type, who placed devotion to the law above all else and had no tolerance for shortcuts or legal fictions.[148] Rebbe, on the other hand, dealt with the real world on a daily basis, whether he was leading the community or representing it to the outside Roman world.

---

145. Gittin 36a–b.

146. See the comment of R. Elijah of Fulda (c. 1650–c. 1720), *Mahara Fulda* on Y. Demai 1:3, s.v. *mahu*; R. Moses ibn Habib (1654–96), ibid., s.v. *Rebbe*; Alon, *Jews in Their Land,* 731–32; Lau, *Ḥakhamim*, vol. 3, 325. Some traditional commentators, notably R. Solomon Sirillio (late fifteenth/early sixteenth century) and R. Elijah of Vilna (1720–1797), known colloquially as "the Gra," argue that the suspension was for but one year; but the talmudic text offers no support for this assertion. See R. Solomon Sirillio, Y. Demai, loc. cit., s.v. *Rebbe baa,* and R. Elijah of Vilna, *Bi'ur HaGra,* loc. cit., *Rebbe baa mishrei.*

147. R. Elijah of Fulda asserts that Rebbe actually gathered many of his colleagues to validate his position, and that R. Pinhas sought to dissuade them, but there is no textual support for this conjecture. *Mahara Fulda* on Y. Demai 1:3, s.v. *mahu.*

148. See the discussion in Lau, *Ḥakhamim,* vol. 3, 321, 324–26.

In many ways their contrasting attitudes and relationship to society foreshadowed the different approaches that have distinguished communal rabbis from their counterparts in yeshivas for the past three centuries. The former, like Rebbe, have tended to approach halakha with a certain tendency toward leniency, so as not to overburden ordinary folk. The latter, like R. Pinhas, reared within the "four cubits of halakha" and never venturing beyond them, have instinctively preferred more rigorous interpretations of the law, with far less concern for its second- and third-order consequences for Jewish society at large.

Rebbe's argument did not carry the day. The rabbis sided with R. Pinhas. Rebbe evidently anticipated that his efforts to terminate *shemitta* might come to naught, and he prepared a more modest, but still radical back-up plan. Basing himself on a report that R. Meir had eaten a leaf in Beit She'an without tithing it,[149] which meant that the area was also exempt from *shemitta* regulations, Rebbe tried to exempt that town and a number of others on the grounds that although those areas had been conquered by Joshua when the Israelites first arrived in Canaan, they had not been resettled during the return of Babylonian exiles under Ezra.[150] They therefore were to be treated as non-Jewish territory, to which *shemitta* did not apply.

Accordingly, "Rebbe exempted Beit She'an; Rebbe exempted Keisarin (Caesarea); Rebbe exempted Beit Guvrin; Rebbe exempted Kfar Tzemach. And Rebbe permitted taking produce immediately upon the end of the seventh year."[151] Beit She'an and Keisarin were both located in what originally had been the western portion of the territory of Menasseh, Beit Guvrin in that of Judah, Kfar Tzemach in that of Naphtali. Given the relatively limited territory that Judaea encompassed upon Ezra's *aliya* from Babylonia, Rebbe's case seemed *prima facie* quite valid.

Rebbe's modified reform fared no better than his original proposal, however. It provoked an outcry among his colleagues, and even

149. See Ḥullin 6a: "R. Joshua b. Zeruz, the son of R. Meir's father-in-law, testified before Rebbe that R. Meir ate a leaf of a vegetable in Beit She'an. Rebbe therefore permitted the entire territory of Beit She'an." Y. Demai 2:1 presents the same report in roughly similar language.

150. See *Mahara Fulda* on Y. Demai 2:1, 12b, s.v. *Beit She'an*.

151. Y. Demai 2:1.

within his immediate family. They challenged his right to permit a place that heretofore had been treated as part of biblical Israel's territory and therefore was subject both to the tithe and to the restrictions of the Sabbatical year. Unfazed, he cited the Scriptural passage "And he [Hezekiah] broke the bronze serpent into pieces." Pointing out that other kings prior to Hezekiah who had ruled after Moses created the serpent and could equally well have destroyed it, he asserted that "just as the Holy One, blessed be He, enabled him [Hezekiah] whereby he might distinguish himself; so in this case He enabled us to distinguish ourselves."[152]

Rebbe stood firm; his decision reflected his recognition of both the political and economic realities within which he had to operate. Still, not everyone was prepared to follow his lead. The Talmud relates that R. Joshua ben Levi, an influential younger contemporary of Rebbe's, instructed his young students not to buy vegetables for him in Beit She'an during the Sabbatical year.[153] Presumably that was his view regarding *shemitta*'s applicability to the other towns as well.

New Rulings on Usury and Robbery

The Torah explicitly issued a wide-ranging prohibition against charging interest on a loan, whether it be "interest on money, interest on food or interest on any item for which interest is taken."[154] The Mishna and Gemara expanded the prohibition to include, for example, gaining advantage by means of the rise or fall of market prices, or charging a higher price for an article sold on credit.[155] Rebbe nevertheless ruled that if one actually did lend funds on interest, he was not to be forced to return the interest to the borrower. As the Talmud reported: "We do not accept what robbers or usurers are

152. Ibid.; compare Ḥullin 6b–7a.
153. R. Joshua was a leading scholar of the generation that succeeded Rebbe; he was reputed to have had frequent meetings with the prophet Elijah, whom Scripture records (II Kings 2:11) as having risen to Heaven on a fiery chariot and who, according to tradition, has roamed the earth ever since.
154. Deut. 22:20.
155. These and other instances are the subject of the fifth chapter of Bava Metzia entitled "What Is Interest" *(Eizehu Neshekh)*.

prepared to restore; and the spirit [i.e., approval] of this teaching was enunciated in Rebbe's days."[156]

The Talmud then recounted a tale to justify this ruling:

> There was a case where a man sought to repent [and make restitution] but his wife rebuked him by saying, "Ne'er-do-well, if you repent [and restore what you took] even the girdle that you are wearing will no longer belong to you." So he held back and did not repent [or restore]. It was at that moment that [the rabbis] ruled: "We do not accept what robbers or usurers are prepared to restore; and the spirit [i.e., approval] of the sages does not rest on whosoever accepts [such interest or articles] from them."[157]

It was not uncommon for the rabbis to promulgate rulings on the basis of a single incident (*maaseh shehaya*); statistical analysis would not begin to be developed as a discipline until late in the seventeenth century. Yet in the case of usurers and robbers who sought to return their ill-gotten gains, the story of the man and his miserly wife was likely not at all the basis for the ruling attributed to Rebbe. Instead, as with his proposal to waive the requirement that farmers leave their land fallow during the *shemitta* year, his motivation was primarily socio-economic. Whatever normative halakha might have decreed, lending at interest had become a central element of the local economy for Jews as much as for non-Jews. Given frequent famines, onerous Roman taxes, and widespread communal impoverishment, if the Jews were forced to return their earnings they would barely subsist.

Rebbe's decision to couple robbers with usurers was based on a different rationale, one that conformed more closely to the Talmud's story of the man who neither returned what he took nor repented. As has already been noted, Rebbe placed a very high premium on repentance. Accordingly, he did not want to discourage those who committed misdeeds, even one as serious as robbery, from undertaking *teshuva*. Moreover, he may not have been referring to actual robbers at all, but rather to those who

156. Bava Kamma 94b. Rashi, ad loc., s.v. *ein,* interprets the phrase "the spirit of the sages does not rest" to mean "he has no spirit of wisdom or piety (*Ḥasidut*) within him."
157. Bava Kamma 94b.

improperly acquired property from others; a modern example might be "con men." In the context of such lesser crimes, Rebbe determined that it was more important to encourage repentance than to recover financial losses. It is noteworthy that in contrast to his positions on *shemitta*, his decisions regarding both usurers and robbers were upheld unanimously.[158]

A Reform Ahead of Its Time: *Pat Akum* (Non-Jewish Bread)

Ever concerned about the welfare of ordinary people, Rebbe proposed to permit Jews to eat non-Jewish bread, thereby abandoning a tradition dating back at least as far as Daniel and codified by Beit Shammai (in one of the relatively few cases where halakha followed that school's position). As has been noted in the case of the starving newlyweds, the land suffered mightily from famine and drought. It was Roman practice to distribute bread to the masses. In desperation, ordinary Jews ate Roman bread; Rebbe sought to remove any guilt on their part for having done so.[159]

As with his other more radical reforms, Rebbe encountered strong opposition from his colleagues. In two places where there were reports of Rebbe's effort to permit the consumption of non-Jewish bread, the later rabbis rationalized his position either by reinterpreting his views entirely or noting that he only meant one could eat such bread in the field, that is, *in extremis* when nothing else was available.[160] It is possible, however, that Rebbe sought to reverse the ban after he had edited the portion of his great work that dealt with this issue.

In any event, over time, the rabbis themselves came around to Rebbe's view that in light of the hard-hit local economy, it was best not to prevent the community from consuming non-Jewish bread. They never actually rescinded the ban. They simply did not force the issue.[161]

---

158. See Maimonides, *Mishneh Torah: Hilkhot Gezeila VaAveida*, 1:13 and *Hilkhot Malveh VeLoveh*, 4:5; Karo, *Shulḥan Arukh: Ḥoshen Mishpat, Hilkhot Gezeila*, 366:1. For a discussion, see Oppenheimer, *Rabbi Yehuda HaNasi*, 88–89.
159. See the discussion in Lau, *Ḥakhamim*, vol. 3, 344–46; see also Y. Avoda Zara 2:8.
160. See Margolies, *Mareh HaPanim*, ad loc., s.v. *ve'imamu*; Avoda Zara, 35b.
161. Lau, *Ḥakhamim*, vol. 3, 346; see Maimonides, *Mishneh Torah: Hilkhot Maakhalot Asurot*, 17:9; Karo, *Shulḥan Arukh: Yoreh De'ah, Hilkhot Maakhalei Ovdei Kokhavim*, 112:1. See also R. Yosef Hayyim, *She'elot UTeshuvot Rav Pe'alim*, vol. 1: *Oraḥ Ḥayyim* (Jerusalem: Salem, 5772/2012), nos. 6–7.

A Ruling on Air Space: Rebbe's Treatment of Syria

As Josephus records, Jews had lived for generations in the Roman province of Syria, especially in Antioch, the provincial capital.[162] The Talmud records a discussion regarding the permissibility of entering "Syria" in ritual purity, since as a general rule, all lands outside Palestine were considered ritually impure. There was a consensus among the rabbis that the territory of Syria, like those of other lands, rendered one who entered it ritually impure. With regard to Syria's airspace, however, there was no agreement. Rebbe ruled that if one entered Syria without actually touching the ground, for example on a palanquin, or in a "box, chest, or portable turret," one was not defiled. R. Yose b. Judah, disagreed, arguing that Syrian air space was no different from Syrian soil. The rabbinical consensus supported Rebbe, as does normative halakha.[163]

Did Rebbe Permit the Use and Consumption of Non-Jewish Oil?

The Mishna explicitly states that Rebbe and his court permitted the use and consumption of non-Jewish oil. At issue is the identity of "Rebbe" in this case. The Mishna as recorded in the Babylonian Talmud refers to "Rabbi Judah the Prince." Though the reference seems clear-cut, both medieval and modern commentators have argued that it is actually a later interpolation, and that "Rabbi Judah the Prince" is actually R. Yehuda Nesia, Rebbe's grandson.[164] It is rare, however, for R. Yehuda Nesia to

162. Josephus writes: "Our Jewish residents in Antioch are called Antiochenes, having been granted rights of citizenship by its founder Seleucus." Flavius Josephus, *Against Apion,* trans. H. St. J. Thackeray (Cambridge, MA and London: Harvard University Press, 1926), II:39. Seleucus I Nicator (359–281 BCE) was the founder of the Seleucid dynasty. See also Josephus, *Antiquities,* 12:3:1. See also A. Kasher, "The Rights of the Jews of Antioch on the Orontes," *Proceedings of the American Academy for Jewish Research* 49 (1982), 69–85.

163. Gittin 8a; Maimonides, *Mishneh Torah, Hilkhot Tumat HaMet,* 11:6. In theory, the laws of ritual purity would mandate that an Israeli soldier who was a Kohen should not enter Syria unless involved in a direct action; a Kohen could, however, participate in an aerial bombing raid without becoming ritually impure.

164. Y. Avoda Zara 2:8; Avoda Zara 35b; Rashi, s.v. *Rebbe UVeit Dino; Tosafot,* Avoda Zara 36a, s.v. *asher*; Urbach, *The Sages,* 133 and *The Halakhah,* 218 all claim the reference is to R. Yehuda Nesia. See, however, Hidary, *Dispute,* 328, and discussion in Y. Avoda Zara 2:8, which refers explicitly to "Rebbe."

be called by his Hebrew equivalent. Moreover, in one case when the Talmud refers to "Rabbi Judah the Prince," at least one major commentator considers the person in question to be Rebbe.[165]

The mishna that appears in the Jerusalem Talmud speaks of "Rebbe." That term was reserved for R. Yehuda Nesia's grandfather. To further complicate matters, the Tosefta refers to "R. Judah." It is unusual for Rebbe to be called by his given name and even more rare for R. Yehuda Nesia to appear as R. Judah in the Mishna.[166]

Finally, the Jerusalem Talmud states that "Rebbe" was referred to as *Rabboteinu* (our Rabbis) on three occasions: with respect to gentile bread; regarding the validity of a bill of divorce (*get*) that a husband granted on condition that he not return from travel within twelve months who then failed to do so; and in the matter of defining whether a miscarried fetus should render the mother ritually impure.[167] In each case *Rabboteinu* ruled leniently: the bread was permitted, the divorce was valid, the mother was pure unless the fetus had human form. The Talmud thereupon criticized the court, calling it "a permissive court."

It is therefore far from clear who actually permitted the use of non-Jewish oil. In any event, whether it was Rebbe or his grandson whose court came in for rabbinical criticism, the ruling stood. Oil became halakhically permissible.

LOOKING TO THE FUTURE WHILE DRAWING FROM POLITICAL EXPERIENCE: A RULING ON TEMPLE PROCEDURE

When Rebbe advocated for reforms, he in general did not explicitly draw upon his worldly experience to buttress his arguments. In at least one instance, however, he did so; it was in the course of a rabbinic debate

165. *Tosafot,* s.v. *VeRabbi Yehuda HaNasi,* Gittin 14b. It is noteworthy that Rashi does not identify "Rabbi Yehuda HaNasi" as Rabbi Yehuda Nesia as he does in the discussion of gentile oil. See also Temura 16a, which also refers to "Rabbi Yehuda HaNasi"; none of the commentators included in the Vilna *Shas* claim that the reference is to R. Yehuda Nesia.
166. On the other hand, see Y. Berachot 3:1, 21a, which refers to "Rabbi Yehuda Nesia grandson of R. Yehuda Nesia"!
167. Y. Avoda Zara 2:8, 11b and Margolies, *Pnei Moshe,* ad loc., s.v. *beGittin*; s.v. *uvesandal.*

over Temple practice. These debates, many of which appear in the order of tractates entitled "Holy Matters"(Kodashim), reflected both the rabbis' hope that the Temple would somehow soon be rebuilt despite all indications to the contrary, and their more practical desire to preserve a record of Temple ritual that would serve as a guide to the priests and people whenever the Temple was restored.

At issue was the proper procedure for "waving" the two lambs and the two loaves of new wheat bread that were brought to the Temple on the festival of Shavuot, signaling permission to use the new wheat crop for loaves used in Temple ritual. The rabbis could not agree as to whether the bread was placed on top of the lambs or under them. Hanina b. Hakhinai proposed a compromise: the bread should be situated between the lambs' thighs so that when the waving took place, the bread was both above and below the lambs. Rebbe took issue with this last position, however. No doubt drawing upon his interaction with high Roman officials and his knowledge of their mores, he asserted that "one does not do so before a mortal king" and asked, "Does one do so before the Kings of kings?" Instead, he postulated, "One holds the bread alongside the lambs and waves them simultaneously."[168] And it was Rebbe's view that prevailed among later decisors.[169]

168. Menaḥot 62a.

169. See Maimonides, *Mishneh Torah: Hilkhot Temidin UMusafin,* 8:11; Avraham di Butan, *Leḥem Mishneh,* loc. cit., s.v. *umanihan*; R. Yosef Karo (*Kesef Mishneh,* loc. cit., s.v. *keitzad*) notes that Maimonides ruled according to Rebbe because "his rationale makes sense."

Chapter 8

Final Days

When Antoninus died, Rebbe exclaimed: The bond is snapped!

Avoda Zara 11b

CARACALLA'S LAST CAMPAIGN

It was not long after he passed through Palestine that Caracalla began his preparations for his operation against the Parthians. These preparations lasted throughout 216; Caracalla commenced his offensive later in the year. The results were hardly promising; Caracalla met with even less success than his father.

The operation suddenly was terminated when one of the Guard Prefects, M. Opellius Macrinus, discovered that he was being targeted for elimination. For some time Caracalla had publicly poked fun at Macrinus "for his lack of military experience and bravery, carrying this to the point of abuse...he [also] accused the prefect of cowardice and a womanly disease." Needless to say, "Macrinus resented these accusations and was deeply offended."[1] Caracalla was playing a dangerous game; it is one to which leaders often succumb. Stalin was known for such behavior; he

1. Herodian, *History of the Empire,* 4:12:1–2.

once made Khrushchev dance before him.[2] It is generally accepted that Stalin's underlings – some of whom, like his foreign minister Vyacheslav Molotov, he may have targeted for liquidation – helped him along to his death.[3] Macrinus went even further. When he intercepted a letter from Rome to Caracalla accusing him of plotting to kill the emperor, the prefect preempted, and had Caracalla murdered by a fellow named Martialis on April 8, 217 CE. When Macrinus thus became emperor, it marked "the first time that a man who was not only from outside the imperial family but also outside the senatorial class was raised to the imperial purple."[4]

The Talmud records that when "Antoninus" died, Rebbe eulogized him with the words "The bond is snapped." Rebbe recognized that something would be lost with Caracalla's passing. The Jewish leader had no particular relationship with Macrinus, who himself showed no special interest in the Jews, other than permitting road construction that had begun under Caracalla to continue. In any event, though Macrinus had bribed his way to winning the Guard's support, he incurred the wrath of the ordinary legionaries, who had venerated Caracalla as a "soldier's soldier" – the highest form of praise that grunts reserve for a general.[5]

Not surprisingly, Macrinus was himself put to death barely a year after he took power and was replaced by a member of the imperial family. His fourteen-year-old successor, Bassianus, also known as Elagabalus, was Caracalla's cousin's son, and therefore could claim to be a royal, whereas Macrinus was not. Bassianus' mother and grandmother – the latter was Caracalla's great-aunt Julia Maesa, Julia Domna's sister – contrived to put him on the throne; Julia claimed that he was Caracalla's illegitimate

2. Nikita Khrushchev, *Khrushchev Remembers,* trans. Strobe Talbott (London: Sphere, 1971), 267. Contemporary leaders likewise should beware, because those they poke fun at may someday turn against them.
3. Michael Wines, "New Study Supports Idea Stalin Was Poisoned," *The New York Times* (March 5, 2003), http://www.nytimes.com/2003/03/05/world/new-study-supports-idea-stalin-was-poisoned.html; Jonathan Brent and Vladimir Naumov, *Stalin's Last Crime: The Plot Against the Jewish Doctors, 1948–1953* (New York: Harper Collins, 2013) 313–14.
4. Goldsworthy, *Pax Romana,* 402.
5. General Omar Bradley, of World War II fame who later became the first chairman of the Joint Chiefs of Staff, was called a "soldier's soldier" by the troops who adored him.

son. He won the support of one of the important legions, the Third Gallic Legion, as well as of the Second Legion; to highlight his connection with the royal family, he called himself Marcus Aurelius Antoninus Augustus.

Elagabalus was a hereditary priest of an identically named Syrian deity, and it was therefore not surprising that he did not hold Jews in the highest regard. A report from the often-suspect *Historia Augusta* notes that he wished that the religious rites of the Jews (and those of Samaritans and Christians) should be performed in his eponymous Temple on the Palatine hill.[6] The same questionable source also records that Elagabalus would serve ostriches – a non-kosher-bird – at dinner, "saying that the Jews had been commanded to eat them."[7]

Elagabalus was married and divorced several times, once to a male slave, and generally engaged in dissolute behavior,[8] much to the disgust and outrage of the Praetorian Guard, the troops, and the common folk. His religious practices also alienated his grandmother, who plotted to replace him with Septimius Severus' great-nephew Alexander Severus. Within four years Elagabalus was dead, as was his mother, both being assassinated by the troops when they appeared before them alongside the more popular Alexander.

Alexander Severus, who ruled for eleven years before he too was assassinated, was especially well disposed toward the Jews, as well as toward Christians. Indeed, he was despised by some precisely because of his positive attitude toward them. Nevertheless, Rebbe's premonition that something had been lost was not inaccurate. Despite his favorable attitude toward the Jews, Alexander appears to have had no particular special relationship with them; he was equally tolerant of Christians. With Caracalla's passing the special relationship between patriarch and emperor had come to an end.

---

6. *Historia Augusta: Antoninus Elagabalus,* 3:5.
7. Ibid., 28:4.
8. Dio Cassius reports that he engaged in cross-dressing and "was bestowed in marriage and was termed wife, mistress and queen." Dio Cassius, *Roman History,* 80:14:4–15:1–4.

AN AGING LEADER

Because the Talmud is ahistorical, it is difficult to identify at which point in his life Rebbe issued particular rulings or articulated certain maxims. In the case of two rulings, however, it is clear that both took place very late in Rebbe's life. They appear on the same page of the Talmud and address two different aspects of the laws governing the eradication of idolatry.

In the first case, R. Yose b. Saul, an early *Amora* much younger than Rebbe, asked him: "May utensils which were used in the Temple of Onias [a Jewish temple erected in Egypt in the third century BCE] be used in the Sanctuary?" Rebbe replied, "They are prohibited," and he then added, "and I had a Scriptural text [upon which to support this decision] but I have forgotten it." Rebbe was famous for his ability to plumb the depths of biblical verses in order to derive halakhic rulings from them. For him to acknowledge that he could not remember what he himself had derived was quite remarkable, but also a sign of serious aging. R. Yose b. Saul quoted a passage that apparently refuted Rebbe's view: "Moreover all the vessels, which king Ahaz in his reign did cast away when he trespassed, we have prepared and sanctified."[9] He asked Rebbe, "Does not 'we have prepared' mean that we immersed them [in a *mikve*], and 'sanctified' that we have made them holy again!" The quote triggered the older man's memory. He exclaimed, "May the blessing of Heaven be upon you for having restored my loss to me! 'Have we prepared' means we have stored them away, and 'sanctified' that we have substituted others for them." The passage was the proof-text for Rebbe's ruling.

Almost immediately after relating this episode, the Talmud records that Rebbe was challenged by his son R. Simeon for seeming to contradict one of his own rulings. Rebbe had expounded to his son that an idolater can annul an idol belonging to himself or to another idolater but not one belonging to a Jew. R. Simeon, clearly puzzled, asked: "My Master, in your youth you taught us that an idolater can annul an idol belonging to himself or to an Israelite! But can the idol of an Israelite be annulled?"

9. II Chr. 19:19.

R. Hillel b. R. Wallas, who greatly admired the patriarch, then explained to R. Simeon that Rebbe was only referring to the case where there was joint ownership of an idol by a Jew and a non-Jew, and that in this particular case Rebbe indeed had reversed himself. "In his youth he held that the Israelite worshipped the idol on account of the heathen, so that when the latter annulled it for himself he annulled it also for the Israelite. In his old age, however, he held that the Israelite worshiped it on his own account, so that when the heathen annulled it he did so for himself but not for the Israelite."[10]

Rebbe's willingness to admit that he had forgotten the reason for his ruling was another demonstration of his basic humility. His ability to change his position demonstrated how flexible and open-minded he could be. It was also a mark of his great intelligence; he judged issues on their merits. His behavior stands as a model for all who serve in the contemporary rabbinate or wish to join its ranks.

REBBE'S LAST DAYS

Rebbe departed from this world the same year as Caracalla, though far more peacefully. He was able to die in his bed, with his sons and students surrounding him. His final instructions provided for the governance of the community once he was gone. Rebbe had combined "Torah and greatness" in his person like few before him; it was in many ways an unnatural combination.[11] He recognized that his position as both a religious and communal leader who also was sufficiently worldly-wise to interact with the highest echelons of Roman officialdom could not easily be replicated. He had no potential successor with the same breadth and scope of authority and attributes. He therefore had no choice but to allocate his various roles to the persons who were best suited to carry them out.

Like the patriarch Jacob, Rebbe showed a marked preference for his younger son, Simeon, though he did not deprive his older son Gamaliel of his place as hereditary leader of the Jewish community. As the Talmud

10. Avoda Zara 52b.
11. Binyamin Lau, *Ḥakhamim*, vol. 4: *MiMishna LaTalmud* (Tel Aviv: Yediot Ahronot, 2012), 25.

records, Rebbe told his retainers to call in the Sages of Israel and in their presence he announced that "Simeon my son is wise, Gamaliel my son will be the patriarch, Hanina son of Hama will sit at the head."

Rebbe's decision may not have gone down well with R. Simeon. When Levi, who was one of Rebbe's confidants, asked why it was necessary to specify that R. Gamaliel would succeed his father, since that should have been obvious, R. Simeon, perhaps because he was disappointed that his father had not chosen him as successor,[12] snapped at him that it wasn't obvious at all. He, Simeon, was the more accomplished scholar and more closely filled his father's shoes. The Talmud then explains that although R. Simeon was the better scholar, R. Gamaliel followed in his father's footsteps more carefully when it came to fear of Heaven and therefore merited the patriarchate.

Rebbe was implying that although Simeon was the more learned of the two brothers and would lead rabbinical deliberations, Gamaliel was certainly well suited to be the community's administrator and its face to the Roman world. His therefore was put in charge of civil matters such as tax collection, fiscal support for the Roman military, and all municipal activities. Simeon, on the other hand, was placed in charge of the yeshiva and all the responsibilities attached to that position: providing halakhic rulings, establishing the order of studies in the yeshiva, and refining the editing of the Mishna. He was also put in charge of granting ordination to deserving students. It was a sensible appointment, given R. Simeon's superior academic knowledge.[13]

Nevertheless, in what certainly must have been a source of frustration for R. Simeon, he was not awarded the deanship of the yeshiva. That title instead went to R. Hanina bar Hama. As has already been pointed out, however, R. Hanina declined the honor in favor of R. Afes who was two and one half years older, and only took over leadership of the yeshiva once R. Afes had passed away.[14]

12. Ibid., 37.
13. Rebbe complimented R. Simeon for his scholarly acuity by calling him "the light of Israel" (*Ner Yisrael*) – Arakhin 9b.
14. The Talmud Yerushalmi, Y. Taanit 4:2, reverses the name as Hami b. Hanina (see, however, R. Akiva Eger, *Gilyon HaShas*, ad loc., who emends the text to read Hanina bar Hama). It also points out that Rebbe had rotated the head of the yeshiva, but

R. Simeon may have been upset by his father's decision to install his brother as patriarch, but he accepted it. The *modus vivendi* that existed between the two brothers contrasted sharply with the friction that existed between the two sons of Septimius Severus. Severus' male heirs hated each other; the relationship between Caracalla and Geta more closely resembled that of Cain and Abel than that of Rabbis Simeon and Gamaliel.

Modern scholars note that only the Babylonian Talmud records the discussion between Levi and R. Simeon. It "underscores a notion which appears many times in the BT (Babylonian Talmud) and, indeed, seems to be peculiar to Babylonian tradition: that the crucial quality of the patriarch, without which he may be considered unworthy of his position, is *ḥokhma*, wisdom and knowledge."[15] In this view, R. Simeon would have had every reason to question his brother's appointment as patriarch, and the Talmud in effect had to "explain" Rebbe's decision.[16] The Jerusalem Talmud, on the other hand, which did not include this colloquy, reflected the Palestinian tradition that the patriarch's secular role was more important than, or equal to, his role as a scholar,[17] or scholarch, that is, the head of a permanent academy.[18]

---

he wanted R. Hama to be its permanent dean. His rationale for not having done so earlier was that R. Hama was from Sepphoris and its townspeople were unwilling to submit to his rulings. Y. Taanit 4:2; see also Frankel, *Korban Ha'eda*, s.v. *trein; middedamakh; umanei; ufarikh*. See Lau, *Ḥakhamim*, vol. 4, 26, who argues that R. Hanina actually was awarded the position of what today would be called communal rabbi. However, the text of the Talmud does not bear him out.

15. Steinmetz, "Must the Patriarch Know 'Uqtzin'?" 164.
16. The Babylonian Talmud's recording of the conversation with Levi, omitted by the Jerusalem Talmud, which was completed more than two centuries earlier, is but one example of a modern scholar's assertion that "the stories of Rabbi Judah's death show many signs of addition and elaboration." Anthony J. Saldarini, "Last Words and Deathbed Scenes in Rabbinic Literature," *The Jewish Quarterly Review* 68 (July 1977), 43.
17. Steinmetz (op. cit., 187) argues that the Palestinian tradition, which was "closer to historical reality," considered the patriarch's primary role to be, in effect, secular. It is arguable, however, that based on the Talmud's own testimony, the two roles were equally as important. See the comments in the preface to this book.
18. A scholarch was the head of a permanent academy. Tannaitic academies appear to have been linked to a particular rabbi; when the rabbi departed the academy closed.

Rebbe left other instructions besides announcing the appointment of his successors. He requested that he not be eulogized in the smaller towns, and by extension villages as well, so as not to disrupt the people's daily routine by having to arrange and attend funeral services.[19] As it happened, all the people from surrounding towns and villages came to the larger cities where the funerals were being held. It was then understood that his intention was not so much to spare the people special exertions on his behalf, but rather to honor the people who indeed went to the trouble of leaving their homes and work, and did so in order to attend his memorial services.

Despite his close relations with non-Jews, Rebbe requested that no gentile touch his deathbed. Instead, Rebbe asked that "those who served me in life should serve me in death."[20] As has been noted, he was referring to Simeon of Efrat and Joseph of Haifa. Both, however, passed away before he did.

Rebbe also ordered that his yeshiva return to its normal schedule of Torah study after thirty days; he did not want the students to disrupt their lessons completely with extended bouts of mourning.[21] He reasoned that he surely was no better than Moses, for whom the people mourned but thirty days. After thirty days, therefore, the scholars returned to some semblance of regularity for the next eleven months by studying Torah at night if they mourned during the day, or in daytime if they mourned at night.

Rebbe told his sons not to live in Shekantsiv, because its citizens were scoffers and would corrupt them. He also told them, more cryptically, not to sit on the bed of a "Syrian woman." Later rabbis, who had a tradition that he said something along these lines, had no real idea what he meant.[22]

The patriarch's academy was tied to the institution, not the individual, similar to Greek academies. See Shaye J. D. Cohen, "Patriarchs and Scholarchs," *Proceedings of the American Academy for Jewish Research* 48 (1981), especially 82–83.

19. Y. Ketubot 12:3.
20. *Midrash Tanḥuma: Parashat Vayeḥi* 3.
21. Rashi, Ketubot 103b, s.v. *vehoshivu.*
22. Pesaḥim 112b. The rabbis of the Talmud advanced several theories: that he was being literal; that he was referring to going to sleep without reciting the *Shema*; or that he instructed his sons not to marry a proselyte. Clearly they had no idea what he was talking about; moreover, he had already married off his sons.

In a lesson that should be heeded by many contemporary Jews, Rebbe also told his sons not to evade the Roman tax, since if caught by the government, it could "deprive you of all that you possess." He advised them not to "stand in front of an ox when it comes up from the meadow because Satan dances between its horns [i.e., it is mad]."[23] This instruction may initially have confused the rabbis as well, though a medieval scholar explained: "This refers to a black ox in the month of Nisan," when the ox gets spring fever and becomes especially violent.[24]

Finally, Rebbe enjoined his sons to continue to respect their stepmother after his passing. As the Talmud indicates, this was not at all self-evident:

> Surely, respect for a parent is a biblical commandment, as it is written, "Honor thy father and thy mother." She was their stepmother. That too is a biblical commandment as [a *baraita*] taught: Honor thy father and thy mother – thy father also connotes the wife of your father [i.e., stepmother] and your mother also connotes the husband of your mother [i.e., your stepfather]...these injunctions apply only when one's own parents are alive but not after death.[25]

Rebbe took the principle of honoring a stepparent one step further by commanding that his wife be respected even when he was gone. It should be noted that the position of women in ancient times was quite precarious.[26] Divorcees and widows were especially vulnerable and often suffered from extreme penury. Rebbe not only did not want his second wife to be reduced to a state of poverty, he wanted her to be treated with respect as the dowager wife of the patriarch. In this regard, as in others, Rebbe was far ahead of his time.[27]

---

23. Ibid.
24. R. Samuel b. Meir (Rashbam), Pesaḥim 112b, s.v. *mipnei.*
25. Ketubot 103a. See also Y. Ketubot 12:3. For a variant account see Y. Kilayim 9:3.
26. It is still precarious in many parts of the world today, and even within some sectors of the *ḥaredi* community.
27. Rubenstein points out that whereas the Yerushalmi lists only four of Rebbe's final requests, that his widow remain in their home, that he not be eulogized, that his servants occupy themselves with his funeral arrangements (Y. Ketubot 12:3), and that

Just as the behavior of Rebbe's sons toward each other differed sharply from that of Caracalla and Geta, so too the contrast between Rebbe's final instructions and those of Septimius Severus, who, unlike Caracalla, also died in his bed, could not have been more striking. Severus' last words reflected the precariousness of his family's position and focused on maintaining the loyalty of the military: "His death-bed advice to his sons and successors was to 'indulge the soldiers and despise everyone else.'"[28] Rebbe too considered his family's position but focused as much, if not more, on his spiritual and moral legacy,

The talmudic description of the scene at Rebbe's deathbed is highly stylized, to the point where some scholars have challenged its veracity. It certainly reflects elements of talmudic stories of the final instructions of other great scholars. For example, Rebbe teaches his sons and/or acolytes a numbered set of things; Tractate Pesaḥim attributes four to him. R. Akiba's instructions to R. Simeon b. Yohai consists of five points; and Rebbe himself received three instructions each from R. Yose b. Judah and R. Yishmael b. Yose.[29]

Similarly, Rebbe provides halakhic guidance to those who have come to pay him their last respects; the Talmud relates that Akavia b. Mehalalel did the same.[30] Rebbe's burial instructions parallel Rabban Yohanan b. Zakkai's last words.[31] Finally, the Talmud's account of R. Hiyya coming not only to say his final farewell to his mentor but to engage him one last time, is similar to the exchange between Hanina b.

R. Hami b. Hanina be appointed to head the yeshiva (Taanit 4:2), the Babylonian Talmud adds several more, all of which "correlate lineage and rabbinic leadership." Rubenstein, *Culture*, 92.

28. Goldsworthy, *Pax Romana*, 330. The quote is from Dio Cassius, *Roman History*, 77:15:2, who wrote, "I give his exact words without any embellishment." Since Dio was in close touch with Severus for many years, and indeed claimed to have been inspired to write his history after exchanging letters with Severus (73:23:1–2), his account of Severus' last words may well be accurate.
29. Pesaḥim 112a–b. See also Saldarini, "Last Words," 32. Y. Kilayim 9:3 has him give three sets of instructions, but R. Hezekiah added a fourth: that he not be buried in multiple shrouds, and the Talmud confirms that he meant that he wanted only a single shroud.
30. Eduyot 5:7.
31. He gave a different set of deathbed instructions. See Y. Avoda Zara 3:1.

Teradion and the dying R. Yose b. Kisma.[32] R. Hiyya saw that Rebbe was weeping and pointed out that if a man "dies smiling it is a good omen for him, but if he dies weeping it is a bad omen... dying of diarrhea is a good omen because most righteous men die of diarrhea." Rebbe replied, "I cry because I will be separated from Torah and the commandments."[33]

Rebbe's final hours were spent suffering from tremendous intestinal pain; R. Hiyya may have referred to diarrhea because it was plaguing the dying man. Rebbe's colleagues announced a day of fasting and prayers for his recovery. They also issued what seemed to be a strange proclamation: "Whoever will announce that Rebbe has passed away should be stabbed with a sword."[34] To their minds, however, the proclamation was necessary. They were convinced that Rebbe's ailments were not just due to his final illness. As has already been noted, the rabbis believed that there was merit to suffering, both for the one who suffered and for the community he led and served. As they saw it, Rebbe therefore had submitted himself to thirteen years of kidney stones and scurvy, from which he was still suffering; yet in all of those years the land had never needed rain to flourish. The rabbis – and perhaps Rebbe himself – correlated the land's good fortune with his own tribulations. The rabbis were simply hoping against hope that Rebbe would recover, not just for his own sake, but for the sake of the entire population.[35]

The Talmud relates that Rebbe's loyal maidservant overheard the rabbis' deliberations and became extremely agitated. She went up to the roof of his house and called out, "The Heavens are seeking out Rebbe as are those on earth, may it be the Lord's will that those below should conquer those above." When she saw how much pain her master was in, that he constantly had to take off his tefillin to relieve himself and then put them on again, she reversed herself: "May it be the will [of the Almighty] that those above may overpower those below."[36]

32. Avoda Zara 18a. See Saldarini, loc. cit., 41.
33. Ketubot 103b.
34. The Yerushalmi variant has the people of Sepphoris pronouncing that they would kill whoever announced Rebbe's passing. Hence Bar Kappara's indirect reply. See Y. Ketubot 12:3, 58a, and Frankel, *Korban Ha'eda*, ad loc., s.v. *Tzipporaya*.
35. Bava Metzia 85a, Ketubot 104a, and Maharsha, *Aggadot*, ad loc., s.v. *hahu*.
36. Ketubot 104a.

It was a talmudic tradition that the rabbis, especially the *Tanna'im*, wore tefillin all day. Later commentators appear to have assumed that this was the case with Rebbe as well. It is doubtful, however, that he did so; he simply had too many responsibilities, not least of which was interacting with the Romans, as well as occasionally traveling around the country to places mentioned in the Talmud such as Simonias, Acco, and Lod, and no doubt to some others as well.[37] In such circumstances, it would have been exceedingly difficult if not impossible for him to keep in place both the hand tefillin, with the precise positioning of the straps around arm and hand, and the head tefillin, which had to be centered high upon the forehead. It is possible, however, that, to the extent the talmudic description of Rebbe's passing is at least a partial reflection of what actually took place centuries earlier, Rebbe's final hours took place in the morning, when he was wearing his tefillin while engaged in the morning prayer. Since one cannot wear tefillin while suffering from any internal pains, Rebbe would have been forced to remove them each time he had to relieve himself. It was after watching him constantly leave his prayers – much as someone at a dinner table who suffers a violent attack of diarrhea must constantly and painfully excuse him- or herself – that the maidservant could stand it no longer and vented her anguish to the heavens.

The rabbis would not stop praying, however, so that Rebbe continued to hang on. So she took a dish and threw it down from the roof. The commotion startled the rabbis, who interrupted their prayers. At that moment, Rebbe lifted his ten fingers and cried out, "Master of the Universe, it is well known to you that I labored in the Torah with all ten of my fingers, and I never profited [from Torah] with even one of my fingers. May it be Thy will that I should rest in peace." A Heavenly voice responded, "He shall come in peace; they shall repose in their resting place,"[38] and Rebbe passed away peacefully.

The story's particular focus on the maidservant reflects once again the Talmud's perception of the loyalty that Rebbe commanded from his household. One part of the story certainly rings true: The rabbis, bereft

---

37. Oppenheimer, *Rabbi Yehuda HaNasi*, 135–36.
38. Is. 57:2.

at the loss of their leader, correlating his physical agony with the prosperity from which the country had benefited, and tending to pay little attention to women's concerns, were certainly not going to cease their prayers at the bidding of a mere maidservant.

Nevertheless, as has already been noted, the maidservant was remembered in later years as a very special person, one at least as knowledgeable as Rebbe's students, and perhaps as expert as some of his colleagues as well. Indeed, when Rebbe's maid threw the dish to the ground to disorient the rabbis momentarily from their prayers, thereby enabling Rebbe to pass from this world, she actually provided guidance for contemporary decisors regarding treatment of patients with a terminal illness who are suffering from excruciating pain. Just as the maid was able to bring on Rebbe's death, because it was clear to her that the rabbis' prayers were neither healing him nor even easing his pain, so too, ruled the great twentieth-century decisor R. Moshe Feinstein, when it is evident that medication will neither save the patient nor ease his/her pain, it is best to let the patient expire.[39]

The first person to see Rebbe after his soul had departed was none other than Bar Kappara. No doubt he had been alerted while in Lod that his teacher was at death's door. Bar Kappara may have been a wiseacre who annoyed Rebbe, but he loved him all the same. He must have rushed to Sepphoris to be with him. The other rabbis, knowing his relationship to Rebbe and not knowing that Rebbe had already died, asked Bar Kappara to look in on him to check on his condition. Bar Kappara found that his teacher was gone. He tore his cloak, turned the tear inward, and pronounced, "The angels and the mortals have each taken hold of the Holy Ark. The angels overpowered the mortals and the Holy Ark has been captured." The rabbis, realizing that he meant that Rebbe had died, asked him explicitly, "Has he died?" And Bar Kappara, always having his wits about him and remembering the rabbinical curse, replied, "You said it, not me."[40] Then, as was the custom since the passing of Rebbe's

39. R. Moshe Feinstein, "Teshuvot BeInyanei Refua: Meniat Refua MiḤoleh Mityasser" (Responses in Medical Matters: Withholding Medication from a Suffering Patient) in *Teḥumin* 5 (5756/1996), 213–14.

40. Ketubot 104a.

grandfather, Rabban Gamaliel II, "incense was burned after his death as if for royalty."[41]

Although he died in Sepphoris, Rebbe was interred in Beit She'arim, where he had spent much of his adult life.[42] He may have arranged for his burial plot either at the time he had moved to Sepphoris or while he was living there.[43] His tomb is to be found in what is now the Beit She'arim National Park, where many catacombs, as well as an ancient synagogue, have been excavated. The cave where Rebbe's tomb was located collapsed in a rockslide and was closed for some time.[44]

The entrance to the cave where Rebbe is interred. The barrier to entry can be seen in both photographs. (Photo: Dov Zakheim)

41. Schafer, *History of the Jews in Antiquity*, 168: Tosefta Shabbat 8:9 recounts: Just as they burn [incense] on [the death of] kings, so they burn for patriarchs... it happened that when Rabban Gamaliel died Onkelos the proselyte burned incense in his memory for seventy years.

42. Ketubot 103b.

43. R. Yosef Hayyim, *Ben Yehoyada*, vol. 3, Ketubot, s.v. *veha*.

44. Excavations near the national park are ongoing. See http://www.asor.org/anetoday/2018/02/New-Excavations-Beth-Shearim.

With the passage of time, Rebbe achieved mythical status in the eyes of the rabbinical class. He was venerated for his ability to mine the Scriptures to deduce the finer points of halakhic legislation. As Rava put it, "He draws water from deep pits."[45] Indeed, it was also taught that "if one sees Rebbe in a dream, he may hope for wisdom."[46] It is therefore hardly surprising that the Babylonian Talmud accorded him superhuman powers. It asserts that on the day that Rebbe died,

> a heavenly voice (*bat kol*) broke through and announced: "Whoever has been present at the death of Rebbe is assured of a life in the world to come." A certain laundryman who would attend to Rebbe on a daily basis, failed to call on that day. When he heard [that Rebbe had passed on] he climbed up to the roof, fell to the ground and died. At that point another *bat kol* broke through and announced: "That laundryman is also assured of a life in the world to come."[47]

Such was the degree of awe with which Rebbe was held by the rabbis who sought to transmit his legacy.

With Rebbe's passing the high point of positive Jewish-Roman relations came to an end. Those relations briefly took a turn for the better more than a century later during the six years (355–361) when Julian the Apostate ruled the eastern provinces of Rome, and the two additional years when he was Rome's sole emperor. With Julian's untimely death, however, any hope of good relations with Rome was snuffed out once and for all.

45. Shavuot 7a.
46. Berakhot 57b.
47. Ibid., 103b.

Chapter 9

Conclusion: A Man of Many Parts

> Rabbi Simeon b. Judah would say in the name of Rabbi Simeon bar Yohai, "Beauty, strength, wealth, honor, wisdom, sagacity, old age, and progeny are fitting for the righteous and fitting for the world."… Rabbi Simeon b. Menassia said, "These seven qualities enumerated by the Sages for the righteous were all embodied in Rebbe and his sons."
>
> *Kalla Rabbati* 8:6 (Avot 6:8)

Rabbi Judah the Prince is a larger-than-life figure in the Talmud. Not only was he recognized as a scholar of the first rank, but the rabbis of following generations were so overawed by his reputation as a man who could mingle with the great and powerful of the Roman Empire that they created an entire mythology that not only had him equal to the Roman emperors, but actually had those rulers subservient to him. Though they could point to other rabbis who had relations with the rulers of their time – Rebbe's students Rav and Samuel in particular – they recognized that the relationships of these later scholars were nowhere nearly as personal as Rebbe's had been with Septimius Severus and his son Caracalla, whom they blended together as "Antoninus."

Rebbe demonstrated better than any other talmudic figure that a Jew could devote him- or herself both to Torah and to worldly matters. His greatest contribution to Jewish life was, of course, the Mishna. Like most men of multiple talents, he somehow found the time to edit that great work even as he continued to lead a major yeshiva, issue halakhic rulings both for the community in Palestine and for Jews living elsewhere in the Roman empire, manage the community's secular affairs, interact with the Romans, and maintain diplomatic relations with the Parthians as well. And all the while he suffered from severe physical ailments that were probably aggravated by sleep deprivation and exhaustion.[1]

His contribution to the study of Torah extended well beyond his editing the Mishna. Rebbe trained a cadre of students who spread Torah knowledge not only throughout Palestine but also in the Diaspora. In particular, his students Rav and Samuel established the most important yeshivas in Babylonia. Rebbe thus can rightly claim to be the primary source for the development of that Diaspora community into the talmudic powerhouse that provided the basis for Jewish practice and custom to this day.

Rebbe's approach to halakha and tradition was based on the rabbinic principle that "a judge only rules what is before his eyes."[2] In modern parlance, that translates as "calling them as one sees them." At times he could issue rulings that were nothing short of radical, such as proposing the abolition of Tisha B'Av, permitting usurers and robbers to keep their gains, and waiving the need to bring tithes from lands bordering historic *Eretz Yisrael*. At times he demonstrated tremendous sensitivity to the plight of the unfortunate, as when he permitted a woman who had been captured by gentiles to marry a priest on the basis of her

1. Maimonides described similar strains on his health to his great translator, R. Samuel ibn Tibbon. He wrote of his need to commute to Cairo every morning to attend to the Sultan, and how he would return home completely exhausted only to find a throng of both Jews and non-Jews waiting to see him, primarily because of medical issues. He barely had time to eat and would go to bed exhausted. He was even hard-pressed on Shabbat when the community looked to him for leadership. See Maimonides, *She'elot UTeshuvot HaRambam: Pe'er HaDor*, 2nd ed., ed. David Yosef, no. 143 (Jerusalem: Machon Yerushalayim, 5754/1994), 278.
2. Nidda 20b. For a discussion of this principle, see Berkovits, *Not in Heaven*, 80–86.

minor child's testimony that she had not been raped. At other times, however, he took a harder line than his colleagues. For example, his view of the Samaritans was much harsher than those of the majority of rabbis. He was prepared to allow a married man to betroth another married woman conditional upon her husband's passing. His colleagues overruled him, because they worried about the deleterious impact of this ruling upon the health of the man's current marriage. Again, his initial position banning the planting of certain types of vegetables even when they were planted at a permissible distance from other crops was stricter than those of the rabbis, who permitted such plantings. Ultimately, he yielded to their views.

It was not that he was inconsistent in being more permissive in some cases and restrictive in others. Rather, he was not dogmatic; he judged each case on its merits, and only on its merits. It is a quality that only true leaders possess.

Yet even as he spread the knowledge of Torah and led his people on the basis of its precepts, Rebbe was a man who clearly was comfortable outside the four ells of the Jewish community. He spoke Greek, preferring it to Aramaic, which over the centuries became canonized as a holy language. He was classically trained. He dressed in the Roman style. He socialized with non-Jews, even gentile priests. And, unlike some contemporary university-trained Jewish parents who discourage their children from receiving the same education that they did, he brought up his children to follow both in his Jewish and worldly footsteps.

Rebbe's life and accomplishments demonstrate that it is possible to make outstanding contributions both to the world of Torah and the world around us. Contrary to the belief in some Orthodox Jewish quarters, these are not either/or choices. Rebbe chose both and excelled in both and did so because, at bottom, he was truly comfortable in his own religious skin. In so doing he offers an example that every modern Jew and Jewess, whatever their talents and capabilities and wherever they might live, can and should strive to emulate.

Appendix 1

Time Line

98–117 CE	Reign of Trajan
115–117	Revolt of Jews in Cyrenaica, Cyprus, and Egypt; Trajan's war against Parthia
117–138	Reign of Hadrian
132–135	Bar Kokhba rebellion
135	R. Judah the Prince born in Usha; legend that R. Akiba dies same day
145	Septimius Severus born in Lepcis, 11 April
138–161	Reign of Antoninus Pius
161–69	Joint reign of Marcus Aurelius and Lucius Verus
162	Severus first comes to Rome
165? 175?	R. Simeon b. Gamaliel II, father of Judah, dies; Judah becomes patriarch
165? 175?	Rebbe moves Sanhedrin to Beit She'arim
169	Severus becomes a Senator, 11 April
169–77	Reign of Marcus Aurelius
175	Revolt of Avidius Cassius; Marcus Aurelius in Palestine
175?	Severus marries Paccia Marciana
177–80	Joint reign of Marcus Aurelius and Commodus
180–92	Reign of Commodus
187	Severus marries Julia Domna
188	Caracalla born in Lugdunum (modern-day Lyon) 4 April

189	Severus becomes proconsul of Sicily
191	Severus becomes governor of Upper Pannonia
192–93	Reign of Pertinax
193	Reign of Didius Julianus
193	Revolt of Pescennius Niger
193–98	Reign of Septimius Severus begins 9 June 193
194	Severus defeats Niger at Issus
197	Severus defeats Clodius Albinus at Lugdunum, 19 February
198–99	Septimius Severus and Caracalla in Palestine; meet Rebbe
198–211	Joint reign of Septimius Severus and Caracalla
200	Rebbe moves Sanhedrin to Sepphoris (Tzipori) from Beit She'arim
ca. 200	Rebbe completes editing of Mishna in Sepphoris
211	Severus dies, 4 February
211–217	Reign of Caracalla
212	Edict of Caracalla (*Constitutio Antoniana*); Jews now Roman citizens
215	Caracalla in Palestine; meets Rebbe
217	Rebbe dies on 17 Kislev and is buried in Beit She'arim

Appendix 2

A Brief Note on Rabbinic Biography

The Talmud is not a historical work. The works of Roman historians, or their Greek predecessors for that matter, are not necessarily more reliable. Herodotus employed heavy doses of his imagination in producing his history of the Persian Wars. Thucydides, generally recognized as providing a more accurate account of the events he described, nevertheless did not shy away from creating monologues that he inserted into the mouths of various figures who made their appearance in *The Peloponnesian Wars,* including Pericles' stirring oration to the Athenians.

The Roman historians were somewhat better, but not much. Plutarch employed what has been termed "characteristic anecdote" without necessarily validating its authenticity.

Of Sallust, the first of the truly great Roman historians (the others being Tacitus and Livy), one scholar notes: "He had little reason to promulgate outright lies in his work. However, Sallust's political career did engender biases … Sallust's work is permeated by rancor against the

Senate and politicians from old noble families. Simultaneously, through his histories Sallust perhaps sought to vindicate his patron, Julius Caesar."[1]

Livy, perhaps the most accurate of the three, was not without creations of his own, such as the speeches he attributed to the Roman generals in the war with Hannibal. Tacitus revealed his biases and fabrications with his anti-Jewish rants, including allegations that

> their…customs, are perverted and abominable, and owe their prevalence to their depravity. All the most worthless rascals, renouncing their national cults, started showering them with offerings and tribute…they feel nothing but hatred and enmity for the rest of the world… [they] are immoderate in sexual indulgence…. The Jewish ritual is preposterous and sordid.[2]

He wrote much more in a similar vein.

All three historians lived and flourished well before Judah the Prince was born, indeed, before the Bar Kokhba revolt. The only two historians who were Judah's contemporaries were Dio Cassius and Herodian. Of the two, the former is generally considered to be by far the more accurate historian, but he too was not above creating anecdotes when it suited him. Later historians were not much better; indeed, it is arguable that the *Historia Augusta*, completed a half century after Rebbe's death, is so full of inaccuracies that it is a throwback to an earlier time. Thus the stories of rabbinic doings are no better nor worse than those of non-Jewish historians on the lives and activities of the Caesars.

Because there are no other sources to validate these biographical sketches, and because of the very nature of these sketches, they have evoked a variety of reactions on the part of those who have studied them. For centuries, until the Enlightenment and the emancipation of Jews beginning in the late 1700s, the stories about the rabbis were all taken at face value. Classic rabbinic commentators often sought to reconcile

1. Julian Barr, "Sallust: Corrupt Politician and Historian," *Crossroads* 6:1 (2012), 58–63.
2. Tacitus, *The Histories*, trans. W. H. Fyfe, ed. D. S. Levene (Oxford: Oxford University Press, 1999), 5:2–3, 233–34.

varying accounts of a given incident; at times, however, they simply ignored the contradictions and continued to cite one or the other tale as the occasion suited them.

Some contemporary Jews, notably those who adhere to the *ḥaredi* or ultra-Orthodox weltanschauung, continue to treat the tales of the rabbis as literal unvarnished truth. Indeed, they believe that all of the Talmud, even stories such as Rabba bar Bar Hana and R. Yohanan's famous tales of sea dragons and other monsters, embodies the Oral Law that God conveyed to Moses simultaneously with the written Torah. As they see it, all is truth, nothing is exaggeration.

At the other extreme are academic scholars, generally but certainly not exclusively from the liberal streams of Judaism or from other faiths. To them rabbinic literature, like the Torah itself, is not the product of a divine hand but rather an aggregation of different texts, edited over time. Naturally, they also do not accept the notion that the Talmud is the written expression of the Oral Law, and they do not hesitate to examine it critically. Moreover, they argue that since the reports of rabbinic doings were often written down centuries after they supposedly took place, the absence of any corroborating evidence (such as archeological finds or non-Jewish sources) renders those reports problematical at best. As one scholar has put it, "Talmudic stories about the rabbinic past...in generic terms are homilies, fables, legal cases or *chriae* rather than historiography."[3] Their underlying, "minimalist" assumption is that the contents of rabbinic lore tend to be closer to inspired fiction than revealed truth. Indeed, some will go so far as to question whether particular rabbis even existed, or whether they are simply fictional national heroes, no different from Hercules, Sir Galahad, Paul Bunyan, and other colorful figures that over the centuries have inspired nations and civilizations.[4]

Some scholars do not necessarily question the existence of rabbinical figures, but argue that tales of their activities were formulated in

3. Seth Schwartz, *The Ancient Jews from Alexander to Muhammad* (Cambridge: Cambridge University Press, 2014), 99. Schwartz articulated his "minimalist" view at length in *Imperialism and Jewish Society, 200 BCE to 640 CE.*
4. For a discussion, see Holtz, *Rabbi Akiva*, 8–12.

Sassanian Persia centuries after they flourished in Palestine, and therefore reflected the values and concerns of the Babylonian *Amora'im* and their immediate successors. Still others would argue that there were only a very few rabbinic scholars and leaders at any one period during the era that spanned five centuries from the destruction of the Temple, and that these rabbis had far less influence over the community as a whole than their literature implies.

It naturally follows that those who adopt the "minimalist" approach to rabbinic literature question not only the details of Judah's interactions with a Roman emperor, but whether he had any political power at all. In their view, "these stories manifestly retroject activities and types of authority possessed by later, mainly fourth-century patriarchs onto one of the dynasty's revered founders.... The historical Judah was a more modest figure, though some elements of the rabbinic stories about him are not implausible."[5]

Finally, some scholars, of whom most belong to the group that calls itself Modern Orthodox, but some are traditionalists from the non-Orthodox movements or even non-Jews, tend to what has been termed the "maximalist" view that many rabbinic tales, especially the biographical ones, contain at least a germ of truth about their subjects.[6] While admittedly these stories are not biographies in the modern sense of that term, they nevertheless contain far more information regarding certain key individuals than laymen and even scholars realize. And this information is not pure fiction.

Those who argue that most if not all the tales of the rabbis were created by the scholars who appear in the Babylonian Talmud or indeed

5. Schwartz, *Ancient Jews*, p. 119. Burton Visotzky takes a similar view, but goes even further in arguing that rabbinic Judaism actually "was invented in the matrix of Roman culture." Visotzky, *Aphrodite*, 12. Visotzky's approach is flippant bordering on irreverence, with interjections such as "wow" and "yikes" that appear geared to a teenage readership.
6. See, for example, Goodman, *Rome and Jerusalem*. Though he dismisses the Antoninus stories as belonging "to the same genre of moralizing folk tales as other rabbinic narratives about gentiles" he also asserts that "it is likely, at the least, that Judah haNasi did have a closer relationship to the Roman government than his predecessors and successors in the rabbinic community" (482–83). See also Oppenheimer, *Rabbi Yehuda HaNasi*, 14–15.

by those who edited and revised that work, base their case on the absence of parallel stories in the Jerusalem Talmud, which is a product of the land in which those stories purportedly took place.[7] Yet the Jerusalem Talmud, as we now have it, is far from complete. It is missing the entire Order of Kodashim, which includes several important tractates such as Zevaḥim, Menaḥot, Ḥullin, and Bekhorot, all of which occupy large numbers of folios of the Babylonian Talmud. Moreover, just as the Jerusalem Talmud expands upon all the *mishnayot* of the Order of Zera'im, and not, like the Babylonian Talmud, merely on those of Berakhot, the same may have been true of the Order of Teharot, about which the latter is silent. Thus, it may well be that the tales of the rabbis that appear in the Bavli are faithful renditions of stories that were first recounted in the Yerushalmi but have since been lost. Moreover, variants of many of the Bavli's stories, including some regarding Rebbe and "Antoninus," do appear in the Yerushalmi or in Genesis Rabba, which also predated the Bavli.[8]

In addition, to assert that the rabbis were a far smaller, less influential group than traditional Jews and many historians have long believed, is to postulate, without evidence, that those named in rabbinic writings were not the leaders of their community. This position simply discounts the significant probability that their many students and followers were referred to anonymously. For example, when the Talmud asserts that Hillel had eighty students, but only two – R. Yohanan ben Zakkai and Yonatan ben Uziel – are named, it does not necessarily mean that the other seventy-eight never existed. It is like claiming that since works by perhaps less than one hundred post-World War II American rabbis have appeared in print, there were no other rabbis or yeshiva students in the United States during the second half of the twentieth century. There is no reason entirely to disbelieve talmudic assertions regarding the rabbis' sway over the general population. The rabbis may well have exaggerated their influence, but the Talmud's recorded cases of townspeople who

7. This argument is a major theme of Jeffrey Rubenstein's *Culture*; see, for example, 7–13.

8. In at least one case where the Yerushalmi and the Bavli recount the same story, Rubenstein is forced to admit that "it is methodologically suspect to explain away a source that contradicts one's theory." Rubenstein, *Culture*, 167n10.

approached the rabbis for their rulings indicates that their influence extended beyond their immediate circle of acolytes.

In the same vein, as one scholar has written with respect to the talmudic reports of interactions between Judah the Prince and a Roman emperor, "the stories would hardly have developed or been invented, had there not been an emperor who had provided a peg upon which to hang them by meeting a Jewish patriarch or a prominent rabbi on friendly terms at some time."[9] At the same time, scholars who accept that there is an element of truth to midrashic tales consciously or unconsciously reflect the views of the tenth- and eleventh-century leaders of Babylonian Jewry, R. Sherira Gaon and his son R. Hai Gaon; of R. Hai's great contemporary, the eleventh-century statesman, general, and talmudic scholar Samuel ibn Naghrillah, known in Jewish history as Samuel the Prince (Shmuel HaNagid); and of R. Abraham son of Maimonides, who flourished in the late twelfth and early thirteenth centuries. In Samuel's words, "*Haggada* is any interpretation that appears in the Talmud on any matter that does not involve a commandment... and one need not derive [halakha] from it [*haggada*] anything other than what appeals to one's intellect."[10]

In other words, when the activities of a particular rabbi are recounted in the literature, one need not accept the specifics. These may not be accurate given the time that has elapsed between the event in question and the talmudic or midrashic report centuries later. Yet one could reason that something did happen along the lines of the incident in question, which simply was distorted with the passage of time, or consciously altered for heuristic, homiletical, or political reasons.

Indeed, one can point to cases where descriptions of similar "meetings" in the non-Jewish world were based to some degree on actual occurrences. A recent study of the inventor, analyst, spy, author, and scoundrel William Playfair offers a case in point. In 1787, Playfair

9. Smallwood, *Jews under Roman Rule*, 485.
10. R. Shmuel HaNagid, *Mevo HaTalmud* (in Vilna *Shas*, first volume 45a), s.v. *haggada*. For citations, and a discussion, see Nathaniel Helfgot, *Mikra and Meaning: Studies in Bible and Its Interpretation* (New Milford, CT: Maggid, 2012), 23 and n. 27.

published *Joseph and Benjamin,* which claimed to be the translation of a French transcript of a secret meeting between Emperor Joseph II of Austria and Benjamin Franklin, when the latter was the American ambassador to France. For years the book was dismissed as a mere fantasy; indeed, the two men never met. But recent research indicates that they were indeed supposed to have met: the meeting was arranged through a third party, but when Franklin arrived at the appointed place Joseph did not appear. By the time the emperor arrived, a disappointed Franklin had departed. Even if the so-called "transcript" was a fiction, it now can be seen to be based on an actual historical incident.[11] So too, one might argue, were the colloquies between Rebbe and the emperors.

Roman sources do not mention Judah the Prince or any other rabbis. Indeed, the only rabbi of the Talmud to be mentioned in an external source is Rabban Gamaliel the Elder, who is variously described in Acts of the Apostles as "a Pharisee, named Gamaliel, a doctor of the law… in reputation among all the people" and as the teacher of Paul of Tarsus "according to the perfect manner of the law of the fathers."[12] Yet it strains credulity to posit that none of the other rabbis existed, that all of their reported activities and pronouncements are pure fiction, and that until the fourth century, when the Theodosian Code mentioned the patriarchate, the scions of Judaea's princely line never served as both leaders of their people and their representatives to the outside world.[13] It simply is too difficult to ignore an entire corpus of literature. This is especially so if the basis for dismissing that literature is itself highly speculative, and often derives from particular interpretations of archeological findings that themselves offer little more than ambiguous evidence for evaluating the veracity of rabbinic texts. On the contrary, the behaviors ascribed to rabbis in later rabbinic literature seem plausible in light of human nature in general and political exigencies in particular.

Writing of Muslim traditions, the eminent Harvard historian G. W. Bowersock notes that "the factional quarrels that have bedeviled Western

11. See Bruce Berkowitz, *Playfair: The True Story of the British Secret Agent Who Changed How We See the World* (Fairfax, VA: George Mason University Press, 2018), 45–46.
12. Acts of the Apostles 5:34; 22:3.
13. Schwartz, *Ancient Jews,* 118.

scholarship on early Islam should be brought to a close.... Minimalism is not the way to throw light on a dark age." He points out that the fact that the traditions were only committed to writing two centuries after the events they described "does not altogether indict them as unworthy of attention. [They] simply remind the historian to be constantly alert."[14] His observations could equally well be applied to rabbinic literature. In both cases, whether addressing the traditions of Islam or those of the Talmud, the particular details recounted in oral tradition for centuries before being committed to paper may be questionable, but the general thrust of these reports offers sufficient truth to obviate being dismissed as mere fantasy.

14. G. W. Bowersock, *The Crucible of Islam* (Boston, MA: Harvard University Press, 2016).

Select Bibliography

I cite numerous passages in both the Scriptures (Tanakh) and rabbinic writings. For the Scriptures, I have generally employed the original JPS translation, and for the Talmud Bavli the Soncino translation, though occasionally I have modified them, translated from Hebrew commentaries, or employed other translations. Unless otherwise indicated, all post-talmudic and midrashic traditional commentators and decisors cited are in Hebrew.

Talmudic and Midrashic Texts

Mishna: Kilayim, Megilla, Yevamot, Ketubot, Sota, Gittin, Sanhedrin, Eduyot, Horayot, Avoda Zara, Avot, *Avot DeRabbi Natan,* Nidda.

Tosefta: Kilayim, Terumot, Shabbat, Pesaḥim, Sota, Sanhedrin, Eduyot, Avoda Zara, Oholot, Nega'im.

Mekhilta DeRabbi Yishmael: Bo, Beshallaḥ (HaShira), Yitro (BaḤodesh).

Talmud Yerushalmi: Pe'ah, Demai, Kilayim, Terumot, Maaserot, Rosh HaShana, Taanit, Megilla, Yevamot, Ketubot, Gittin, Nedarim, Sanhedrin, Avoda Zara.

Talmud Bavli: Berakhot, Shabbat, Eiruvin, Pesaḥim, Yoma, Beitza, Rosh HaShana, Taanit, Megilla, Mo'ed Katan, Ketubot, Nedarim, Sota, Gittin, Kiddushin, Bava Kamma, Bava Metzia, Bava Batra, Sanhedrin, Makkot, Avoda Zara, Horayot, Eduyot, Menaḥot, Ḥullin, Arakhin.

Midrash Tanḥuma: Vayeshev, Miketz, Vayeḥi.
Midrash Rabba: Genesis Rabba, Leviticus Rabba, Ecclesiastes Rabba.
Pesikta DeRav Kahana: R. Kahana's Compilation of Discourses for Sabbaths and Festal Days, trans. William G. (Gershon Zev) Braude and Israel J. Kapstein (Philadelphia: Jewish Publication Society of America, 1975).
Yalkut Shimoni.
Midrash HaGadol.

Commentaries: Mishna

Maimonides/R. Moshe ben Maimon. *Introduction to Order Zera'im.*

Commentators: Yerushalmi

Frankel, R. David Herschel. *Korban Ha'eda.*
Loeb, R. Elijah ben Judah. *Mahara Fulda.*
Margolies, R. Moshe. *Pnei Moshe.*
Sirillio, R. Solomon. *Commentary on Seder Zera'im.*

Commentators: Bavli

Adels, R. Samuel Eliezer Halevi (Maharsha). *Ḥidushei Halakhot VeAggadot.*
R. Elijah Ben Solomon (Gaon of Vilna). *Commentary on Gittin.*
Meiri, R. Menaḥem ben Shlomo. *Beit HaBeḥira: Berakhot,* ed. Shmuel Dickman. Jerusalem: Makhon HaTalmud HaYisraeli HaShalem, 5725/1965.
R. Nissim Girondi (Ran).
R. Samuel Ibn Naghrillah / R. Shmuel Hanagid. *Mevo HaTalmud.*
R. Shlomo Yitzḥaki (Rashi).
R. Shmuel Ben Meir (Rashbam).
Sofer/Schreiber, Abraham. *Tosafot Ḥakhmei Anglia Al Masekhtot Beitza, Megilla, Kiddushin.* Jerusalem: n.p., 1970.
Tosafot. Various authors.
R. Yosef Hayyim, *Ben Yehoyada,* vol 3.
Zakheim, R. Zvi Hirsh. *Zvi HaSanhedrin,* vol. 3. Brooklyn, NY: Gross, 5752/1992.

Commentators: Midrash

Ben Joseph, Enoch Zundel. *Eitz Yosef.*

Decisors and Halakhic Commentators

di Butan, R. Avraham. *Leḥem Mishneh.*

Encyclopedia Talmudit (1951–).

Feinstein, R. Moshe. *Igrot Moshe: Oraḥ Ḥayyim*, vol. 2. Brooklyn, NY: Moriah, 1963.

———. *Oraḥ Ḥayyim*, vol. 3. Brooklyn: NY: Moriah, 1973.

———. *Oraḥ Ḥayyim*, vol. 4:20. Bnei Brak: Yeshivat Ohel Yosef, 5741/1981.

———. "Teshuvot BeInyanei Refua: Meniat Refua MiḤoleh Mityasser" (Responses in medical matters: withholding medication from a suffering patient), *Teḥumin* 5 (5756/1996).

Ḥayyim, R. Yosef. *She'elot UTeshuvot Rav Pe'alim*, vol. 1: *Oraḥ Ḥayyim.* Jerusalem: Salem, 5772/2012.

Isserles, R. Moses. *She'elot UTeshuvot HaRema*, rev. ed., ed. R. Dr. Asher Ziv, no. 123. Jerusalem: Mossad Harav Kook, 2018.

Kagan, R. Israel Meir. *Mishna Berura.* Jerusalem: Torah Le'am, 5720/1960.

Karo, R. Yosef. *Shulḥan Arukh: Oraḥ Ḥayyim, Yoreh De'ah, Ḥoshen Mishpat, Even Ha'ezer.*

———. *Kesef Mishneh.*

Klein, R. Menashe. *Mishneh Halakhot: Mador HaTeshuvot: Mahadura Kamma*, vol. 6. Brooklyn, NY: Mishne Halachoth Gedoloth Institute, 5758/1998.

Landau, R. Yeḥezkel. *She'elot UTeshuvot Noda BiYehuda HaShalem, Even Ha'ezer*, vol. 1. Jerusalem: Machon Yerushalayim, 5754/1994, *Mahadura Tinyana.*

Maimonides/R. Moshe ben Maimon. *Mishneh Torah: Introduction; Hilkhot Temidin UMusafin; Hilkhot Maakhalot Asurot; Hilkhot Gezeila VaAveida; Hilkhot Malveh VeLoveh; Hilkhot Tumat HaMet.*

———. *She'elot UTeshuvot Pe'er HaDor*, ed. David Yosef, 2nd ed. Jerusalem: Makhon Or Hamizrah, 1994/5754.

Schachter, R. Hershel. *Nefesh HaRav.* Jerusalem: Reishit Yerushalayim, 5755/1994; Heb.

Schreiber, R. Moshe. *Ḥatam Sofer: Oraḥ Ḥayyim.* Bnei Brak: Kodesh Mishor, 1990.

Segal, R. David Halevi. *Turei Zahav,* in Karo, *Shulḥan Arukh: Even Ha'ezer.*

Sherman, R. Avraham-Ḥayyim. "Bedika Ḥozeret Shel Giyur BeVeit Din Aḥer" (Repeat investigation of [a] conversion in another rabbinical court), *Teḥumin* 31 (5771/2011).

Sonenfeld, R. Yosef Hayim. *Torat Hayim: Teshuvot Rabbi Yosef Hayim Sonnenfeld,* 3rd ed. Jerusalem: Machon Re'em, 5765/2005.

Sperling, R. Abraham Isaac. *Taamei HaMinhagim UMekorei HaDinim,* no. 847. Jerusalem: Eshkol, 5732/1972.

Waldenberg, R. Eliezer Yehuda. *She'elot UTeshuvot Tzitz Eliezer,* vol. 4, 2nd ed. Jerusalem: n.p., 1985.

———. *She'elot UTeshuvot Tzitz Eliezer,* vol. 5, 2nd. ed. Jerusalem: n.p., 1985, *Introduction: HaRiformim VeHeikhaleihem BaHalakha.*

Weingarten, R. Yoav Yehoshua. *Ḥelkat Yo'av,* vol 1, no. 1, cited in *Encyclopedia Talmudit,* vol. 37.

Yosef, R. Ovadya. *She'elot UTeshuvot Yabia Omer,* vol. 2, 2nd ed., *Even Ha'ezer.* Jerusalem: n.p, 5746/1986.

Books

Adler, Marcus Nathan, ed. and trans. *The Itinerary of Benjamin of Tudela.* London: Oxford University Press, 1907.

Alon, Gedaliah. *The Jews in Their Land in the Talmudic Age (70–640 C.E.),* trans. and ed. Gershon Levi. Cambridge, MA and London: Harvard University Press, 1980.

Beard, Mary. *SPQR: A History of Ancient Rome.* New York and London: Liveright, 2015.

Berkovits, Eliezer. *Not in Heaven.* Jerusalem and New York: Shalem Press, 2010.

Birley, Anthony R. *Septimius Severus: The African Emperor,* rev. ed. London and New York: Routledge, 2010.

Braverman, Jay. *Jerome's Commentary on Daniel: A Study of Comparative Jewish and Christian Interpretations of the Hebrew Bible.* Washington, DC: Catholic Biblical Association of America, 1978.

Brown, Jeremy. *New Heavens and a New Earth: The Jewish Reception of Copernican Thought.* Oxford and New York: Oxford University Press, 2013.

Cohen, Shaye J. D. *From the Maccabees to the Mishnah,* 2nd ed. Louisville, KY and London: Westminster John Knox Press, 2006.

Dio Cassius. *Roman History,* trans. Earnest Cary. Cambridge, MA and London: Harvard University Press, 1914.

Ellenson, David and Gordis, Daniel. *Pledges of Jewish Allegiance: Conversion, Law and Policymaking in Nineteenth- and Twentieth-Century Orthodox Responsa.* Stanford, CA: Stanford University Press, 2012.

Eusebius. *Ecclesiastical History,* trans. C. F. Cruse. Peabody, MA: Hendrickson, 1989.

Feldman, Louis H. *Studies in Hellenistic Judaism.* Leiden and New York: E. J. Brill, 1996.

Goldsworthy, Adrian. *How Rome Fell.* New Haven and London: Yale University Press, 2009.

———. *Pax Romana: War, Peace and Conquest in the Roman World.* New Haven, CT and London: Yale University Press, 2016.

Goodman, Martin. *Rome and Jerusalem: The Clash of Ancient Civilizations.* New York: Vintage, 2007.

Grant, Michael. *The Severans: The Changed Roman Empire.* London and New York: Routledge, 1995.

Gruen, Erich S. *Diaspora: Jews Amidst Greeks and Romans.* Cambridge, MA and London: Harvard University Press, 2002.

Halbertal, Moshe. *Maimonides: Life and Thought,* trans. Joel Linsider. Princeton, NJ and Oxford: Princeton University Press, 2014.

Hammer, Reuven, trans., intro., and commentaries, *The Classic Midrash: Tannaitic Commentaries on the Bible.* New York and Mahwah, NJ: Paulist Press, 1995.

Herodian. *History of the Empire,* vol. 2, trans. C. R. Whittaker. Cambridge, MA and London: Harvard University Press, 1970.

Hidary, Richard. *Dispute for the Sake of Heaven: Legal Pluralism in the Talmud.* Providence, RI: Brown, 2010.

Historia Augusta. Vol. 1, trans. David Magie. Cambridge, MA and London: Harvard University Press, 1921.

———. Vol. 2. Cambridge, MA and London: Harvard University Press, 1924.

Holtz, Barry. W. *Rabbi Akiva: Sage of the Talmud*. New Haven and London: Yale University Press, 2017.

Horovitz, H. S. *Corpus Tannaiticum… Pars Tertia: Siphre D'Be Rab,* reprinted as Haym Shaul Horovitz, *Kovetz Ma'asei HaTanna'im… Ḥelek Shlishi: Sifrei DeVei Rav*. Jerusalem: Or Olam, 5768/2008; Heb.

Jellinek, Aharon, ed. *Beit HaMidrash,* vol 6. Vienna: Winter Brothers, 5638/1878; Heb.

Jerome. *Commentary on Daniel,* trans. Gleason L. Archer. Eugene, OR: Wipf and Stock, 2009.

Josephus, Flavius. *The Jewish War,* ed. Gaalya Cornfeld. Grand Rapids, MI: Zondervan, 1982.

———. *Against Apion,* trans. H. St. J. Thackeray. Cambridge, MA and London: Harvard University Press, 1926.

Lau, Binyamin. *Ḥakhamim* vol 3: *Yemei Galil*. Tel Aviv: Yediot Ahronot, 2008; Heb.

———. *Ḥakhamim* vol. 4: *MiMishna LaTalmud*. Tel Aviv: Yediot Ahronot, 2012; Heb.

Levin, Dr. Binyamin Menashe, ed. *Igeret Rav Sherira Gaon: Nusaḥ Sefarad VeNusaḥ Tzorfat*. Haifa: Itzkovski, 1921.

Lewis, Naphtali, and Reinhold, Meyer, eds. *Roman Civilization vol. II: The Empire*. New York: Harper&Row, 1966.

Lieberman, Saul. *Tosefta Kipshuta: Order Zera'im,* vol. 2. New York: Jewish Theological Seminary Press, 2001: Heb.

McLynn, Frank. *Marcus Aurelius: A Life*. Cambridge, MA: Da Capo, 2009.

Margalioth, Mordekhai, ed. *Encyclopedia of Talmudic and Geonic Literature: Being A Biographical Dictionary of the Tannaim, Amoraim and Geonim,* vol. 1. Tel Aviv: Chachik, 1960; Heb.

Oppenheimer, Aharon. *Rabbi Yehuda HaNasi*. Jerusalem: Mercaz Zalman Shazar, 2007; Heb.

———. *Rabbi Judah ha-Nasi: Statesman, Reformer, and Redactor of the Mishnah*. Tubingen: Mohr Siebeck, 2017.

Rosenfeld, Ben Zion. *Torah Centers and Rabbinic Activity in Palestine 70–400 CE: History and Geographic Distribution,* trans. Chava Cassell. Leiden and Boston, MA: Brill, 2010.

Rubenstein, Jeffrey L. *The Culture of the Babylonian Talmud*. Baltimore, MD: The Johns Hopkins University Press, 2003.

Schafer, Peter. *The History of the Jews in Antiquity: The Jews of Palestine from Alexander the Great to the Arab Conquest*, trans. David Chowcat. Luxembourg: Harwood, 1995.

Schwartz, Seth. *Imperialism and Jewish Society, 200 BCE to 640 CE*. Princeton: Princeton University Press, 2001.

Sebag Montefiore, Simon. *Jerusalem: The Biography*. London: Phoenix, 2012.

Secunda, Shai. *The Iranian Talmud: Reading the Bavli in Its Sassanian Context*. Philadelphia: University of Pennsylvania Press, 2014.

Smallwood, E. Mary. *The Jews under Roman Rule: From Pompey to Diocletian: A Study in Political Relations*, 2nd ed. Atlanta, GA: SBL, 2014.

Stern, Menahem, ed. *Greek and Latin Authors on Jews and Judaism: From Tacitus to Simpliciius*. Jerusalem: The Israel Academy of Sciences and Humanities, 1980.

Strauss, Barry. *Ten Caesars: Roman Emperors from Augustus to Constantine*. New York: Simon & Schuster, 2019.

The Authorized Daily Prayer Book of the United Hebrew Congregations of the Commonwealth, 4th ed., trans. with commentary Chief Rabbi Sir Jonathan Sacks. London: Collins, 2007.

Urbach, Ephraim E. *The Sages: The World and Wisdom of the Rabbis of the Talmud*, trans. Israel Abrahams. Cambridge, MA and London: Harvard University Press, 1975.

———. *The Halakhah: Its Sources and Development*, trans. Raphael Posner. Tel Aviv: Modan, 1996.

Visotzky, Burton L. *Aphrodite and the Rabbis: How the Jews Adapted Roman Culture to Create Judaism as We Know It*. New York: St. Martin's Press, 2015.

Zakheim, Dov S. *Nehemiah: Statesman and Sage*. New Milford, CT and Jerusalem: Maggid, 2016.

Articles and Internet Sources

Aberbach, Moshe. "Ḥizkiyah Melekh Yehuda VeRabbi Yehuda Hanasi: Heksherim Meshiḥiyim" (Hezekiah King of Judah and Rabbi Judah the Patriarch – Messianic Aspects). *Tarbiz* 53:3 (5744/1984), 353–71; Heb.

Agus, Aharon. "Some Early Rabbinic Thinking on Gnosticism." *The Jewish Quarterly Review* 71 (July 1980), 18–30.

Bar Am, Aviva. "Ancient Tzipori." *The Jerusalem Post* (January 25, 2010), http://www.jpost.com/Israel-Guide/Top-Tours/Ancient-Tzipori.

Barnes, T. D. "The Family and Career of Septimius Severus." *Historia: Zeitschrift fur Alte Geschischte,* vol. 16 (March 1967), 94–107.

Basser, H. W. "Allusions to Christian and Gnostic Practices in Talmudic Tradition." *Journal for the Study of Judaism in the Persian, Hellenistic, and Roman Period* 12:1 (1981), 87–105.

Boyarin, Daniel. "Literary Fat Rabbis: On the Historical Origins of the Groteque Body." *Journal of the History of Sexuality* (April 1991), 551–84.

Buchler, A. "Der Patriarch R. Jehuda I und die Griechish-Romichen Stadte Palastinas." *Jewish Quarterly Review* 13 (July 1901), 643–740.

Cohen, Shaye J. D. "Patriarchs and Scholarchs." *Proceedings of the American Academy for Jewish Research* 48 (1981), 57–85.

Demsky, Aaron. "Abbaye's Family Origins – A Study in Rabbinic Genealogy." http://iijg.org/wp-content/uploads/2014/02/WUJS_Aaron_Demsky.pdf.

Epstein, I. "Introduction to Seder Kodashim," in Rabbi Dr. I. Epstein, ed., *Zebahim,* trans. Rabbi Dr. H. Freedman. London: Soncino, 1988.

Felton, D. "Advice to Tyrants: The Motif of 'Engimatic Counsel' in Greek and Roman Texts." *Phoenix* 52 (Spring-Summer 1998), 42–54.

Fonrobert, Charlotte Elisheva. "When Women Walk in the Way of Their Fathers: On Gendering the Rabbinic Claim for Authority." *Journal of the History of Sexuality* 10 (July–October 2011), 398–415.

Golinkin, David. "Should we continue to fast on Tisha B'Av and the other three fasts which commemorate the destruction of the Temple?" (June 17, 2010). http://www.schechter.edu/should-we-continue-to-fast-on-tisha-bav-and-the-other-three-fasts-which-commemorate-the-destruction-of-the-temple-1/.

Goodlatt, David. "Al Sippur HaKesher Neged Rabban Shimon ben Gamliel HaSheni" (The story of the plot against Rabban Simeon b. Gamaliel II). *Zion* 49:4 (1984), 349–74; Heb.

Goodman, Martin. "Trajan and the Origins of Roman Hostility to the Jews." *Past & Present* 182 (February 2004), 3–29.

Hadas, Moses. "Rabbinic Parallels to Scriptores Historiae Augustae." *Classical Philology* 24 (July 1929), 258–62.

Hammond, Mason. "Septimius Severus, Roman Bureaucrat." *Harvard Studies in Classical Philology* 51 (1940), 137–73.

Harrer, G. A. "The Chronology of the Revolt of Pescennius Niger." *Journal of Roman Studies* 10 (1920), 155–68.

Jakobovits, Chief Rabbi Lord Immanuel. "The Social Fabric of Faith," in *The Authorised Daily Prayer Book of the United Hebrew Congregations of the Commonwealth:* Revised and Enlarged Centenary Edition. London: Kuperard, 1998, 17–18.

Kasher, A. "The Rights of the Jews of Antioch on the Orontes." *Proceedings of the American Academy for Jewish Research* 49 (1982), 69–85.

Lieberman, Saul. "Palestine in the Third and Fourth Centuries." *The Jewish Quarterly Review* 36 (April 1946), 329–370.

———. "Achievements and Aspirations of Modern Jewish Scholarship." *Proceedings of the American Academy for Jewish Research* 46/47, part 1 (1979–80), 369–480.

Naiweld, Ron. "There Is Only One Other: The Fabrication of Antoninus in a Multilayered Talmudic Dialogue." *The Jewish Quarterly Review* 104 (Winter 2014), 81–104.

Neusner, Jacob. "Some Aspects of the Economic and Political Life of Babylonian Jewry, Ca. 160–220 C.E." *Proceedings of the American Academy for Jewish Research* 31 (1963), 165–96.

Paz, Yakir. "'Meishan Is Dead': On the Historical Contexts of the Bavli's Representations of the Jews in Southern Mesopotamia," in Geoffrey Herman and Jeffrey L. Rubenstein, eds., *The Aggada of the Bavli and its Cultural World.* Providence, RI: Brown University Press, 2018, 47–101.

Philo. "On the Embassy to Gaius," in *The Works of Philo,* trans. C. D. Yonge. Peabody, MA: Hendrickson, 1993, 757–90.

Saldarini, Anthony J. "The End of the Rabbinic Chain of Tradition." *Journal of Biblical Literature* 93 (March 1974), 97–106.

———. "Last Words and Deathbed Scenes in Rabbinic Literature." *The Jewish Quarterly Review* 68 (July 1977), 28–45.

Schiffman, L. H. "The Samaritans in Tannaitic Halakhah." *The Jewish Quarterly Review* 75 (April 1985), 323–50.

Schwartz, Joshua. "The Morphology of Roman Lydda." *Jewish History* 2 (Spring 1987), 33–66.

Shapiro, Marc B. "Another 'Translation' by Artscroll, the Rogachover and the Radichkover." *The Seforim Blog,* http://seforim.blogspot.com/2018/06/another-translation-by artscroll.html.

———. "The Hanukkah Miracle." *The Seforim Blog* (April 27, 2017), http://seforim.blogspot.com/2017/04/the-hanukkah-miracle.html.

Segelman, R. Micah. "The Status of Minority Opinions in Halacha." *The Journal of Halacha and Contemporary Society* 71 (Pesach 5776/Spring 2106), 60–81.

Simkovich, Malka Z. "Uncovering the Truth About Chanukah." *TheTorah.com* (November 27, 2013), http://thetorah.com/uncovering-the-truth-about-chanukah/.

Smallwood, E. Mary. "Domitian's Attitude toward the Jews and Judaism." *Classical Philology* 51 (January 1956), 1–13.

Steinmetz, Devora. "Must the Patriarch Know 'Uqtzin'? The Nasi as Scholar in Babylonian Aggada." *ATJ Review* 23/2 (1998), 163–89.

Swidler, Leonard. *Biblical Affirmations of Woman* (Philadelphia: Westminster, 1979), 106–10.

Urbach, Ephraim E. "The Rabbinical Laws of Idolatry in the Second and Third Centuries in Light of Archeological and Historical Facts." *Israel Exploration Journal* 9, no. 3 (1959), 149–65.

Wallach, Luitpold. "The Colloquy of Marcus Aurelius with the Patriarch Judah 1." *Jewish Quarterly Review* (January 1941), 259–86.